# PROVING BIBLICAL NAZARETH

Evidence for the Key Sites of Jesus

View to Catholic Church of the Annunciation with conical dome, nestled in the historic village site of Nazareth.

Book 2: Study Resource Edition

## TREVOR HARRIS

Key-line Christian Research Pty Ltd

**THE NAZARETH SERIES**
**Proving Biblical Nazareth - Evidence for the Key Sites of Jesus**
Book 2: Study Resource Edition
Revised 1st. Edition 2017
ISBN  978-0-9925506-1-5  (Print B&W soft cover)

National Library of Australia Cataloguing-in-Publication entry
Dewey Number:  232.9

ISBN  978-0-9925506-2-2  (Print Colour soft cover)
ISBN  978-0-9925506-3-9  (ebook)

Copyright © 2017
Author Trevor E. Harris

Published by:
Key-line Christian Research Pty Ltd
P.O. Box 3205
Norwood, South Australia, 5067
Australia

All rights reserved. No part of this book may be used or reproduced by any means, graphic, electronic, or mechanical, including photocopying, recording, taping or by any information storage retrieval system without the written permission of the publisher except in the case of the brief quotations embodied in critical articles and reviews as permitted under the Copyright Act.

**Disclaimer:** All coordinates given in this book are nominal *Google Earth* positions which are not quite as accurate as the *Global Positioning System (*GPS). All maps produced are for illustrative purposes only.
Google maps produced under the conditions of *"Google Maps".* Data from Mapa GISrael ORION-ME. Historic base maps are from the *Palestine Exploration Fund* (PEF) Survey 1880, courtesy of the Israel Antiquities Authority (IAA).

Cover and book layout design by Anna Dimasi
Illustrations by Trevor Harris, Meg Stephens and Andrew Blaney

Front cover features current view of modern Nazareth seen through the lens of the Annunciation of Mary with the visit of the angel Gabriel. Modified engraving image by Gustave Dore. *Refer* page 4.

The New King James Version (NKJV)  is used for all Bible quotes unless stated otherwise in the text.
Copyright © 1982 by Thomas Nelson, Inc., Nashville TN, USA.
Used within the terms and conditions stated by the publisher.
All other credits are listed in the text and Reference Section.

# CONTENTS

| | |
|---|---|
| Forewords | vi |
| Preface and Introduction | ix |

## SECTION A: THE MYSTERY OF NAZARETH CITY .................. 1

**Chapter 1: The controversial city of Jesus** — 3
  1.1 Nazareth: the lost city — 5
  1.2 The Galilee and the Nazarenes — 13
  1.3 The intriguing explanation — 18

**Chapter 2: Nazareth city at Tel Yafia** — 23
  2.1 Defining Nazareth city-polis — 24
  2.2 Yafia's story in the archaeology — 30

**Chapter 3: Traditional Nazareth hamlet–village** — 35
  3.1 The town built by theology — 36
  3.2 The sites of Mary and Joseph — 41
  3.3 The devout Christian village of Nazara — 47

**Chapter 4: Two Nazareths: the evidence** — 53
  4.1 Persecutions and preserving the name — 54
  4.2 How Nazareth city was lost in time — 60
  4.3 How Nazareth city became Yafia — 63

**Conclusion to Section A** — 65

## SECTION B: WHERE JESUS DECLARED HIS GOSPEL OF LIBERTY — 67

**Chapter 5: The early years of Jesus** — 69
  5.1 At school in Nazareth city — 70
  5.2 Jesus the apprentice and carpenter — 73
  5.3 Teaching parables by experience — 75

**Chapter 6: Locating Nazareth city synagogue** — 79
  6.1 No synagogue in the hamlet — 80
  6.2 Nazareth Synagogue: spiritual and physical factors — 83
  6.3 The proposed locality — 88

**Chapter 7: Jubilee Declaration of Liberty** — 91
  7.1 Joshua's altar and Jesus' synagogue — 92
  7.2 The Jubilee and Gospel declaration — 94

**Chapter 8: The Nazareth plot to kill Jesus** — 97
  8.1 The hometown rejection of a prophet — 99
  8.2 The execution site: a proposal — 101
  8.3 The premature attempt to kill Jesus — 104

**Chapter 9: Christian synagogue in Jewish Nazareth** — 107
  9.1 Yafia's Jewish synagogue or Byzantine church? — 108
  9.2 Count Joseph's testimony and his Nazareth church — 110
  9.3 The workshop of Joseph the carpenter? — 119

**Conclusion to Section B** — 121

## SECTION C: HOW NAZARETH UNLOCKS LOWER GALILEE ..... 123
### Chapter 10: Bible site mapping and Zebulun — 125
10.1 Bible sites: nomination and mapping — 126
10.2 Zebulun's boundaries and the Galilee — 130
10.3 Did Jacob and Moses make false prophecies? — 132
### Chapter 11: The Roman–Jewish War evidence — 137
11.1 Jewish fortifications and the Roman strategy — 138
11.2 Jotapata: the 'Masada' of Galilee — 141
### Chapter 12: Identifying biblical Japhia — 145
12.1 Tel Yafia is not biblical Japhia — 146
12.2 Joshua's Japhia — 149
12.3 Josephus' Japhia — 151
### Conclusion to Section C — 153

## SECTION D: FOUR SITES OF THE MESSIAH ..... 155
### Chapter 13: Prophetic mountain near Nazareth — 157
13.1 Bible site mapping — 158
13.2 Sarid: key set-out point — 158
13.3 Reclaiming Mount Kedumim for Jesus — 162
### Chapter 14: A Levite city that points to Jesus — 167
14.1 Unique city layout of the Levite priests — 169
14.2 Daberath and 'The Word' — 172
### Chapter 15: Cana of Galilee — 175
15.1 The miracle at a Jewish wedding — 176
15.2 Tel Yodfat is Cana of Galilee — 180
15.3 The Cana wedding site: a proposal — 182
### Chapter 16: Locating the Transfiguration — 187
16.1 Which holy mountain? — 189
16.2 St. Elias Orthodox Church — 192
16.3 Jesus' transfiguration: a site proposal — 194
### Conclusion to Section D — 196

## E: GEOGRAPHIC SPATIAL SUMMARY ..... 197

## E: SUMMARY ..... 203
1. The Story of Nazareth — 204
2. Some reflections — 206
3. Afterword — 207
4. Conclusions — 208

## F: APPENDICES ... 211
  1. Biblical archaeology: an explanation   212
  2. Nazareth 27 AD: demographics and the critics   217
  3. Joshua's altar: sacred Mt. Ebal   222
  4. Sites of Zebulun: Lower Galilee   231
  5. Border sites near Zebulun   235
  6. Levite cities archaeology   238
  7. Jewish fortifications in Lower Galilee   241
  8. A Catholic source for Bible sites   245

## REFERENCE SECTION ... 253
  Abbreviations, Terminology and Glossary   253
  Alpha-numeric code for sites   256
  List of Tables   256
  Summary: Alternative site nominations   257
  Credits for Illustrations   258
  Bibliography   261
  Index   267

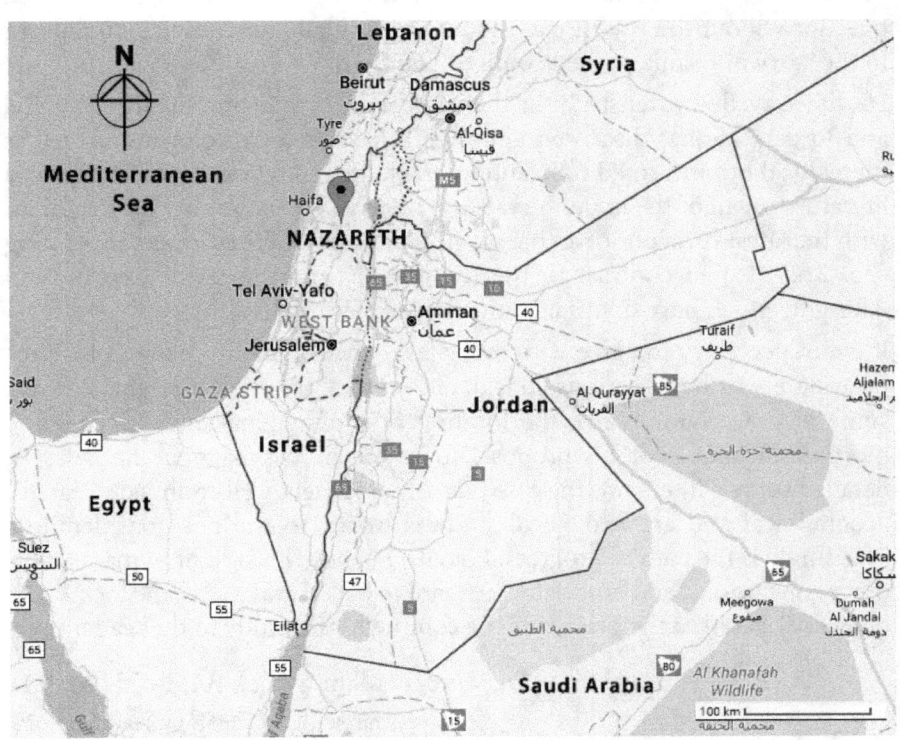

Nazareth (labeled by author) is located in northern Israel.
Base map Google Maps. Map data © 2016 Mapa GISrael, ORION–ME.

v

# Foreword by a historian

It has become commonplace in our modern world for atheists and sceptics to attempt to poke holes in the Bible in whatever way they can. I must confess that even with my own experience in archaeology I was surprised when Trevor Harris drew my attention to a "hit piece" by an atheist author, René Salm, alleging that Nazareth did not exist in New Testament times. The claim is that parts of the Gospels are fiction and unreliable.

Trevor has done an in-depth study, partly in response to Salm's allegations, but more broadly to ascertain the identity of Biblical sites in the Galilee region. Hence the study is essentially positive, and a genuine advance in what is a continuing puzzle to archaeologists and geographers. The identity and location of many Biblical sites remain a mystery for some villages and cities. Trevor has bitten the proverbial bullet in regard to a number of these sites, and has shown ability in thinking outside of the traditional framework.

This study is mainly occupied with the Lower Galilee, the ancient tribal territory of Zebulun, and locations near the Sea of Galilee, and many site proposals are put forward. He does venture further south and has raised questions about the traditional mountains of Ebal and Gerizim, significant in the story of Joshua in the Promised Land.

He has travelled extensively in the Middle East, and particularly in Israel and Jordan. He has discussed issues with leading archaeologists as well as many local but informed folk, and interacts with the leading archaeological literature on all of the issues he raises. Likewise, he shows that he is familiar with the latest revisions of archaeological periods and their respective dating (pp. 212–216) in contrast to the traditional time frames of Kenyon and Albright, which have dominated the field for far too long.

It is not necessary to agree with every last conclusion, but many of his proposals are worthy of serious consideration, and may well be right. For me, some of the proposals like the location of Mount Ebal and Cana require more verification. For his proposal for a Nazareth synagogue he awaits a detailed survey. It remains the case that any argument well-founded in careful geographical and archaeological study is worthy of serious consideration. This surely is the path of progress. Equally, I believe he is right in many of his other conclusions, and especially in regard to his central thesis: the location of biblical Nazareth. I therefore heartily commend this study to the reader.

Dr Murray Adamthwaite, BA, BD, MA, PhD.
Historian with archaeology qualifications.
Bible College lecturer, theologian and linguist.
Former lecturer, University of Melbourne, Australia.

# Foreword by a Bible scholar

I am pleased to recommend Trevor Harris' thorough contribution to the study of the hometown of Jesus. To those who would deny that Nazareth even existed, he has provided more than ample evidence that such a denial is untenable. However, this is more than just proving that Nazareth existed. He has gone to lengths to explain how and where the attempt to stone Jesus by his fellow citizens took place.

In his use of historic sources, he has not hesitated to call upon many New Testament passages as witnesses. This is as it should be. Too often one encounters cavalier rejection of the reliablity of the gospel accounts by scholars who are far less critical of non-Christian sources that are not nearly as well-attested.

Of particular interest to me is the in-depth attempt to connect the church reported as built in the early Fourth Century by Count Joseph with excavated remains of a possible Jewish Christian synagogue.

Trevor has allowed his research to carry him well outside the geographic boundaries of Nazareth, and the reader will find discussions of many other sites that Jesus would have known in his youth and where he would later pass and perform miracles.

There is necessarily a healthy amount of speculation that requires further research. Some of the key sites are recommended for further archaeological investigation. The total package is a welcome contribution to moving forward the scholarly discussion of the city of Nazareth.

> Ray Pritz, PhD (Hebrew University) Jerusalem.
> Lecturer Hebrew University.
> Former Director Bible Society in Israel.
> Resource educator, Translations Department, United Bible Societies.

## About the author

Trevor Harris received his Honours degree in Architecture in 1971. During his undergraduate period he took a year (1969) off to hitch-hike around the world on a low budget of $A10 per day in today's value. Part of that journey included time in the Middle East and the lands of the Bible. This was the start of a long passion for evidence of the archaeology and history of the Bible.

A Masters degree in Urban and Regional Planning was completed in 1976. This gave training in mapping, topographic analysis and planning criteria that is essential in evaluating historic site proposals. Both of these degrees contained a large portion of historical studies which is one of his great passions. He has been an architect and planner for 23 years in Government and 21 years in his own private practice.

He was converted to the Christian faith in 1965 which sparked his passion for Bible study. This has developed over the years resulting in the formation of a research company dedicated to publishing information on Bible sites (www.biblekeylines.com). Seven research trips have been made to Middle East countries to gain information and establish contacts.

The Middle East is not short on controversy when it comes to history and geography. This was illustrated when he arrived in Israel in 1969 just ten days after another Australian back-packer tried to burn down the famed Al Aqsa Mosque on Temple Mount in Jerusalem, causing a huge reaction in the Islamic world. While sleeping rough in a Tel Aviv park, Trevor was arrested and interrogated. Was he linked to a wider terrorist conspiracy, the police wanted to know?

Research in the Middle East requires an understanding of the Jewish and Islamic religions and valuable contacts in both these cultures have been made. There are three broad traditions in the Christian faith; Catholic, Orthodox and Protestant, and Trevor values and respects the contributions of each.

## Acknowledgements

Foremost is the support of my wife, Maureen and her patience with a husband often glued to the computer. Her gift for prayer has been essential with some of the dangers of field trips. Next is Meg Stephens who has been indispensable in developing illustrations and managing data records. Acknowledgement must also be given to my friends and confidants, who helped with photography, travel and counsel. In particular mention is made of Frank Eames, Malcolm Graetz, Bill Wright, Andrew Lothian and Antony Scammell.

# PREFACE

This book is a response to many questions that have been raised over the years regarding the city of Nazareth as to its size and location. This is the site named in the New Testament and claimed as the place of the divine incarnation of Jesus Christ, the place where he grew up and lived for most of his life. This locality would have implications if Jesus was the actual Messiah and his coming the subject of particular prophecies.

There have been many books written about Nazareth theologically and historically, so why should there be another? Whilst each author brings assumptions and insight, my research has found that most authors have not been able to address four very fundamental questions.

1. **If biblical Nazareth was a city, where was it?**

   Definite archaeological evidence of this Gospel city needs to be proven. The scant remains at the traditional Nazareth location show only a very small hamlet in the time of Jesus. How can this be reconciled with the stories in the gospels?

2. **If Nazareth was only a small hamlet, how can the story of the members of the local synagogue rising up to kill Jesus, be explained?**

   If Jesus grew up with a small devout local community he would have worshipped with them. The family synagogue became the place where they reacted to his teaching with violence. Can archaeological evidence and the topography provide the answer to this very extraordinary event?

3. **Why have key sites in the Galilee region, including that of Japhia (Yafia) near Nazareth, been incorrectly located?**

   There has been debate on some Bible sites in Galilee for a long time. Is there a way that some of the debate can be resolved? Can solving the puzzle of Nazareth's location lead to unlocking the mystery of other sites?

4. **If Jesus was in fact the promised Messiah, is there any significance in the location of sites associated with him?**

   Jesus is a controversial figure in history who made challenging claims. Is there any geographical correlation between Old Testament and New Testament sites? For Christians, connecting events in the life of Jesus with Old Testament locations is a form of *prophetic mapping*. This topic, with its questions, is addressed in the following chapters. The results of the research are there to be examined and tested. Indeed the accounts of the Bible are enriched when some of the sites are identified, enabling a reconstruction of the events.

## From the author

My interest lies in investigating links between spiritual events as they are recorded in the Bible and the actual geography of the Middle East region. This particularly includes the so-called *'Promised Land'* of Abraham. In this book, attention is given to the Israelite tribal area of Zebulun, which the gospels relate to the first coming of the Messiah. One of my favourite mottos is *'The Land is the fifth Gospel'*. It is a concept attributed to both St. Cyril (313–386 AD), a bishop of Jerusalem, and famed Christian scholar Jerome (347–420 AD). The motto was summarised by archaeologist Bargil Pixner:

> Five gospels record the life of Jesus. Four you will find in the books and one you will find in the Land they all call holy. Read the fifth gospel and the world of the four will open to you. [1]

## To the readers

There is vigorous academic debate on topics discussed in this book. I hope that some of the proposals, with the supporting evidence, will shed more light on these issues. People in large numbers from many nations and cultures travel to Nazareth and the Galilee annually. Some are curious about the historical sites and where significant biblical events occurred. They want to see for themselves and ask the questions, is it true, and how do we know?

- I believe that the original Hebrew *Old Testament* and the Greek *New Testament* are historically reliable. [2] The Bible, because of its profound claims, is rightly subject to scrutiny as to its reliability. That scrutiny also applies to locations where biblical events occur. This book gives new insight, with examples, of how some biblical sites can be verified.
- When the draft edition of my proposals was circulated in 2014, it had a very mixed response, particularly amongst various contacts made in Nazareth. Some were fascinated and excited by the implications. Others felt unsure, with their mindset and assumptions being challenged. I want readers to consider the facts about the physical sites of the life of Jesus and how they have amazing connections to the Land promised to Abraham.
- Some readers want the story or narrative emphasised and others want the facts and reliable evidence. An effort has been made to bring both needs together to assist those with an interest in the Bible. Specifically I seek to help researchers, teachers and students. I hope it will encourage more reading on the topics and further investigation of some of the sites.

---

1 Pixner, B 1992, *With Jesus through Galilee According to the Fifth Gospel*, Rosh Pina, Israel, Corazin Publishing, backcover.

2 In this book *Bible* is used generically. It includes the Old Testament, also known as the Hebrew Bible. There are two main versions of the Old Testament, Masoretic text (MT) and the Septuagint text (LXX). The Christian New Testament is also included.

*Preface*

Front entrance of the Catholic Church of the Annunciation, the proposed site of the visit of the angel Gabriel to the Virgin Mary. Located in the centre of traditional Nazareth.

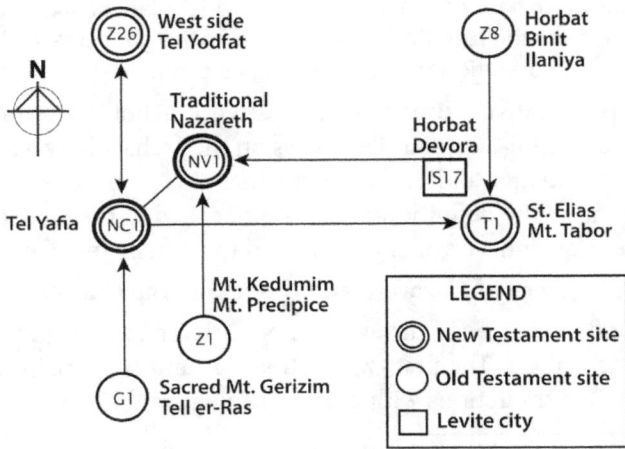

Diagram of geographic spatial relationships of eight existing significant sites. They are the key sites of this book and can be compared with Illus. E.01 on p. 198.

xi

# INTRODUCTION

When Roman Governor Pontius Pilate nailed the legal plaque on Jesus' cross according to the Roman custom, it included the words *'Jesus of Nazareth'*. This Jesus is a fascinating figure, with all four gospels declaring unambiguously that he is the Messiah. If he was the Messiah, and the subject of many prophesies, are there prophetic illustrations in the names and locations of sites with which he was associated?

One of the great themes of the Bible for Christians is the linking of the Old Testament to the New Testament. It is summed up with a profound quote by noted theologian Saint Augustine (354–430 AD): "The New is in the Old contained. The Old is in the New explained".[1] This topic is explored with particular Bible sites of significance. The starting point is the controversy of the city of Nazareth.

**The Atheist challenge**

The Atheist Press of America published a book by René Salm entitled *"The Myth of Nazareth – The Invented Town of Jesus"*. A case was presented that based on the archaeology, there was no city of Nazareth in the time frame of Jesus (4 BC–30 AD). Many questions were raised, but the conclusion was that the gospels were not reliable and there was even the suggestion that Nazareth was invented as part of a conspiracy by Christian writers. In the Introduction it was stated:

> A battle has raged over the Nazareth evidence from ancient times, ever since problematic claims were made about the town. That which is problematic must be doubly defended, and it is not coincidence that the myth of Nazareth has needed hiding under a thick blanket of tradition ... The repercussions of the resulting reassessment of the gospel record upon the traditional interpretation of Christian origins can hardly be exaggerated.[2]

These very provocative claims caught my attention, but in reading the book I found myself sharing some similar views on the archaeology. However there was one fundamental and crucial error that was overlooked. That was an understanding of the definition of Nazareth, called in the Greek text a *polis*. This book explains this error and how it led to a totally incorrect conclusion.

**Solving the mystery of Nazareth and unlocking the Galilee**

There is good evidence for the story of Nazareth and its significance in the region of the Galilee. The first two sections (A and B) explain how to solve the apparent contradictions with the archaeology and historical sources.

---

1   Mears, HC 2011, *What the Bible is all about*, Regal, Ventura, California, USA, p. 24.
2   Salm, R 2008, *The Myth of Nazareth – The Invented Town of Jesus*, American Atheist Press, Cranford, New Jersey, USA, p. xvi.

When Nazareth is solved it unlocks other sites in the Galilee in the tribal area known as Zebulun. It begins to solve the puzzle of some of the mystery sites of the Bible. This in turn helps to identify some sites associated with the ministry of Jesus. Sections C and D give the evidence for these proposals. When these sites are mapped, along with the archaeological data, interesting correlations can be made on the locations as shown on page xi.

**Confirmation of Bible sites**

Modern day researchers still face the challenge of determining the correct nomination of Bible sites. However there are scholars who claim the original texts of the Old and New Testament are unreliable and the product of human manipulation. They downplay any divine inspiration and even suggest parts of the text are corrupt. Claims are made of wrong spelling, illogical order and unreliable authorship. The following chapters explore this topic in the context of some of the sites associated with Jesus. Evidence is presented to show that the texts are reliable when all the factors are correctly understood.

**The objective**

The objective of the book is to address the four main questions that are listed in the preface. Each of these raises other questions that require further investigation. When a site is correctly identified there is often correlation from a number of sources. This is similar to the old biblical adage that the truth of a matter is to be confirmed with two or three witnesses (Deut. 19:15 and 2 Corinthians 13:1). This will be shown in the examples illustrated with supporting data from a range of disciplines.

**Methodology and technical information**

The methodology for the site proposals has two stages:

- The first is to critically evaluate the current range of nominations with the assumptions made by relevant scholars.
- The second is supporting a particular proposal based on the biblical descriptions, followed by the historical and archaeological evidence, the topographical requirements and the planning logic. The latter two areas are often missing in site nominations. My experience in these disciplines has been used to provide support for some of the proposals.

Extensive appendices and footnotes have been provided to give relevant technical information. This material may be daunting to some readers but encouragement is given to press through. Reading the chapter title pages and the two summaries first, could help to gain an overview.

# Important explanatory notes

### Alpha-numeric code for sites
Every site listed has been given an alpha-numeric code, e.g. Z1. A code number is used throughout the text and in all illustrations to assist in cross-referencing. The letters relate to the tribal area where it is located: Z is Zebulun, A is Asher, N is Naphtali and IS is Issachar (*see* Reference Section).

### Coordinates for sites
To assist readers viewing the sites *Google Earth* coordinates are provided. The latitude and longitude are given as degree-minutes-seconds (hyphenated). It must be noted that there are always variations between *Google Earth* and the actual *Global Positioning System* (GPS). In most cases the margin of error is not significant with the proposals. The variations are complex to measure due to the nature of Google Earth's dynamic visual representations. Variations of up to 10 metres (33 feet) are common and sometimes even higher figures can occur.

### Measurement systems
This is an international edition so both SI metric and US imperial are used.

### Hebrew and Greek meanings
There are many references to Hebrew and Greek meanings. To reduce the need for footnotes Strong's Concordance has been used due to its simplicity.[3] Strong's reference number has Hebrew as (H----) and the Greek as (G----).

### Historical time frames
The concept of using BCE (Before the Common Era) and CE (Common Era) is used in some scholarly circles. Due to the significance of the subject matter involving Jesus Christ the traditional chronology letters of BC (before Christ) and AD (anno Domini) have been used. In this book AD sites are termed *historic* and BC sites are termed *ancient*.

### Common terminology and abbreviations
Jewish historian Josephus Flavius (37–c.100 AD) gave detailed descriptions of the Jewish war with the Romans in 67–71 AD. His book references are denoted in the text as *Life*, *Ant.* (Antiquities), and *Wars*.

'Promised Land' and 'Land' are used to denote the region given to Abraham (Gen. 12:7). 'Law' is used to denote the Jewish Torah. 'PEF' is the Palestine Exploration Fund. 'IAA' is the Israeli Antiquities Authority. *Refer* page 253.

### Electronic footnotes
All electronic footnotes accessed and checked June to September 2016.

---

[3] Strong, J 2001, *The New Strong's Expanded Exhaustive Concordance of the Bible*, Red letter Edition, Thomas Nelson Publishers, Nashville, TN, USA. Selected due to its Web availability.

# SECTION A

# THE MYSTERY OF NAZARETH CITY

It is very doubtful whether the beautiful mountain village of Nazareth was really the dwelling place of Jesus. No such town as Nazareth is mentioned in the OT, in Josephus, or in the Talmud … Was Nazareth originally the name of a town (or village) at all?

*Encyclopedia Biblica,* 1899, entry for Nazareth.

---

This section seeks to answer some questions about the size and location of the city of Nazareth from 4 BC–30 AD.

The gospels clearly state that Nazareth was a large city with a good sized population. The current archaeological surveys in the traditional location do not support this. This has resulted in questions, similar to that quoted above, as to its existence and size at the time of Jesus.

Compelling evidence will show that the story of this city can be reconstructed. Indeed the mystery of the lost city of Nazareth can be solved.

A.01 The inscriptions on the plaque of Jesus' cross. 'Jesus of Nazareth – King of the Jews' in Hebrew, Greek and Latin. Image source unknown.

A.02 Historic photograph of traditional Nazareth by Fadil Saba, 1920s. Credit Wikimedia Commons.

# CHAPTER 1

## THE CONTROVERSIAL CITY OF JESUS

> Now Pilate wrote a title and put it on the cross.
> And the writing was:
> JESUS OF NAZARETH, THE KING OF THE JEWS.
> Then many of the Jews read this title, for the place where Jesus was crucified was near the city; and it was written in Hebrew, Greek *and* Latin.
>
> John 19:19–20.

---

If the terminology of the gospels is reliable, there must be good evidence in support of this plaque, known as a titulus, ordered by the Roman governor Pontius Pilate. There are scholars of many different disciplines and belief systems who have queried, debated and challenged the understanding of Nazareth in the time of Jesus.

This chapter introduces the debate and the reasons why it is controversial. The name 'Jesus of Nazareth' takes on a whole new meaning when all the facts are ascertained. Witnesses to his crucifixion would have fully understood the geographical part of the plaque, even if they did not understand the messianic title attached at the end.

A.03 Luke's Gospel describes the encounter of the Virgin Mary with the angel Gabriel.
"The Annunciation" by Gustave Dore, circa 1866.
Courtesy of the Pitts Theology Library, Candler School of Theology, Emory University, USA.

## 1.1 Nazareth: the lost city

**The controversial Gospel account.** Luke 1:26–38 (verses numbered).

[26] Now in the sixth month the angel Gabriel was sent by God to a city of Galilee named Nazareth, [27] to a virgin betrothed to a man whose name was Joseph, of the house of David. The virgin's name was Mary. [28] And having come in, the angel said to her, "Rejoice, highly favored one, the Lord is with you; [5] blessed are you among women!"

[29] But when she saw him, she was troubled at his saying, and considered what manner of greeting this was. [30] Then the angel said to her, "Do not be afraid, Mary, for you have found favor with God. [31] And behold, you will conceive in your womb and bring forth a Son, and shall call His name Jesus. [32] He will be great, and will be called the Son of the Highest; and the Lord God will give Him the throne of His father David. [33] And He will reign over the house of Jacob forever, and of His kingdom there will be no end."

[34] Then Mary said to the angel, "How can this be, since I do not know a man?" [35] And the angel answered and said to her, "The Holy Spirit will come upon you, and the power of the Highest will overshadow you; therefore, also, that Holy One who is to be born will be called the Son of God. [36] Now indeed, Elizabeth your relative has also conceived a son in her old age; and this is now the sixth month for her who was called barren. [37] For with God nothing will be impossible." [38] Then Mary said, "Behold the maidservant of the Lord! Let it be to me according to your word." And the angel departed from her.

This account would have been verbally given to Luke by Mary when he was doing his research for his gospel. The details of the angel Gabriel's visit to the young Mary raise issues that I wish to address in Section A.

- In the original Greek text the writer refers to a large city named Nazareth which is described as a *'polis'* (v. 26).
- The home of the Virgin Mary is the location for the announcement of Gabriel, also known as the *Annunciation*. The reference "and having come in" (v. 28) clearly implies the residence of Mary. The *Incarnation* (where the divine takes human form) occurs there some time after with Mary's full consent and cooperation. Being a devout Jew she would have prayed for years for the coming of the Messiah. Her obvious surprise was more to do with her being chosen by God and the appearance of an angel.
- The *virgin conception* (v. 31,33) and the divine titles propose this Jesus to be the *Messiah*. That is, the *Saviour* or *Promised Redeemer* of the Old Testament (v. 31,32). This has considerable theological implications.
- The location of this event is significant and can be defined as a primary Messiah site. It is a key focal point in the *salvation* plan of God.

## A large city required

There is verifiable archaeological evidence of a small dispersed rural hamlet in the locality of the Catholic Church of the Annunciation in Nazareth about 4 BC. However, there is no evidence of a large city as described by Luke's terminology. A large city is also required for later events described in the gospels. This city seems 'lost' for historical evidence and 'lost' in archaeological remains, a mystery site! This apparent ambiguity has caused some to doubt other descriptions in the gospels and challenge the reliability of the authors. As mentioned previously, there are even claims of a conspiracy. In this book I will unravel the mystery, and provide evidence that the 'lost' city has indeed been found. I will show that the name 'Jesus of Nazareth' used consistently in the New Testament is a title of great substance and importance. The words Roman governor Pilate placed on the legal plaque of the cross of crucifixion were:

"JESUS OF NAZARETH, THE KING OF THE JEWS" (John 19:19).

Thus he specifically and legally described him as from a known city, not the product of an insignificant, humble and impoverished hamlet. How do we reconcile the gospel references to Nazareth as a city to the archaeological evidence of a rural location? What is the explanation for this puzzle?

## Lost cities of the Middle East

First we might consider some background on the topic of searching for lost cities. I have been fascinated by accounts of sites that have been lost in time. As an architecture student I spent a year hitch-hiking around the world to see some of these sites. I smuggled myself into western Cambodia, despite the border embargo due to the Vietnam War, to see the former hidden city of Angkor Wat. This city was looted and abandoned in 1431 AD and parts became overgrown by the jungle. The 're-discovery' was in stages by locals (1564 AD) and Europeans (1586–1860 AD).

The Middle East contains lost sites that have captured the hearts and the imaginations of generations of people. The starting point is the account of the "city and tower" of Babel recorded in the book of Genesis (11:1–9) and alluded to in Sumerian legends. Scholars have debated the reliability of this record for centuries. The story was deemed credible enough to inspire the 1992 official poster and motto of the fledgling European Union. The poster depicted Dutch artist Pieter Brueghel's famous painting of the Tower of Babel and the motto read *"Europe: Many Tongues One Voice"*.[1] The tower story allegedly even influenced the design of a European Parliament building.[2]

---

[1] This poster was protested against and was soon withdrawn. A revised motto for the European Union was adopted in the year 2000 as "Unity in Diversity."

[2] It is curious that the architects of the European Parliament in Strasbourg designed what has been described as a visually unfinished tower building which they described as "an unsettled snapshot of geometry". The architects for the building were "Architecture Studio" Paris. Statement on their website <www.architecture-studio.fr/en/projects/str2/european parliament.html>.

Historians debated whether the ancient Greek writer Homer was correct in describing the city of Troy. Homer's vivid account of the Greeks with their wooden horse secretly entering a major citadel was thought by some to be fiction. People were amazed when the remains of this city were found in western Turkey in 1868 AD. In recent times one of the most visited sites of the Middle East is the historic city of Petra in Jordan. It was known to the local Bedouin tribes, but 'hidden' from the inquisitive eyes of outsiders for many centuries. It was not until 1812 AD that a daring Swiss explorer, Johann Burckhardt, eventually found an entry and brought a description back to the Western world.

A.04 Babylon City with Tower of Babel at the rear. An alternative explanation for the 'Hanging gardens' of Babylon has been proposed. Credit Wikimedia Commons.

## Nineveh and its 'hanging gardens'

The following example is very relevant to the search for lost sites, and has application in the topics of this book. There was debate at the start of the nineteenth century on the location of the royal Assyrian city of Nineveh that is mentioned in the Old Testament. This city was made famous by the visit of the prophet Jonah, best known for his association with a large sea creature. Much later the biblical prophet Nahum foretold the destruction of the city, about ten years before this actually occurred in 612 BC (Nahum 3:6). Nineveh eventually became lost in location and time and critics came to doubt the accuracy of the story of Jonah and the size of the city. Nineveh's discovery near Mosul in northern Iraq in 1842 AD caused quite a stir. The site was huge in size, 750 hectares (1,900 acres) and had been buried in soil and sand for over two thousand years.

Recently a British Assyriologist, Stephanie M. Dalley made a controversial proposal by suggesting that the famous *Hanging Gardens of Babylon* were, in fact, located in Nineveh.[3] Compelling evidence for this nomination indicates that a large, multi-tiered garden complex once existed there. It is even depicted on the ancient Nineveh palace panels now on display in the British Museum. The large irrigation system required to maintain such a garden has been revealed and proven. Dalley believes that this magnificent garden, first recorded by its creator King Sennacherib (reign 705–681 BC), has been incorrectly linked to Babylon a century later. Her claim is that archaeologists and historians may have made a wrong assumption with certain written accounts. This theory would explain why no large garden remains of one of the seven wonders of the ancient world have been found at Babylon.

The debate on the historical records has begun, but the key to solving the puzzle was the questioning of prevailing assumptions. This book also raises questions about some of the assumptions made for Bible site nominations. Scholars have been assuming some of the sites for a very long time, even when the evidence is not clear-cut and even contradictory. The preceding examples mentioned illustrate a great truth in historical research. If a wrong assumption is made about a site, and its time frame, it will hinder its correct identification. All history, as well as the reliability of its writers, has to be evaluated and reviewed in the light of any verifiable information. This now brings us to the question of traditional Nazareth – a site of great debate.

**What the scholars say**

The following quotations clearly illustrate the consensus that the traditional locality of the hamlet of Mary and Joseph in 4 BC was very small.

From a Christian theologian:
> While it comes as a surprise to some people, the historical existence of Nazareth at the time of Jesus has been a controversial topic ... In the case of first-century Nazareth, religious scholars tend to talk up the size of Nazareth, while sceptics tend to question whether Nazareth even existed at the time.

Jenks, G 2013, *The Quest for the Historical Nazareth*, School of Theology, Charles Sturt University, St. Francis Theological College, Brisbane, Australia. *Refer* Bibliography.

From an archaeologist:
> The remains from the Late Hellenistic to Roman town were limited to numerous silos ... cisterns, immersion pools and storage caves – and the surrounding agricultural terraces bear witness to a thriving agrarian economy upon which the town was based.

Negev, A and Gibson, S (eds) 2001, 'Nazareth', *Archaeological Encyclopedia of the Holy Land*, Continuum, New York, USA, p. 362.

---

3   Dalley, S 2013, *The Mystery of the Hanging Garden of Babylon: An Elusive World Wonder Traced*, Oxford University Press, Oxford, UK.

From a Christian archaeologist:
> Since most of this was empty space in antiquity, the population would have been a maximum of about 480 at the beginning of the 1st century a.d. Nazareth lay beside Yafa or Yafia.

Strange, J 1992, 'Nazareth', *Anchor Bible Dictionary*, Yale University Press, USA.

From a Jewish encyclopedia:
> It is evident from John 1:46 that Nazareth was an obscure place. During the Biblical period Japhia was the important town of the locality and attracted to itself all the notice of historians.

Singer, I and Barton, G 'Nazareth', *Jewish Encyclopaedia*, <www.jewishencyclopedia.com/articles/11394-nazareth>. *Refer* Bibliography.

From an atheist scholar:
> [Comment on Nazareth remains]: They may suggest that the community was founded by Torah-observant Jews. We must keep in mind that in the earliest stage of the village relatively few people were involved – probably less than one hundred. After all, it was the beginning of the settlement. Everyone certainly knew everyone else very well and, indeed, it is probable that the earliest settlers (and the later ones?) were related by blood.

Salm, R 2008, *The Myth of Nazareth – The invented town of Jesus*, American Atheist Press, Cranford, New Jersey, USA, pp. 183–184.

A.05 A critique of Nazareth published by Atheist Press of America.

## Some responses to the scholars' evidence:

It may surprise some readers that the atheists were not the first to propose doubts on the existence and meaning of the city of Nazareth. In 1899, *Encyclopedia Biblica*, edited by liberal scholars of the day, stated in its reference to Nazareth:

> It is very doubtful whether the beautiful mountain village of Nazareth was really the dwelling place of Jesus. No such town as Nazareth is mentioned in the OT, in Josephus, or in the Talmud ... Was Nazareth originally the name of a town (or village) at all?[4]

> **In conclusion, the common belief is that the traditional site of Nazareth in the time of Jesus was a very small Jewish community in a mainly rural setting.**

---

4  Reference: en.wikisource.org. (2016), *Encyclopaedia Biblica/Naphisi–Nebai*–Wikisource, the free online library, <en.wikisource.org/wiki/Encyclopaedia_Biblica/Naphisi–Nebai#NAZARETH>. Editors of this edition adhered to the *higher critical* school of scholars at the turn of the century.

This problem has resulted in a number of explanations summarised in the following three quotations regarding 4 BC–27 AD Nazareth:

**1. An invented or later city**

Sceptics have argued there is proof that such a city named Nazareth city did not exist. René Salm questions if the gospel writers were deluded or lying:

> If Nazareth did not exist in the time of Jesus, then questions quickly arise: Why did the evangelists place him there? If Nazareth was a persistent and recurrent invention in the gospels, then we leave the realm of error and enter the realm of elaborate fiction. [5]

This extraordinary claim for deception, in my opinion, is not convincing. The correct location with evidence would totally refute this suggestion.

**2. A misunderstood site**

Some Christian scholars, who seek a rationale, claim Nazareth was never a city, and that the gospel writers Luke and Matthew lacked local knowledge. The Catholic archaeologist Bargil Pixner wrote:

> Luke probably did not have the local knowledge of Nazareth, which according to the archaeological excavations, was at the time of Jesus, hardly more than a hamlet that probably belonged to the larger village of Japhia … The description that Luke provides does not fit the local situation. [6]

My response is that Pixner's observation that the hamlet was part of Japhia is archaeologically correct, but mistaken on labelling. More explanation on this important point will be given.

**3. A hidden site**

There are Christians who hope that remains of a city may eventually be found. Maybe it is buried under modern Nazareth city? Perhaps it will be found in the Nazareth Valley basin still largely un-excavated? It could even have 'moved' to a nearby hill or valley that is still to be revealed? These points were raised by Norman Geisler, author of a book on biblical archaeology, who wrote:

> First there has been little archaeological work completed in the Nazareth area since most of the ancient city lies under the modern city of Nazareth … Even if there was no material data uncovered at Nazareth from the early first-century AD it does not eliminate Nazareth as a historical city … it is not uncommon that Nazareth's location moved somewhat over time. [7]

I agree this is a very plausible approach. However, finding the correct site for Nazareth city and its urban and regional definition can solve the mystery. This is what has driven my own research on the topic.

---

5 Salm, R, op. cit., p. xii–xii.

6 Pixner, B 1991, *Paths of the Messiah*, (ed.) Riesner, Rainer, Ignatius Press, San Francisco, USA, p. 428.

7 Quotation: normangeisler.com. 2016, *Is Jesus' Hometown (Nazareth) a Myth?* Geisler, Norman, <normangeisler.com/is-jesus-hometown-nazareth-a-myth/>. Author of *The Popular Handbook. of Archaeology and the Bible.*

## Are the gospel writers reliable?

*The Holy Land Oxford Archaeological Guides* makes a controversial statement under its section called Nazareth:

> The evangelists do not agree as to where Mary and Joseph lived before the birth of Jesus. Matthew implies that it was BETHLEHEM Matt. 2, but Luke says it was Nazareth Luke 2:4–5. It is more probable that Matthew is correct.[8]

This quotation illustrates that even archaeology textbooks take a theological position on the reliability of the gospel writers. What is the evidence for such a claim? When it comes to naming the city of Jesus there are four gospel writers who make reference to it. An explanation, why there are four gospels is that the story of Jesus' life was addressed to four prevalent world-views at that time. Matthew relates to the religious (Hebrew) culture. Mark appeals to the pragmatic (Roman) perspective. Luke as a Hellenised Jew, addresses the intellectual (Greek) mindset. John enlightens the conceptual universal world-view. They are still applicable, in similar ways, to today's equivalent world-views. Central to all their approaches is the requirement to write a record based on the truth of the events and their locations. The claims they made were bold and radical and there was plenty of opposition from a range of authorities. If there was any fabrication of misleading facts on the actual site of Nazareth at that time, critics then would have pointed that out.

## St. Luke, the researcher and historian

A.06 The Evangelist Luke – physician, historian, by artist G. Reni 1621 AD. Credit WikiArt.org.

Luke very clearly indicates that his writings are thoroughly researched. The introduction to his gospel states (Luke 1:1–2):

"Inasmuch as many have taken in hand to set in order a narrative of the things which have been fulfilled among us, just as those who from the beginning were eyewitnesses and ministers of the word delivered then to us".

He then immediately launches into the whole story of the incarnation, the birth of Jesus and references to Nazareth. Luke would have consulted with the Virgin Mary, the apostles, Jesus' relatives, the disciples and the other eyewitnesses from Galilee.

---

8   Murphy-O'Connor, J 1998, *The Holy Land,* Oxford Archaeological Guides, J Cunliffe, B (ed.) Oxford University Press, Oxford, UK, p. 375.

It has been debated whether Luke actually travelled to the Galilee, but it is highly likely that he would have. He records the name of Nazareth eight times in his gospel and seven times in his Book of the Acts.

**St. Matthew, the tax collector and administrator**

Matthew mentions the location of Nazareth four times in his account of the life of Jesus. He was Jewish and a resident of the Galilee region where he was a tax collector before his call to discipleship. A taxation officer would be well acquainted with the business community of the Galilee and the surrounding districts. He would also have good insight into the municipal system of government in Galilee. It is very likely that he would have visited Nazareth with its status of polis at some time.

A.07 The Apostle Matthew was a resident of Galilee. Icon courtesy of www.conventofsaintelizabeth.org.

**St. Mark, the scribe of St. Peter**

Mark makes five references to Nazareth in his gospel. Mark is a more difficult writer to define as there is debate on his identity. Some link him to John Marcus mentioned in the New Testament. Others suggest he was one of the seventy disciples connected to the wider ministry of Jesus. Both of these suggestions are not accepted. My support is for the reference by the early Christian writer Papias whom some scholars support as a contemporary of the Apostle John. Papias indicates that Mark was the scribe attached to the Apostle Peter:

> Mark became Peter's interpreter and wrote down accurately, but not in order, all that he remembered of the things said and done by the Lord. For he had not heard the Lord or been one of his followers, but later, as I said, a follower of Peter.[9]

Thus Mark is recording the eyewitness accounts of St. Peter who was from Galilee. He is probably the Mark mentioned as a "son" in 1 Peter 5:13.

---

9  Maier, PL 2007, *Eusebius The Church History*, Kregel Publications, Grand Rapids Michigan, USA, p. 114. Papias is dated to c.70–163 AD. He was a companion to the famous martyr Polycarp. He became a bishop of Hieropolis which is near Ephesus in Turkey. He is acknowledged as a reliable source for comments on the origin of the gospels.

**St. John, the Galilean fisherman**

John was a Jewish Galilean who recorded Nazareth five times. He ran a fishing business with his father Zebedee and bother James at Bethsaida on the Sea of Galilee. His travels in Galilee would mean he would be familiar with the location of the city and probably had occasions to visit.

All the gospel writers' terminology on Nazareth are consistent. The claim that the gospel writers were mistaken about the existence of the city of Nazareth does not hold water. More comments are given in Appendix 2.2.

## 1.2 The Galilee and the Nazarenes

A brief historical overview of the Galilee region needs to be understood. Each successive era can be labelled with archaeological or political empire terminology and correlated to biblical events [10] (*refer* Appendix 1).

**TABLE 1: Historical periods of the Galilee**

| Period * | Events in the Galilee region |
|---|---|
| **Bronze Age** Ends 1120 BC | Joshua leads Israel into the Promised Land in 1451 BC at the end of the Middle Bronze Age. The Galilee is given to three tribes called Zebulun, Naphtali and Asher. The time of Israel's Judges is the Late Bronze Era. |
| **Iron Age Kingdoms** 1120–732 BC | United Kingdom of Israel starts with King Saul in 1095 BC. King David rules from 1048 BC and conquers the Galilee. Solomon reigns from 1015–975 BC. 975 Israel divided into two and the Galilee is part of the Northern Kingdom. |
| **Eastern Empires** 732/22–332 BC | In 732 BC the Assyrians commence their conquest of the Galilee. The Israelites were decimated in the Galilee and Gentiles filled the vacuum. Rule by Assyrians 722–586 BC Babylonians 586–539 BC Persian 539–332 BC. |
| **Hellenistic** 332–63 BC | Greek rule with Alexander the Great. The Galilee under the influence of pagan culture. A Jewish conquest of Galilee by the Maccabees in 101 BC. Jewish migrants, including Nazarenes from Judea settle in the Galilee. |
| **Early Roman** 63 BC–135 AD | Roman rule commences in 63 BC. This period ends with the Second Jewish War 135 AD. Persecution of Jews by Romans. Includes the life of Jesus Christ (4 BC–30 AD) centred in the Galilee. Includes the Christian Apostolic Age. |
| **Late Roman** 135–325 AD | A time of persecution of Christians by Romans and Jewish authorities. Start of the Jewish Mishnah period 200 AD in Galilee. A decline of settlements. |
| **Byzantine** 325–638 AD | Emperor Constantine's conversion results in a Decree of Tolerance in 313 AD and reduces religious persecutions. Jewish Talmud writers based in Galilee. Growth of Galilean Christian sites and pilgrims from other countries. |
| **Islamic** 638–1099 | Arab rule Umayyad (Mecca)–Abbasid (Baghdad). European pilgrims decline. |
| **Crusader** | European rule (1099–1291). Revived Christian sites and pilgrimage. |
| **Islamic** 1291–1917 | Rule by Ayyubid–Mamluke (Cairo)–Ottoman (Istanbul). Limited pilgrimage. |
| **Modern** | British Mandate (1917-1948). State of Israel 1948. Revived Christian sites. |

10 Jones, FN 2005, *The Chronology of the Old Testament,* 15th Edition, Master Books, Green Forest, AR 72638, USA.

\* Dates based on Murphy-O'Connor, J op.cit. pp. 2-5 (Exception of lower Iron Age date of 1120 instead of 1200 BC based on other scholars proposals. eg. Prof. Israel Finkelstein. Some also date the Early Roman. Era from Herod's reign (37 BC) and not Pompey's invasion (63 BC).

## Digging up the past

In the nineteenth century Palestinian archaeology was still in its infancy. Sites were being uncovered and the difficult task of identifying the biblical names began. Scholars did not always agree on some of these nominations, but a start was made to uncover the secrets of the Promised Land. Christians were also keen to gain more information on sites associated with the life of Jesus. There had been a rise in that century of debate about the reliability of the Bible and the historicity of Jesus. An American explorer and Bible scholar named Edward Robinson (1794–1863) travelled extensively in Palestine and sought to identify some of the sites. He was described as the father of biblical geography and in 1841 he published his research and site proposals. [11] His intent was noble but unfortunately some of his nominations were not accurate and have led to incorrect site assumptions.

## Jewish migration to the Galilee

A.08 Map of the Promised Land.

The northern region of Israel is also known as "the Galilee". Excavations in that region began to reveal Jewish sites at the end of the Late Hellenistic era. In 140 BC a revived Jewish kingdom was set up in Judea by a patriotic group called the *Maccabees*. In 101 BC this kingdom conquered the former northern kingdom of Israel. This occurred after a very long period of abandonment by the Israelites. After this event Jewish immigrants began establishing communities in what was predominately a Gentile culture. They brought their distinctive features and pottery that can be observed in the Galilean archaeological record.

Included in this group were the forebears of the *Virgin Mary*, who according to tradition, settled in the region of a city called Sepphoris, located just north of Nazareth. Sepphoris became the capital of the Galilee and had both Gentile and Jewish sectors. Near the time of Joseph and Mary's return from Egypt it had a large building program. Most of the funding was from the newly appointed King Herod Antipas, who reigned from 6–39 AD. He was a prolific builder, just like his notorious father, King Herod the Great.

---

11 Robinson, E and Smith, E 1841, *Biblical Researches in Palestine, Mount Sinai and Arabia Petraea*, vol. III, Crocker and Brewster, Boston, USA, p. 200.

The migration to the Galilee included Jews from many backgrounds and their motives would also be diverse. For some the decision was probably political, fuelled by a revived sense of nationalism. To others the move would be commercial with new opportunities for business. Significantly, there were groups where the reason for their migration was religious, to fulfil the mandate of recovering the Promised Land of Abraham (Gen. 12:7). Part of this religious migration involved groups of devout Jews keen to establish their own, independent identity.

Included in this category were the *Essenes* who are documented in historical accounts. Josephus noted their piety and wrote that they "esteem that the rewards of righteousness are to be earnestly striven for" (*Ant*.18.1.5). The Essenes were devout and practised a very communal lifestyle. To them it was very important to preserve their spiritual heritage and not come under the influence of pagan Greek culture. Before the first Roman War they had settlements throughout the land and Josephus comments that they numbered about four thousand in Israel in his day.

## Pious pioneers and Nazarenes

A.09 King David's statue Jerusalem.

Another group of particular relevance for this book are the *Nazarenes* or *Nazoreans* who were a distinct group of Jews claiming direct bloodline ancestry all the way back to King David. The meaning of *Nazorean* is derived from the Hebrew word *netser* which means a *little branch, shoot* or *sprout*. The Nazarenes saw themselves as little branches connected to King David who was *the Branch*. They would have been appreciative of their spiritual heritage. It is no different today when people proudly trace their lineage back to any recognised royalty. Some of the Nazoreans established devout settlements in the Galilee.

## The Nazareth colony

There was a tradition of clusters of Nazarene/Nazoreans forming in the Nazareth environs with archaeologist Bargil Pixner claiming they had a marked presence in the period, starting around 100 BC. He describes them as "a group of the Davidic Nazorean clan".[12] This group gives its name to a particular settlement that is called Nazareth. Pixner affirms this connection with his statement: "one can assume with some degree of certainty that

---

12 Pixner, B op.cit., p. 30.

Nazara/Nazareth ("little Nezer") got its name from a Davidic clan".[13] One of the early colonies decided to name their settlement to show their distinctive ancestry. They take the root meaning of *Nazara* (G3478) to get *Natserat*, the settlement of the *Branch*. The pioneers would have been both pious in lifestyle and devout in belief, and this information, we will see, is the first clue in solving the mystery of Nazareth city.

**Isaiah and the Messiah**

Isaiah made a number of prophecies about the Messiah and one of them is linked to the Hebrew root meaning of Nazareth. Specifically Isaiah 11:1-2 proclaimed: "There shall come forth a Rod from the stem of Jesse. And a Branch shall grow out of his roots. The Spirit of the LORD shall be upon Him".

Matthew in his gospel clearly links Jesus as the Messiah, with the city of Nazareth. He points out that it is part of a master-plan over many centuries. "And he [Joseph] came and dwelt in *a city called Nazareth*, that it might be fulfilled which was spoken by the prophets, *He shall be called a Nazarene*" (Matt. 2:23). [italics added]

**Jesus of Nazareth: the Nazarene**

Jesus is described with two Greek words derived from Nazara. The first is *Nazarenos* (G3478) which is used as an adjective showing he was connected to his city. The second is *Nazoraios* (G3480) which is a proper noun that was more of a title that implies an aspect of spirituality connected to his Davidic ancestry. (Many versions translate these terms interchangeably.) Due to the lack of an archaeological identification of this city, some scholars emphasise that Jesus' title has more to do with his lineage than his place of residence. Pixner further proposed: "Therefore the title 'Nazorean' does not refer so much to the hometown of Jesus as with his Davidic lineage".[14] However, if the city could be identified, the two aspects would finally come together. That is how the Jewish Matthew in his gospel clearly understood it. The title of *'Jesus the Nazarene'* combines the messianic meaning of the prophecy with the geographical location of his large native city. Prophetic geographic pointers will be shown to illustrate this aspect in the subsequent sections.

**Yeshua mi-Natserat**

In the culture of that day a Jewish male was identified in two ways:

**1. Patronymic:** An individual's name with 'son of' attached to the father's name was used. For Jesus it could have been *Yeshua ben Yosef*, yet he is not described as such. He was the legal son of Joseph but not by bloodline, to make a theological point.[15]

---

13 Pixner, B, op.cit., p. 30.

14 Pixner, B, op.cit., p. 29.

15 The Christian understanding is that Joseph was the legal, "adopted" father of Jesus. Mary is the natural mother by bloodline and the incarnation of the Messiah is a sovereign action of God.

**2. Geographic:** Using his name with the largest city or town publicly known at the time in the area where he lived. In the case of Jesus this, in Hebrew, is *Yeshua mi-Natserat* meaning Jesus of Nazareth. Yeshua (i.e. Jesus) was a common name in that period, and the narrowing down to a specific city for identification purposes was useful. This was his common description rather than 'Jesus, son of Joseph'. [16]

### Who called him Jesus of Nazareth?
Many people in the New Testament have been recorded as using the title *'Jesus of Nazareth'*. If this was part of a conspiracy, as suggested by some scholars, it had to be a far reaching one, as it would have involved Jewish and Roman authorities as well as his believers. Listed below are examples of occasions where this title or epithet was used:
- Four apostles: Peter (Acts 3:6), John and Philip (John 1:45), and Paul (Acts 26:9).
- Three believers: Mark (Mark 1:9), Luke and Cleopas (Luke 24:19).
- Demons in a spiritual encounter (Mark 1:24).
- Temple guards at his arrest (John 18:7).
- Jerusalem crowd welcoming him on Palm Sunday (Matt. 21:11).
- The servant girl of the high priest Caiaphas to Peter (Matt. 26:71).
- Governor Pilate when labelling the plaque on the Cross (John 19:19).
- An angel after his resurrection (Mark 16:6).
- Jewish enemies at a Jewish Sanhedrin trial (Acts 6:14).
- Jesus, when introducing himself, at the conversion of the Apostle Paul (Acts 22:8).

### Early labelling of Christians
The early disciples of Jesus were not called Christians at first. It was not until about 47 AD that this label was used, and that was outside Palestine in Antioch, a place now located in modern south-western Turkey (Acts 11:26).
- The Arabs, from earliest times, have referred to the followers of Jesus as *Nasara*. This term can be seen as recognition of his ancestry, or of his geographic home city, or both.
- The very early Jewish references use the term *Notzrim* to denote Jewish Christians. Some suggest this comes from an understanding that Jesus came from a geographic location with *'netzer'* in the name – Nazareth. The suggestion is they would not be keen to link it to his Davidic ancestry. Notzrim has become a generic Jewish term for Christians generally and is often used as such by Jews in modern day Israel.

---

16 Jesus the Nazarene, which has debated meaning, would be Yeshua ha-Natserati or ha-Notsri. He is mentioned as "son of Joseph" in John 1:45 by the Apostle Philip. The context was to identify his family and city of origin. He was called son of Joseph by the rulers of his synagogue (Luke 4:22). On several occasions he was called 'Son of David' which was one of his messianic titles.

## 1.3 The intriguing explanation

My proposal is that there are two sites that share the same name of Nazareth. This is the second and vital clue to the mystery of Nazareth.

Listed in Table 2 opposite are the biblical references that can distinguish the two sites from one another.

- One list refers to Nazareth as a large urban city centre (denoted NC).
- The other list refers to the traditional residence of Mary and Joseph. It is in an outlying hamlet (denoted NV) within the city-polis limits of Nazareth.

On the map below are indicated the two locations that are 2,500 metres (2,700 yards) apart by direct measure.

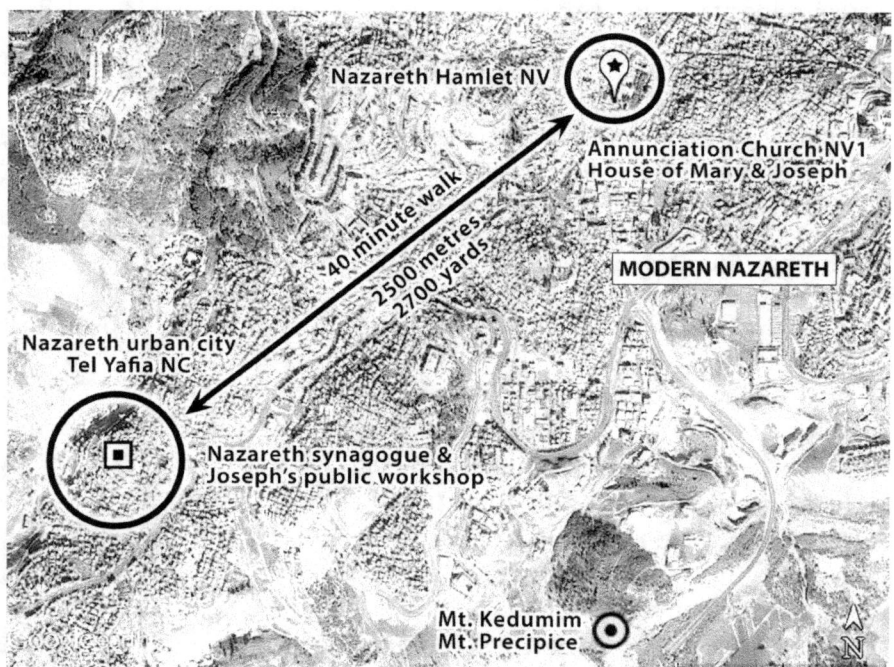

A.10 Map showing relationship of the original Nazareth city urban centre with the adjacent hamlet of Joseph and Mary.
Base map Google Earth. Image © 2015 DigitalGlobe.

*The controversial city of Jesus*

**TABLE 2: Bible verses explaining the two Nazareth locations.**

**NAZARETH HAMLET – VILLAGE (NV)**
A very small hamlet 4 BC. Traditional location of house of Mary and Joseph. Became a village after 30 AD.

2,500 metres – 2,700 yards
40 minute walk

**NAZARETH CITY (NC) URBAN CENTRE**
(1st Century AD)
Currently named as Tel Yafia. or Mar Yarkob

### SITE NC
### EVENTS RECORDED AT THE URBAN CITY OF NAZARETH

1. Joseph has a workshop/residence somewhere near the city of Nazareth (*Matthew 13:55*).

2. Jesus helps his father in the Nazareth city workshop (*Luke 2:51–52*).

3. Joseph and Mary had close family relatives in the city of Nazareth (*Matthew 13:55–56*).

4. Nazareth was a large city with leaders of questionable reputation (*John 1:45–46*).

5. Jesus taught in the city synagogue and was rejected (*Matthew 13:54–58*).

6. Jesus returned to the city synagogue to make his Jubilee Declaration (*Luke 4:16–22*).

7. Leaders pushed Jesus outside the city walls, towards an execution site on the ridge of the city (*Luke 4:28–30*).

### SITE NV
### EVENTS RECORDED AT THE HOUSE OF MARY AND JOSEPH IN NAZARETH HAMLET

1. The Incarnation. Mary is chosen to be the mother of Jesus. The event occurs in a house (*Luke 1:26–38*).

2. Mary leaves her house to visit Elizabeth her cousin in Juttah in Judea (*Luke 1:39*).

3. Pregnant Mary returns to her house from Judea (*Luke 1:56*).

4. Joseph takes Mary as wife in her home in the hamlet (*Matthew 1:24–25*).

5. Joseph and Mary leave their home to travel to Bethlehem for the birth (*Luke 2:4*).

6. Joseph and Mary return to their home in Nazareth with baby Jesus (*Luke 2:39*).

7. After a short stay in their home, the Holy Family flees to Egypt (*Matthew 2:13–15*).

8. Joseph and Mary return from Egypt to their house at Nazareth (*Matthew 2:22–23*).

9. Jesus matures in the hamlet and city of Nazareth (*Luke 2:51–52*).

10. Joseph dies at his home and is buried somewhere nearby (implied).

11. Jesus travels from his home to be baptised by John the Baptist in the Jordan (*Mark 1:9*).

12. Jesus relocates with Mary early in his ministry from his Nazareth home to Capernaum (*Matthew 4:12–13*).

## THE URBAN NAZARETH CITY AT TEL YAFIA (NC)

- A historic suburb of modern Nazareth spelt as Yafia, Yafi'a or Yafa.
- Archaeological evidence shows it was a large Jewish city in Jesus' time.
- Civic and religious centre of about 5,000 people in 4 BC–30 AD.
- The place of Joseph's main workshop but not his family home.
- The location of Mary and Joseph's synagogue.
- A city that would be well known to the inhabitants of Israel in 30 AD.
- Incorrectly endorsed as Old Testament Japhia (Jafa, Yafa) by Edward Robinson in 1841 AD. Yafia is also the same as Japhia in Hebrew.
- Not all scholars have accepted this as the location of biblical Japhia.

Nazareth is known as Joseph and Mary's home city, but they did not live in the central urban section. This centre was located on the hill of Yafia. Surveys have confirmed the remains of the required large Early Roman period city. The IAA (Israel Antiquities Authority) has named the hill *Mar Yarkob* based on a medieval tradition. Another description would be *Tel Yafia*.

The city usually included the nearby surrounding villages and hamlets up to the halfway point towards the next city. Nazareth was a new city that started developing some eight to nine decades before the time of Jesus. For this reason it is not recorded in the Old Testament.

The proposal of this site as that of Nazareth city will cause some reaction in archaeological circles, because it is popularly known as the city of Japhia. This was one of the border sites of Zebulun named by Joshua. My proposal is there is another location which meets Japhia's biblical requirement.

Scholars have nominated Tel Yafia as the *'Japha'* of historian Josephus, who describes a fierce battle there between the Romans and the Jews in 67 AD. His descriptions will be used to show support for my nomination.

The map Illus. A.14 is important as it shows the urban and regional spatial definition of the city of Nazareth. When this is understood the Gospel's city terminology makes sense.

---

**IMPORTANT NOTE**

In this book **"Tel Yafia"** will be used and consistently refers to the central **City of Nazareth** site. It is the main **urban centre** occupying a historic hill. This label is used despite its variable status and names through history.

*The controversial city of Jesus*

# THE HAMLET–VILLAGE IN NAZARETH (NV)

- The Catholic Church of the Annunciation today is the most likely location for the event involving Mary and the angel Gabriel.
- This Church will also be shown as the locality of the house of Mary and Joseph in a Jewish hamlet in 4 BC before it grew to a village.
- The site is a 30–40 minute walk to the nearby urban city of Nazareth. It was outside the urban centre, but within the geographical city limit.
- The hamlet site grew over the centuries due to extensive pilgrimage.
- It became known as the City of Nazareth after the original city centre nearby was destroyed circa 630 AD.

There is evidence of a long period of veneration at the traditional *Catholic Church of the Annunciation*. The site remains from the Early Roman era are very minimal.

As pointed out by modern researchers, archaeology to date does not support the Church of the Annunciation as part of a large Jewish city from 4 BC to 30 AD. However this locality is the small isolated hamlet of Joseph and Mary located approximately 2,500 metres (2,700 yards) north-east of the walled city site. Significantly it is *within the accepted geography of Nazareth* city-polis environs in an outer rural zone.

The archaeological remains for this settlement reflect only a small number of inhabitants in the first century AD. After 30 AD it was occupied by *Judeo-Christians* which later included descendants of Jesus' relatives.

During the first three centuries, when Christians were persecuted, this site remained small. With the growth of Byzantine Christianity from 313 AD onwards, and the arrival of pilgrims over the succeeding centuries, the settlement became a village and eventually a flourishing town.

In modern times, this city has boomed with the influx of visitors and pilgrims from all over the world. It is estimated in that over one million people per year have visited Nazareth in recent times.

---

**IMPORTANT NOTE**

In this book, to avoid confusion, this locality will be called **"traditional Nazareth"**. It will also be referred to as the **hamlet or village of Nazareth.** This name is used to distinguish it from the urban city site to the south-west.

A.11 View of modern day Yafia facing south. It shows the prominent hill profile. NC2 indicates a Byzantine site with intriguing remains explained in Chapter 9.

A.12 View of Tel Yafia facing east towards Mt. Kedumim and Mt. Tabor. The hill was once the urban centre of Nazareth city with its circuit walls. The Franciscan Church (NC1) and the Byzantine site (NC2) are key locations. Base Map Google Earth Image © 2016 DigitalGlobe.

# CHAPTER 2

## NAZARETH CITY AT TEL YAFIA

### The City of the Branch

*And being warned by God in a dream,
he [Joseph] turned aside into the region of the Galilee.
And he came and dwelt in a city called Nazareth, that it might be fulfilled
which was spoken by the prophets,
"He shall be called a Nazarene".*

Matthew 2:22–23.

---

The mystery of this prophecy of the lost city of Jesus is found in a suburb of modern Nazareth. This suburb, known today as Yafa or Yafia lies 2.5 kilometres (1.55 miles) from the traditional home of Mary and Joseph. *'Tel'* is Hebrew for a mound of historical ruins and buried within Tel Yafia's foundations are the proven remains of a city at the time of Jesus. A description of the city of Nazareth can be made when the main characteristics of a Galilean Jewish city in the first century are understood with this site.

## 2.1 Defining Nazareth city-polis

**Yafia is not Japhia according to some scholars**
Tel Yafia: 32-41-16 N. and 35-16-30.3 E.

When American explorer Edward Robinson supported the site of Tel Yafia as that of biblical Japhia in 1841, it robbed the site of its true origin as Nazareth. This nomination was accepted by other scholars at that time.[1] However, since then a number of scholars from a range of disciplines have rejected the nomination, based on topographic logic.[2] The details and their reasons for rejection are given in Chapter 12. Before considering how to describe this city, it is necessary to understand how a Jewish city in the Galilee in the Early Roman Era was defined spatially. This is a key aspect in understanding the gospel accounts and how to solve the mystery.

**Urban and regional city limits**
Jewish sites are differentiated from pagan and Roman sites by a number of factors. In archaeology certain pottery types; the absence of pig bones; and remains of ritual baths called mikvah are among the site indicators. Studies on the demographics of Jewish Galilean cities and villages in Roman times have been done to show the size of their populations. Uzi Liebner has a hierarchy of six settlement types based on the size of Galilean ruins.[3] These sites are ranked in our terminology as large city, city, town, village, hamlet or villa. The city is known in Greek terminology as *polis* (G4172). Israeli Professor Ze'ev Safrai has commented on this definition in the time frame:

> The polis enjoyed for the most part, autonomy. Even if the Roman authorities attempted in some ways to limit this privilege, the city still retained a highly developed mechanism for independent self rule.[4]

Polis has the root words *"polys"* (G4183) which means many, or high in number and *"polus"* which includes great and large. Hence a settlement with a relatively large size and population for that time period is required. A polis could include nearby villages (*Gk. kome*) and hamlets (*Gk. mikro chorio*). The size and status of the 'polis' in Galilee varied but there were three zones within them.

---

1. For example Dr. William Smith Bible Dictionary (1884). Scholars who travelled there and wrote in support were C.W. Van de Velde (1851), L.F. de Saulcy (1850), Rabbi J.Schwarz (1850). *Refer* 'Japhia' *McClintock and Strong Cyclopedia. Refer* Bibliography.

2. Yigal Levin (Israeli Bible Geographer) has rejected the nomination. Other scholars also rejecting the nomination include Martin Noth, Zecharia Kallai, Nadav Na'aman, Zvi Gal, Carl Keil and Robert Hubbard. *Refer* Chapter 12.

3. Liebner, U 2009, *Settlement and History in Hellenistic, Roman and Byzantine Galilee*, No.127, Mohr Siebeck, Tubingen, Germany, p. 85. A dunam is 1000 square metres. Very small (0.5-3 dunam), small (4-10), medium (11-20 dunam), medium large (21-40 dunam), large (41-60 dunam), very large (61-90 dunam).

4. Safrai, Z 2003, *The Economy of Roman Palestine*, Routledge, London and New York, Section II. 4, p. 19.

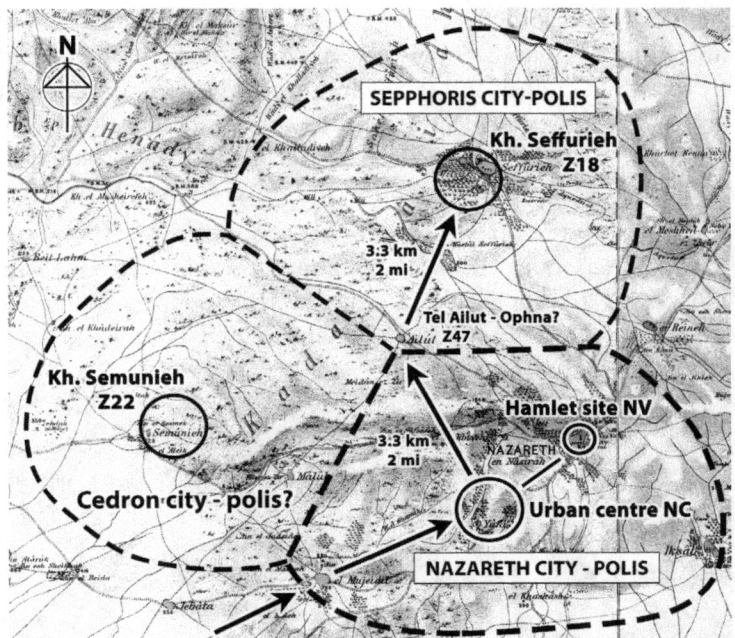

A.13 Notional regional map 4 BC. Boundary limits of Nazareth city with two adjoining cities. The arrows indicate the main road connections. PEF base map.

## The three city-polis zones

- *The walled city* was the central urban core having a secure perimeter with gates. It was often erected on a prominent, elevated location.
- *The suburbs* were adjacent to the walled section on the nearby slopes. They would provide support facilities and trades for the city.
- *The outer perimeter* contained hamlets and villages in a rural setting and included agricultural facilities. The perimeter was within convenient walking distance of the city centre.

Each city centre gave its name to the locality and this definition included the nearby rural zone. However, when Jewish cities were adjacent to each other there was a requirement to define the exact boundary. The logical position would be the approximate halfway point between two city centres. There are two cities in close proximity to Nazareth shown in Illus. A.13. To the north was the well-known capital of Sepphoris and the headquarters of King Herod Antipas and to the west was Cedron.[5] Further to the east was the well documented historic city of Daburiya (Daberath). The southern limit probably extended to the start of the Jezreel Plain which had its own cities.

---

5  Cedron in the Septuagint is Joshua's Kitron which is explained in Appendix 4. It is not Shimron as traditionally proposed by some. On the east it probably extended to Iksal in the direction of Tabor. Further to the east was the well-known city of Josephus known as Dabaritta (Daberath).

Archaeological surveys between Sepphoris and Nazareth have revealed a discernible cultural boundary between the two cities. The Nazareth side is distinctly Jewish in culture and the Sepphoris side is more multicultural. As noted by archaeologist Ken Dark from his surveys: "This along with other evidence strongly suggests that a Roman period cultural boundary existed between communities nearer Sepphoris and those nearer Nazareth".[6]

The Nazareth city limits from the centre are about three kilometres (1.86 miles) to the north, south and west and about four kilometres (2.5 miles) to the east. Allowing for topographical influences the total city-polis area can be approximated to about 35 square kilometres (8650 acres).

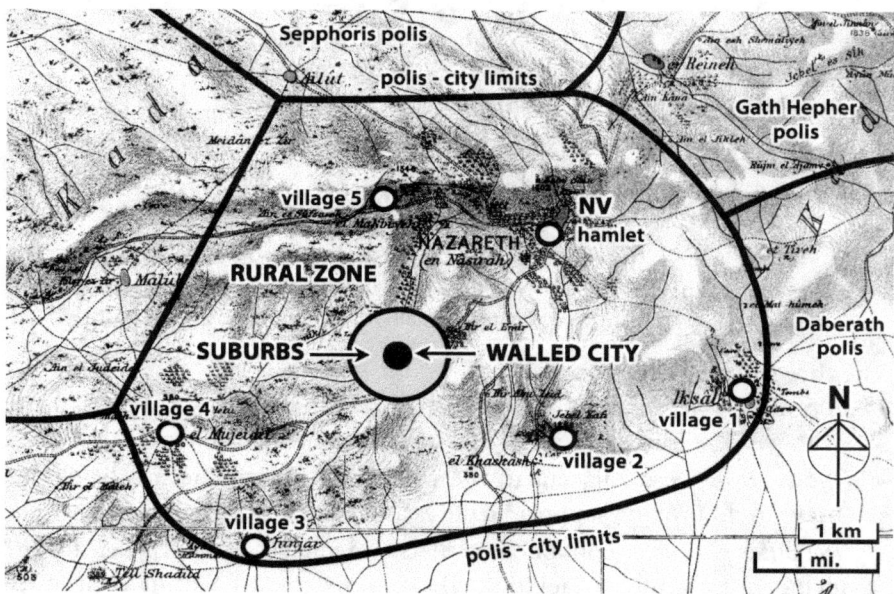

A.14 Proposed boundary limits of Nazareth city 4 BC showing the urban centre with the rural zone adjacent. The hamlet of Joseph and Mary (NV) was included. PEF base map.

**A critical definition**

From Illus. A.14. it can be understood that the little traditional hamlet where Mary and Joseph lived was within the city limits. It was located in the outer perimeter zone and not in the central walled city. However, a citizen residing in the hamlet would still identify them-self as a resident of the city. The historic Jewish understanding of the semi-rural perimeter was that its residents were part of the city. This was the case in the first century as described by Prof. Ze'ev Safrai: "Essentially, a polis can be defined as a self ruled settlement

---

6  Christianorigins.div.ed.ac.uk, CSCO 2016, *Dr. Ken Dark on Galilean Archaeology*, New College, University of Edinburgh, UK. Full article Dark, KR 'The Roman Period and Byzantine Landscape between Sepphoris and Nazareth', *Palestine Exploration Quarterly* 140.2, 2008. pp 87-102.

possessing the necessary institutions required of the *polis* ... *During the Roman period the polis ruled over the adjacent rural territory*".[7] [italics added]

This understanding continued into the following centuries and is proven in a quote from the *Jerusalem Talmud*: "And so it has been taught: Those which are near a city and are part of its landscape – lo, they are in its status".[8]

So the gospel terminology can be clearly shown as geographically reliable for supporting the traditional location of the house of Mary and Joseph.

### A description of Nazareth city-polis

The plan below is a proposal of how Nazareth City urban centre could have been based on the topography. (Archaeological remains within dashed zone.)

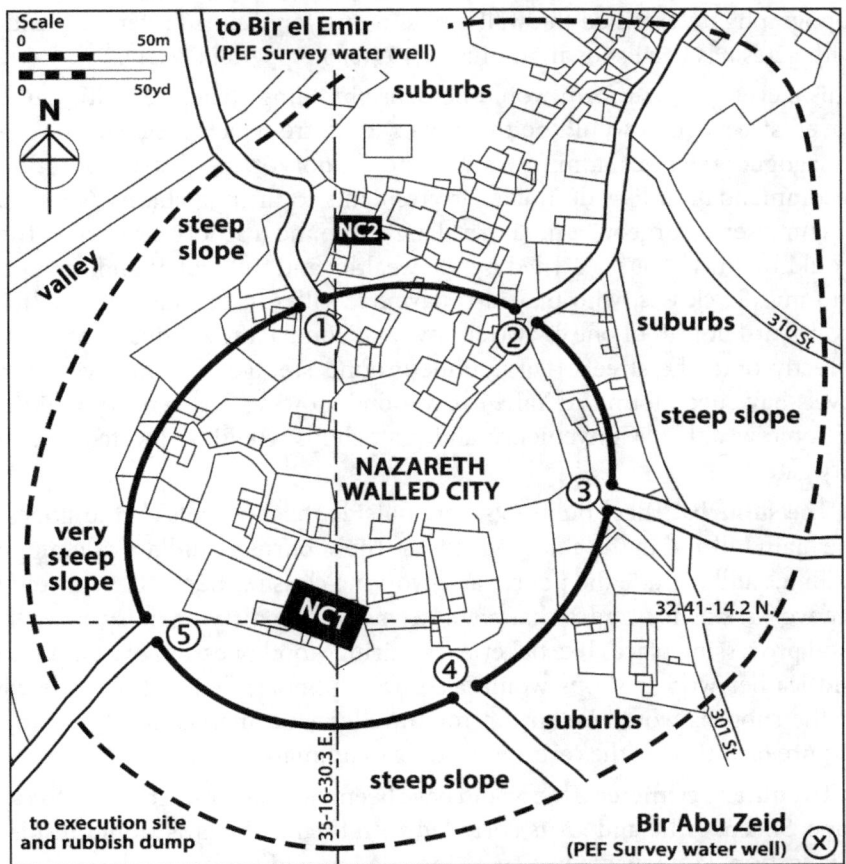

A.15 Proposed upper city walls with gates numbered and suburbs dashed 27 AD. Base map by author is Yafia town plan 1951. *Refer* p. 89. The Franciscan compound (NC1) and the Byzantine remains (NC2) are sacred sites that are explained further.

---

7  Safrai, Z, op. cit., p. 15.

8  Talmud, Megillah, *The Talmud in the Land of Israel*, Chapter1.1, IV.A Item C, <books.google.com.au/books?id=lh995zXhEPgC>.

Based on the understanding of Galilean Jewish cities in the Early Roman period, along with Tel Yafia's archaeology and topography, a reconstruction of Nazareth polis can be made.

**1. The walled city.** The main urban centre was located at Tel Yafia and the archaeology survey estimates the site covers an area of 50 dunams [9] which is five hectares or nearly 12.5 acres. This site has two components, the walled sector at the centre on the most elevated position, and the surrounding slopes which would contain the suburbs. In larger sites the elevated section of a city was called the upper-city or in Greek terms an acropolis. The stone walls with gates occupied the ring of the top plateau and this circuit may have included the bare walls of some of the town-houses to provide security. The topography determined the wall position and for Yafia a preferred position with gates has been shown on Illus. A.15 (*refer* Appendix 8.1.1).

This elevated urban form would be dense building structures with narrow, paved streets. This would be the city civic centre which included the main synagogue, religious administration and school for the district. A Talmud recommendation lists desirable city residents to include charity workers, a circumciser, a surgeon, a notary, a slaughterer and a school-teacher. [10] There would be town-houses owned by the wealthy and influential and the upper and middle classes, who may also have had villas in the surrounding hills. Courtyard houses of one or two storeys and compact row-houses would face directly onto the streets. Large underground storage silos involving three levels have been found in Yafia excavations showing first century buildings of some wealth. [11] Convenience and craft shops would be located near the city gates.

**2. The suburbs.** These buildings were outside the city walls on the slopes of the main hill and in the adjacent valleys. The suburbs would provide support facilities and include the poorer and working class residents. Here would be the workshops for trades that were deemed to be dirty or noisy, as well as food processing places like bakeries requiring wood piles and ovens. Butcher and leather-worker shops would also be in popular demand. On the edge of the suburbs would be an inn for travellers and merchants. They would require facilities for the care and feeding of animals.

**3. The outer perimeter.** This would have been the previously mentioned rural zone. Sheep, cattle and goats corralled with their shepherds would reside in this section. Poultry would also be included providing food and eggs.

---

9   Gal, Z 1992, *Lower Galilee During the Iron Age*, Dissertation Series. American Schools of Oriental Research, Eisenbrauns, Winona Lake, Indiana, USA. p. 13.
10  Babylonian Talmud, Folio 17B.
11  Alexandre, Y 2012, 'Yafi'a', *Hadashot Arkheologiyot*, Israel Antiquities Authority Report.

There would be olive groves and vineyards and the required presses to process their produce. Roman era remains of agricultural terraces, field towers, farmhouses and limestone quarries for building stone have been found near Yafia and traditional Nazareth.[12]

**The city water supply.** This factor is crucial to all settlements. Some houses would collect rainwater from their flat roofs and then store it in cisterns. At Nazareth springs and wells were the primary source of water for the city. The IAA Report notes that:

> A main water source of the village is a spring Ein Sufsafa in the valley to the north of the Yafi'a hill, which supplies the Bir el-Amir well at the foot of the hill.[13]

A spring is indicated at the top of the IAA Illus. A.16. (NC6). Two wells were shown on the 1877 PEF map for Yafia to the north and the south-east (noted on Illus.A.15). Other wells are likely to have existed in the floor of adjacent wadis in earlier times.

> Nazareth was a large city in the time of Jesus. It was a centre for worship, administration, education, commerce and industries.

A.16 Yafia aerial view of excavation sites. Mar Ya'akub (as labelled in the centre) means Saint Jacob (James in English). Courtesy of the IAA. NC6 added by author.

---

12 Atrash, W 2009 'Nazareth (West)', *Hadashot Arkheologiyot*, Israel Antiquities Authority Report.
13 Yardenna, A, 'Yafi'a', op. cit.

## 2.2 Yafia's story in the archaeology

### Early history
The secrets of the history of Nazareth City have been revealed by the excavations in Tel Yafia. A pottery survey reported by archaeologist Dr. Zvi Gal showed the probable sequence of events.[14] After the time of Joshua's conquest, at the end of Middle Bronze II era, a very minimal settlement was formed on the hill. The settlement may have been started by devout Israelites of the tribe of Zebulun. Some tombs from that era have been found nearby showing some permanence of the settlement. In the time of King David and Solomon in the Iron Age, it remained a very small village, hence no reference in the Old Testament.

After the Assyrian invasions from 732 BC the settlement was abandoned for over six hundred years. Jewish settlers only arrived here again in the Hellenistic time of the Maccabees around 100–80 BC. The oldest coin found at Tel Yafia is dated back to Alexander Janneus in 76 BC. This gives a potential clue on the foundation era of the site. As discussed previously, it is proposed that this revived pioneer site was started by Nazarenes who called their settlement Nazareth, which grew into a city.

### A Jewish city
The *Israel Antiquities Authority* (IAA) has confirmed the evidence that this was a devout Jewish settlement. Their report states:

> The Late Hellenistic pottery reflects the renewed settlement at Yafia at the end of the second or the beginning of the first century BCE. [circa 110 to 90 BC]. The identification of the new settlers as Jews from Judea is supported by the similarity of some of the vessels to Judean pottery forms from the Hasmonean period ...
>
> This Jewish identity is further supported by the continuity of settlement into the early Roman period ...
>
> The chalk stone bowls and cups date to the Early Roman period and are characteristic of the Jewish population, reflecting a concern for ritual purity.[15]

This is very crucial information. The city was founded by devout Jews from Judea and extends into the time frame of Joseph and Mary. The IAA Report clearly shows the occupation in the required Hellenistic–Early Roman era. Nazareth as a city began to flower in this period and it expanded and developed to the size required for it to be called a polis by 4 BC. Being a good-sized Jewish city means that Nazareth provided a range of facilities for worship, education, commerce, industry and agriculture.

---

14 Gal, Z 1992, op. cit., p. 13. A limited survey in the southern and eastern sector revealed Middle Bronze IIB 9%, Iron Age I 11%, Iron Age II 22%, Hellenistic 14%, Roman 14%, Byzantine 30%.

15 Alexandre, Y 2012, Yafi'a, op. cit.

*Nazareth city at Tel Yafia*

## The evidence for Nazareth City

The IAA Report
vol.124, 2012.
It shows clear confirmation of a large Jewish city of the Early Roman Era, the required time frame for Jesus' life.

Illustrations and photos used courtesy of the
Israel Antiquities Authority.

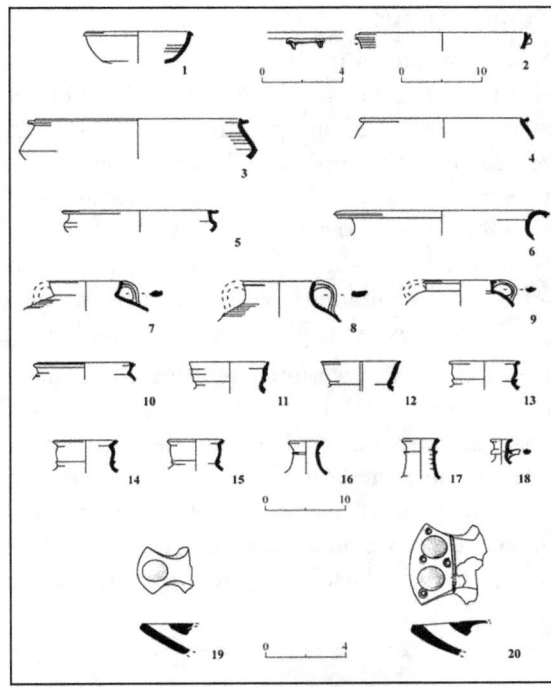

A.17 Early Roman era pottery Tel Yafia.
The pottery remains shown on the left have evidence of a devout Jewish population at this site.

A.18 Silo 105 & Shaft 106.
Photo Assaf Peretz. IAA.

A.19 An excavation view.
Photo Assaf Peretz. IAA.

## How big was Nazareth in the time of Jesus?

Having established that the site was significant in size in 27 AD, the question is, how many people actually lived there? If this is answered it will shed light on events recorded in the gospels. A detailed demographic estimate is given in Appendix 2. Yafia's tel of five hectares (12 acres) would easily support two thousand people within the urban area. A further estimate of about three thousand in the adjacent rural area means Nazareth city-polis was about five thousand people. This means that it was quite large for a city at that time and can be compared to the royal capital city of Sepphoris located to the north with an estimated 10–16,000 residents given by demographers. [16]

In the same appendix the size of the congregation attending the central Nazareth synagogue has been calculated as about 1,280 worshippers. This active religious community enables us to have a better understanding of events related in the gospels, for example the large group of dissidents and leaders who are hostile to Jesus' preaching. It can show how he was missed by his parents in a large convoy, at age twelve, on a return trip from Passover in Jerusalem. It justifies the required client base to support Joseph's public workshop in the city.

A.20 IAA report Nazareth building remains at Tel Yafia. Photo Assaf Peretz. Courtesy IAA.

A.21 Early Roman remains found under the Catholic Church in Yafia. This site is located in the suburban area of Nazareth city in 27 AD.

---

16 Fiensey, DA and Strange, JR 2014, *Galilee in the Late Second Temple and Mishnaic Periods*, Volume 1, Life, Culture and Society, Fortress Press, Minneapolis, USA, p.183.

## Responding to the 'silent' evidence

Critics have commented that Nazareth is not mentioned by Josephus or in the Talmud. The archaeological evidence of Nazareth (Tel Yafia) provides a good explanation to these two historical sources.

**1. Josephus.** He spent some time living in the Galilee fighting the Romans and wrote his accounts about 73 AD. There were 204 villages or towns in his understanding of the Galilee in the first century (*Life* 45.235). Modern surveys support Josephus' tabulation as many Roman era villages and towns of reasonable size have been found. However he only listed 45 settlements in his accounts; the fact that Nazareth city was not on the list is no surprise as he listed only a fifth of the sites. [17] It is not a problem that Nazareth was not on the list as there were many other Galilean sites not named.

**2. Talmud.** There is no mention of the name of Nazareth in the writings of the Jewish Mishnah and Talmuds (200–400 AD). The decline and eventual demise of Nazareth city probably started after the defeat of the Roman War in 67 AD. The IAA Report notes: "There was almost no evidence for activity at the site in the second and third centuries CE [AD]." [18] In the Mishnah era circa 200 AD, activity at the site was very minimal and this is why it is not mentioned. The *Jerusalem Talmud*, written later, listed for the Galilee 66 names out of 204 settlements, which is less than a third of the total nominated. The fact that Nazareth was not listed does not mean it did not exist as other similar sites are not named. This explains why there is a lack of literary references and gives more insight into the story of Nazareth.

## The revived Jewish site

After a period of abandonment the Byzantine remains show it was resettled. There was a revival of the site after Roman Emperor Constantine's *Edict of Tolerance* in 313 AD. This imperial decree for the empire helped not only Christians but also Jews to start or renew settlements in the Galilee. During Constantine's reign (306–337 AD) there was increased building activity in Palestine. Twenty four years later he was succeeded by Julian the Apostate (reign 361–363 AD) who was anti-Christian and favoured the Jews. His short reign may account for another boost of renewed vigour of Jewish Nazareth. The IAA Yafia Report gives more confirmation:

> The quarrying activity at the site, dated on the basis of both pottery and coins to the fourth century CE [AD] indicates that renewed building activities were undertaken in the village. [19]

---

17 Whiston's translation of Josephus has "two hundred and forty" sites but modern scholars translate it as 204 sites. If 204 sites it is 22% and if 240 sites it is 19%.

18 Alexandre, Y 2012, Yafi'a, op. cit.

19 ibid.

Nazareth once again developed into a very devout Jewish town. This fact was recorded by a visiting bishop Epiphanius in 377 AD, who noted that the town was still very resistant to Christianity.[20] This site experienced revived growth and it was not until 630 AD that the town was again to be abandoned. The story of the final destruction and demise is explained in Chapter 4. There are limited remains of life on the site during the following Arab and Crusader eras. The hill site under different names continued as a village into the Medieval–Ottoman period (1291–1917 AD). In the nineteenth century Yafia was recorded as an Arab village with mainly Christian residents.

A.22 View of Tel Yafia hill facing North. NC1 indicates the peak location of the Franciscan Church, the proposed locality of the original Nazareth Synagogue.

**Yafia today**

Modern Yafia has expanded significantly from the original historic village on the hill. The prominent high hill profile is shown in Illus. A.12 and A.22. It is now a large suburb in the south-west of the larger Nazareth Municipality. The mainly Arab population is over eighteen thousand residents, with about seventy percent Muslim and thirty percent Christian, and its mosques and churches are well-attended.

Unfortunately much of the modern development has covered most of the original remains, yet a number of significant sites have been found. Deep in the foundations of Tel Yafia lie more answers to the mystery of Nazareth. The fascinating evidence of Yafia's true identity must be made known and its unique heritage and importance needs to be preserved and promoted.

---

20 Epiphanius, Donato Baldi 1935 Franciscan Cyberspot, <www.nazareth.en.custodia.org/default.asp?id=5952>.

# CHAPTER 3
## TRADITIONAL NAZARETH HAMLET–VILLAGE

### The town built by theology

> Now in the sixth month the angel Gabriel was sent by God to a city of Galilee named Nazareth, to a virgin betrothed to a man whose name was Joseph, of the house of David. The virgin's name was Mary.
>
> Luke 1:26–27.

---

Historical evidence gives support to the traditional Catholic site of the Annunciation of Mary with the angel Gabriel. It was located in a very isolated and sparse hamlet in 4 BC. The subsequent archaeological remains give a testimony of a small community for several centuries. The recorded accounts show this belonged to the first Judeo-Christian church in Nazareth, which was founded by Jesus' relatives.

A.23 Watercolour of Nazareth Village, 1839 by David Roberts. Credit Library of Congress. USA. LC-USZC4-3449.

## 3.1 The town built by theology

The claim of the divine incarnation of Jesus is one of the central tenets of the Christian faith, and also one of the most controversial. If Jesus was the Messiah, then sites associated with his life would have great spiritual significance. The location of his birth at Bethlehem is accurately foretold in Micah 5:2, but there is no mention of Nazareth in the Old Testament. So what evidence is there that the venerated location, in what today is called traditional Nazareth, is correct? The book by René Salm claims that there was a conspiracy regarding Nazareth and that the traditional site is a town built by theology.[1] The conspiracy claim can be shown as incorrect, but his description of the traditional site's growth due to theology is very accurate.

At the centre of the settlement is the *Catholic Church of the Annunciation*, which, based on prophetic mapping shown later, is supported as the correct location of Mary's residence. When visiting this large basilica that today dominates the Nazareth city skyline, it is very obvious that the site is a major pilgrimage destination. Group after group file through the doors and provide a kaleidoscope of ethnic representatives from all round the world.

---

1   Salm, R *The Myth of Nazareth*, op. cit., p. 299.

A leading Italian ecclesiastical architect Giovanni Muzio was selected to design the building. The project was the subject of much controversy and construction spanned from 1960 to 1968. He had the challenge to create a structure that preserved the old historic remains, and yet provided a new, modern space. This has been brilliantly achieved with a three-tiered structure centred on the traditional sacred grotto area. There are, in fact, remains of four previous places of worship in the church:

1. The limited remains of the first early *Judeo-Christian* church. [2]
2. A plan outline of the *Byzantine* Church dating back to the fifth century.
3. Walls from the twelfth century *Crusader* church can be clearly seen.
4. Evidence of the *Franciscan* structures built in 1715, 1877 and 1911 AD.

The large conical dome that hovers over the transept is full of symbolism and creates a sense of majesty befitting the importance of the site. When all the geographical facts and the archaeology are understood, this site's historical importance becomes more apparent. My mapping will show how the location has prophetic pointers, confirming its spiritual significance, preceding the coming of the Messiah by over fourteen hundred years. *Refer* Illus. E.03 p. 199.

A.24 View of the Catholic Church of the Annunciation located in Nazareth. Pilgrims visit this site from all around the world.

---

2   There is debate on the definition of the early Jewish converts to Christianity. Some sources denote them as Judeo-Christian reflecting their Jewish origin. That emphasis would be on their Judean bloodline. Other sources use Hebrew Christian to show a wider classification of converts outside of Palestine where the Jewish factor may have been religious and cultural, cf. Hellenistic Jews. In this book it is taken as a wider cross section of Jews. *Refer* Chapter 3.3.

## Defining Nazareth as a hamlet

In the book of Joshua, reference is made to "cities with their villages" (Josh. 19:16), when describing named sites. The early Israelite cities consisted of a central walled section and the outlying settlements nearby would be the villages. The archaeological surveys of traditional Nazareth shows it did have a minimal settlement in the time of Joshua and the era of Kings David and Solomon (Iron Age) but definitely not a city.[3] In the previous chapter the Roman era city was defined as including the adjacent hamlets and villages that lay nearby to the central urban area. The question that now needs to be asked is, what was the status of the settlement in which Mary and Joseph resided? Was it a defined village or was it merely a tiny hamlet in Early Roman times?

The definition of a *hamlet* varies according to different cultures. For example, in Britain a hamlet used to be understood as a "small village usually without a church."[4] In the New Testament the Greek word *'kome'* (G2968), meaning village, is never used in the context of Nazareth when referring to Jesus' residence. However, it is used in the description of his Galilean ministry where it is said that he "went about all the cities and villages, teaching in their synagogues" (Matt. 9:35). A village could be large enough to warrant its own synagogue. The traditional Jewish requirement for establishing a congregation was for at least ten mature, learned men of the Law to give oversight. The synagogue of Jesus was in the *'polis'* so it can be assumed that his settlement was more of a hamlet than a village. It was not large enough to justify its own synagogue.

Extensive studies have been conducted on the different levels of Jewish settlement in the Galilee. A hamlet requires a site of somewhat less than five hundred people and this perfectly describes the early settlement of Mary and Joseph. Archaeologists have suggested that, judging by the remains found thus far, it was a hamlet of up to three hundred people. Others have a lower figure: "In the time of Jesus the population may have been fewer than 300 persons, and we might imagine that the majority of them would have been children".[5] This suggests a figure of forty to fifty families in the wider

---

3  Gal, Z, *op. cit.*, p. 15.

4  *The Concise Oxford Dictionary* 1964, Clarendon Press, Oxford, UK, p. 555. *The National Geographic Encyclopedia* offers a modern figure less than 500 people. Estimates vary in different studies for first century Palestine hamlets. Arieh Ben David proposes less than 500 people in Fiensy, D and Strange, J, op. cit., p. 183.

5  Jenks, G, op. cit., p. 10. Stange, J 'Nazareth' *Anchor Bible Dictionary*, op. cit. gave a figure of 480 residents. A similar figure of 400 residents is supported in Reed, JL 2002. *Archaeology and the Galilean Jesus*, Trinity Press International, Harrisburg, Pennsylvania, p. 131. The key issue is the population 4 BC–30 AD and the figure after that period.

locality with most making a living in rural activity. This means there were less than a hundred adults which is a good figure for the definition of a hamlet in Early Roman times. On this point of smallness, there is agreement by most scholars as shown by the quotations in Chapter 1. This hamlet's locality does not grow significantly until the Byzantine era in the fourth century.

**Nazareth village reconstructed**

An interesting complex in recent years has been developed about six hundred metres (656 yds.) to the west of the hamlet site. It is called the *Nazareth Village* and is located on an ancient farm that dates back to the first century BC.[6] A team of archaeologists led by Stephen Pfann and Ross Voss have explored and developed the site which opened in the year 2000. At the centre of the project is the re-creation of a typical Galilean village with houses, workshops and a synagogue. Locals are employed and dressed to depict aspects of the Jewish lifestyle of that period. It is a very popular site with visiting tourists seeking a glimpse of what life would have been like in Jesus' time.

**A description of Joseph and Mary's hamlet**

The archaeological record of the traditional hamlet is illuminating as it proves the small Jewish population. Recovered first century purity vessels of the time show that this hamlet shared a common level of devoutness. The hamlet site originated after 40 BC and remained very small in the time of Joseph and Mary. In fact, only a few residences may have been nearby to them during their occupation, but they were part of a more dispersed rural hamlet. They would have been a close-knit community and everyone would have known each other.

The main activity of the residents would have been agriculture and supporting trades, and the small hamlet would have had a strong dependence and connection with the urban centre. The distance between the hamlet and the city centre was a thirty to forty minute walk. The residents of the hamlet would have seen themselves as residents of the city-polis despite their more remote location in a rural setting.

God did not intend that the special incarnation event was to occur in the middle of a walled city, as such a site could have been 'contaminated' by previous residents. The incarnation event required a spiritually prepared site with a discrete location. After Jesus' earthly ministry, the physical separation from the city centre became crucial in preserving the memory of Mary's residence. Persecution in subsequent centuries would have put the location at greater risk if it was within the walls of a Jewish city (*refer* next chapter).

---

6   The Nazareth Farm website <www.nazarethvillage.com/>. It does not claim to have remains of a hamlet but does show evidence of agricultural facilities and terraces dating to Hellenistic and Early Roman period. The Early Roman hamlet is noted in Jenks, G, op. cit., p. 8.

*Proving Biblical Nazareth*

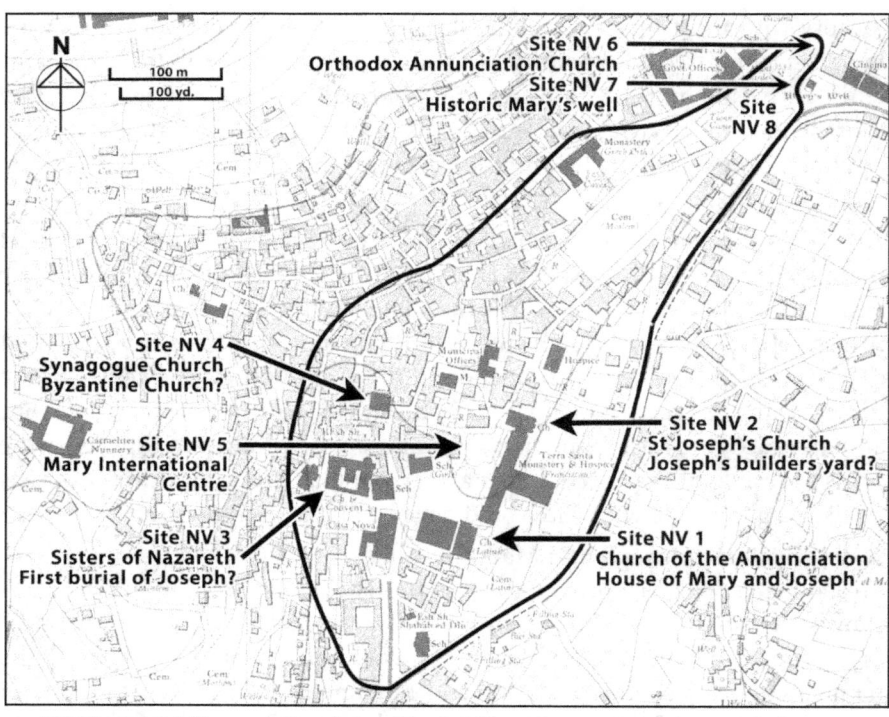

A.25 Nazareth Village outline defined by B. Bagatti Survey. Sacred sites labelled with alpha numeric code for reference. Base map credit National Library of Australia.

A.26 Internal view of the historic Catholic Church of the Annunciation. The altar area marks a traditional location of Mary's residence in 4 BC.

## 3.2 The sites of Mary and Joseph

If the existence of Nazareth city is controversial, it should not be a surprise that the exact location of Gabriel's annunciation and the incarnation event with Mary are subject to lively debate. A related question is the possible location of the eventual family home of Mary with Joseph. Most agree they are all somewhere in the hamlet of Nazareth, but where specifically? There are four current sites shown on Illus. A.25 to consider. An understanding of the events with the required sites and archaeology can be made.

**TABLE 3: Sacred sites at traditional Nazareth**

| Code | Building | Traditional nominations | Proposed nominations |
|---|---|---|---|
| NV1 | Catholic Church of the Annunciation | 1. House of Mary's mother<br>2. Site of the annunciation and incarnation | 1. Mary's house at the time of the annunciation and incarnation<br>2. Becomes the family home with Joseph and Jesus |
| NV2 | Church of Joseph's Workshop | 1. Joseph's home/workshop<br>2. Home of Joseph and Mary<br>3. Church of the Nutrition | 1. Joseph's builder's yard |
| NV3 | Convent of the Sisters of Nazareth | 1. Church of the Nutrition<br>2. House of a "Just man" (?) | 1. Mary's relative (forebear?)<br>2. Joseph's first burial site |
| NV6 | Orthodox Church | Annunciation of Gabriel | Byzantine site |

**Note:** The numbers indicate the sequence. The *Church of the Nutrition* is a Byzantine tradition of Mary and Joseph's residence with two nominations.

### The Catholic Church of the Annunciation (NV1)

Location: 32-42-7.4 N. and 35-17-52.6 E. A messianic location that can also be described as a prophetic site. Surveys have been conducted at this site by archaeologists and the long history has been determined.[7] Remains of occupation to the north of the site from the Bronze and Iron Age have been found. If this site was planned by God as the location for a very significant event, it is possible that in the centuries preceding, God led devout people and prophets to go to the location. They would discreetly camp nearby and conduct sessions of prayer. A good candidate for such an activity would be Elijah who for a time was a resident of the region (*refer* Appendix 8.2.1).

### A young virgin's house

The angel Gabriel's visit is recorded as *'having come in'* suggesting a residence to make his announcement (Luke 1:28). The gospels note that Joseph and Mary were betrothed, but not cohabiting at the time of Gabriel's visit. Mary was a teenager and still a virgin. Joseph was from Judea and tradition suggests that he was not a wealthy man, so the question is, who provided Mary's residence? Franciscans propose it was her mother's house.

---

[7] Bagatti, B 1969, *Excavations in Nazareth*, vol.1, Franciscan Printing Press, Jerusalem, Israel.

Another logical explanation is that Mary's parents, (Anne and Heli), would have arranged for a dwelling (existing or newly built) for their betrothed daughter. This was an acceptable cultural practice in that era. Heli (known as Eliachim= Joachim) and Anne are named in the *Protoevangelium of James*.

It is also highly likely that Mary's mother and a domestic helper would be present in this house at the time of Gabriel's visit as witnesses. A young virgin would not occupy the house on her own before the end of the betrothal. More comment on this explanation is in Appendix 8.2.1-6. Joseph was most likely residing at that time at his public workshop in Nazareth city. Joseph only moved there after it became obvious that Mary was pregnant (Matt. 1:18–25).

**An early site of Christian devotion**

A.27 Internal view of the communion altar table and grotto in the Catholic Church of the Annunciation.

Mary and Joseph were resident from 4 BC to 27 AD, except for their sojourn in Egypt, and this thirty year window is a relatively small period in terms of archaeology. We do not know the size of their residence and no clear-cut remains of the original walls have been found. However there is evidence of occupation of the site in the required period. An IAA article on the location notes: "Many storage pits and cisterns, some which *date from the Early Roman period,* were found in the compound of the Church of the Annunciation".[8] [italics added]

After the relocation by Mary and Jesus in 27 AD the house would be seen as a sacred precinct and therefore a discrete place of devotion. Jesus' relatives would have taken ongoing responsibility as caretakers for the required preservation. An important point, not always understood, is that Mary's house was a unique residence. She knew its significance and only

---

8 Antiquities.org.il. 2016, Israel Antiquities Authority, <www.antiquities.org.il/article_eng.aspx?sec_id=25&subj_id=240&id=1638>. In an interview 19 November 2014 with Fr. Eugenio Alliata, Professor of Christian Archaeology, he mentioned that archaeologist B. Bagatti (who he had worked with) claimed some traces of Early Roman pottery were found at the site of the Church of the Annunciation near the grotto area.

trusted Christians would have gained entry in the early decades after her vacating the site. After the Apostolic Age (30–100 AD) this site has relics of particular attention. The Franciscans claim they have evidence that shows the earliest venerated structure associated with the site dates back to a Judeo-Christian synagogue in the second century. Their website gives examples including a baptismal basin, mosaics and agricultural facilities along with pilgrim graffiti. [9] There is clear evidence that this was an early Christian site and that Mary's name has been found on graffiti associated with it. [10]

Critics have challenged this site as the house of Mary by pointing out that two grottos under the church have the remains of burial sites. There is no proof that they existed before 30 AD and after that date it was no longer a residence. However the graves can be explained as they have cultural Jewish *kokhim* features from the Roman era. They are likely to have been used by Judeo-Christians who settled in the locality in the first few centuries. Kokhim graves provided a place of decomposition of the body for about a year and also the storage of the remaining bones in stone boxes known as ossuaries.

**The pilgrim accounts**

The earliest recorded account of a visit to the church is the Spanish pilgrim Egeria who visited in 383 AD and wrote:

> In Nazareth is a garden in which the Lord used to be after his return from Egypt, (Pet. Diac. Lib. P4) and there is a big and very splendid cave in which she (that is Holy Mary) lived. An altar has been placed there. [11]

Historian and archaeologist Joan Taylor has commented on this eyewitness account, "One may wonder, at this stage, if there was not some small structure connected with the cave: a consideration that should be borne in mind when looking at the archaeological evidence". [12] This shows it was still a modest site but was attracting pilgrim attention. Two years later, in 385 AD, the site was visited by St. Jerome and his companions Paula and Eustochium. He wrote of the visit in 404 AD but no mention of a large building was made. In 431 AD there was an *Ecumenical Church Council* meeting at Ephesus and on this occasion it was decreed that Mary was to be honoured as *Theotokos*– the natural mother of God. The report from that Council used the term:

---

9  christusrex.org. 2016, *Nazareth: Basilica of the Annuncuation Archaeological Excavations*, <www.christusrex.org/www1/ofm/san/TSnzz04.html>.

10 Briand, J 1994, *The Judeo-Christian Church of Nazareth*, Franciscan Printing Press, Jerusalem. p. 23. My proposal is that Mary's room was located at the position of the current open altar under the dome, not the traditional site of the grotto cave some metres to the north.

11 Quoted by 'Peter the Deacon' in Taylor, JE 1993, *Christians and the Holy Places – The myth of Jewish-Christian origins*, Clarendon Press, Oxford, UK, p. 226.

12 ibid. p. 226. St. Helena's biographer (anonymous 9th century) mentions she helped preserve a structure at Nazareth. This could be dated to about 330 AD towards the end of her life.

"Theotoke (a Greek word meaning 'she who has given birth to God or to a god')."[13] It is no surprise that later pilgrims report a more developed site at Nazareth. The Piacenza Pilgrim recorded of her visit of 570 AD: "St. Mary's house is now a basilica and many beneficial effects come to those who can touch her clothes".[14]

The archaeology of the church of the Byzantine era has been dated to somewhere after 400 AD. A case can be made that following the Ephesus Church Council it provided the impetus for a basilica structure which may have been built as early as 440 AD. The next major event was the invasion of the Persians in 614 AD which is explained later. This was followed by the Arab invasion of 638 AD which drastically affected pilgrim numbers. A large church was built around 1100 AD after the Crusader invasion and remains of its base walls are observable today, though most was destroyed in 1263 AD.

**Mary's room?**

For seven centuries pilgrims from all around the world have travelled to Loreto in Italy to a huge basilica that sits on top of its hill. Contained within its walls are the intact remains of a modest stone wall room said to be part of the original house of Mary. There is much controversy about this structure, and the means by which it was transported from Palestine to Italy after 1291 AD. This account would require the walls to be housed within the Byzantine and Crusader church structures. Archaeological examination has shown that the stones could be from the Nazareth area and the period of when the stones were cut could very well be the Early Roman Era. There are strong opinions for and against on this matter. Saint Francis of Assisi (1181–1226 AD) made claims about this structure in Italy with its sacredness and its location.[15]

His order of Franciscan monks became the inheritors of the original sacred site in Nazareth and they have been faithful custodians of it since 1275 AD. Pilgrimages to Nazareth continued during the Medieval Era and in 1715 a substantial church was rebuilt on the site. This remained until the current structure was erected by the Franciscans in 1968.

> **The mapping shown later will support the traditional Catholic site as the location of Mary's room at the time of the incarnation. This location is a very significant messianic site.**

---

13 Third Ecumenical Council, *Prolegomena*, <www.intratext.com/IXT/ENG0835/_PV.HTM#7K>.

14 Murphy-O'Connor, J., *The Holy Land*, op. cit., p. 375.

15 This tradition is well documented in Catholic sources. The story of Loreto raises many questions on the origin of the structure. The claim is that Saint Francis predicted the transfer of the remains before the event.

## The memory of Joseph

There are three sites of interest associated with Joseph the carpenter and two are dealt with in this segment. The third is explained in Chapter 9.3.

### St. Joseph's Church (NV2)

Located 100 metres (110 yards) north of the Church of the Annunciation, is a church commemorating Joseph and his workshop. The Franciscans even claim that this site could be the location of the family home of Joseph and Mary due to the Early Roman remains and evidence of later veneration. My proposal is that Joseph had his main workshop in urban Nazareth. There is another explanation for this site being in close proximity to the family home. A carpenter, like Joseph would require a large compound for sheds and a stable for at least one donkey to operate his trade. His sheds would provide a place to store and dry a large amount of timber. This would be a logistics base where Joseph and Jesus worked together to supply their public workshop in the city. The family home was set in a fairly isolated location with access to trees for Joseph's timber needs (*refer* Appendix 8.2.7). There would be land where they could also grow their own vines, fruit trees and vegetables. After 30 AD this site would be ideal for any caretakers in the apostolic era and remains from this period have been found there.

### Convent of the Sisters of Nazareth (NV3)

Located 100 metres (110 yards) west of the Church of the Annunciation is a site with a long history. An archaeological survey was conducted in 2004 and the results have been published. [16] This showed that this site was originally a Jewish residence in the earlier Early Roman Era. After it was abandoned it was partly quarried. Later an interesting *'rolling stone'* tomb dated to the second half of the first century AD was located within the site. There is good evidence that this house and tomb site then became incorporated into a Byzantine chapel. [17] A local tradition, of unknown date and origin is that this was once a great church and that it contained the remains of a saint or 'just man'. It can be suggested that this may have

A.28 Convent of the 'Sisters of Nazareth'. Rolling stone tomb – St. Joseph's first burial site?

---

16 Dark, K 2012, 'Early Roman–Period Nazareth and the Sisters of Nazareth Convent', *The Antiquaries Journal* 92, The Society of Antiquaries of London, UK.

17 The archaeologist Ken Dark has proposed this site as the Church of the Nutrition (early home of Jesus) mentioned by a pilgrim Abbot Adomnan in 670 AD. Dark, K 2012 'The Byzantine Church of the Nutrition in Nazareth rediscovered' *Palestine Exploration Quarterly* 144 (3). pp. 164–184.

been the initial burial place of Joseph the carpenter as he has to be buried somewhere in the locality. Given his status, such a tomb, with its dating, would be suitable, and could explain the early veneration of the site. There is an account that his remains were relocated to Bethlehem (*refer* Appendix 8.2.8). If this is correct the most likely period would be during the Crusader era before 1263 AD. The archaeology of this site and its proximity to the proposed house of Mary raises an interesting scenario. Was this the residence of a forebear of Mary whose vacated site provided some of the stone for her residence, and then a place of burial for Joseph? Some decades later his burial was made more secure yet accessible with the rolling stone tomb.

**Mary's neighbour? – excitement and debate (NV5)**

In 2011, the *Mary of Nazareth International Center* was opened. This project gained support from twelve major Christian denominations in Israel. The aim was to have a centre that promoted an understanding of the Virgin Mary from different perspectives using modern media presentations. The location is about 60 metres (65 yards) from the Catholic Church of the Annunciation. In the course of the site preparation, an amazing discovery was made of the remains of a historic residence. What excited the local Christians was the IAA report that linked parts of it back to the Early Roman period. Yardenna Alexandre, the archaeologist involved, has made interesting observations:

> The discovery is of the utmost importance since it reveals for the first time a house from the Jewish village of Nazareth and thereby sheds light on the way of life at the time of Jesus. The building that we found is small and modest and is most likely typical of the dwellings in Nazareth in that period.[18]

The courtyard site with rooms, a cistern and a cave has been shown to be Jewish. It recently caused quite a stir as the Israeli Antiquities Authority has dated this site as from 100 BC–100 AD, which includes Mary's timespan of circa 19 BC–42(?) AD. These dates would make the residents potential neighbours in the time of Mary, Joseph and Jesus. The remains have been taken to show the case for a village setting for Nazareth. The debate goes on, but the dates point to another interesting topic.

A.29 Early Roman Era remains found at the International Mary Center. Could this have been one of Mary's neighbours?

---

18 Israel Antiquities Authority 2009, *For the Very First Time: A Residential Building from the Time of Jesus was Exposed in the Heart of Nazareth*, <www.antiquities.org.il/article_eng.aspx?sec_id=25&subj_id=240&id=1638>.

*Traditional Nazareth hamlet-village*

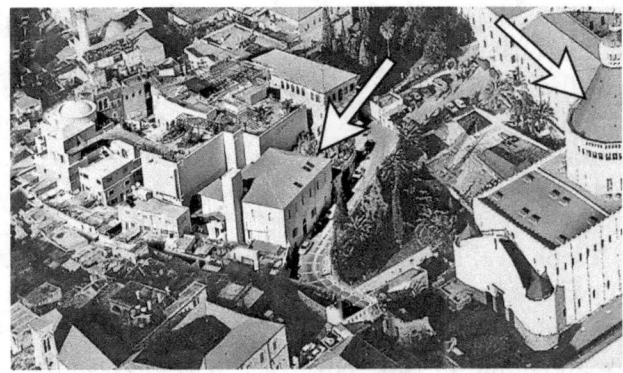

A.30 Mary of Nazareth International Center on the left and the Church of the Annunciation on the right. Courtesy www.cimdn.org. Left arrow indicates the ruins position and it's proximity to Mary's proposed house.

## 3.3 The devout Christian village of Nazara

In the second century the Christian scholar Africanus reported there were two Jewish villages in Galilee named as Nazara and Cochaba, quoted later in the text. They were occupied by descendants of Jesus' relatives who provide key information on the story of Nazareth. They occupied the traditional site of Nazareth which is visited by pilgrims from around the world today. The case for the history of early Christian Nazareth can be plotted with support from the archaeology of the first three centuries.

**The first church in Nazareth**

The gospels indicate that the Apostle John took care of Mary after 30 AD (John 19:27) and a strong tradition states that they eventually resided near to Ephesus in Turkey. After her death in about 42 AD, Mary's residence would have come into the custodianship of surviving relatives at Nazareth. This was common practice in the culture for extended family relationships at that time. There is record of these initial relatives based in Nazareth shown in Illus. A.32. Some are described in our English versions as *'brothers'* and *'sisters'* of Jesus. The Greek word used is *'adelphoi'* (meaning 'from the same womb') which in the Jewish culture could include brothers, half-brothers, step-brothers and cousins. This matter has been a subject of controversy regarding Jesus' family from the second century onwards. A careful reading of biblical texts given on page 49 shows the case that they were cousins. This was the understanding of early church scholars such as St. Jerome. It must be emphasized that Jesus gave responsibility of the care of his mother to the Apostle John, *not to any other family member*. Mary's parents, Anne and Heli, are the common denominator heading up a family that produced cousins to Jesus. These cousins are named as James, Joseph (Joses), Judas (Jude) and Simon (Mark 6:3 and Matthew 13:55).

James is well-known as the son of Alphaeus, one of the twelve original apostles, and called James "the Less". He became the bishop-leader of the

Hebrew Christian church based in Jerusalem until he was martyred in 62 AD.[19] His brother Judas (also known as Jude), is considered by some scholars as the author of the book of Jude in the New Testament, where he identifies himself as the "brother of James" (Jude 1:1). Another much younger brother was Simon who succeeded James as bishop of Jerusalem. According to the chronicler Hegesippus (110–180 AD), he led the Christians away from Jerusalem before the Roman attack in 70 AD and also their return in about 107 AD. Joseph (No. 15) was a half brother indicated in Illust. A.32. These brothers would have the initial responsibility of the preservation of Mary's house, but it would not be promoted as a tourist site for pilgrims!

So the first Judeo-Christian church in Nazareth would have been initially pioneered by James the Less as bishop (based in Jerusalem) with brothers Jude and Joseph (Joses) as leaders initially in Nazareth. Mary's residence, because of its great importance, probably became a special house of prayer in the Apostolic Age. It would be the nucleus of a small cluster of residences that included descendants of the initial relatives of Jesus and other Jewish converts. This pious Judeo-Christian community had a pioneer influence in the early church. There are also records (e.g. St. Jerome) of their various denominations' interaction with the Gentile part of the Christian Church into the fourth century.

There is also another reference for this first century church of Jesus' relatives. The persecution by Roman emperor Domitian (89–96 AD) was recorded by Hegesippus and quoted in the writings of historian Eusebius.

A.31 'James the Less', a cousin of Jesus. His father was Alphaeus not Joseph. Wikimedia Commons.

---

19 Recorded by Josephus (*Ant.* 20.9.1). There has been debate on defining the Hebrew Christian Church. Joan Taylor has challenged some of the assumptions by B. Bagatti. A good exposition is given in: Pritz, R 1988 *Nazarene Jewish Christianity*, The Hebrew University, Jerusalem, 1988.

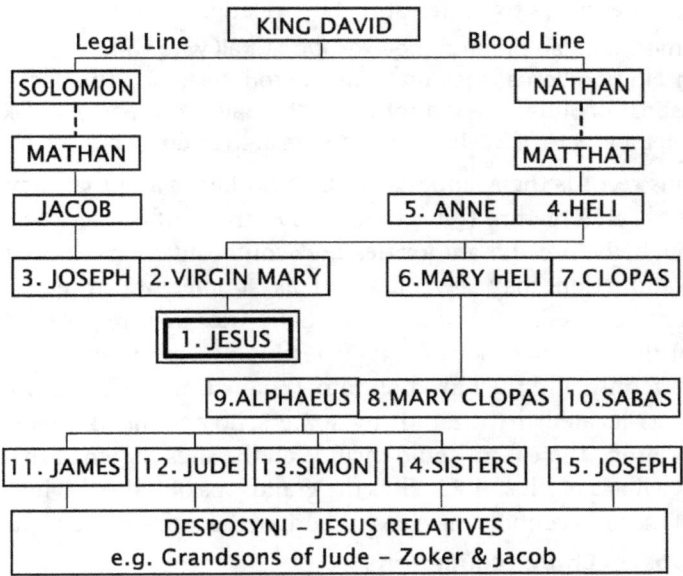

A.32 – Family tree of Jesus

1. Jesus the *"son of Mary"* (Mark 6:3).
2. The Virgin Mary, mother of Jesus (Luke 1:31).
3. Joseph, husband to Mary (Matt.1:16). A son (in-law) to Heli (Luke 3:23).
4. Heli, a descendant of King David, known also as Joachim (=Eliachim).
5. Anne the wife of Heli. The 'adelphoi' (from same womb) in the relating.
6. Mary Heli, *"His mother's sister, Mary the wife of Clopas"* (John 19:25). She shares the same name with her much younger sister the Virgin Mary.
7. Clopas the husband of Mary Heli and uncle to Jesus (John 19:25).
8. Mary Clopas the niece to the Virgin Mary and first cousin to Jesus. *"Mary the mother of James"* (Mark 16:1). The *"other Mary"* (Matt. 28:1). First marriage to Alphaeus a widower and father of St. Matthew. Remarries Sabas. She solves the mystery of the three Marys in the gospel accounts.
9. Alphaeus, father to *"James the Less"* (Luke 6:15) & Matthew (Mark 2:14).
10. Sabas the father of Joseph Barsabas (Acts 1:23). A cousin by re-marriage.
11. James "the Less" apostle listed as 'brother' to Jesus (Matt. 13:55, Gal. 1:19). Alphaeus his father (Matt. 10:3) a Mary is mother (Mark 15:40). A cousin to Jesus. Author NT Book of James. First Jerusalem bishop (Acts 21:18).
12. Jude (Judas, Theudas) listed as a *'brother'* of Jesus (Matt. 13:55). Jesus' cousin. Known as the *"brother of James"* (Jude 1:1). Author Book of Jude.
13. Simon listed as a *'brother'* of Jesus (Matt. 13:55). Later became a bishop.
14. No names given for *'sisters'* of Jesus (Matt. 13:55). They are cousins.
15. Joseph (Joses) listed as a *'brother'* of Jesus (Matt. 13:55). He is a cousin. Candidate to replace Judas Iscariot, named Joseph Barsabas (Acts 1:23).

His account describes two interesting later relatives of Jesus:
> The same Domitian ordered the execution of all who were in David's line, and an old tradition alleges that some heretics accused the descendants [grandsons] of Jude — the brother of the Savior, humanly speaking — claiming they were of David's family and related to Christ himself. [20]

Hegesippus records their names as Zoker and James and that they owned a plot of land of 39 plethra (8 hectares or 20 acres). After their betrayal they were brought before the authorities and confessed their bloodline. Upon closer examination they were deemed as simple, non-threatening farm workers and released. [21] Eusebius noted that: "After their release they became leaders of the churches, both for their testimony and because they were of the Lord's family, and they lived on into Trajan's time". [22] The farm has been proposed as located in Nazareth by some scholars and the hamlet is the logical location. Their farm could include all the sites shown at the southern end of the village of Illus. A.25. Thus the grandsons of Jude who lived into the start of the second century may have inherited the estate of Mary and Joseph.

**The Desposyni Church community**

Scholars have indicated: "Slender evidence suggests that a Judeo-Christian community survived in Nazareth during the C2 and C3 AD". [23] Nazarenes are recorded as still in existence in circa 220 AD with the account of a visit by the historian Sextus Africanus. These Nazarenes are called *Desposyni* which in Greek means *belonging to the Master*. Eusebius confirmed Africanus' Desposyni account a century later, explaining that they were:
> so called because of their relation to the Saviour's family. Living in the Jewish villages of Nazareth and Cochaba, they went through the rest of the land, explaining the above genealogy of their descent and quoting from the book of daily records as much as they could. Whether or not this is true, no one could give a clearer explanation, and the Gospel record, in any case, is true. [24]

This account specifically names the existence of a Judeo-Christian (Nazarene) village called Nazareth in existence in the second century. It was clustered around the traditional location of Mary and Joseph's residence.

---

20 Maier, P., *Eusebius The Church History.* op. cit., p. 94.

21 ibid p. 95 The farm land size given in Eusebius *Church History* 3.20. See also Bauckham, R 2015, *Jude and the Relatives of Jesus in the Early Church*, Bloomsbury Publishing, London, UK, p. 95.

22 ibid p. 95. Trajan reign 98–117 AD. Nazareth as proposed farm location Negev, A op.cit. p. 363.

23 Murphy O'Conner J., op. cit. p. 374.

24 This is Eusebius' account of Africanus' visit in Maier, PL, op. cit., p. 38. Some translations give the two sites as "villages of Judea" rather than "Jewish villages". Maier and other scholars prefer "Jewish villages" and the logic would support the Galilee. The Jewish village of Cochaba is proposed as a site known today as Kaukab near Tel Yodfat in Galilee (*Refer* Chapter 15. 2. 5).

The third century was marked by relentless persecution but the ongoing testimony of the Nazarenes and Desposyni continued. There are accounts of Desposyni being bishops in the church in Iraq in the second century.[25] There is a report of a Nazarene arrested in 250 AD in Pamphylia in Turkey. He was a former resident of Nazareth named Conon and claimed a direct ancestry from Jesus' family. He was brought before the Roman authorities in the reign of Emperor Decius and condemned to a cruel death:

> According to the acts of his martyrdom when questioned in court as to his origin and his ancestry, he replied: *'I am of the city of Nazareth in Galilee, I am of the family of Christ* whose worship I have inherited from my ancestors, and whom I recognize as God over all things'.[26] [italics added]

This Conon is recognised by some churches as a martyr and his name is recorded in the current Church of the Annunciation by a mosaic provided by a deacon with the same name dating back to early fifth century.[27]

**A discrete location**

A reconstruction of the evidence can now be made. The main road from the Jezreel Plain passed west of the urban centre of Nazareth, then northwards via Ha-Horesh and Ilut (Z47 *refer* page 25) to the main capital of Sepphoris (Z18). Parts of this road have been found. This made the hamlet of Joseph and Mary an isolated locality, being two kilometres (1.24 miles) to the east of this route. Today we would call it a low-profile site. The archaeological evidence shows it remained small for a long time which would suit the persecuted community of early Judeo-Christians. It was only later when pilgrimages grew that this Nazareth village became part of the regional road system.

**The important oral tradition**

The historical references to the existence of a 'Nazarene' Nazareth in the second and third century, is valuable and beneficial information. It gives a good explanation of how the oral tradition of some of the sites associated with Jesus could be preserved for the first three centuries. This is a very important consideration in understanding who would have informed the later Byzantine (Gentile) Christians which locations were correct. The Byzantines were keen to establish dedicated places of veneration of Jesus life and consultation with his local living relatives would be obvious.

---

25 The claim is supported by Bible scholar Richard Bauckham and by a Syrian historian Bar Hebraeus. There is also a claim of a meeting between some Desposyni and Pope Sylvester in 318 AD. Questions have been raised on the credibility of this claim made by a Catholic priest in Martin, M 1981, *The decline and fall of the Roman Church*, G.P. Putnam's Sons, N.Y., USA.

26 Baulkam, R., op. cit., p. 95.

27 Part of the debate on Conon is that there are several Conons recorded in history. Refer for more information: johnsanidopoulos.com. 2015, *Holy Martyr Conon the Gardener* Mystagogy Resource Center, <www.johnsanidopoulos.com/2015/03/holy-martyr-conon-gardener.html>.

*Proving Biblical Nazareth*

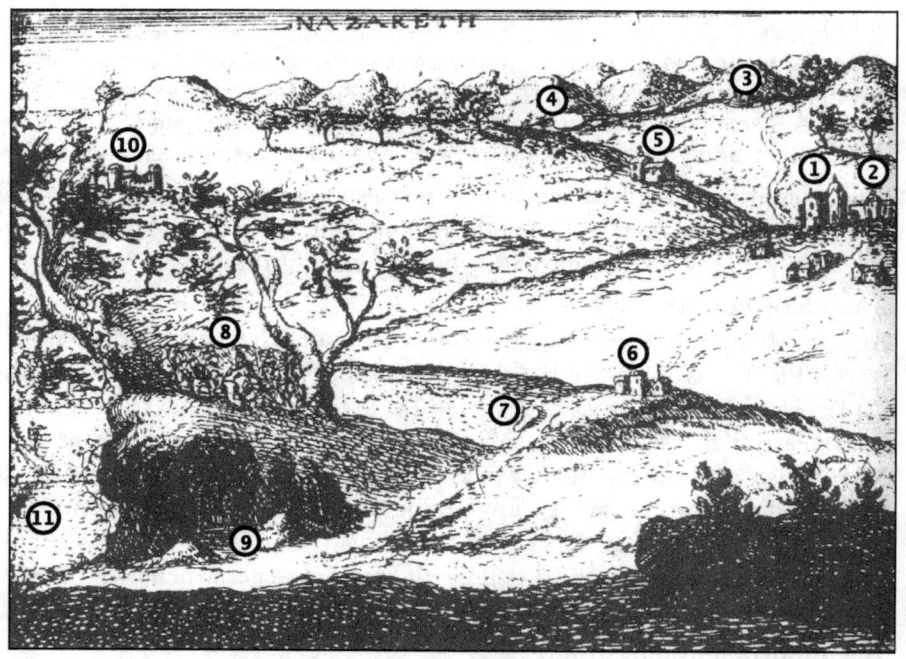

A.33 The Holy Places of Nazareth according to Fr. A. Gonsales 1673 AD.
1. Nazareth Annunciation Church (NV1) 2. St. Joseph's Workshop (NV2)
3. Mary's well (NV7) 4. The Lord's table 5. Synagogue (NV4)
6. Mary's Fright Convent 7. Mary's fright site 8. Precipice of Christ (Z1) 9. Little Chapel
10. Sappha (Jaffa of Nazareth) 11. Plain of Esdraelon (Jezreel).
Image courtesy Studium Biblicum Franciscanum, Jerusalem.

This historical postcard shows sites of significance to Medieval pilgrims.
Numbers have been enhanced by the author.
It indicates the nearby location of Yafia (10–Sappha, Jaffa) sacred sites.
The significance of two of these sites (NC1 and NC3 in Illust. B.16) in Yafia
to the story of Nazareth can be explained.

# CHAPTER 4

## TWO NAZARETHS: THE EVIDENCE

> Philip found Nathanael and said to him,
> "We have found Him of whom Moses in the law,
> and also the prophets, wrote–
> Jesus of Nazareth, the son of Joseph."
> And Nathanael said to him,
> "Can anything good come out of Nazareth?"
>
> John 1:45–46.

---

The fascinating story of Nazareth can be told when all the verifiable evidence is considered together. It requires an understanding of two sites with the same name but side by side. Both sites have a unique history and can help answer many of the questions posed by scholars over the centuries.

## 4.1 Persecutions and preserving the name

Persecution against Christians from 30 AD to the Edict of Tolerance by Constantine in 313 AD varied considerably across the Roman Empire, ranging from ostracism to martyrdom. It included brutal pogroms in the reigns of Nero (54-68 AD), Domitian (81-96 AD), Trajan (98-117 AD) and Diocletian (284-305 AD). Several of these Emperors, such as Decius (149-151 AD), were determined to eradicate the bloodline of King David. Any Jews with a direct bloodline to King David, that is Nazarenes, were to be hunted and executed. Christian sites needed to be very low-key for the first three centuries after Jesus' death. Deliberate pagan edifices were erected by Emperor Hadrian (117-138 AD) over the sacred Christian sites of the Nativity in Bethlehem and the Calvary site in Jerusalem. Extreme care was required for Christians and their faith was tested in many ways. They were seen as a threat to the political and religious order of Rome. There was also persecution from Jewish religious authorities. One of the early and relentless Jewish persecutors of Christians was a man called Saul of Tarsus, who in his own words (Acts 26:10-11) said:

> This I also did, in Jerusalem, and many of the saints I shut up in prison, having received authority from the chief priests; and when they were put to death, I cast my vote against them. And I punished them often in every synagogue and compelled them to blaspheme; and being exceedingly enraged against them, I persecuted them even in foreign cities.

A.34 'The conversion of St. Paul' on the road to Damascus. Engraving by Gustave Dore, circa 1866 AD. Credit WikiArt.org.

Saul was present in Jerusalem at the stoning of Stephen, the first recorded Christian martyr. Eventually he was dramatically converted, and then re-named as the well known Apostle Paul. Herod Antipas also ordered the execution of the Apostle James son of Zebedee in 44 AD due to his faith (Acts 12:1-2). Most of the original apostles were to die for their faith and nearly all died at the hand of the ruling religious or political elite in other lands. However, this did not suppress the Christian movement – rather it is said to have fuelled its growth.

Nazareth seemed to accept Jesus as a good natured carpenter, but could not believe in him as the Messiah. They could not recognise its most famous citizen as he did not meet their theological expectations. The first century saw an increasing divide between the Hebrew Christian church and the Jewish religious authorities. It led to condemnations at Jewish councils and the claim that Christians were heretics. [1] There were critics and scholars opposing the gospels, so if there were any inaccuracies in the names and places mentioned by its authors in the first century, this would have been made known. [2] There is no known record of any questioning of Nazareth's existence by any Jewish scholar.

St. Luke reported on the Roman and Jewish authorities being evangelised by the apostles. The first recorded Roman convert was a centurion called Cornelius, at Caesarea Maritima on the Mediterranean coast circa 41 AD (Acts 10). Twenty years later the Apostle Paul was held in prison for two years in this same Caesarea and eventually had an audience with the visiting King Herod Agrippa II. In his address Paul used the term "the name of Jesus of Nazareth" (Acts 26:9) as the one whom he now worshipped. Caesarea, where the audience took place, was 50 kilometres (30 miles) from Nazareth and there was no query as to which city Jesus came from. It can be suggested that its existence was known in 61 AD. King Agrippa was a capricious ruler and Paul would not invoke an 'invented' site as part of his argument.

**Two theologians who lived near Nazareth**

Origen (185–254 AD), was an early Church writer and influential theologian who lived near Nazareth in Caesarea for many years. He wrote gospel commentaries and when referring to Gabriel's visit he notes, "to a town of Galilee named Nazareth". [3] Justin Martyr (100–165 AD) was a Christian teacher who was born in Palestine (Nablus) and travelled around it. They both were Gentiles who had good pagan educations before their conversion. These two scholars mention Nazareth, confirming that it existed in their understanding and they would have been aware of any critics of their day about the site. They would also be in contact with the Nazarene Desposyni in the Christian Nazareth hamlet/village who preserved the oral traditions.

---

1 There has been strong debate over the centuries on the topic of when official expulsions of Jewish Christians from synagogues occurred. Some scholars point towards the end of the first century and culminating with a curse pronounced at a Council of Jamnia. The terminology for heretics, including Christians, by the Jewish authorities was *mimim* and pronouncements against them are documented in historical sources.

2 Fragments of Matthew's Gospel dating to the middle of the first century have been found in Egypt.

3 Origen 1996, *The Fathers of the Church*, Catholic University of America Press, Washington, DC. USA, p. 24. Justine Martyr reference in *Dialogue with Trypho* 1, Chapter 78.

## The historian who visited Nazara (Nazareth) in 220 AD

Sextus Africanus (160–240 AD) travelled through Palestine and mentions Nazareth in 220 AD as Nazara, a real site that existed in his time. He is definitely referring to the village site as he states Jesus' relatives as coming from there, as explained previously. From his account it is clear there is a Christian village at the site with Jesus' relatives that is seen as Jewish and not as Gentile. They had preserved the original name for the first two centuries.

## The Bible geographer who records Nazareth

Eusebius (circa 260/263–340 AD) was a prominent early church chronicler. Critics have tried to throw doubt on the existence of Nazareth by claiming it was not highlighted by Eusebius, who was a bishop at nearby Caesarea. Three examples of his acceptance of Nazareth can be noted from his work.

### 1. The Incarnation

In Eusebius' early Book 1, *The Person and Work of Christ*, he affirmed the importance of the physical incarnation of Jesus. He supports the gospels describing it as "the miracle of his birth". [4]

### 2. Nazareth on the list of sites

His geographical compendium, known as the *Onomasticon*, (324 AD) states:

> Whence the Christ was called a Nazorite (our Lord and Saviour was called). Formerly (as a taunt called) the Nazarenes are now called Christians. It is even now in Galilee (a village) opposite Legeon fifteen miles to the east near Mt. Thabor (named Nazara). [5]

A.35 Eusebius – Bishop of Caesarea, circa 314–339 AD. Wikimedia Commons.

This clearly demonstrates a real village site named Nazara at a measurable distance. The fifteen Roman miles is 22 km (13.6 US miles) and Legeon is the site of Legio which has been recently excavated near Tel Megiddo. The straight line distance from Legio to Nazareth village is 18.4 km (11.4 miles) and the distance between Legio and the Nazareth city site is 15.9 km (9.8 miles). This indicates that the village site is the intended one of the *Onomasticon*. It shows the distance by walking the actual roads from Legio to Nazareth village is accurate at fifteen Roman miles.

---

4   Maier, PL, *Eusebius,* op. cit., p. 26.
5   Wolf, CU 2006, *The Onomasticon of Eusebius Pamphili.* No. 749. *Refer* Bibliography.

## 3. Confirmation of Nazara village

Eusebius agreed with, and quoted Africanus when referring to Nazara and the Desposyni. He clearly believes there was a 'Jewish' village by that name with Jesus' relatives – evidence that it is not a fabricated or ficticious location.

### A major policy change

During Eusebius' time as bishop in Caesarea, the dramatic conversion of Emperor Constantine occurred. This event ushered in great changes for the Christian Church and Constantine made his famous *Edict of Tolerance* in 313 AD. Constantine was a great friend of Eusebius and there is recorded correspondence between the two. Constantine was also very keen to see the identification and restoration of Christian sacred sites and the building of new churches. His instructions to Eusebius included a profound new policy:

> Therefore, remind the churches over which you preside, as well as the bishops, presbyters and deacons presiding in other localities whom you know, to give serious attention to church buildings: either to repair the existing ones or to enlarge them, or, if necessary, to build new ones. You yourself and others through you will ask for what is needed both from the provincial governors and from the prefects. For they have been told to provide with all readiness what is said by your Holiness.[6]

This new policy of tolerance was to have a marked impact on the two sites of Nazareth. The Jewish city site eventually began to be revived by devout Jews. In Chapter 9 it will be shown that a remarkable Hebrew Christian church was later built there with the endorsement as shown in the quotation above.

### The theological factor

A historical statement of faith quoted by Tertullian known as the Old Roman Creed stated Jesus was "born of the Virgin Mary". Constantine and Eusebius attended the pivotal Church Council of Nicea in 325 AD which stated that Jesus "came down and was incarnate and was made man".[7] This important tenet meant that the conception was divine and that this event was central to the gospels. This led to pilgrim interest in the location of the original house of Mary and any evidence in support of it. At that time there was a rise in the influence of Gentile Christianity and a decline in the role of Hebrew Christian groups in Palestine. It is not clear exactly when this occurred, but scholars suggest it was in the fourth century. The Gentile Byzantine Church would eventually inherit this site.

---

6   Theodoret, 2012, *The Sacred Writings of Theodoret.* Jazzybee Verlag: Chapter XIV. Letter written by the Emperor Constantine regarding the building of churches in Palestine.

7   Newadvent.org. 2016, 'Nicene Creed', *Catholic Encyclopedia.* Refer Biblography. After the Eucumenical Coucil at Constantinople in 381 AD it added "incarnate by the Holy Ghost of the Virgin Mary".

## Jerome: the resident scholar of Palestine

Jerome (347–420 AD) is acknowledged as a great scholar of the early Church. He was a gifted linguist and translated the New Testament from Greek into Latin. When Jerome edited the four gospels, he translated the Greek word *polis* (city) from the original account, to *civitem* (city) in Latin. To the learned Jerome Nazareth was clearly meant to mean a city. If there were any doubt about the existence or size of the city then he would have raised it. After all, he had made a visit to the traditional hamlet site in 385 AD and used the Latin word *viculus* (small village) to describe the settlement.[8] This confirms that the hamlet site only grew to a small village in the first 400 years.

A.36 Jerome, by artist Ghirlandalo, 1480 AD. Wikimedia Commons.

Jerome endorsed visiting sites associated with Jesus' life. He wrote in one of his letters, regarding his sojourn in Palestine, that "it is still our duty as believers to worship on the spot where the Lord's feet once stood to see for ourselves the still fresh traces of His birth, His cross and His passion".[9] Later in his life, Jerome was concerned about some of the unsavoury connections involving pilgrimage to the Holy Land. In particular he is quoted as saying that visitors to Jerusalem had started to attract "prostitutes, play actors, and buffoons"[10] which was not good for the spiritual city.

## The Caesarea Inscription

In 1962 a curious find was made at Caesarea Maritima, the well known city of King Herod the Great, named in honour of his patron Caesar Augustus. Archaeologists uncovered a fragment of stonework at a historic synagogue that had ancient Hebrew writing on it. When linguistic experts analysed the letters, they noted that it appeared to be part of a list of towns that had a roster of priests dating back to the Late Roman era.[11]

---

8   Jerome's statement on Nazara found in his translation of Eusebius *Onomasticon*. His description in Latin was "viculus contra Legionem" which means a small village (or hamlet) opposite Legio. Found in Jerome's book *Sancti Eusebii Hieronymi Stridonensis* Presbyteri Operum tomus tertius, <books.google.com.au/books?id=I0f1ulTpQJcC>, p. 255.

9   *Church Fathers Letter* No. 47 (Jerome) No. 47.2.

10  Jerome, The Principal Works of St. Jerome, Schaff, P (ed.), *Christian Classics Ethereal Library*, NPNF 2.06, <www.ccel.org/ccel/schaff/npnf206.html>. p. 308.

11  This is not to be confused with another inscription also known as the Nazareth Inscription

*Two Nazareths: the evidence*

After the second Roman war of 135 AD, the priestly families were expelled from Judea. These families migrated north to Galilee and eventually to particular towns named in the early Talmudic period (200–330 AD).[12] The rostered list in chronological order had been displayed on synagogue walls. They have been deciphered by Professor Michael Avi-Yonah and generally accepted as dated to near the fourth century AD.

## The Priestly Course at Nazareth

The most intriguing name that appeared on the list was *'Nazareth'* giving evidence outside the gospels that the city did exist. The relevant line is:

"The 18th course Hapizzez Nazareth".[13]

This indicates that there was a town named Nazareth that had families of priests who were on a roster (known as *courses*) of religious duties in the Galilee. We do not know the numbers, as the Tel Yafia site was very minimal in this era. However it is likely they would have been pioneers for the revived Jewish town at the start of the fourth century AD.

A.37 Hebrew text showing fragment found in Caesarea listing Nazareth. *Refer* Credits.

A.38 Israeli Government Mint Medallion showing the Nazareth fragment.

## The controversial government medallion

Soon after this find there was hot debate and some questioned the date. It was even claimed to be a hoax perpetrated by Christians.[14] The professional integrity of the scholars involved was challenged.[15] The controversy has not

---

(11 cont.) found on a first century Roman era marble tablet. It has a Greek text claimed as describing a decree by one of the Caesars. It is currently in the Louvre, Paris.

12 Tuccinardi, E 2010, *Nazareth the Caesarea Inscription and the hand of God*, Salm, R (trans.), p. 10. Tuccinardi supports the Nazareth listing as accurate for the Caesarea Inscription.

13 Inscription given on the Israeli Mint medallion located on the fragment depiction side. In the Hebrew Bible the name is also known as Aphses from the time of King David (1 Chronicles 24:15).

14 Tuccinardi, E., op. cit.

15 Salm, R 2013, *Is the Caesarea inscription a forgery?* Mythicist Papers, <www.mythicistpapers.com/2013/06/10/is-the-caesarea-inscription-a-forgery/>.

deterred the Israeli Government, with the support of scholars, from claiming that the find was genuine. In 1981 the Israeli Mint (ICMC) issued bronze and silver commemorative medallions with a graphic of modern Nazareth on one side. On the reverse side was the depiction of the fragment with the Hebrew letters spelling 'Nazareth' from the fourth century. Even this proof of the naming of the city outside of the gospels does not diminish the sceptics' challenge as they still demand, quite rightly, to know exactly where this town site was located.

**The fact of a Jewish town**

There may be debate on this find in Caesarea, however some sceptics agree that a very devout Jewish town called Nazareth existed at the start of the fourth century. This was proof of the Jewish settlement revival in the Galilee. As noted by one of the sceptics:

> The inscription also reveals that in Middle Roman times Nazareth was strictly Jewish, for a priestly course would not have settled in a small mixed town of both Jews and Gentiles.[16]

Most scholars seem to be in agreement about the revived Jewish town named Nazareth. However, Nazareth's strong Jewish population was resistant to Christian influence as recorded by a visit by Bishop Epiphanius in 377 AD. His account will be commented on further. The nearby Christian village of Nazareth mentioned by Jerome in 400 AD had been attracting Gentile pilgrims after Constantine's Edict of Tolerance in 313 AD.

It might seem curious that two sites with the same name can exist side by side. A good modern era example is Berlin, the capital of Germany. After World War II in 1946 it was divided into two distinct cities known as East and West Berlin. Both had separate governments and economic systems for forty-five years. Each had its own identity and tensions between the two were real. This can now be compared to a historical period in Nazareth.

## 4.2 How Nazareth city was lost in time

The story of how Nazareth city was lost can be summarised into three phases over a long period of time.

**Phase 1: The destruction of the city**

Towards the end of the Byzantine era in Palestine, in the sixth century, there was a shift to a much more rigid form of control from Constantinople. This led to increased tensions between Jews and their Christian Byzantine rulers. In 614 AD a dramatic chain of events started with the Persian invasion by King Chosroes II. A leading Israeli archaeologist noted it was:

---

16 Salm, R, *The Myth of Nazareth*, op. cit., p. 278.

described in historical sources as a most violent military raid that dramatically affected the political and administrative stability of Byzantine Palestine, involving large scale damage to churches and a mass killing of the local Christian population.[17]

The Persian campaign was particularly directed against Christians. Some of the Jews sided with the Persians and participated in massacres of Christians, and it is claimed that some deaths even occurred in Nazareth:

> In 614, however, the Persians invaded Palestine from the north, Jews of Nazareth apparently joined Chosroes II in destroying churches and murdering Christians in Jerusalem.[18]

This can be seen as residents from the Jewish city taking out their animosity on the Christian village of Nazareth nearby. Archaeological reports detail the extent of the massacres in Judea and bones in mass grave sites are still seen today.[19] Some fourteen years later in response to the Persian–Jewish attack, the Byzantines, led by the Emperor Heraclius, entered Palestine. His campaign resulted in a revenge on the Jews and this was particularly meted out to the residents of the Jewish city of Nazareth. The city was decimated and abandoned: "In revenge, the emperor Heraclius *reluctantly singled out Nazareth for special punishment*".[20] [italics added]

The Byzantine campaign of 629–630 AD was short-lived as it was followed by the Islamic Arab invasion of Palestine in 638 AD. This invasion sealed the displacement of the Jews of Nazareth City.

**The lament of a Jewish poet**

Nazareth City was totally lost after the decimation in 630 AD. Another fascinating piece of evidence helps solve the puzzle. A famous Jewish poet named Eleazar ben Killir (or Kalir) wrote poems of lamentations about the displacement of the Jews from Palestine. He made a special reference to the priestly class of Nazareth:

"And to the ends of the earth was dispersed the priestly class of Nazareth".[21]

A.39 Street sign in modern Tel Aviv named after poet El'Azar (Ha) Kalir.
Credit Wikimedia Commons.

---

17 Avni, G 2010, *The Persian Conquest of Jerusalem (614 c.e.)—An Archaeological Assessment* p. 35. <www.jstor.org/stable/27805159)>.

18 Taylor, J, op. cit., p. 229.

19 Avni, G, op. cit., pp. 2–7.

20 Taylor, J, op. cit., p. 229.

21 Eleazar ben Killir quotation as noted by Tuccinardi, E, op. cit., p. 1.

This quote contains two important facts. Firstly, the dispersal of Jewish residents of a city named Nazareth at some point in history. Secondly, the confirmation of the existence of a priestly class in the devout Jewish city. There is debate on the time frame of Eleazar the poet's life with some sources putting it around 570–640 AD.[22] These dates would place him in the time after the Byzantine campaign in 629–630 AD. Some scholars date him later but there is agreement that his works under the title of *Lamentations* were recited in synagogues for many centuries after his death.[23] Eleazar's quote must clearly relate to the Byzantine period, as the priestly class can only be ascribed to the priestly rosters as noted in the section above. This is a reference to a good-sized town not a hamlet. It is not the Christian town recorded by pilgrims nearby in the same era.

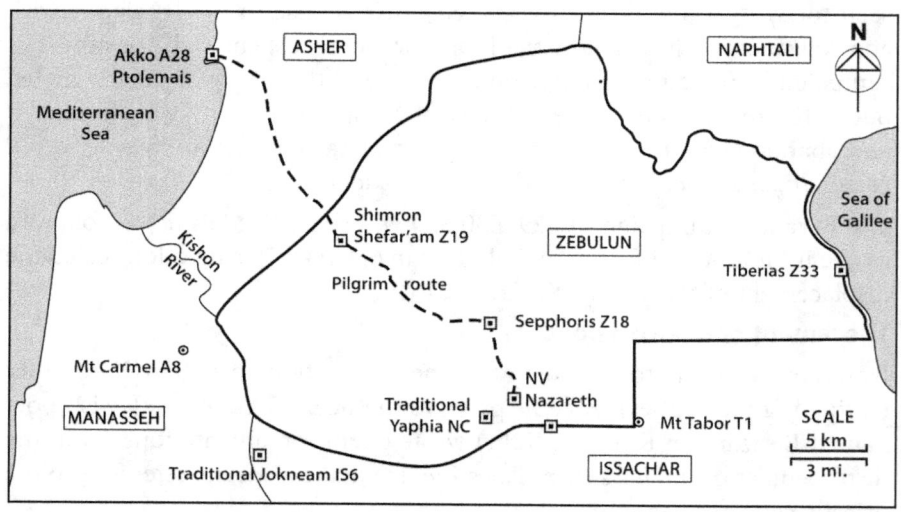

A.40 Map showing the Pilgrim route from Akko to Nazareth via Shefar'am (Shimron Z19). Outline of the tribal area of Zebulun explained in Chapter 10. The traditional location of Yafia (Yaphia or Japhia) (NC) is located nearby to Nazareth.

---

22 Jewish Virtual Library 2016, *Kallir. Eleazar*, <www.jewishvirtuallibrary.org/jsource/judaica/ejud_0002_0011_0_10643.html>. *Refer* Bibliography.

23 ibid.

## 4.3 How Nazareth city became Yafia

The next part of the story of Nazareth city shows how, with the destruction of the main site in 630 AD, the original name was eventually lost and replaced over time. The name may have survived in the following centuries with the local oral tradition, but after the Crusader invasion in the twelfth century names began to change. Two particular names get connected with Tel Yafia.

**Phase 2: From Shefar'am to Safra to Yafia**

The first name is *Safra* which starts as *Shimron* or *Simonias* on the border of the Galilee (Z19. Illus. A.40). After the second Roman war of 135 AD it acquired its current name Shefar'am which means *Horn of the nation*. It became a sacred pilgrimage city to Jews and Christians as the traditional burial place of the prophet Malachi. Later it also became important with the erection of a church honouring the Apostles James and John, known as the sons of Zebedee. It became a legend and even claimed to be their birthplace.

During the time of the Crusaders Shefar'am became known as *Safra*. Some time after the defeat of the Crusaders in 1291 AD, the name of Safra, with its legend, was transferred to the village on Tel Yafia.[24] The archaeologist Fr. Bellarmino Bagatti noted, regarding the transfer of the two apostles' birthplace legend, that: *"This privilege then passed onto Yafia near Nazareth where it remains until our day"*.[25] [italics added] A crucial piece of information.

In the Medieval Ottoman period Safra became a Christian Arab village and the legend of James and John was embedded in the local folklore. The Israeli Antiquities Authority (IAA) officially names Tel Yafia as *Mar Ya'akub* in honour of the Apostle James (Yarkob) and the medieval tradition.

**From Japheph to Japhia**

The second name is *Japheph* which explains how Japhia became connected to Tel Yafia. A curious site near Nazareth is described in records of the Crusader period of the village of Japheph (*refer* Appendix 8.5):

> Documents of the Crusader period actually speak of a church dedicated to the Virgin in the village of Japheph situated "juxta mensam Domini" which was destroyed in 1187.[26]

A site that meets this location requirement is the historic town known as Ilut, 3.5 kilometres (2.17 miles) to the north-west of traditional Nazareth.[27]

---

24 Safra had other spelling and name variations including Sapha, Saron and Sasron.

25 Bagatti, B 2001, *Ancient Christian Villages of Galilee*, Jerusalem: Franciscan Printing Press. Jerusalem, p. 106.

26 ibid., p. 80. The Latin quoted means "nearby the altar table of the Lord" which was a site in western traditional Nazareth.

27 Ilut or Ailut (based on a historic Hebrew name of Ayyatalu) could also have been a Nazarene village with its Hellenistic–Roman remains. It is marked as Z47 on map Illus. A.13.

The mention of *Japheph* explains how the name of *Japha* became associated with the area near Tel Yafia, just over three kilometres (1.86 miles) to the south. Some Medieval period accounts also link the name *Jaffa* to *Sappha* shown in Illus. A.33. By the eighteenth century the name of *Yafa* seems to be fixed to the Arab village on the hill in the outskirts of traditional Nazareth.

### Phase 3: Edward Robinson and Yafa

The mistake was compounded in 1841 when the noted American explorer Edward Robinson described his visit to *Yafa village*. After observing the historical remains and its name, he endorsed it as biblical *Japhia*. He wrote:

> The little village of Yafa, as we have seen, lies somewhat more than half an hour S.W. of Nazareth ... The name seems to identify it with the Japhia of Scripture ... the Japha fortified by Josephus, was probably the same, a large strong village of Galilee. [28]

A.41 Edward Robinson (1794–1863) American explorer of Palestine who nominated Bible sites. Wikipedia Commons.

The suggestion is that *Safra* is very similar to *Safa*, and the possible local link of *Japheph* as *Jafa*, caused the incorrect label that was to prove fatal to the story of Nazareth. Robinson's observation was well intentioned, but in contradiction to the clear information in the Bible and Josephus' accounts. Since the publication of Robinson's travels his scholarly authority resulted in changes to most Bible maps. *Yafa* (or *Jafa*) is shown as a suburb in Nazareth to this day. However this nomination of *Jafa/Japhia* has not been fully accepted by all scholars. It has robbed '*Yafa*' of its significance as the large urban city of Nazareth.

In summary Nazareth city has been lost for nearly fourteen hundred years. The first phase was physical. The second phase was by a complete transfer of the name *Safra* from another city in the Medieval Era. The last phase was by adopting the local name of *Jafa*, a misplacement in the seventeenth century. *Jafa* is also *Yafa*, and has become fixed, but the error must be corrected.

---

28 Robinson E and Smith, E, op. cit., p. 200.

*Two Nazareths: the evidence*

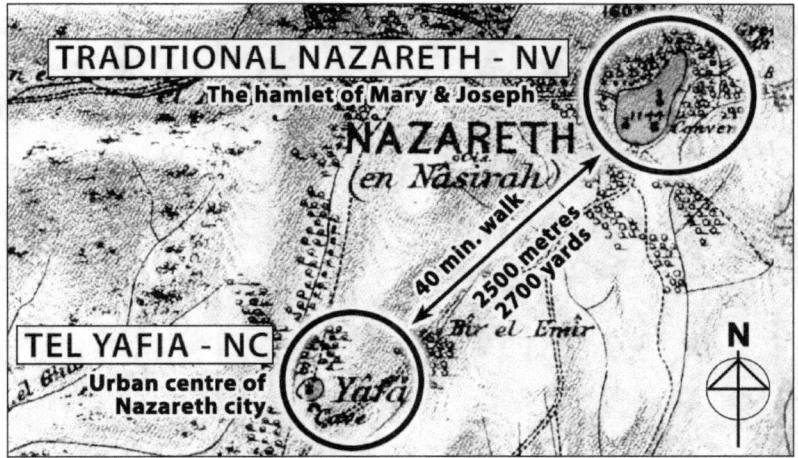

A.42 Map showing the close connection between traditional Nazareth and the site of Yafia to the south-west. PEF base map.

## Conclusion to Section A

The critics have made a bold claim that:

> the existence of Nazareth two thousand years ago can be proved or disproved by digging in the ground. Because the archaeology of a site is empirically demonstrable. "Nazareth" is in a category apart. To this day, *it preserves the explosive potential to either prove or disprove the gospels' accounts.* Upon that determination depends a great deal, perhaps even the entire edifice of Christendom.[29] [italics added]

This section has sought to address many of the challenges raised by scholars. When all the evidence for the two sites associated with Nazareth is correctly interpreted, the mystery of this city is solved. The above accounts of history are more easily understood when the concept of two sites is made clear.

Archaeological evidence confirms these two distinct sites in the required time frames. Indeed, part of the answer has been found by digging in the ground. The biblical references can also now be more clearly understood. The descriptions of the devout Jewish city of Nazareth that became lost in time had a geographical location at Tel Yafia. The Christian hamlet nearby, however, grew and preserved the name of Nazareth in history. Claims of a conspiracy can be shown to be unfounded. The story of Nazareth is a fascinating one with all its controversies. The preservation of the truth of its significance in the life of Jesus is important.

---

29 Salm, R, op. cit., p. xi. This book by René Salm also has an extreme claim on the back cover. "Apologists and all other professional Christians are going to be out of work unless they can disprove this book – or find ways to suppress it." Frank Zindler, past president *American Atheists*.

B.01 'Jesus unrolls the book in the Synagogue' painting by James Tissot, circa 1886. It was in Nazareth city that Jesus made his declaration of the Gospel as Messiah. Credit: Brooklyn Museum photograph 2007.

# SECTION B

## WHERE JESUS DECLARED HIS GOSPEL OF LIBERTY

*Cause the progeny [descendant] of David your servant, to blossom quickly. Let him shine in your deliverance, for we await your salvation every day.*

Historic Jewish prayer of the Amidah No. 15 "Blessing of David".

---

This section proposes the location of two intriguing sites in Nazareth city associated with the Messiah.

The first is a locality for the synagogue where Jesus made his famous declaration of 'Good News' of Liberty in the Jubilee year of 27 AD. The synagogue would require a location of spiritual significance if he were the Messiah. A fascinating prophetic pointer towards this locality is proposed.

The second is the location of Joseph the carpenter after he found out about Mary's pregnancy. He was visited by an angel who told him that this event was the coming of the Messiah and he was to name the child Jesus. Remains of a church have been discovered that might hold the clue.

B.02 Jesus grew up in a rural hamlet of Nazareth city learning carpentry from Joseph.
The author commissioned this artwork by Margaret McEntee and it has the title
*"The Prophetic Cross-beam"*.
The aim was to illustrate that Jesus was a practical trades-person.
Many historical examples of religious art depict him as unreal and inappropriately
dressed in flowing robes.

# CHAPTER 5
## THE EARLY YEARS OF JESUS

*Then He went down with them
and came to Nazareth, and was subject to them,
but His mother kept all these things in her heart.
And Jesus increased in wisdom and stature,
And in favor with God and men.*

Luke 2:51–52.

---

Theologians have been puzzled by the small amount of information in the gospels on Jesus' early life in Galilee. However, with the correct location of some of the sites, and our understanding of life in first century Galilee, a clearer picture emerges. This can be used to understand some of the deeper meanings of his parables and that they were based on real-life experiences.

## 5.1 At school in Nazareth city

### Jesus' mystery years

There are only three references to Jesus after his family's return from Egypt when he was a small boy until his baptism at nearly thirty years of age (Luke 3:23). Theologians call them the 'mystery' or 'missing' twenty-two years with reference to his life in Nazareth. Many questions have been raised by scholars, such as Professor James Charlesworth, about the context of Jesus' growing up and ministry:

> How does archaeological research help re-create Jesus' time and place?
> How do these new insights help us understand Jesus' life and actions? ...
> How do archaeological discoveries help us re-create his social environment?
> How do they assist us better to understand Jesus' teachings? [1]

Jesus was born in Bethlehem of Judea in late 4 BC. After the mandatory forty days of purification for Mary required by the Jewish Law, he was taken to the temple in Jerusalem for dedication. Here he was prophesied over as a baby by two devout Jews known as Anna and Simeon (Luke 2:22–38). After this ceremony they returned home: "So when they had performed all things according to the law of the Lord, they returned to Galilee, to their own city, Nazareth" (Luke 2:39).

Shortly after returning, possibly several months, Joseph was warned by an angel to flee to Egypt (Matt. 2:13). Ruthless Herod was starting to organise a future campaign to kill all male infants in the Bethlehem region under the age of two years. (Any links like Joseph to the royal line would also be at risk.) The arduous trip of over 500 kilometres (310 miles) was probably in the spring of 3 BC. Jesus would be about three to four months old and the circumstances would have exposed him to suffering at a tender age. The Greek word used for his age was *'paidon'* which means he was a very young infant. While Joseph and Mary stayed in Egypt, they would have been part of the Jewish diaspora there in the first century. Their circumstances would mean they were part of the impoverished lower class. Part of their stay would likely be in the Goshen location of their ancestors' sojourn from where the Exodus occurred.

This sojourn was prophetic, as recorded by Matthew 2:15, "Out of Egypt I called my son" (Hosea 11:1). The Greek word used here for son is *'huios'*, which means a mature child with developed moral traits. He was probably seven or eight years of age when his parents returned from Egypt. Joseph did not return to his ancestral home of Bethlehem because Herod's son, the cruel Archelaus, was still ruling in Judea (Matt. 2:22). This fact tells us that the return had to be before 6 AD when Archelaus was deposed.

---

[1] Charlesworth, JH 2006, *Jesus and Archaeology*, Eerdmans Publishers, Grand Rapids, Michigan, USA, p. 13.

## Jewish education

After being in Egypt, "the Child grew and became strong in spirit, filled with wisdom; and the grace of God was upon Him" (Luke 2:40).

They returned to their family home (cared for by friends or relatives) on the outskirts of Nazareth's urban centre in the Galilee. At that time Galilee was being ruled by one of Herod's sons known as Herod Antipas, whom Jesus was to meet twenty-five years later. Upon returning to his city he would need to continue his Jewish education. At that time, the synagogue was also the location of schools for the instruction of children. Studies have identified the first part of the Jewish education system near that time.

> It was the parent's duty to send their children to the bet ha-sefer (the elementary school) ... the city was obligated to provide an instructor and a place for study ... and funding the education system.[2]

The *Mishnah*, a historical Jewish book, indicates that elementary education was from five to twelve years. So on the days when Joseph walked from his house to his city workshop, a journey of thirty to forty minutes, the boy Jesus would often have accompanied him. He would have attended a good-sized school with his fellow students. At the end of classes, he would have returned to Joseph's workshop and probably helped with jobs and the clean-up, then they would make the return journey home together. At the school they were taught to read and write, and also given grounding in matters of the Law and the Prophets, key to their growing in wisdom.

B.03 The Catholic Church and school in modern Yafia. Jesus went to the Nazareth school in this same locality.

They would be taught the history of Israel and of their forebears. Jewish society placed importance on a good basic education and on maintaining their own distinct culture, despite the foreign occupation by Rome.

Students would have been told the stories of the prophets. These would have been made vivid as some historical events had happened near their city. An example is the story of Elijah and the confrontation with the prophets of Baal, with the site of the encounter viewable from Nazareth towards Mt. Carmel (1 Kings 18:16–17:40). The story of Barak and Deborah and

---

2   Urman, D and Flesher, P (eds) 1998, *Ancient Synagogues – Historical Analysis and Archaeological Discovery*, Brill Academic Publishers, Leiden, Netherlands, p. 186.

their great battle with Jabin, the king of the Canaanites, happened on the Jezreel Plain just south of their city (Judges 4:1–23). Joseph and Mary would have understood some of their genealogy and would have told Jesus that he was of the line of King David. His parents were devout and they would have taught him how to pray as a young child.

**How Jesus got 'lost'** (Passover, 10 AD. Luke 2:43–47.)
> His parents went to Jerusalem every year at the Feast of the Passover. And when He was twelve years old, they went up to Jerusalem according to the custom of the feast. When they had finished the days, as they returned, the Boy Jesus lingered behind in Jerusalem. And Joseph and His mother did not know it, but supposing Him to have been in the company, they went a day's journey, and sought Him among their relatives and acquaintances. So when they did not find Him they returned to Jerusalem, seeking Him. Now so it was that after three days they found him in the Temple, sitting in the midst of the teachers, both listening to them and asking them questions. All who heard Him were astonished at His understanding and answers.

B.04 Anxious Joseph and Mary entering the Temple to find Jesus talking to the teachers. Part detail engraving by Julius Carolsfeld. Credit Pitts Theology Library.

Jesus' age gives us a vital clue, as this denotes the maturing or increasing accountability of a male who should by now have a working knowledge of the Law (Torah) and be fulfilling the commandments. This compares with the modern Jewish tradition of the *Bar Mitzvah* meaning 'Son of the Covenant'. The puzzle of the above account is how Jesus got 'lost'. The explanation can be given, that after celebrating Passover the family are part of a caravan or convoy of friends and relatives returning home on a three day journey to their home city. *Synodia* is the Greek word used for "company" in the passage which means a large troop of people and animals travelling together.

Jesus' parents would have seen him at the early morning muster. A company from a city would have involved a large number of teenage boys who would help with the animals. Hence he was easily missed by the other boys when they were quizzed at the end of the first day by the anxious parents: "Have you seen Jesus?" Joseph and Mary would have been in the advance party and the teenagers and animals at the rear. Before moving out on the first day Jesus probably receives a strong prompting by God to stay in Jerusalem.

He stayed with his relatives and spent three days in the Temple. He was relating intellectually to the amazed teachers who would be aware he was from the Galilee, and not trained in their higher level of theological schools. Jesus was faced with a decision to obey his natural parents (as listed in the Law) or the prompting of his *Heavenly Father*. This was a crucial spiritual test which he would preach on later with his disciples (Matthew 10:37).

### Growing in wisdom and stature

Following the above story we are told that "Jesus increased in wisdom and stature, and in favour with God and men" (Luke 2:52). The teenage years are when the growth in "stature" (maturity and physique) and "favour" (personality and relationships) occur. The wisdom aspect was cultivated through an understanding of the Scriptures. After the age of twelve years boys were responsible for their actions and were expected to participate in the worship life of the synagogue. The synagogue service before and after 70 AD involved the reciting of a certain set of prayers known as the *Amidah*, which means 'standing up' (to pray). These prayers had their origin in the great reforms of Ezra in the fifth century BC. The prayers were formalised in the Talmud period and the fifteenth (of eighteen) was known as "Birkat David" – the blessing of David. It involved requesting the coming of the descendant of King David who would be the Messiah. A modern translation reads: "cause the progeny [descendant] of David, your servant, to blossom quickly. Let him shine in your deliverance, for we await your salvation".[3]

We do not know the exact wording of the prayers from 9 to 26 AD. Prof. James Charlesworth has made the point that "the Amidah in basic content, order, and number, though not in wording, was set before the fall of Jerusalem in 70 CE".[4] The messianic hope was strong in Jewish prayers and growing up, Jesus would have prayed a very similar prayer to the above with his congregation. This is spiritually powerful, as we will see later, this location was to be the stage for the revelation of the "progeny of David"!

## 5.2 Jesus the apprentice and carpenter

Teenage boys were apprenticed to their father or another relative to learn a trade or profession at about fifteen years of age. There is some uncertainty as to how broadly the Greek word 'tekton' applied to Joseph and Jesus (Matt. 13:55 and Mark 6:3). The common translation in the gospels is 'carpenter' and even today that trade can cover a wide range of activities. The Greek meaning can include a person with a craft, or a general builder, and many scholars

---

3  Hoffman, LA 1997, *My People's Prayer Book: The Amidah*, Jewish Lights Publishing, Woodstock, Vermont, USA, p. 142, </books.google.com.au/books?id=9_akQQPpS9IC>.

4  Charlesworth, JH 2006, *Resurrection: The Origin and Future of Biblical Doctrine*, T&T Clark, London, UK, p. 15.

*Proving Biblical Nazareth*

B.05 A recreation of Joseph's workshop is popular with tourists.
Author's photo courtesy of the Nazareth Village. www.nazarethvillage.com

seem to agree that it involved working with timber in some form. Christians over the centuries have commented on the boy Jesus growing up preparing wood and working with timber. He probably carried many beams and planks as part of his trade. He was a carpenter who hammered in many nails and was involved in constructing many frames and scaffolds. Jesus was a man who would become renowned as the one who carried his own cross beam, part of the way, as required of a Roman execution (John 19:17). He was a man who would eventually be nailed to a timber cross, the framing system so cruelly used by Roman law for crucifixion.

As every trades-person will tell you, it is not just the skill that counts when making a living, but it is also about getting and retaining clients. Jesus would have watched how Joseph acquired his customers and how he handled their different temperaments and expectations. He would have learnt the importance of patience and persistence. This was all part of his growing in wisdom and stature. In his work and in his relationships, he was a source of blessing by favour to others. Having served his apprenticeship, Jesus would gradually have been given more responsibility in the business. This would have required him to travel in the region around Nazareth, finding new clients and visiting building sites. Historical tradition suggests that Joseph was quite old by the time Jesus was twenty, so this would result in more responsibility being given to him as the only son.

**The hometown public workshop**

Joseph is described as a carpenter and obviously part of his home would have included a workshop and builder's compound. But a bigger question arises on this matter. If his residence was in a very small hamlet, how does he gain enough customers to support his family for twenty years until his death some time before 27 AD? He would most likely have had a workshop located in the Nazareth urban centre with its large population that would give easy access to supplies and proximity to clients. Trades at that time tended to be located outside, but near, the gates of a city. It is probable that this was where Joseph had his basic bachelor's room before his betrothal to Mary. Under Jewish law he begins in *'erusin'* or betrothal. After moving into the family home and having marital relations it becomes *'nissuin'*. A site locality proposal for the workshop is detailed in Chapter 9.3.

## 5.3 Teaching parables by experience

At some point in his adult years Jesus must have received recognition of his training in matters of the Jewish Law to be called a rabbi or teacher (Mark 9:5). It would be with elders in the local Essene community rather than from the Pharisees (*Ant.* 18.1.5). An important principle in his ministry was how he used parables to teach people the truths of God and his kingdom. It can be illustrated that nearly all the examples that he used in preaching came from his real life experience of growing up and working in the Galilee. Some relevant examples include the following:

**The city on a hill**

"A city that is set on a hill cannot be hidden" (Matt. 5:14). Did Jesus have a particular site in mind? There are several sites that meet that description in his locality with settlements perched on high hills. For example, Sepphoris, just over five kilometres (three miles) to the north and Tel Gath Hepher, a similar distance to the north-west, were built on hilly summits. However, the best illustration would have been his home city of Nazareth. It was located at the top of the hill 50 metres (164 feet) above the adjacent valleys. At night this site would have glowed with oil lamps lighting the streets and houses. By day, its stone buildings and walls would have sparkled in the sun and Jesus would have seen this many times.

**Two builders**

The parable of the two builders is another example. A wise man "built his house on a rock: and the rain descended, the flood came, the winds blew and beat on that house, and it did not fall, for it was founded on the rock" (Matt. 7:24–27). The "foolish man", however, "built his house on the sand" and under the same conditions a big collapse occurred. Jesus spent sixteen years of his life as a carpenter with his father's business. If he was travelling to Akko (Ptolemais at that time) on the coast he would have crossed the Akko Plain. This plain was subject to annual flooding by the Naaman River and had some very sandy sections and other parts with stable rocky layers. This plain receives strong winds and rain directly from the Mediterranean Sea, so it is possible that there may have been examples of the two types of building conditions used in the parable.

## The cost of building

As a carpenter he would have been aware of the importance of weighing up building costs:

> For which of you, intending to build a tower, does not sit down first and count the cost, whether he has enough to finish it – lest, after he has laid the foundation, and is not able to finish, all who see it begin to mock him (Luke 14:28–30).

These towers are not big castles, but stone structures used for agricultural purposes, such as watchtowers and strongholds. They also could be mill sites for making oil and wine that included storage silos. Evidence of these structures have been found in the Galilee. As a carpenter, his keen eye would have seen examples of unfinished structures in his travels. He would know of the mocking of those with incomplete funds. Jesus was teaching his followers to weigh up the implications of starting an activity.

## Warfare

Jesus also taught of a king weighing up the odds before going out to war. The Galilee had witnessed three successive military invasions in the century before Jesus' birth: the Jewish Maccabean war with the Seleucids (101 BC), the Roman invasion of the Galilee by Pompey (67 BC) and Idumean King Herod the Great's invasion of Galilee to replace the Hasmonean Kingdom (38–37 BC). This shows the context of Jesus' illustration:

> Or what king going to make war against another king, does not sit down first and consider whether he is able with ten thousand to meet him who comes against him with twenty thousand (Luke 14:31).

B.06 Jewish king Janneus who invaded Galilee in 101 BC.
Wikimedia Commons.

B.07 Herod the Great led his army into Galilee in 37 BC.
Wikimedia Commons

Researchers have come up with variable estimates of Herod's army from ten to forty thousand troops.[5] Stories of these campaigns and locations would have been spoken from father to son. Some of Jesus' audience would have been young men when their fathers told stories of Herod's war campaign in the Galilee in 38–37 BC.

---

5  Kasher, A 1990, *Jews and Hellenistic Cities in Eretz-Israel*, Paul Siebeck, Tubingen, Germany, p. 190. Kasher gives an estimate of Herod's army as 10,000 to 13,000 troops.

## Politics

During Jesus' life the political ruler of the Galilee, known as a tetrarch, was Herod Antipas, who governed from 4–39 AD. Antipas ruled the Galilee from stronghold sites at Sepphoris, Tiberias, Jotapata and quite possibly Magdala. Sepphoris, the capital, was an adjacent city just north of Jesus' home. He would have been well acquainted with the way King Herod dealt with his subjects, as people would talk about their leaders just as they do today. When Jesus called Herod, *"that fox"* (Luke 13:32), it was based on first-hand reports and knowledge of his activities. However, he was not to have a face-to-face meeting with him until the famous encounter in Jerusalem, just prior to his crucifixion, when Pilate sent him to Herod during his trial. Herod Antipas had travelled to Jerusalem for the Passover and was residing in a villa-palace near the Antonia Fortress (Luke 23:8–12).

B.08 Herod Antipas, ruler of the Galilee. Jesus described him as a 'fox'. Part detail by J. Tissot c.1890. Credit Brooklyn Museum.

## Agriculture

The Galilee was rich in agriculture and vineyards covered the many hilly slopes, attended by vine-dressers. He used vineyard workers for a teaching on grace involving labour: "For the kingdom of heaven is like a landowner who went out early in the morning to hire labourers for his vineyard" (Matt. 20:1). Wheat fields such as those in the nearby Jezreel Valley had sowers:

> Then he spoke many things to them in parables, saying: "Behold, a sower went out to sow. And as he sowed, some seed fell by the wayside and the birds came and devoured them" (Matt. 13:3–4).

The Netofa Valley, two hours' walk to the north of his home, was ideal for pasturage. "If a man has a hundred sheep, and one of them goes astray, does he not leave the ninety-nine and go to the mountains to seek the one that is straying?" (Matt. 18:12). In his contact with shepherds, he would have heard stories of lost sheep in the adjacent high hills. He knew how to communicate with the locals because he was one of them. The nearby Galilean localities provided good settings for his teaching.

B.09 A shepherd with his flock in a recreated historic site. Author's photo courtesy Nazareth Village. www.nazarethvillage.com.

**Prejudice and love**

When Jesus made the annual Passover journey from Nazareth to Jerusalem he would regularly have passed through the territory known as Samaria. He would have made the journey over twenty-two times and would be acquainted with the tension that existed between Jews and Samaritans. It is not at all surprising that he used a Samaritan to give one of the greatest illustrations on love. The parable of the Good Samaritan is one of the great teachings that has meaning in every culture (Luke 10:29–37).

**A ministry based on experience**

After his father's death, just before turning thirty years of age, Jesus left his Nazareth home to be baptised by a relative named John. This was done in the Jordan River east of Jericho. At his baptism, "the Holy Spirit descended in bodily form like a dove upon Him, and a voice came from heaven which said, 'You are my beloved Son: in You I am well pleased'" (Luke 3:22).

This is *God the Father* commending the character of *God the Son*, now in human form. However, this endorsement must include all his preceding physical work as well with his deeds, actions and attitude as a human. His life experiences at Nazareth under-girded how he related to his followers and gave his teachings.

# CHAPTER 6

## LOCATING NAZARETH CITY SYNAGOGUE

*Then Jesus returned in the power of the Spirit to Galilee, and the news of Him went out through all the surrounding region. And He taught in their synagogues, being glorified by all. So He came to Nazareth, where he had been brought up. And as His custom was, He went into the synagogue on the Sabbath day, and stood up to read.*

Luke 4:14–16.

---

Jesus and his parents were devout Jews and the above account indicates they worshipped regularly in the city synagogue. Modern research has given more information on the features and locations of synagogues. When the principles of town planning, prophetic site mapping and the archaeology of Tel Yafia are considered, a locality for the synagogue can be proposed.

B.10 A reconstruction of a Jewish synagogue with the three tiered seating around the perimeter. Author's photo courtesy of the Nazareth Village. www.nazarethvillage.com.

## 6.1 No synagogue in the hamlet

The Nazareth synagogue was the location of several key addresses by Jesus but is there evidence of where it might be located? When pilgrims visit traditional Nazareth they are shown a structure with the inscription "Synagogue Church" and are told this was where Jesus made his declaration. As explained previously, the hamlet cannot be the actual location of Jesus' hometown synagogue. However, this structure requires further comment. Jewish custom required a minimum of ten learned men in the congregation to form a synagogue or assembly.[1] It can be said with reasonable confidence that there was not a local synagogue in Joseph's hamlet. The gospel text reads "as was his custom" when reference is made to the city synagogue (Luke 4:16). This indicates that his family synagogue was located in the city.

A requirement under Jewish Law was a limit on the distance that could be travelled on the Sabbath. There were variations, but a common figure given was two thousand cubits (890 metres, 973 yards), which was the distance Israel had to keep away from the *holy Ark* when they crossed the Jordan (Josh. 3:4). This figure shows that the house of Mary and Joseph was over the Sabbath walk limit from their synagogue. The explanation is that preceding every Sabbath, before the sunset occurred, Joseph and his family

---

1 The learned would be men familiar with the Jewish Law or Torah. Some sources add "at leisure" to indicate they were not full time in other pursuits.

would journey to Nazareth city centre, and stay with relatives to observe the Sabbath. The most likely relatives they stay with would be the cousins mentioned in Chapter 3 and listed in Matthew 15:35. They are named as residents of the city by the synagogue leaders. Joseph, Mary and Jesus would attend one of the worship sessions in the synagogue, and after the following sunset, make the journey back to their home on the outskirts.

## The pilgrim accounts

The first recorded historical account of a synagogue in traditional Nazareth was made by a Byzantine pilgrim in 570 AD:

> We travelled on to the city of Nazareth, where many miracles take place. In the synagogue there is kept the book in which the Lord wrote his ABC, and in this synagogue is the bench on which he sat with other children. [2]

This account shows there was a synagogue site promoted in the hamlet location. The reference to Jesus' book on display is ridiculous and had more to do with catering to the growing pilgrim trade. Another account is found in 1137 AD with the mention by Peter the Deacon that: "Inside the city, the synagogue where the Lord read the Book of Isaiah, is now a church". [3] This was confirmed one hundred and fifty years later by another pilgrim saying that, "There is still in (Nazareth) the synagogue – but it is converted into a church". [4] It is not specified where this Byzantine and Crusader era structure was located, but a good clue is found in the writings of Franciscan scholar Quaresmius who wrote about his visit to Nazareth in 1639 AD. He indicated that it was "north-west of the Church of Saint Joseph on the way to Saint Mary's Well". [5] This suits the building known today as the "Synagogue Church" which stands in this locality.

## The 'anointed' Synagogue Church

Location: 32-42-11 N. and 35-17-49 E.

So there are accounts of a structure spanning many centuries, and a case can be made that it was located in the Old Market or Suq area of Nazareth. The question is, does the existing building meet that requirement? When speaking to local Christians about this church they comment that it is an *anointed* site. They use that term to indicate that they have experienced the spiritual atmosphere and significance of the location. This also means they believe it must have some previous importance.

---

2  Piacenza Pilgrim, Travels 5, Wilkinson, J (trans.) quoted in Murphy-O'Connor, J, op. cit., p. 375.
3  Pringle, D 1998, *The Churches of the Crusader Kingdom of Jerusalem*, vol. II, Cambridge University Press, Cambridge, UK, p. 146. Quoting Peter the Deacon.
4  ibid. p. 146. Nazareth pilgrim Burchard of Mount Sion.
5  A report on the unpublished excavation by Roland de Vaux at the Synagogue Church in Nazareth, Israel, Dark, K 2009, *Reading Medieval Studies* 35, p. 94.

## The archaeology

The existing structure is slightly below ground level and constructed with rusticated masonry in a barrel vault shape. The oldest parts of the structure date back to the medieval period and this would pre-date 1771 AD, when the Franciscans gave the site to the Melkite Christians. A test pit excavation was done inside the church by Roland de Vaux in 1945 and he noted:

> The discovery of a layer with 'pre-Crusader' (perhaps either Roman–period or Byzantine) pottery beneath the underlying church walls suggests that this area of the present city was perhaps occupied prior to the existing structure.[6]

The current structure is not the synagogue that existed in the time of Jesus. However, the locality could have, from the third century onwards, contained a structure that was a place of worship, as noted in later pilgrim accounts.

B.11 Interior view of traditional Nazareth Synagogue. A spiritual site, but not the one associated with Jesus.

### Another interpretation

This locality was part of the small Judeo-Christian community explained in Chapter 3. This group, and other parts of the Hebrew Christian community in Palestine, went into decline in the fourth century AD. With the growth of Gentile Byzantine Christianity in this century the dynamic of Nazareth hamlet went into a transformation. The Jewish city nearby was hostile to Christians as explained in Chapter 4. A need to relate gospel events to what was called Jesus' hometown required a synagogue location. This is where the description of a site nearby in 570 AD takes on significance. The old market area became the de-facto location for the 'city' with the residence of Mary and Joseph 170 metres (185 yards) away.

Thus this Byzantine area becomes a place of devotion for pilgrims dating from the fourth century or earlier. The anointing on the Synagogue Church is that its environs was the place where early Judeo-Christians, including Jesus' relatives lived and prayed. Later it became a place where pilgrims came to pray which has continued for over sixteen hundred years. It is not the location of the actual synagogue, but it has kept alive the memory of the gospel event. For these reasons it has great spiritual significance. Research leads me to propose a more accurate locality of the Nazareth synagogue.

---

6   ibid. p. 95.

## 6.2 Nazareth Synagogue: spiritual and physical factors

Studies have been made of the design and features of ancient synagogues in the Galilee.[7] A feature of a Jewish synagogue could include a text carved on a dedication stone. These stones have been found on synagogues, with some located on the portal of the doorway. An example of such a plaque found in Jerusalem dates back to the first century. Written in Greek it was inscribed as a foundation stone of priest Vettanos who "constructed the synagogue for the reading of the law and for the teaching the Commandments".[8] Similar blessing texts have been found on some Galilean synagogues e.g. Huqoq: "Blessed are all the people of the town who adhere to all the commandments". We do not know if there was one inscribed at the Nazareth synagogue.

### The spiritual divide in Nazareth

The city Jesus grew up in was very Jewish, but what was the real spiritual condition of the city? As stated previously, the first generation of Nazarenes would have been devout and had given the name to the site. However, as the settlement grew and became a city it came at a cost spiritually. The increased population was not all Nazorean and a wider cross-section of people formed. The emergence of the sect of the Pharisees also gained more influence in the larger Jewish cities. In contrast, the devout Essenes tended to be more communal and preferred to live in rural villages. Eventually, a divide between the more pious residents and the more legalistic Pharisees developed. The existence of these two sects of Judaism was reported on by Josephus in the first century (*Ant.* 13.5.9). He confirmed "the Pharisees have delivered to the people a great many observances by succession from their fathers, which are not written in the law of Moses" (*Ant.* 13.10.6). This criteria sets the scene for accounts of Jesus' interaction with the Pharisees.

B.12 A 'Seat of Moses' found at Chorazim in Galilee. Jesus said Pharisees sought these seats of honour in synagogues.
Courtesy BiblePlaces.com.

---

7   Urman, D and Flesher, P (eds) 1998, *Ancient Synagogues–Historical Analysis and Archaeological Discovery*, Brill, Boston, USA.

8   *A Greek Synagogue Inscription from Jerusalem,* American Schools of Oriental Research, <www.jstor.org/stable/1354801>. This would be for a Hellenistic Jewish Synagogue.

### The Nazareth leaders and teachers with a reputation

Larger Jewish cities had schools of theology often administered by the Pharisees, and part of their role was the education and religious order for the city. In Appendix 3 it is calculated that the Nazareth congregation was about thirteen hundred people. This congregation would require a certain number of learned men, or rabbis, to expound the Law and most of them were probably Pharisees. This has been estimated to be twenty or more rabbis. A city was also required to have a court of justice with a group of judges to administer laws.[9] Insight into the questionable moral qualities of some of the judges in Nazareth was shown when there was an attempt to kill Jesus as discussed in Chapter 8.

A curious reference to Nazareth is made in the Gospel of John. When a disciple called Philip told his friend Nathanael he had found the Messiah, the reply was: "Can anything good come out of Nazareth?" (John 1:43–48). Some say this related to the low character traits of the Nazareth population, but it does not say that. It is in the context of a claim of the Messiah coming from that city. A better and more logical explanation would be that the theological teachings and moral standards of some Nazareth leaders were not highly regarded by Nathanael. Later, when Nathanael actually met Jesus, he was commended as "an Israelite indeed in whom there is no deceit" (John 1:47). Nathanael was a man with high moral principles who was a resident of the Galilee, and who knew Nazareth's religious reputation. Thus, Nathanael was questioning if this particular city's leaders and teachers could produce the *'The Messiah'* – the *'Promised One'* from God. It also implies a sizeable group of candidates giving more evidence in support of a large city.

### The physical factors

Surveys have been made on a list of historic synagogues in Israel. Most of the examples are from the period after 70 AD, but some of the sites before that date are found in Masada, Jericho, Capernaum, Tel Rekhesh and Gamla.

### Prominent location in the city

After 70 AD Jewish texts, known as *Tosefta*, recommend that synagogues "are built only at the highest point of the town".[10] There may have been a preference for a high location but discovered sites show this was not always the case. The question is what could be applicable in the case of Nazareth at

---

9  In the Jewish Mishna a town of at least 120 families had the requirement of 23 judges to act as a jury. This was dated after 200 AD and the requirement before 70 AD is not clear, but the principle would be similar. This also suggests a town requiring over 600 residents to form a court known as a lesser Sanhedrin. Jewishvirtuallibrary.org. 2016, Tractate 'Sanhedrin: Chapter 1', *Jewish Virtual Library*.

10 Horbury, W (ed.) 1999, *The Cambridge History of Judaism*, vol. 3, Cambridge University Press, Cambridge, UK, p. 278.

*Locating Nazareth city synagogue*

Tel Yafia? Nazareth's devout pioneers in the first century BC probably would have located the first synagogue in a prominent position in their village. This would be logical practice as it was the nucleus and focal point for the community. The gospel gives a clue when it states that the synagogue of Nazareth was located within the city and Jesus was "thrust out" of it when they tried to kill him (Luke 4:28).

B.13 The peak of Tel Yafia facing west. NC1 indicates the historic Franciscan Church and its prominent locality.

**The orientation of the synagogue**

The orientation of Jewish synagogues has resulted in vigorous debate by scholars, as part of the problem is in defining what constitutes orientation. Archaeologist Lee Levine has noted that synagogues could be oriented by several criteria.[11] One was the orientation to Jerusalem, which was used after 70 AD. If the meeting hall did not face Jerusalem it was possible to stand, and turn in that direction to do the prayers of the Amidah. In the Talmud it was recommended to orientate west with an eastern entrance similar to the Tabernacle in the book of the Exodus. Some architects were influenced by the site contours in the placement of the building, while others made a point of facing a topographical feature. It seems in the first century, before the Talmud period, there was no rigid criteria for orientation:

> Without a universal floor plan, it is clear that each community valued and required different architectural or functional features, and the design of a synagogue was decided upon by the leaders of the community rather than according to an established synagogue standard.[12]

---

11 Levine, LI 2005, *The Ancient Synagogue – the first thousand years*, Yale University Press, London, UK, p. 326.

12 Murray, D 2015, *The Ancient Synagogue in Israel & the Diaspora*. Ancient History Encyclopedia, <www.ancient.eu/article/828/>. Most of the synagogues excavated in the Galilee reflect one of the above criteria. There are seven Israeli synagogue sites dating before 70 AD. A recent one is at Tel Rekhesh. Masada synagogue orientates to Jerusalem and Herodium orientates to the west.

We do not know what criteria was used for the synagogue in Nazareth. It could be toward the west like the Tabernacle or towards Jerusalem. It may even orientate towards Mt. Kedumim as this will be shown as a spiritual site.

**The facilities of a synagogue**

Very large Jewish cities like Sepphoris and Tiberias had more than one synagogue. However, it is proposed there was one main central synagogue in Nazareth city. This building would also be the headquarters for the outlying synagogues in the villages of the polis. Synagogues had both religious and civic roles and were essentially communal facilities:

> The synagogue (bet kneset) is one of the main institutions characteristic of the public and religious life of the Jewish people from as early as the Hasmoneans ... it was the most prominent – and often the only public structure in the Jewish cities.[13]

Evidence suggests that these buildings could include space for children to be taught, toilets and ablutions, staff facilities and other amenities. Atrium courtyards were also provided in some locations as a congregating point, taking benefit of the climate of the region.

**A size for the Nazareth synagogue**

Fortunately, there is evidence of an actual synagogue from the first century at Gamla in the Golan near the Galilee. It was buried after the Roman attack in 67 AD. Illus. B.14 shows its size and the three tiered seating rows. This seating has been measured and calculated to provide for 344 people.[14] Based on this criteria a proposal has been made for the Nazareth synagogue which is detailed in Illus. B.15. This plan has certain assumptions and slightly more space than Gamla. Note on this layout the location of Moses' seat, the ark cabinet where the holy scrolls were kept and a lectern position. The number of the Nazareth congregation has been estimated as about 1,280 souls and an assumption of seating for 400 people has been made. This means the seating would be adequate for three services on the Sabbath. That requires a meeting hall of approximately 400 square metres (43 US squares) which could be 25 x 17 metres (82 x 55 feet) based on the Gamla plan precedent. Allowing for the support facilities and a courtyard, a site of about 1,000 square metres (108 squares), and preferably fairly level, needs to be considered.

---

(12 cont.) The debatable site at Capernaum appears to be north-south. The Jericho synagogue appears arbitrary to the south-west. Gamla appears to be determined by the topography and orientated to a nearby high hill.

13 Urman, D and Flesher, P, *The Communal Functions of the Synagogue in The Land of Israel in the Rabbinic Period* in Safrai, Z, op. cit. p. 181.

14 Spigel, CS 2012, *Ancient Synagogue Seating Capacities,* Mohr Siebeck, Tubingen, Germany, p. 80. The seating calculations vary according to a number of assumptions explained by Spigel. Gamla's population has been estimated at 3,000 to 4,000 before the destruction. ibid. p. 84.

*Locating Nazareth city synagogue*

## GAMLA SYNAGOGUE

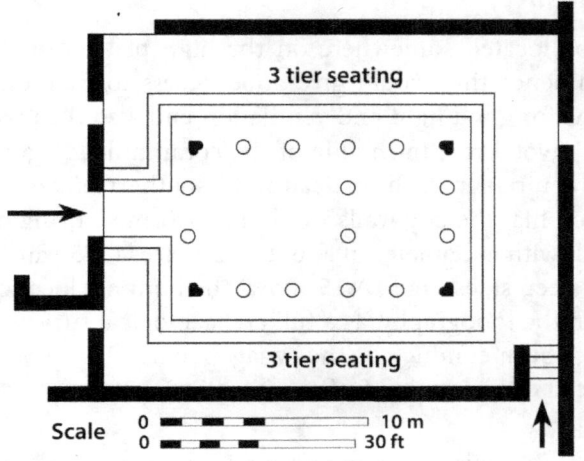

B.14 Gamla Synagogue in the Golan existed until 67 AD. The hall size was 22 x 17m or 72 x 55 feet. Note the three tiered seating which has been calculated for 344 people based on assumptions by a scholar. *Refer* Credits.

## NAZARETH SYNAGOGUE - A PROPOSAL

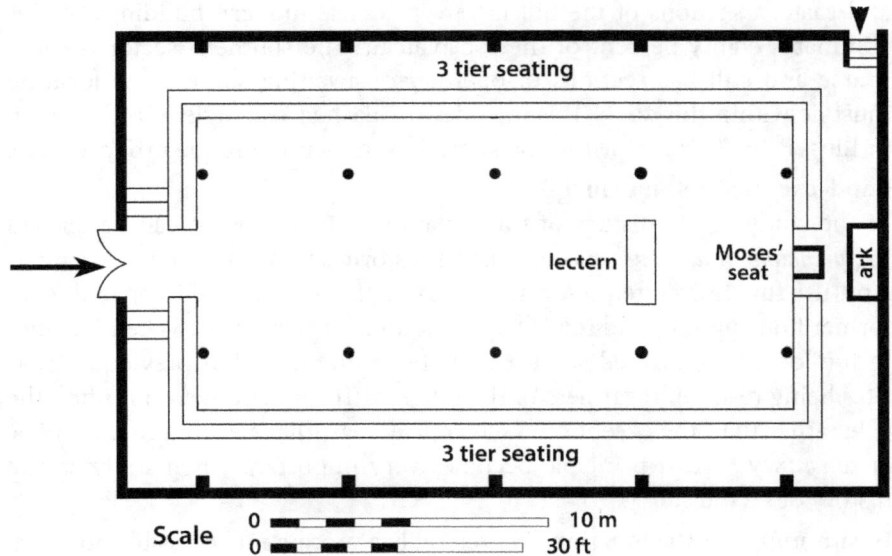

B.15 Author's plan for a Nazareth Synagogue. 27 x 17 metres – 88 x 55 feet (approx). Three tiered seating for 400 people could be provided. Extra overflow bench seats could be put at the side walls. A timber frame structure for the internal posts is proposed to reduce the visual impact.
Jesus would have read from the Isaiah scroll at the lectern.

## 6.3 The proposed locality

The synagogue would be located somewhere on the high plateau of the town on a site of prominence that would give good access to everyone. The location would allow for good light and ventilation and also illustrate its importance with the pivotal role in the life of the community. A good location that meets this requirement is the plateau at the southern end of Tel Yafia. [15] It can be assumed that the city walls would have formed a ring on the top section of the hill with a diameter of about 160 metres (175 yards), taking advantage of the steep sides. Illus. A.15 shows the nominal location of the city walls based on the topography, as a full archaeological survey of the top perimeter has not been conducted. The synagogue must have been within this zone – a crucial consideration (*refer* Appendix 8.1.2).

### The archaeological criteria

The IAA has recognized Tel Yafia to be archaeologically significant, but unfortunately the hill has been extensively built on in recent decades. No remains of an Early Roman era synagogue have been reported to date while preparing foundations for existing buildings. The northern, western and eastern sections of the hill have very dense modern buildings so this eliminates eighty percent of the top plateau. The southern sector is more sparse and still has sections of open space awaiting survey. The location must lie within this zone. This includes the dashed rectangle of NC1 shown in Illus. B.16. This is a prime consideration in identifying the proposed site.

### Land-use succession principle

In the study of the history of town planning there is what can be termed the *principle of land-use succession*. On historic sites over many eras similar land-use functions often re-occur. For example, houses tend to be built over former housing sites and roads tend to follow former tracks. When it comes to the location of sacred sites, it is quite common to find previous sacred sites being re-used, regardless of the religion. This phenomenon is often the rule rather than the exception. One archaeologist has referred to it as a *law of constancy*. [16] This principle becomes very important when studying the history of sacred sites.

**In summary for the location:** 1) preferably a prominent accessible position; 2) within the walls of the historic city; 3) not where existing modern buildings are located; 4) on a reasonably large plateau of at least 1,000 square metres (108 squares); 5) possibly a location with a history of spiritual significance.

---

15 The report by the Israel Antiquities Authority (IAA) Alexandre, Y 2012, *Yafi'a*, op. cit. supported this location as the site of Japhia, which is recorded as being a walled site by Josephus.

16 Pixner, B, op. cit., p. 117. Pixner refers to statements by archaeologist Michael Avi-Yonah on the "law of constancy" for holy places.

*Locating Nazareth city synagogue*

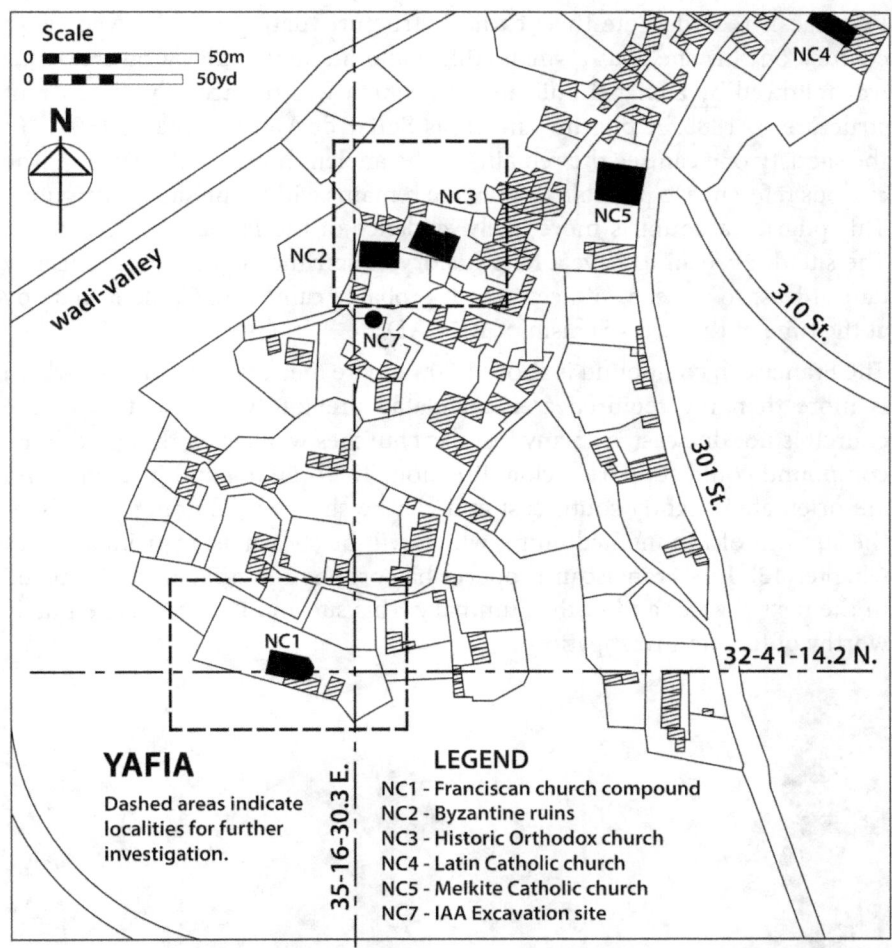

B.16 Yafia showing church locations. Author map based on information in the Yafia town survey 1951 AD. *Refer* page 109, footnote No. 5.
Courtesy of the Institute of Archaeology, Hebrew University, Jerusalem.

## The Franciscan Church compound (NC1)

Church location: 32-41-14.2 N. and 35-16-29.6 E.

This site is a good candidate to start to consider the remains of the synagogue. It meets all the five criteria listed previously. (Refer Illus. A.15). Located on the high point in the south-west corner of the historic city, the large compound is known as the *Church of the Holy Apostles*. Tradition has it to be the original residence of the sons of Zebedee, the Apostles James and John. The mistaken assumption of this legend was explained in Chapter 4. The history of this site has been documented by archaeologist B. Bagatti. [17]

---

17 Bagatti, B 2001, *Ancient Christian Villages of Galilee,* Franciscan Printing Press, Jerusalem,

Franciscan records note their earliest structure, dating to the seventeenth century on this site, was a small edifice and an altar under a fig tree. This was followed by a chapel built in 1766 which was replaced by the current structure in 1885. A pilgrim known as Sodar de Vaulx wrote in 1891: "In the sacristy one can see the remains of the ancient house of Zebedee".[18] The curious reference to possible Roman era remains within the site is intriguing. This pilgrim account is more likely evidence of the Franciscan structures. The site does seem to have a long history of spiritual significance that may date at least to the eleventh century. It probably came into Catholic custody at the time of the Great Schism of 1054 AD.

The Franciscan compound is about 1,200 square metres (130 squares), which is more than the required area calculated previously. Orientation of the church is not due east, as many historic churches were, even though the site compound could support such a direction. The building and its compound are orientated slightly south-east and can be shown as aligning directly to the summit of Mount Kedumim, which will be shown as a spiritual site in Chapter 13. This Franciscan property has prophetic significance discussed in the next chapter and in the Summary. This site and its locale is definitely worthy of further investigation.[19]

B.17 Franciscan Church in Yafia commemorating the Apostles James and John. The orientation of the building and compound is towards Mt. Kedumim.

---

(17 cont.) Israel, p. 80.

18 ibid. p. 81.

19 There are moves afoot to redevelop this site which would require an archaeological survey. Two archaeologists have indicated [to the author] a willingness to be involved in an excavation.

# CHAPTER 7
## JUBILEE DECLARATION OF LIBERTY

"The Spirit of the Lord is upon Me,
Because He has anointed Me
To preach the gospel to the poor;
He has sent Me to heal the brokenhearted,
To proclaim liberty to the captives
And recovery of sight to the blind,
To set at liberty those who are oppressed;
To proclaim the acceptable year of the Lord".

Luke 4:18–19.

> This event can be described as a pivotal one in the life of Jesus. This is where he is prophetically linking a passage in the book of Isaiah to himself, the Messiah announcing the Gospel of Liberty. This event would strongly suggest a location of importance. It may be due north of another site of significance to Jews and Samaritans, the altar and memorial of Joshua on Mount Ebal.

## 7.1 Joshua's altar and Jesus' synagogue

> Now Joshua built an altar to the LORD of Israel in Mount Ebal as Moses the servant of the LORD had commanded the children of Israel. As it is written in the Book of the Law of Moses, an altar of whole stones over which no man has wielded an iron tool. And they offered on it burnt offerings to the LORD; and sacrificed peace offerings. And there in the presence of the children of Israel he wrote on the stones a copy of the law of Moses which he had written (Joshua 8:30–32).

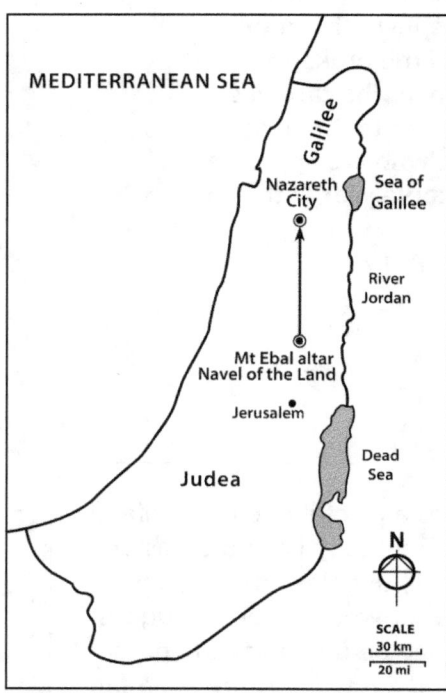

B.18 The altar site at Mt. Ebal is shown in Appendix 3 as "The Navel of the Land". It prophetically aligns to the north with Jesus' Nazareth city in 27 AD.

The crucial challenge of the above account is to locate a site on Mount Ebal with an altar and sacred precinct where the Law of Moses was inscribed on stones. Mount Ebal was also commonly known as the *Mount of Curses* in consequence of the effects of sin. However it is not a cursed hill, but the offerings named point to the requirement to make sacrifices with blood to make peace with God. Moses had also instructed Joshua that they were to "rejoice before the LORD your God" (Deut. 27:7) at this altar site because it illustrated the grace of God who forgives sins. Afterward at another ceremony, with six tribes on Mt. Ebal and six tribes on Mt. Gerizim, they marked the covenant birth of the Israelite nation in the Promised Land.

*Jubilee Declaration of Liberty*

B.19 Sacred Tell er-Ras on biblical Mt. Ebal (Samaritan Gerizim) is proposed as Joshua's altar in the Promised Land. The longitude (marked) aligns with the original Nazareth city.

## Mount Ebal as a sacred altar site (G1)

Location: 32-12-24.4 N. and 35-16-30.3 E. At this point it is relevant to demonstrate that the longitude of the sacred site on traditional Mount Gerizim, known today as Tell er-Ras, bisects the city of Nazareth to the due north. This implies it is a prophetic marker. It also aligns with the Franciscan compound shown in the previous chapter. (Illus. A.15 shows the longitude position.) Appendix 3 has more information on the following:

- The Samaritan account of the preceding Bible passage was that the altar was on Mount Gerizim and not on Mount Ebal. However this can be shown as a later alteration by the Samaritans. They are correct about the altar but they made a changeover with the names.
- The proposal is that traditional Mount Gerizim, is in fact, Joshua's Mount Ebal and there is a good biblical explanation for this nomination. This site was known as the *'Navel of the Land'*, translated from *Erez Tabbur* in Hebrew (Judges 9:36 and *refer* Illus. B.19. and F.08).
- A biblical *navel* can be defined as a centre point geographically and also spiritually. This altar navel can be accurately located by latitude and longitude. The longitude of this site is of particular interest in this book.
- This gives support to Jesus' claims of being the Messiah. Jesus and Joshua share the same name of Yeshua in Hebrew, meaning *deliverer* or *rescuer*. Joshua would have been marking a prophetic location when he positioned his altar and Law memorial. He selected a prominent and spectacular part of the ridge within the confines of the Levite city of Shechem.[1] They would be the logical custodians for such a sacred site in Israel.

---

1  Biblical Shechem is known as Tel Balata an agreed site in modern Nablus. *Refer* also Ch.14.1.

## 7.2 The Jubilee and Gospel declaration

> So He came to Nazareth, where He had been brought up. And as His custom was, He went into the synagogue on the Sabbath day, and stood up to read. And He was handed the book of the prophet Isaiah. And when He had opened the book, He found the place where it was written:
>
> *"The Spirit of the LORD is upon Me, Because He has anointed Me To preach the gospel to the poor; He has sent Me to heal the broken hearted, To proclaim liberty to the captives And recovery of sight to the blind, To set at liberty those who are oppressed; To proclaim the acceptable year of the LORD."* [italics added]
>
> Then He closed the book, and gave it back to the attendant and sat down. And the eyes of all who were in the synagogue were fixed on Him. And He began to say to them, "Today this Scripture is fulfilled in your hearing". So all bore witness to Him, and marvelled at the gracious words which proceeded out of his mouth. And they said, "Is this not Joseph's son?" (Luke 4:16–22).

**The setting**
This was the holy *Day of Atonement* known as *Yom Kippur*. On this occasion it also marked the start of a Jubilee year. Jesus was a member of a large city congregation and he had attended these holy services regularly for eighteen years. The synagogue would have had packed seating for the estimated four hundred people at the service. There would have been about twelve males of similar age to Jesus associated with the congregation.[2] He was known, but not in any exceptional way, with this number of peers. He was also known to the ruling authorities, but not esteemed due to his working class status.

**Jesus and the Day of Atonement**
This great festival is still considered to be the most solemn in the Jewish calendar. From his teenage years Jesus would have stood with his fellow male citizens in his synagogue on the Day of Atonement to pray. They would have faced Jerusalem and solemnly prayed for God's plan of salvation and the answer to the sin of the world. The Messiah would be facing towards the place of his eventual crucifixion, praying for the great plan of salvation! The Jewish synagogue location where the Messiah regularly prayed would be spiritually potent. This is a good example of the Hebrew word *moed* (H4150) used to denote a special appointed time, meeting and place.

---

2  Assumption: Congregation of 1300 adults has 650 males. Age range, 13 to 70 years gives an average of 12 of the same age for each year.

*Jubilee Declaration of Liberty*

## 'The Day' and acceptable 'Year of the Lord'

This gospel event is very significant as Jesus is claiming to be the *'anointed one'* of God. The event would be the fulfilment of an ancient prophecy by Isaiah.

> "The Spirit of the Lord God is upon Me because the Lord has anointed Me To preach good tidings to the poor; He has sent Me to heal the broken-hearted, To proclaim liberty to the captives, And the opening of the prison to those who are bound; To proclaim the acceptable year of the Lord" (Isaiah 61:1–2).

This is the announcement of a powerful Messianic Kingdom that will result in great joy, hope and healing. It includes the promise of freedom from spiritual bondages and oppression. This was the Gospel declaration of an answer to the human dilemma of the effects of sin.

## The Jubilee

The declaration of the *"acceptable year of the Lord"* is a reference to the start of the *Year of Jubilee*. Every fifty years the Day of Atonement was celebrated in a special way and that year would be called a Jubilee year. The Jubilee year was defined as from the *Day of Atonement* of the 49th year to the same on the 50th year (Lev. 25:8–9). This day was the tenth day of the seventh month called Tishri in Hebrew, which would often correspond closely to the month of September or early October. In the Old Testament the Jubilee had certain characteristics. Israelites were commanded not to oppress one another; there was the resting of the land from agriculture, rules for the selling of houses, the cancelling of debt to the poor, the freeing of servants, and a theme of releasing and renewing (Lev. 25:18–55).

B.20 A shofar was blown to announce the start of Jewish festivals. This would have been done on the Jubilee when Jesus preached. Engraving by H.D. Northrop. Credit Wikimedia Commons.

B.21 The famous 'Isaiah Scroll' found at Qumram dates to circa 150 BC. The text has been found to be identical to our version today. Jesus would have read from a similar scroll in the Nazareth synagogue. Credit Wikimedia Commons.

### Jesus returns as a former resident of Nazareth

"In this year of Jubilee each of you shall return to his possession" (Lev. 25:13). This statement in the Law means that people were expected in the Jubilee year to return to the location of their family inheritance. Joseph, before his death, probably gave his city workshop (outside the city walls), to a relative who lived in the city. It would appear that Jesus gave up his property rights to the family workshop (if any) by the time he left Nazareth (Luke 9:58). The Hebrew word used for possession is *achuzzah* (H272), which indicates some ownership of land. Mary and Jesus would still be owners of their outer residence site even though they did not live there at the time.

### The time and date of the Jubilee Declaration

The year-date of Jesus' declaration has been reliably computed by Bible chronologist Professor Floyd N. Jones.[3] His calculation is based on Joshua leading the Israelites over the Jordan River in September 1451 BC. The first seven years were spent conquering the Land so the start of the Jubilee cycle was September 1444 BC. This means the first Jubilee was in 1395 BC and the thirtieth Jubilee was on the evening of the tenth of Tishri 27 AD. Thus Jesus made his declaration towards the end of September 27 AD, approximately a year after his baptism in the Jordan River. This computes well with other dates in the chronology of Jesus, where he is born towards the end of 4 BC, and dies at Passover in 30 AD (Gregorian calendar).

---

3   Jones, FN, op. cit., p. 289.

# CHAPTER 8

# THE NAZARETH PLOT TO KILL JESUS

**So all those in the synagogue,
when they heard these things,
were filled with wrath, and rose up
and thrust Him out of the city;
and they led Him to the brow of the hill
on which their city was built,
that they might throw Him down over the cliff.**

Luke 4:28–29.

---

A popular quote that was made by Jesus is his reference that "prophets" are not often honoured by their fellow citizens. It gets used in many different contexts today. Jesus was well known to his fellow residents as he was the local carpenter's son from the hamlet on the city fringe. Later when he gave his prophetic declaration and teaching there was a violent reaction, particularly from the rulers. A full reconstruction of the story can be made and related to the topography of Nazareth.

B.22 'The plan to kill Jesus' by Jerome Nadal, 1595 AD. It depicts the enraged citizens' attempt to push Jesus off a cliff near the city.
Credit *"Illustrations of the Gospel Stories"* catholic-resources.org.

## 8.1 The hometown rejection of a prophet

Jesus could prove that he was a Nazarene of the messianic line of David, as well as a rabbi. The gospel records that there was a strong reaction when Jesus preached on his first return visit after relocating to Capernaum. Although he was no longer a resident of his hometown, he had a legal right to speak.

> When he had come to his own country, He taught them in their synagogue, so that they were astonished and said "Where did this Man get this wisdom and these mighty works? Is this not the carpenter's son? ... Where then did this Man get all these things?" So they were offended at Him. But Jesus said to them, "A prophet is not without honor except in his own country and in his house". Now He did not do many mighty works there because of their unbelief (Matt. 13:54–58).

It is noteworthy that in this passage the name of Nazareth is not used. The translation has used his "own country". In the original Greek the word is "*patris*", which is better understood as "hometown" and is used to describe where his own synagogue was located. This illustrates that it is the family synagogue being named. Jesus had been a resident, along with the rest of his family, which gives added meaning to the quote of "house" he uses. His fellow citizens were offended at his wisdom because he was considered working class.

**The declaration and violent reaction**

Jesus' second return visit to the Nazareth synagogue was far more dramatic. On this occasion it was the solemn Day of Atonement and this coincided with the declaration of the gospel at the evening start of the Jubilee as discussed previously. Jesus' implied claim of being the Messiah caused great surprise. He had quoted the Isaiah prophecy (Isaiah 61:1-2) and stated he was the fulfilment of it. This caused some initial elation in his fellow worshippers.

At a further Sabbath session, probably the next day, the congregation asked for signs of healing to be done. However, Jesus gave more teaching on the rejection of prophets and the importance of true faith in God. Some of the congregation, particularly the leaders, took strong exception to his teaching. This resulted in a marked change in temperament and increasing indignation, leading to volatile anger:

> So all those in the synagogue when they heard those things, were filled with wrath, and rose up and thrust him out of the city, and led him to the brow of the hill on which their city was built, that they might throw him down over the cliff. Then passing through the midst of them, He went His way (Luke 4:28–30).

The reaction was indeed so violent that there was an attempt to kill him. The evidence for the locations of the attempted execution events can be given, but first some historical background with comments.

**Mount Precipice (Z1)**

There are at least three localities offered as sites of execution based on traditional Nazareth.[1] None are sheer cliffs so scaffolding would have been required for an effective execution. Tourists are directed to a very steep hill south of Nazareth known as Mount Precipice, with plaques denoting the tradition of a proposed execution site. This is one of the most popular of the suggested sites, due to the dramatic cliff overlooking the Jezreel Valley. The spectacular views from this rocky promontory are breathtaking, but it is not the correct site. The ridge does not connect topographically to either of the Nazareth settlements as required by the gospel. Mount Precipice was also known in medieval times as *Saltis Domini* – the Leap of the Lord, but Jesus does not leap to save himself in the gospel account.[2] A further comment: Why make an ideal picnic and lookout site a place of execution?

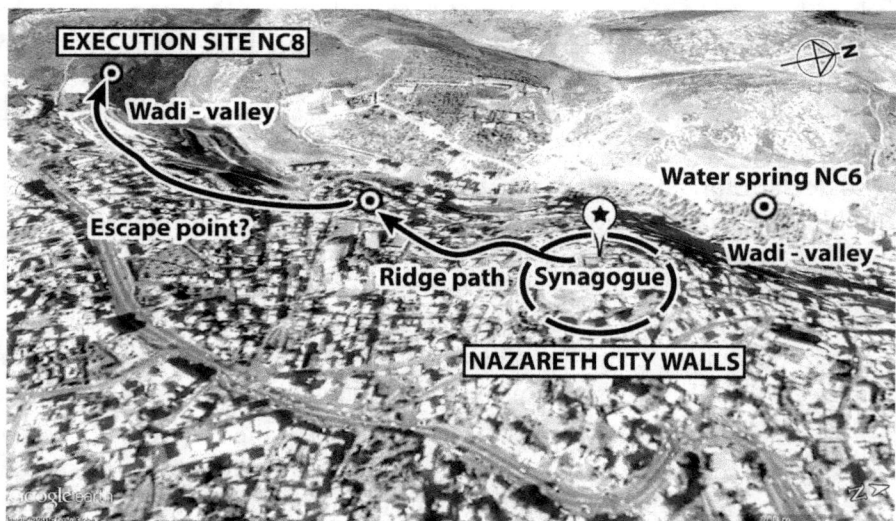

B.23 Tel Yafia showing route from the city towards the execution site, 1,000 metres (1,100 yards) to the SW. Base map Google Earth. Image © 2015 DigitalGlobe.

---

1  An Orthodox tradition locates the place of execution on one of the hills to the east of their church in traditional Nazareth, such as the Hospital Hill. This scenario is not supported, as it also does not connect topographically to the original site of Nazareth city. Mensa Christi on Nebi Sain ridge is located north of the Church of the Annunciation and has been proposed because it is on the same topographical ridge as the traditional site of Nazareth. However if the city is not in the traditional location, as has been shown, this cannot be correct.

2  Associated with this mountain is the Church of Mary's Fright but this is a medieval structure and tradition.

## 8.2 The execution site: a proposal

A nominal locality at 32-40-52 N and 35-15-56 E. just over one kilometre (1100 yards) south-west of Tel Yafia. (Adjacent to a residential area so discretion is required.) Access via main road No. 75 to the last traffic circle and petrol station in Yafia. Partially viewable south-west from that station's balcony and behind an existing dump facility. Such sites which are described as a *'stoning place'*, were well known in Jewish law, as the setting used to perform the death penalty by a variety of methods. Most large cities had these sites as detailed in the Mishnah. The following are the logistical requirements:

**The common ridge with the city**

Luke states that the city of Nazareth was on the same ridge (Luke 4:29) as the execution site. Traditional Nazareth, the hamlet site, in fact is located in a hollow, not on a ridge. The Greek word used for "*brow*" can be translated as 'ridge' and it is the same word used for eyebrow, denoting the profile of the prominence. The brow is the cusp of a ridge with a steep slope falling away from it (*refer* Appendix 8.3.1).

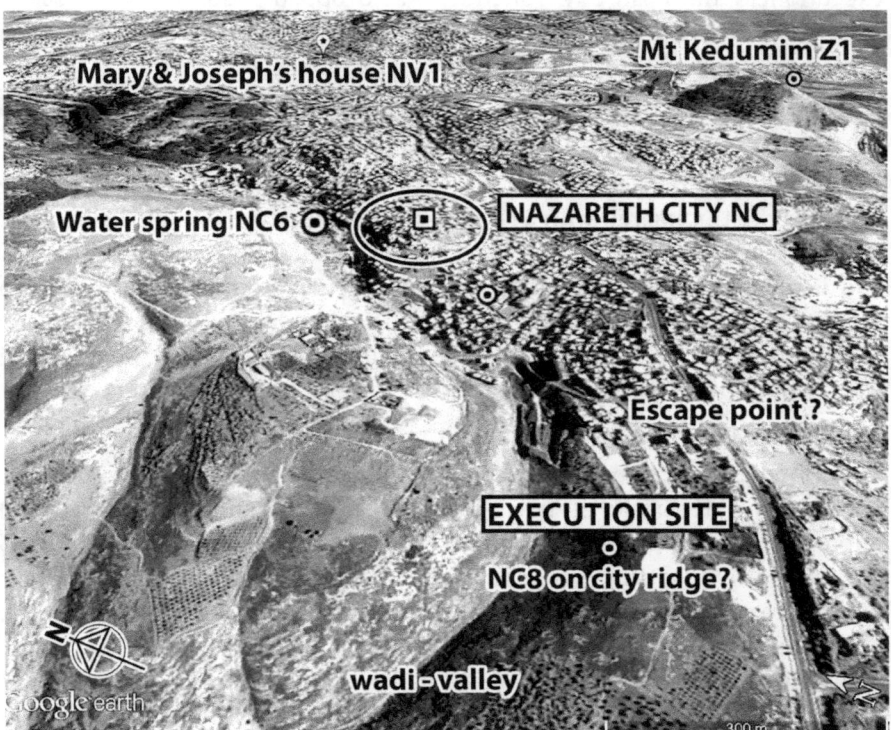

B.24 Nazareth city from the south showing the ridge connecting the city and the execution 'stoning' site (NC8) as required in the gospel account.
Base map Google Earth. Image © 2015 DigitalGlobe.

## South-westerly from the city: water and sanitation

The question is whether the execution site was north or south of the city. The city water supply was north-west of the city (NC6). The watercourse flows south-west, so it seems logical that an execution site would be below the flow of a water source for sanitation and health reasons. Nazareth was a large city, which would have required a good sewage disposal system. The fall of the watercourse to the south shows that this is the logical direction for any unclean activity. Jewish laws required certain purity rules within their settlements (Deut. 23:14). A ritually unclean area would be required to be well away from the city. One of the Israelite measures for sanctity was the two thousand cubit distance, which is just under 900 metres (985 yards) (Joshua 3:4). This would be a very good distance to place a ritually unclean site away from the city walls and the proposed location is just over that limit.

## The Jewish 'Stoning' place

The answer to understanding the execution site is a deep crevice in the ridge with a scaffold system attached to the edges. This would give safety to the executioners and ensure the offender was dropped headlong (Illus. B.27). The Greek used in the text means "cast down headlong" (G2630) which explains this action. The later era *Babylonian Talmud* reported:

"The stoning area's height was that of two men. One of the witnesses pushed him on his loins" (*Mishnah Sanhedrin 6:4*).

This would require a minimum fall of about 4.5 metres (15 feet) from the waist height tipping rail with a landing on a stone pavement. This fall would quickly render the offender unconscious or dead. They were then checked and if not dead witnesses participated in a group stoning to ensure death as prescribed in Deut. 17:7. Most Jewish cities would have such a dedicated execution site. This was seen as a quick and humane way to be executed with community justice.

## The evidence today

The proposed execution site, just north of the ridge road, is located near the current outer limits of Yafia's suburbs near bushland. As shown in the photos, this ridge is still steep today. It would only have required a deep crevice in the ridge-slopes for the drop to be made, not a massive cliff face. A number of factors have changed the profile of this ridge today. Historic seismic activity or earth tremors are well known in this region. This, along with natural erosion over many centuries has changed the surface profile and modified the original crevices. The site would have fallen into disuse after the Jewish city was abandoned in the seventh century. Housing development is currently occurring in this location making any identification difficult.

*The Nazareth plot to kill Jesus*

B.25 View from Franciscan compound (NC1) towards proposed execution site (NC8). Located on the southern side of the Yafia valley.

B.26 View from proposed execution site to Tel Yafia. Note the steep valley slopes showing the 'brow' of the ridges. Arrow indicates proposed Nazareth Synagogue locality. The distance is just over the 2000 cubits if required for ritual purity.

## 8.3 The premature attempt to kill Jesus

Luke's Gospel (4:30) states that to escape, Jesus "passed through the midst of them." The question is, how does he make his escape? He obviously escapes successfully before they reach the execution site. The answer lies in the topography, the time frame of the event and the direction that the vigilantes are moving. The required orientation is south-westerly out of the city. This ridge path heads towards a slight dip that connects to a higher section more southward again. The entire route is connected to the same eastern ridge of the Yafia watercourse, as can be seen in the Google Earth illustration B.24. This area would have been more rugged and rocky with crevices in 27 AD.

**A reconstructed scenario**

With the preceding factors, a convincing narrative of the dramatic events can be made. The Day of Atonement was at the end of September in 27 AD (sunset to sunset on the next day). That evening at sunset the trumpet (shofar) was sounded to commence the very sacred day and assembly. This was the service when Jesus made his Jubilee declaration, much to their amazement. The following day was still the holy day and services continued in the synagogue. Jesus also gave teaching that afternoon and on this occasion some attendees took strong exception to his message. No execution could be attempted on that day, as it was against the Law to do work, including executions, on a holy day. As the sun set that evening, the holy day was ended with a trumpet blast and some members of the synagogue made their way home. Refreshments may have been taken for those remaining.

But there was a group that was not happy, in particular the large group of leaders, probably Pharisees and their friends. They were "filled with wrath" (v. 28) and formed a circle around Jesus. An animated discussion occurred and they confronted him. How dare he, the local carpenter's son, challenge them on matters of faith. The rulers took counsel and deemed him to be worthy of execution. There was no legal trial as was required by Jewish law, but what we in Australia call a *kangaroo court*, an unjust hasty trial, such was the intensity of the wrath against Jesus.[3] If the seating of the synagogue was four hundred, then a large crowd of two hundred could be involved, with ring leaders whipping up the emotions.

With fading light and darkness falling, burning torches would have been produced to give light. Eventually Jesus was seized, but not bound, and physically escorted from the synagogue precinct. He went voluntarily, and

---

[3] Jewish law required a fair trial with witnesses before anyone could be sentenced to death. It also required a number of judges to preside over such a trial. The haste and manner of this event seems to add support to the previous reference of Nazareth's leaders' moral character. As Nathanael had said, "Can anything good come out of Nazareth?" (John 1:46).

*The Nazareth plot to kill Jesus*

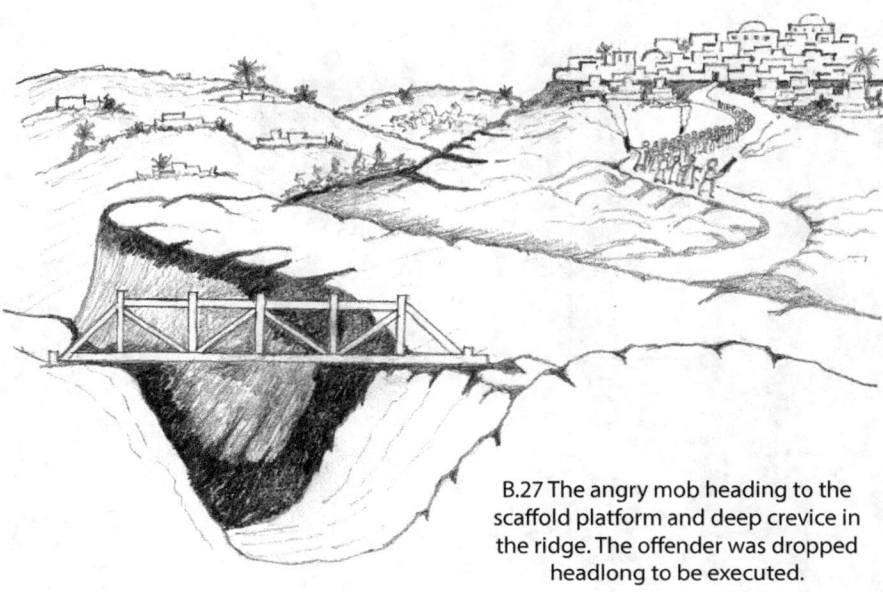

B.27 The angry mob heading to the scaffold platform and deep crevice in the ridge. The offender was dropped headlong to be executed.

was "thrust outside the city"(v. 28). Emotions were running high, as the mob with flickering torches made their way outside the city into the darkness. They moved south-westerly along a narrow path towards the city execution site that was located on the east bank of the deep wadi-valley. This valley echoed the howling and yelling of the mob. The execution site was some distance away, requiring a fifteen to twenty minute walk. There were rocky parts and deep crevices in this ridge and the path required very careful navigation to prevent a trip or fall.[4] Heading towards the city sewage dump the pungent odour filled the air. They were moving toward the deep crevice with scaffold planks and railing that formed a platform with a sheer drop. To the sensitive the "sense" of death would also hover over this locality.

The crowd was pushing and shoving (v. 29) and highly agitated. At a point in the walk before reaching the platform, near a rocky part of the pathway Jesus simply stopped. In the poor light, those pushing behind took their eyes off him to navigate the rocky section. They pressed on past him, not noticing his action. As they marched ahead Jesus quietly stood until the last marcher passed him in the poor light. He then slipped away and returned to his home in Capernaum. This is how, "passing through the midst of them, He went His way" (v. 30). It was not a bizarre leap as one tradition suggests.

---

4   Aspects of this scenario have been influenced by an account given in Appendix 8.3.2.

*Proving Biblical Nazareth*

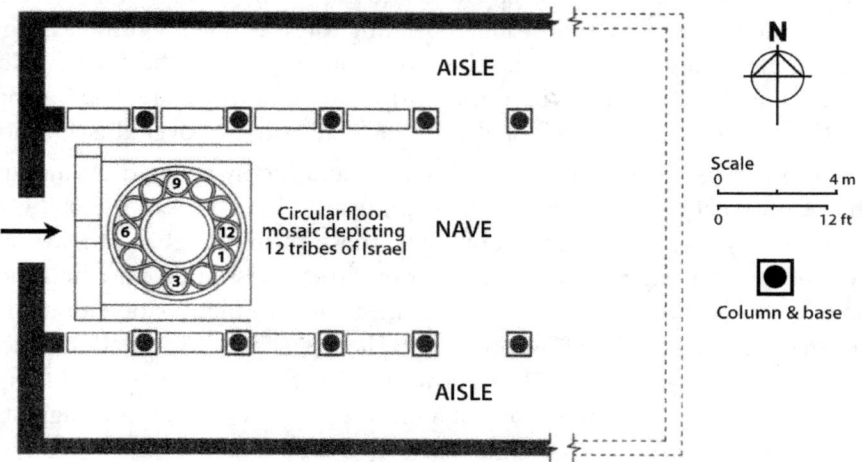

B.28 Archaeological excavation of Yafia 'Synagogue', 1951. Note the stone capital located in front of the standing worker. Photo courtesy of the Israel Exploration Society.

B.29 Yafia 'Synagogue' plan drawn by author based on E.L. Sukenik archaeology report. Note the 12 circular mosaics and their sequence on the floor that gives vital clues.

# CHAPTER 9
## CHRISTIAN SYNAGOGUE IN JEWISH NAZARETH

> But while he thought about these things,
> behold an angel of the Lord
> appeared to him in a dream, saying,
> "Joseph, son of David, do not be afraid
> to take to you Mary your wife, for that which
> is conceived in her is of the Holy Spirit.
> And she will bring forth a Son,
> and you shall call His name Jesus
> for He will save His people from their sins".
>
> Matthew 1:19–21.

The above account indicates that the naming of the Messiah occurred at the residence of Joseph the carpenter and not the future family home. This chapter examines an intriguing sacred Yafia site that may hold the answer to Joseph's residence. It is the proposed Hebrew Christian church built by a converted Jew known as Count Joseph. The location has connection to other sites of prophetic significance. A photo of the excavation and the plan of this building is shown on the left.

## 9.1 Yafia's Jewish synagogue or Byzantine church?

This segment seeks to identify the locality of the public workshop of Joseph the carpenter. My proposal is that it must be located somewhere in the urban centre of Nazareth. It was not in the isolated hamlet where it would be difficult to do business. Before this can be explained, two significant sites need to be identified to give possible clues.

B.30 Northern view of St. George Orthodox Church (NC3) Yafia.

B.31 Arabic dedication plaque. The Orthodox Church stone lintel shows Byzantine Christian symbols.

**The Orthodox Church at Tel Yafia (NC3)**
Location: 32-41-19 N and 35-16-31.2 E. (Illus. B.16 and B.34).

On the northern slopes of Tel Yafia's hill are two Orthodox churches, one is recent and the other is historic. Archaeologist Fr. Bellarmino Bagatti has researched the historic church and he dates the current building back to 1905–07.[1] A recovered plaque found in 1946 states that a former structure was there in 1755 AD. (The Ottoman era equivalent Islamic date is 1123 AH.) The Arabic plaque in Illus. B.31, now prominently displayed, is translated, "With the abundance of your mercy, I enter into your house. Orthodox Church of St. George 1123".[2]

What is most intriguing is that the door lintel below that plaque has evidence of secondary use, that is, it is much older than the building in which it has been incorporated. This lintel, as shown in the photograph, is clearly historic, and has obvious Christian symbols which were noted by Bagatti.[3] The carvings include a cosmic cross popular in the Byzantine times, a chalice and two ampulle, which are vessels for consecrated water or oil. What is the explanation for these historic Christian carved motifs found in a church within ancient Nazareth city?

---

1 Bagatti, B, *Ancient Christian Villages of Galilee*, op. cit., pp. 81–82.

2 ibid., p. 82.

3 ibid., p. 82.

*Christian synagogue in Jewish Nazareth*

A Byzantine sacred building with interesting features has been discovered adjacent to the historic Orthodox Church.

B.32 Interior of St. George Orthodox Church (NC3).

**Discovery of an ancient 'synagogue'**
In 1921 Louis Vincent, a priest and archaeologist, investigated several other ancient carved lintels in the Yafia village: "One was decorated with a menorah, and the other with a wreath flanked by two eagles." [4] These lintels had been incorporated into later structures, and his conclusion was that these were Jewish in origin. This find led to the excavation of what was proposed as a synagogue adjacent to and just west of the historic Orthodox Church. This excavation was conducted in 1950 by N. Avigad and E.L. Sukenik for the Hebrew University in Jerusalem. A detailed report was produced and the conclusion was that this synagogue showed *"that a substantial Jewish community continued to live at Yafa until the fourth century of the Christian era"*. [5] [italics added] However, the excavators noted there were curious anomalies in the design and artwork of this building.

B.33 Remains of Byzantine column and frieze found adjacent to the Orthodox Church.

**The dating**
Based on the floor's mosaic tile artwork found on site, Sukenik concluded: "I should be inclined to date it somewhere towards the end of the third century C.E. and not later than the beginning of the fourth". [6] This gives us a date around 300 AD for the art inspiration for the motifs. The style can be described as Late

---
4  Negev, A and Gibson, S, (eds) 2001, 'Japhia', op. cit., p. 255.
5  Sukenik, EL 1951, *The Ancient Synagogue at Yafa near Nazareth*, Preliminary Report, The Hebrew University of Jerusalem, Jerusalem, pp. 11–13.
6  ibid., p. 18. The marks the beginning of the art influence which would extend into the 4th. Cent.

Roman to Early Byzantine. In this period, style changes were appearing after Emperor Constantine's decree of tolerance in 313 AD. The Byzantine starting date in the Galilee is about 330 AD, so a date range for the structure could be between 300–350 AD.

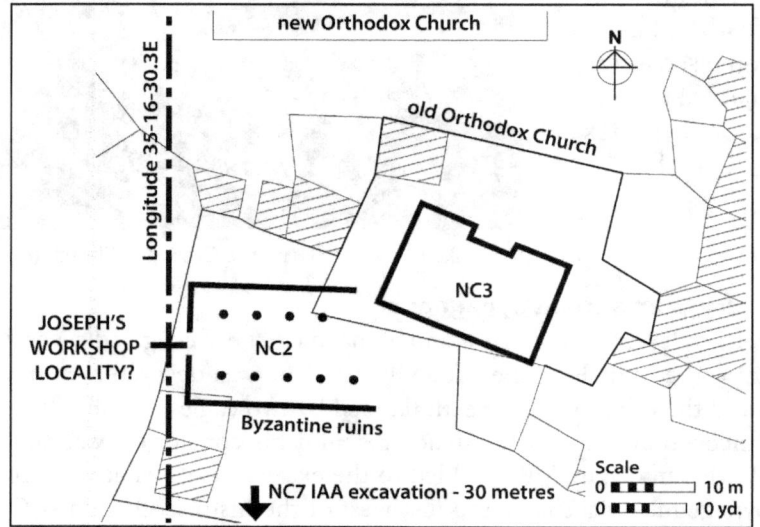

B.34 A sacred site (NC2) adjacent to Orthodox Church in Yafia (NC3). Overlay by author based on map B.16 in the archaeology report. It is speculated this locality may have contained Saint Joseph's public workshop.

**A controversial proposal**

The archaeology report makes note of certain anomalies with this building. The dating can be used to give an answer to the mystery of this unusual building. The proposal is that this structure is in fact, the famous Hebrew Christian synagogue of a certain *Count Joseph*, recorded in history. There is compelling evidence for this claim, but first we need to know more about this Joseph.

## 9.2 Count Joseph's testimony and his Nazareth church

On July 22nd each year, some Christians in Israel commemorate a very interesting historical figure in their tradition. They celebrate the memory of a person known as 'Count Joseph of Tiberias'. He is not to be confused with Saint Joseph the carpenter, the adopted father of Jesus. The title of 'count' came from an imperial honour bestowed on him by Emperor Constantine. An excellent summary of this intriguing figure has been given by scholar Gunter Stemberger.[7]

---

7   Stemberger, G 2000, *Jews and Christians in the Holy Land*, T&T Clark Ltd, Edinburgh, UK.

Count Joseph was a convert from Judaism in the fourth century who intended to build a Christian church at Nazareth. The debated question is whether in fact he did it as he planned. If he did, where was this church located and is there any evidence to prove it? His life story makes for interesting reading and there is a case that he indeed achieved his aim as we read about his testimony. The information comes from a Cyprian bishop named Epiphanius (315–403 AD) who wrote of visiting and staying with Count Joseph at Beth Shean (Scythopolis) in northern Israel in 360 AD.

He wrote of his host, "in regard to his public life he lived in accordance with the Jews, we discussed both his way of life and how he was converted to Christianity". [8] Count Joseph was born in about 290 AD into a wealthy Jewish family. He became a devout and educated Jew and served the local Jewish patriarch of Tiberias. Some scholars propose this patriarch to be a known figure called Judah III, who died in 320 AD. However, just before the patriarch's death, Count Joseph witnessed secretly through a keyhole a visit by a local Christian bishop who came disguised as a doctor. The bishop baptised the patriarch in secret on the pretext that the large amount of water required in the room was for medicinal reasons. After Judah's death, Joseph ventured into the patriarch's library and found to his surprise it contained a variety of Christian books. Included in the shelves was the:

> Hebrew version of Matthew and Hebrew translations of John and Acts. Joseph read these, was again troubled, but "he was hardened in heart". [9]

This was the start of Joseph's difficult journey of faith. He claimed that Jesus appeared to him personally in a dream, but he still was unconverted. Joseph later became ill and Jesus appeared to him again. This time there was a partial softening in his attitude and a healing resulted. Later his heart hardened again and the sickness returned, nearly causing him to die. A Christian persuaded him again to have true faith in Jesus Christ. Count Joseph responded and tried another test to see if Jesus was all powerful. He went out and conducted an exorcism in the name of Jesus on a local demonised man. This man was known to take his clothes off and run around naked. Joseph's exorcism was successful but even this was not enough to convince him to wholeheartedly accept the Christian faith. He was still sceptical and in need of more persuasion.

He remained in the employ of fellow Jews who later sent him to Cilicia near Tarsus in Turkey. He was performing financial administration, but these

---

8   Pritz, R 1985, 'Josephus of Tiberius– the Legend of a 4th Century Jewish Christian', No.2, *Mishkan – A Theological Forum on Jewish Evangelism*, Jerusalem, Israel, p. 39. Quoting Epiphanius.

9   ibid., p. 40. Quoting Epiphanius.

*Proving Biblical Nazareth*

B.35 Constantine, as depicted in a mosaic at the Hagia Sophia, Istanbul, 532–537AD. Patron of early church building in Palestine. Credit Wikimedia Commons.

duties led to some friction with one of the Jewish synagogues. The local Christian bishop gave the count a copy of the gospels to read and he was caught reading these books, which angered the local Jews. The end result was he was thrown into the Cydnus River (modern name is Berdan) and nearly drowned. Joseph was rescued by Christians, and went on to be baptised, and became a true believer in about 333 AD.

**Constantine's imperial decree**

Several years later he travelled to Constantinople to meet the Emperor Constantine where he shared his testimony. The story of his journey of faith impressed Constantine:

> The good emperor (Constantine) made (Joseph) a count and added that he could ask of him whatever he wanted. Joseph asked for nothing but to receive this great gift from the emperor, that he be permitted by means of imperial edict *to erect churches to Christ in the villages of the Jews. Indeed, no one had ever been able to build churches there*, because neither Greek nor Samaritan nor Christian was found in their midst.
>
> This (rule) indeed they have that no other race may be next to them. This is true especially in Tiberias, in Diocesarea also known as Sefforis, *in Nazareth* and in Cafarnaum. He only built a small church ... in Tiberius, *but he fulfilled his building wishes in Diocesarea and some other cities.* [10] [italics added]

The last half of Joseph's life was spent zealously building Christian churches in the Galilee. The correlation here is that the window of building these churches is approximately 340–361 AD. Stemberger proposes that,

> Joseph's conversion should be dated to between 324 and 337, because of his meeting with Constantine that occurred shortly afterwards. His meeting with Epiphanius happened under Constantius, that is, before 361. Epiphanius finished the Panarion in which he tells this tale, around 377. [11]

Epiphanius says that Joseph was about seventy years of age at the time of their meeting. This clearly again illustrates support for the two Nazareth settlement sites explained previously. The Nazareth Jewish town site, as

---

10 'Epiphanius', Donato Baldi, 1935, *Enchiridion Locorum Sanctorum, Jerusalem*, pp.2–3, Franciscan Cyberspot, <www.nazareth-en.custodia.org/default.asp?id=5952>.

11 Stemberger, G, op. cit., p. 74.

described by Epiphanius above was resistant to Christian residents. It was only by imperial decree that a site could be found and a Hebrew Christian church built there. It was not to be located in the existing Christian village some distance away as they had their own church.

### Evidence for Count Joseph's Church (NC2)
Location: 32-41-18.8 N. and 35-16-30.8 E. (Illus. B.34). Adjacent to and west of the historic Yafia Orthodox Church. There is no current access as it is re-buried with a residential block on piers (pilotis) directly above.

Count Joseph's plan was to build in the city of Nazareth, but he would have been aware of the potential hostility from residents if his site was located within the town wall zone on the plateau at the top. A more logical position would have been outside these walls, but still as near as possible to them. This is the case for this site as it is about 50 metres (55 yards) downwards from the crown of the hill on the northern side.

B.36 Author with column base and capital from Yafia Byzantine sacred archaeological site.

The construction time-frame for Count Joseph's Nazareth Church is 340–345 AD. This is based on a number of factors. [12] It can be noted that a major earthquake was recorded circa 363 AD in the Galilee. It is not clear what impact that it had on any of Joseph's churches. [13]

### The architecture
The capitals and bases of the central columns were found during excavation of the site. Some have suggested these capitals are Corinthian in style due to the leaf-like profile used, but this is not correct. The capitals have been

---

12 Factors in calculating the building time frame:
- The calculated time frame of all of the Count's building activity is 340–361 AD if we assume that all the projects had been commenced before he meets his biographer.
- It is likely that it was before the Jewish uprising against the Roman Emperor Gallus at nearby Sepphoris in 351–352 AD.
- It is probable that it occurred before the short anti-Christian reign of Roman emperor Julian the Apostate of 361–363 AD.
- The period nominated for the building's artwork was 300–350 AD.

13 Damage occuried to varying degrees in the Galilee. There is debate about the extent of damage at Sepphoris nearby as some claim the damage there was also due to the destruction from reprisals of the Gallus Revolt in 352 AD. The effect in Nazareth is not known or documented. No evidence of seismic disturbance to the Yafia site was noted in the 1951 survey report.

B.37 Yafia Aeolic capital. The style is used in Jewish synagogues.

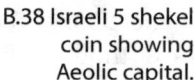

B.38 Israeli 5 shekel coin showing Aeolic capital.

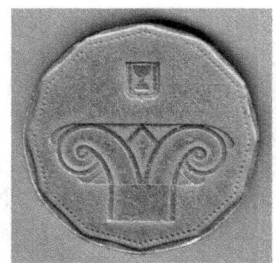

carefully examined and photographed and are better described as Jewish in style. These remains have the classic Aeolic scroll detail found in many earlier Jewish buildings, pottery and crafts. It is depicted on the modern Israeli five shekel coin. There is a thesis that this motif developed back in the Kingdom period in Israel.[14] The scroll detail has been suggested as symbolic of the scroll of the Law that is a central feature in Jewish culture.

Another comment is the carved lintel re-used in the Orthodox Church described previously. It has obvious Christian symbols of the Byzantine era that were used in the fourth century. It is possible that it was part of Count Joseph's Church and was re-used in the building adjacent. However this cannot be proven as to its origin, but a likely possibility.

**The unusual 'deviant' plan**

The archaeological survey revealed a rectangular structure 15 metres (50 feet) wide and an estimated length of about 19 metres (62 feet). Two rows of internal columns "make it clear that the synagogue was a basilical structure orientated from west to east"[15] (Illus. B.29). Comments have been made on the surprising orientation of this Yafia synagogue as it is clearly facing east with western entry. This is unusual for Jewish synagogues, and there is a suggestion that it was a broad-house plan where the congregation faced the long side (south), but that is not logical for this plan. One history researcher commenting on this and other sites wrote, "the synagogue of Japhia in the Lower Galilee … 'deviant' in their orientation … their prayer direction was apparently eastward".[16]

If we understand that the building is Christian it becomes apparent why it is considered 'deviant'. The plan is similar to many early Christian buildings which usually faced east.

---

14 Lipschits, O 2014, *The Origin and Date of the Volute Capitals from the Levant*, Bible History Daily, <www.biblicalarchaeology.org/daily/news/proto-aeolic-capital-associated-with-judahs-longest-spring-tunnel/>.

15 Sukenik, EL, op. cit., p.14.

16 Urman, D and Flesher, P (eds), op. cit., p. 149.

Christian synagogue in Jewish Nazareth

This point was picked up by the excavating archaeologist Professor E. L. Sukenik when he observed that, *"the structure at Yafa could be the remains of a church or a pagan temple"*.[17] [italics added]

This is a profound admission reinforcing my proposal that this is Count Joseph's Church. Nevertheless, Sukenik's conclusion that it was a synagogue, and not a church, was based solely on a circular floor mosaic.

### The circle mosaic of the tribes of Israel

*Refer* Illus. B.39. The surviving floor mosaics have been described as "fine workmanship and particularly rich in motifs"[18] and support the proposal that the patron builder was wealthy. The western end floor mosaic has a central circle with twelve interlacing circles with figures around it. Whilst there has been extensive damage to the mosaics enough of two of them can still be seen to debate its meaning and generate controversy.

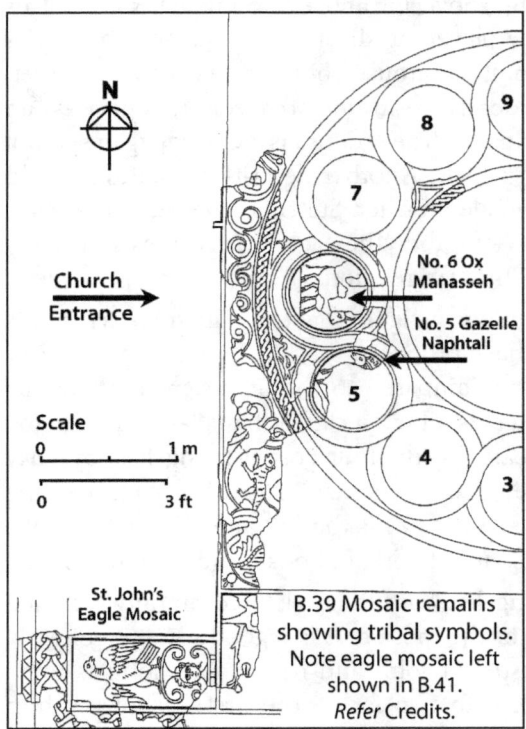

B.39 Mosaic remains showing tribal symbols. Note eagle mosaic left shown in B.41. *Refer* Credits.

It has even been proposed that the mosaic images may represent some Zodiac cycle showing a pagan influence found in other synagogues.[19] After careful examination of the evidence Sukenik came to the opinion that:

> The riddle was solved when it occurred to me that we had here no zodiac cycle but a new motif – the twelve signs of the tribes of Israel.[20]

Sukenik's key conclusion was based on an identification of Manasseh's tribal symbol (No. 6) of the ox at the due west circle, which is also the position of the tribe's camp sites in the Exodus sojourn.

---

17 Sukenik, EL, op. cit., p. 23. This quote is an extraordinary confirmation by the excavator that the site indeed could be Christian and not Jewish.

18 ibid., p.18.

19 Magness, J 2003, 'Helios and the Zodiac Cycle in Ancient Palestinian Synagogues', *Symbiosis, Symbolism, and the Power of the Past*, Eisenbrauns, Winona Lake, Indiana, USA, pp. 363–389.

20 Sukenik, EL, op. cit., p. 23.

Adjacent is a part image of a horned animal (No. 5) which is difficult to identify.[21] If the tribal order listed in the Christian book of *The Revelation* is used, the symbol could be a gazelle or deer, which is the symbol for Naphtali. Count Joseph culturally identified himself as a Jew, but his new found faith was that he was a Christian who had found the Messiah. His mosaic circles of the twelve tribes would be based on the order in the Book of Revelation (Rev. 7:5–8).[22] That book contains Manasseh and Joseph (Ephraim) but makes no mention of the tribe of Dan. This interpretation is supported if it was a Hebrew Christian building. What better mosaic to see at the entrance to the building than the foundational Old Testament tribal symbols of the congregation's spiritual inheritance?

**The eagle mosaic– John the Evangelist's symbol.**
*Refer* Illus. B.41 and B.40. The other curious mosaic found on the floor in the south-west corner was an eagle hovering above a young man's head. This mosaic was removed and is now placed on display at the Israel Antiquities Authority Museum in Jerusalem. It has aroused hot debate because it is seen by some as a pagan motif and described in one archaeology report as "an eagle standing on a stylised Medusa".[23] The Medusa is a Greek pagan symbol of a woman with hair made of snakes. Another description states it could be a Greek *gorgon* or hideous female monster. Sukenik labelled it as Helios, the Greek personification of the sun-god. The eagle was seen as spiritually symbolic in pagan, Jewish and Christian religions.

The correct interpretation lies in an intriguing fact of Christian art that is well documented. Theologians have proposed that the *'four living creatures'* described in Ezekiel 1:10 can be compared to the living creatures of the book of *The Revelation* (4:7) listed as a lion, a calf, a man's face and a flying eagle. These symbols were allocated to the four gospel evangelists by early church father Irenaeus in the second century. The consensus became Matthew is the man, Mark is the lion, Luke is the calf and John is the eagle. Early examples are seen in Christian artwork, in books, and church motifs.

The association of John the Evangelist, with the eagle is commonly accepted and is the answer to the riddle of the mosaic. It is a good example of early Christian art depicting the Gospel of John and his symbol. John is often portrayed in Christian artwork with two faces. The first is showing him as a young man with shoulder length hair and no beard. This is John the Evangelist as a young man, because he was known as the younger son of

---

21 Sukenik noted that this symbol position did not fit the order in the Jewish Midrash.
22 The order is 1. Judah 2. Reuben 3. Gad 4. Asher 5. Naphtali 6. Manasseh 7. Simeon 8. Levi 9. Issachar 10. Zebulun 11. Joseph 12. Benjamin.
23 Negev, A and Gibson, S, 'Japhia', op. cit., p. 255.

*Christian synagogue in Jewish Nazareth*

B.40 Celtic Lindisfarne Gospels circa 750 AD. Depicts a young St. John the Evangelist with his symbol of the eagle. Courtesy British Library.

B.41 Yafia mosaic depicting a young man's face with scroll and eagle. It is proposed this depicts St. John.

B.42 Detail of B.43. St. John without a beard depicting him as the younger brother of James.

B.43 Detail of B.41. Compare features of this mosaic with Lindisfarne artwork adjacent.

Zebedee and his older brother was James. The second face portrays John as a very old man, balding and with a beard. This is the face of the Apostle John as the author of the book of *The Revelation* at the age of ninety-nine years.

A good example of this concept of a young John is found in the magnificent *Lindisfarne Gospels*.[24] These gospels were recently put on display in Britain (2013) and are considered one of the high points of Anglo-Celtic Christian art. A closer look at the Lindisfarne illustration shows two elements, the Evangelist John with a scroll and the soaring eagle holding a gospel book. Clearly both images depict John and his Gospel.

A case can be made that the mosaic found at the Yafia site signifies the head of John encased in his gospel scroll (with the curled motif top and bottom). The surmounted eagle clearly portrays this is *John the Evangelist*. Joseph was first introduced to Christianity after reading the Gospel of John in Hebrew. If he was the patron for this site, why would he not acknowledge John with a gospel illustration near the entrance to the Church.

**Who destroyed this structure?**

Professor Sukenik raised a telling question from his excavation:

> It seems clear that the synagogue was violently destroyed. Perhaps when Christianity became dominant in Palestine, the fanatical followers of the new religion could not suffer the existence of a Jewish community with such a splendid synagogue so near to Nazareth.[25]

His report showed Arab period remains on top of the site, indicating the destruction may have occurred some time before 638 AD. There are two possible explanations for the destruction:

- The Byzantine decimation of Nazareth city in 630 AD as detailed in Chapter 4. Did they see it as more Jewish than Christian in its motifs?
- The Arab conquest of Palestine in 638 AD caused destruction of some sacred sites, both Jewish and Christian.

**The summary explanation**

The floor plan and the mosaics with St. John show the Christian origins of this structure. The Jewish features are cultural and support a Hebrew Christian influence. This site gives strong support to the claim that Yafia is Nazareth city, where Count Joseph sought to build a church as recorded in history. He did not build the church or basilica at traditional Christian Nazareth as suggested by some scholars. His heart was set on evangelising his own Galilean Jewish citizens.

---

24 *St. John the Evangelist* in the Lindisfarne Gospels, London, British Library, MS Cotton Nero DIV, f209v.

25 Sukenik, EL, op. cit., p. 18.

*Christian synagogue in Jewish Nazareth*

B.44 A 2015 excavation 30 metres south of proposed Count Joseph's Church showing clear evidence of Early Roman remains (NC7 on maps). IAA Report vol. 127. Photo Omar Zidan. Courtesy of the Israel Antiqities Authority.

## 9.3 The workshop of Joseph the carpenter?

Matthew's Gospel records that after the incarnation event, Joseph was in a quandary regarding a pregnant Mary with whom he had not yet lived.

> Then Joseph her husband, being a just man, and not wanting to make her a public example, was minded to put her away secretly. But while he thought about these things, behold an angel of the Lord appeared to him, in a dream, saying "Joseph, son of David, do not be afraid to take to you Mary your wife, for that which is conceived in her is of the Holy Spirit. And she will bring forth a Son, and you shall call His name Jesus, for He will save His people from their sins" (Matthew 1:19–21).

This text confirms that Joseph was a Nazarene, being a descendant of King David, and he was to be the adopted father of Jesus the Messiah. The relevant question in this passage is where was Joseph located when this angelic event occurred? He is clearly not in the dwelling occupied by Mary his betrothed wife ('erusin' under Jewish law). Joseph would be resident somewhere in the city sector before occupying the family home. The city was his place of business as a carpenter. The narrative has obvious prophetic significance as it involves the second naming of the Messiah. The first occasion had been by the angel Gabriel with Mary in the future family home in the hamlet.

## The logistics
(*Refer* Illus. B.34. and Appendix 8.1.3.) It is possible that this sacred locality marks the vicinity of the workshop of Joseph the carpenter in 4 BC. The logic is as follows:

- Devout Count Joseph would have prayed for guidance for the location of his church. There may have been a local Christian tradition, passed down that preserved the spiritual significance of the site.
- A significance is implied with the adjacent building of the Orthodox Church. They inherited the site after the Great Schism in 1054 AD.
- The proposed site is on the northern slopes of the city. Joseph's future home residence was north-east of the city centre so it is possible that his public workshop was located somewhere on the northern side.
- This is a logical place for a trades-person to do business being near the gates to the city. The position is 50 metres (54 yards) from the probable walls at the crest of the hill. This position is between two possible city gates, one north-west (toward the well-spring of the city) and the other north-east toward his future residence (*refer* NC2 on city plan A.15).
- The site is within the defined suburban area (*refer* Appendix 8.1.3).
- An archaeological survey has recently been done 30 metres (33 yards) to the south of this site (NC7).[26] The results of this survey confirmed, "Silos and underground cavities associated with *a settlement from the Early Roman period* were exposed in the excavation". [Italics added] This shows remains close by in the required time frame.
- Even if remains of a workshop were found it would still be speculative that it belonged to Joseph. However of particular interest is the long continual religious history of the site shown in the first two points above.

## Summary
The interpretation of the Yafia 'Synagogue' is solved when the builder is identified as Count Joseph and his Church at the Jewish city of Nazareth. Joshua's altar on Mt. Ebal is on a longitude close to the position of the church of Count Joseph. This raises an interesting speculation for the location of Saint Joseph's workshop.

The key question of identifying gospel sites was mentioned in Chapter 3. The point made was that the relatives of the Virgin Mary and Jesus, known as the Desposyni, existed into the fourth century. It would not be difficult to suggest that the oral tradition for such an important site could be preserved by the relatives and made known to Count Joseph. They would be a possible guide to the locality where the name of the Messiah was given. It is Jesus in English but related to Yeshua (Joshua) in the Hebrew.

---

26 Zidan, O 2015, Yafi'a, *Hadashot Arkheologiyot*, Volume 127, p. 3.

## Conclusion to Section B

- The early life of Jesus is more clearly understood when the evidence of his localities are identified. His family home was in a more rural part of the city. His early life in Galilee provided the setting for many of his teaching parables.
- He was part of a large worshipping congregation in Nazareth city and observed all the Jewish festivals. His lowly social status and occupation meant that he was not a candidate for an anointed leader according to the rulers of his synagogue. The story of their violent reaction and attempt to execute him can be clearly understood and related to the topographical features described in the gospel.
- Three centuries later a converted Jewish aristocrat named Count Joseph of Tiberias had the vision of building a Judeo-Christian synagogue in Jewish Nazareth. The archaeology shows that he achieved his aim and remains can still be seen today. A question can be raised whether this site points to a previous spiritual significance, possibly the locality of the workshop of Joseph the carpenter.

C.01 Joshua carried out a topographic survey of the Promised Land and allocated tribal regions. 'Joshua dividing the land of Canaan' by Henry Northrop in "Treasures of the Bible". International Publishing Company 1894. *Refer* Credits.

> "These are the areas which the children of Israel inherited in the land of Canaan ... Their inheritance was by lot, as the Lord had commanded by the hand of Moses ... and they divided the land". Joshua 14:1–5.

# SECTION C

## HOW NAZARETH UNLOCKS LOWER GALILEE

*About this time it was that Vespasian sent out Trajan against a city called Japha, that lay near to Jotapata, and that desired innovations, and was puffed up with the unexpected length of the opposition of Jotapata.*

Josephus, Jewish historian *Wars* 3.7.31.

---

This section includes critiques and an evaluation of the traditional Bible nominations of Zebulun. Alternatives are also offered for some of these sites. The eyewitness evidence by Josephus in his account of the war with the Romans gives important and crucial information on this topic.

When Nazareth city is correctly nominated at Tel Yafia it requires another location for biblical Japhia (Japha) to be proved. It starts a domino effect for the other sites of the Lower Galilee.

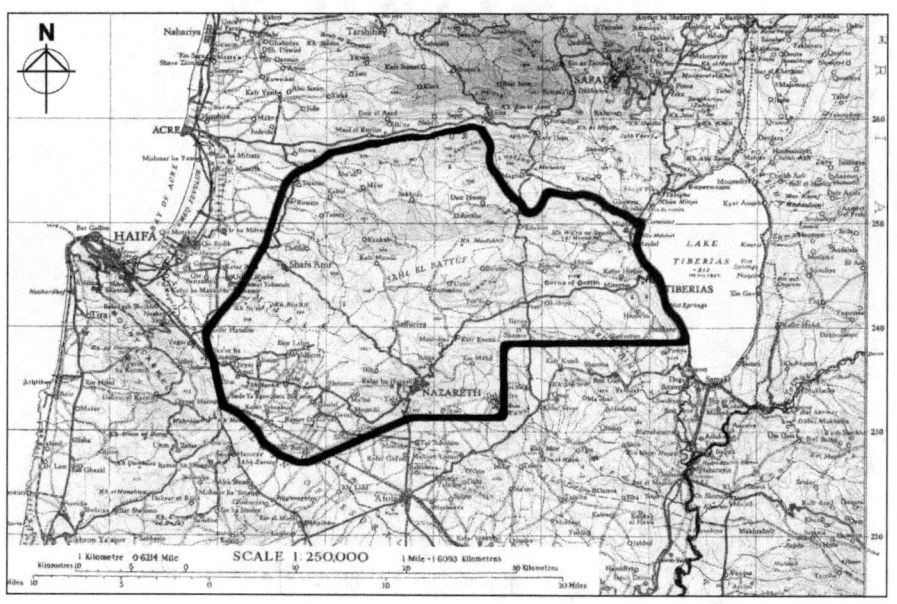

C.02 Showing the proposed logical perimeter for Zebulun's boundary. It contains the geographical area historically known as Lower Galilee. Base map is the British Survey of Palestine, 1946.

> "As for that Galilee which is called Lower, it extends in breadth from Tiberias, to Zabulon, [sic] and the maritime places, Ptolemais, is its neighbour".
>
> Josephus *Wars* 3.3.1(38).

# CHAPTER 10
## BIBLE SITE MAPPING AND ZEBULUN

*And leaving Nazareth, He came and dwelt in Capernaum, which is by the sea, in the regions of Zebulun and Naphtali, that it might be fulfilled which was spoken by Isaiah the prophet saying "The land of Zebulun and the land of Naphtali ... The people who sat in darkness have seen a great light, And upon those who sat in the region and shadow of death Light has dawned".*

Matthew 4:13–16.

---

The tribal region of Zebulun had a special place in the plan of God. It was to be the location of the Messiah's home. Here was to be the location of some of his proclamations of the Gospel of an answer to the problem of death. Put another way, this message was to do with the hope of release from the human condition of sin and the promise of eternal life. Defining Zebulun helps clarify some of the sites and shows some prophetic connections.

## 10.1 Bible sites: nomination and mapping

### The revival of biblical geography in Palestine

The province of Palestine in the Turkish Ottoman Empire saw many changes in the nineteenth century. It began as a relatively poor region with many villages existing at a subsistence level, according to accounts of early western travellers. The Ottoman census of 1800 AD recorded there were 246,300 Muslims, 83,000 Jews and 21,800 Christians. By the end of the century the number of Muslims had doubled, the number of Jews tripled and the number of Christians stayed much the same.[1]

In the nineteenth century across Europe and North America the *'Great Awakening'* of religious revival saw a rediscovered interest in Bible study. With this was a renewed interest in the accuracy of the Bible and the location of many of the listed sites. Churches began to sponsor explorers and a significant figure in this regard was American Edward Robinson noted previously. Christians were interested in locating sites associated with the life of Jesus. They were building on a long tradition of some historic sites recorded by the Catholic and Orthodox sources over many centuries.

Among the persecuted Jewish communities of Europe and Russia there also was an increased desire to return to their heritage homeland. One of the emotive debates that continues today is the extent of the boundaries of the Land promised by covenant to Abraham. Even more controversial was the question of whether that covenant still applied. Increased Jewish immigration led to an interest in discovering the names and locations of sites in the Old Testament. Was there evidence of the sites recorded in the Book of Joshua? Could the special allocated cities of the Levite priests be found? Where were the routes travelled by the patriarchs?

In this century, the embryonic discipline of archaeology began to flower and flourish with committed scholars and researchers. Napoleon commissioned Pierre Jacotin to do the first Palestine land survey in 1799 which was made public in 1817. The stage was set for much field work and excavations began to reveal hidden sites long buried in the layers of ruins. When sites were uncovered the need to identify the biblical name of the site was the challenge. Also of significance was the pioneer work of the British Palestine Exploration Fund Survey of 1871 to 1877. The nominations depended on many assumptions and it is not surprising that in the course of time more than one nomination started to occur for some discoveries.

---

1 Jewishvirtuallibrary.org. 2016 'Population of Israel/Palestine (1553-Present)', *Jewish Virtual Library*. Refer Bibliography.

*Bible site mapping and Zebulun*

C.03 Watercolour by Claude Conder 1872, showing the PEF survey group in Palestine. Courtesy of the Palestine Exploration Fund, London.

## How Bible sites are nominated

Bible site nomination is the discipline that seeks to identify sites mentioned in the text of the Old and New Testaments. Bible sites can be categorised in different ways. One approach is to divide them as follows:

**1. Identified:** Sites that have verifiable evidence from a range of sources (e.g. the original city of Jerusalem (Jebus) and the Mount of Olives).

**2. Debated:** Are those locations or features where there is some uncertainty and there are many in this category. Some have agreement on the general locality but there is debate on the specific location (e.g. three Calvary sites in Jerusalem). Others have quite different nominations over a wide region (e.g. for the Exodus at least seven Red Sea crossing sites and six Mt. Sinai peaks).

**3. Unknown:** Sites where the current information makes the proposing of a location difficult. It includes places where the record of an event is described, but the exact location is difficult to verify (e.g. Moses' personal encounter with the *burning bush* in Sinai). There are also sites where the historical information is difficult to interpret or in some cases lost (e.g. Tower of Babel).

When the correct location is confirmed, it is often possible to show evidence that correlates from different sources. The analogy is with a crime scene. At first the scenario may not be clear, but when all the evidence is considered and correctly confirmed, the facts become more obvious.

Scholars have used a number of criteria to establish the names of Bible sites. Yohanan Aharoni listed three criteria for identifications: 1) historical sources; 2) Hebrew name meanings; and 3) the archaeology.[2] The New Testament would include Greek and Roman names. A fourth can be added and that is the topographical requirement, often missing in many site proposals.

---

2  Aharoni, Yohanan 1979 *The Land of the Bible: A Historical Geography* (ed.) Rainey AF, The Westminster Press, Philadelphia, USA, p. 12.

## 1. Historical sources

The Hebrew Bible, being one of the ancient sources, is taken as the starting point. There are also historical documents such as the Jewish Talmud. Travellers of the distant past have left named accounts of their journeys. However a study of Bible encyclopedias reveals that it is not uncommon for there to be more than one nomination for a location. There are proposals and then counter-proposals from scholars, even from the same discipline. The point to state, is that some Bible sites can, and need to be, re-evaluated.

## 2. Hebrew name meanings

The root of each Hebrew word has a number of derivatives that give a richer understanding of that word. In Palestine, the historic Arabic names can also be linked to the Hebrew due to their common Semitic language origins. These names have been well researched, particularly with the work of the Palestine Exploration Fund, who consulted local residents for information.

## 3. The archaeology

This is a crucial consideration, but there are differences in the assumptions and interpretations. In archaeology circles there is debate on some of the time frames. When researching this subject it becomes apparent there are strong differences in opinion amongst scholars. My proposal is that Joshua's cities, considered and named in this book, are related to the archaeological period known as the end of the Middle Bronze Age (*refer* Appendix 1).

## 4. Topographic logic

Topography involves the study and mapping of the shape of the physical land. The original descriptions made in the Book of Joshua were eyewitness accounts after a detailed land survey commenced in 1450 BC. Some topographic logic should be found in the listing order of the sites in the Bible. This can then be compared to the accurate information we now have on the featured terrain.

### Bible site mapping challenge

Bible site mapping plots the spatial relationship of sites to the geographic features of the land. Some Bible mappers have acknowledged that there are traditional site nominations that can be challenged and re-evaluated. This was strongly commented on by one researcher, J. Maxwell Miller who wrote:

> it must be conceded that biblical site identification is a problem area in contemporary scholarship. Analysis of ... lines of reasoning by which site identification have been made (and are still being made) reveals methodological uncertainty and in some cases blatant misuse of evidence.[3]

---

3 Miller, JM 1983, *Site Identification: A Problem Area in Contemporary Biblical Scholarship.* Zeitschrift des Deutschen Palästina-Vereins Bd. 99., p. 119.

*Bible site mapping and Zebulun*

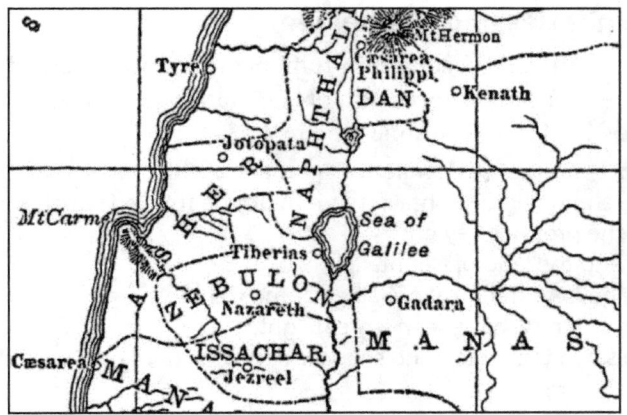

C.04 Early 19th. Century KJV Bible map showing Zebulun extending to the Sea of Galilee. This was accepted until Robinson's endorsement of Yafia in 1841.

## Incorrect Zebulun maps

When readers consult a Bible it is common for an appendix of maps to be provided. This is to help the reader get orientated and to have a better understanding of the geography related to the historical accounts. However, some of the nominations have led to errors in the maps produced. [4] If one site is incorrectly nominated it affects other sites. Put another way, a wrong nomination can rob another site of its significance. This has been the case with the maps of Zebulun. Further explanation is given in Chapter 12.1.

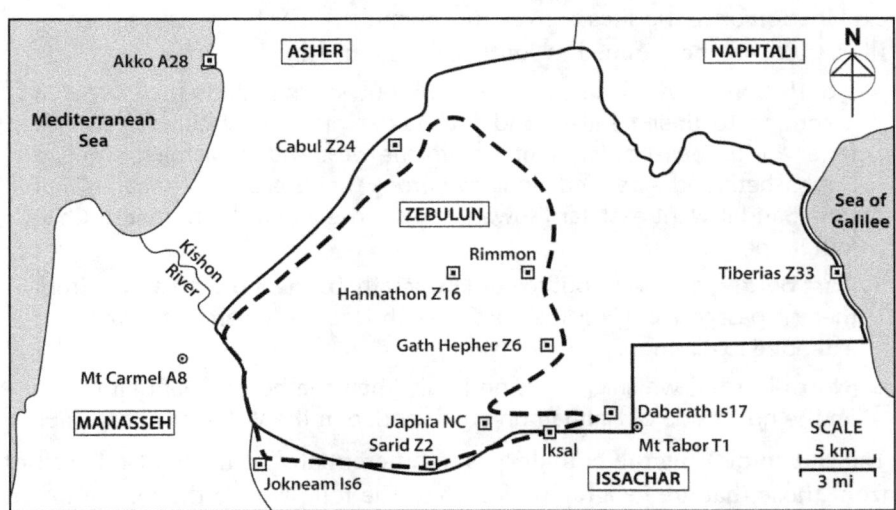

C.05 Map comparing traditional Zebulun (dashed) with proposed boundaries (solid). Traditional Zebulun found in modern Bible maps makes it a small land-locked enclave.

---

4   ibid. Researcher JM Miller commented that some Bible map producers paid "too little attention to methodology, made site identifications on the basis of inadequate evidence, and thus produced distorted biblical maps".

## 10.2 Zebulun's boundaries and the Galilee

Jesus of Nazareth grew up in tribal Zebulun in fulfilment of a prophecy. At age thirty he relocated residence to Capernaum of Naphtali to give meaning to Isaiah 9:1, as the Apostle Matthew summarised in 4:13–16:

> And leaving Nazareth, He came and dwelt in Capernaum, which is by the sea in the regions of Zebulun and Naphtali, that it might be fulfilled which was spoken by Isaiah the prophet, saying:
> "The land of Zebulun and the land of Naphtali,
> By the way of the sea, beyond the Jordan, Galilee of the Gentiles:
> The people who sat in darkness have seen a great light,
> And, upon those who sat in the region and shadow of death
> Light has dawned".

The gospel writers are clear in proclaiming that Jesus was the Messiah and that his coming was to be a blessing to the Israelites and the Gentiles. The headquarters for his dynamic ministry was the Galilee. His second residence was at Capernaum near the well-known *"Way of the Sea,"* an international trade route that passed on the western side of the Sea of Galilee.

### The defining of Zebulun

Most of the sites discussed in this book are found in tribal Zebulun or on its border, so its definition is relevant. (The exception is Joshua's altar at Mount Ebal.) The border sites are listed in Joshua 19:10–14 and a detailed explanation of all the sites is given in Appendix 5. The border sites, shown on Illus. C.06, can be grouped as south, east and north:

> [**South border**] And the third lot came out for the children of Zebulun according to their families, and the border of their inheritance was as far as Sarid. Their border went toward the west and to Maralah, went to Dabbasheth and extended along the brook that is east of Jokneam. Then from Sarid it went eastward toward the sunrise along the border of Chisloth Tabor,
>
> [**East border**] and went out toward Daberath, bypassing Japhia. And from there it passed along on the east of Gath Hepher toward Eth Kazin and extended to Rimmon,
>
> [**North border**] which borders on Neah. Then the border went around it on the north side of Hannathon and it ended in the Valley of Jiphthah El.

The clue to plotting the boundary is to differentiate the named twelve cities from those that are geographic features. The following is the logical order.

**South border.** Crucial to the explanation is that Sarid, detailed later, is a mountain peak and orientation set-out marker. The south-western border runs to the Kishon River. From Mount Sarid again it travels east to Chisloth Tabor on the southern slopes of Mount Tabor.

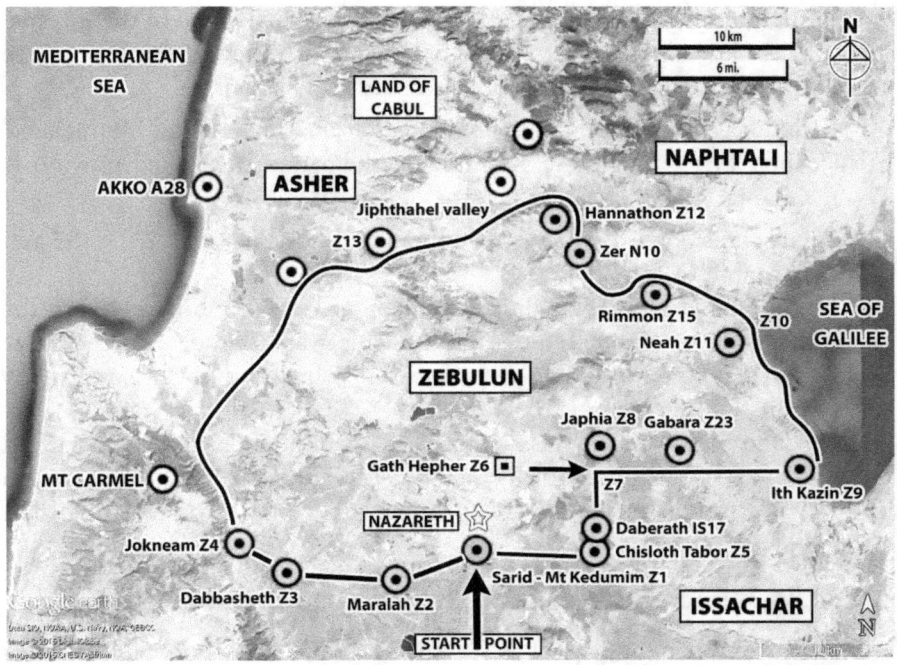

C.06 Proposed boundaries of Zebulun based on Bible sites that have topographic logic. The information of these sites is explained in Appendix 5. Base Map Google Earth. Image © 2016 Digital Globe.

**East border.** It heads north past Daberath, towards Japhia, then turns east from Gath Hepher towards the western side of the sea of Galilee. Then along the seashore to the estuary of the River Zalmon. This is near Neah which refers to the seismic cliffs at Har Arbel and Har Nitai.

**North border.** The River Zalmon (Nachal Tsalmon) is clearly the northern boundary when compared to the other features. Hannathon is Mount Camon, the highest peak in the Lower Galilee. The valley of Jiphtah-El is known today as the Beit Kerem valley.

**West border.** Defined by the eastern border of the tribe of Asher. It was the edge foothills contour facing the coastal plain of Akko.

This demonstrates the topographic logic of the order as listed in the Book of Joshua. Zebulun can be identified as the well-defined geographical region known in ancient and modern times as the *Lower Galilee.* Josephus confirms this understanding in the first century when he stated in *Wars* 3.3.1 (38–40): "As for the Galilee which is called Lower, it extends in breadth from Tiberias to Zabulon [sic], and the maritime places, Ptolemais [Akko], is its neighbour".

When the border is correctly identified the mystery of some of the internal sites of Zebulun can be solved. Three of the sites are relevant to proposals in this book and are listed as Shimron, Jokne'am and Kitron.

1. Included cities: "Kattath, Nahalal, *Shimron*, Idalah and Bethlehem" (Joshua 19:15. Map F11). Shimron is Shefar'am mentioned previously in Chapter 4.
2. Levite cities: *Jokneam*, Kartah, Dimnah and Nahalal (Josh. 21:34-35 and *refer* Map F.14).
3. Unconquered city: "Nor did the inhabitants of Zebulun drive out the inhabitants of *Kitron*" (Judges 1:30). This was a large Middle Bronze II fortification located at Tel Shimron which has been incorrectly nominated *(refer* Appendix 4.2).

All the components of the jigsaw puzzle for Zebulun can make sense when the pieces are clearly positioned. Further investigations and confirmation can be made on an aspect of Bible prophecy involving two very important prophetic figures.

## 10.3 Did Jacob and Moses make false prophecies?

The tribal emblem or flag of Zebulun is a ship, based on biblical texts (Numbers 2:2). Both patriarch Jacob and prophet Moses made predictions about the tribe of Zebulun. In fact there are five specific predictions that can be explained as correct. Both prophets made reference to being adjacent to a Sea (Heb. *Yam*), meaning a large body of water. They could be accused of making a false prophecy if most modern Bible maps are correct which show no sea anywhere near Zebulun's borders. Their tribal area is shown as a small land-locked enclave and has caused commentators to offer excuses and disclaimers.[5] With the right boundaries, attention can now be given to show how the prophecies of Jacob and Moses were absolutely correct.

**Patriarch Jacob and Zebulun**

Just before his death, the patriarch Jacob made two statements in the final allocation of the Land of Zebulun. Jacob was one hundred and forty seven years old when he made his pronouncements to his sons (Gen. 49:1-28). This was made in Egypt in 1689 BC before the 'Promised Land' lottery of 1445 BC, the Land promised to his grandfather Abraham (Gen. 12:1-3). Jacob's prophecy to his son Zebulun regarding his allotment stated:

---

5   Regarding the definition of Zebulun in *International Standard Bible Encyclopedia*, 'Zebulun'. "The details given are confusing. It is to be observed that this does not bring Zebulun into touch with the sea, and so is an apparent contradiction with Genesis 49:13 and also with Josephus". Other theories include it was not geographical but more to show the benefit of maritime trade nearby, e.g. commentaries by Derek Kidner and Carl Keil.

"Zebulun shall dwell by the haven of the sea, He shall become a haven for ships, and his border shall adjoin Sidon" (Gen. 49:13).

C.07 Jacob blessing his grandchildren with his son Joseph and wife Asenath. Artist Rembrandt 1656 AD. Credit Wikimedia Commons.

## Dwelling by the sea

Josephus, writing c. 73 AD in *Ant.* 5.1.22(84), states that his understanding of the Zebulun boundaries is that they extended from the Mediterranean Sea to the Sea of Galilee:[6]

> Issachar, which had its limits in length, Mount Carmel and the River (Kishion) but its limit in breadth, was Mount Tabor. The tribe of Zebulon's [sic] lot included the land which lay as far as the Lake Genesareth, and that which belonged to Carmel and the sea.

By his description it is very obvious that he saw the eastern border as along the western shore of the Sea of Galilee.

## The haven for ships

Three tribes benefited from the freshwater Sea of Galilee. The boundary map shown in Illus. C.08 shows a large part of the seashore was given to Zebulun. Stretching from modern Kinneret to the River Zalmon (Nachal Tsalmon) estuary (Z10) gives a number of port options. Local historian Mendel Nun's book on the stone quays of the sea shows remains of four harbour sites[7] indicating the shoreline could fulfil Jacob's prophecy of a haven for ships.

---

6   Josephus' understanding of the western border in Roman times was the coastal Mediterranean Akko plain as a neighbour that belonged to Asher. *War* 3.3(38). Joshua's account denotes the western border as near the coastal plain of Asher (Josh.19:27).

7   Nun, M 1993, *Ancient stone anchors and net sinkers from the Sea of Galilee*, Kibbutz Ein Gev. Tourist Department and Kinnereth Sailing Co., p. 7. These stone quays are difficult to date.

## Alongside to Sidon: The Land of Cabul

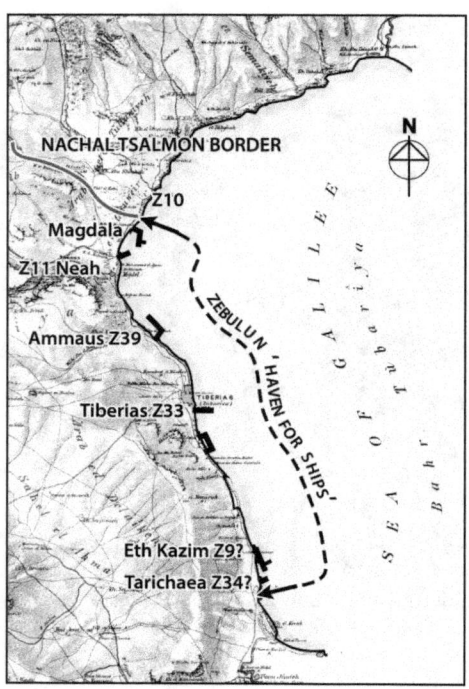

C.08 Galilee Sea shoreline of Zebulun showing Jacob and Moses' prophecies were correct topographically. PEF base map.

This curious reference of Sidon in the prophecy can be rightly understood with the story of the *Land of Cabul*. When King Solomon built his magnificent Temple and palaces in Jerusalem, he required enormous amounts of materials and good skilled workers. He turned to one of his relatives by marriage, King Hiram of Tyre, for skilled trades and timber resources. Tyre was a Sidonian colony located south of Sidon (in modern Lebanon) on the Mediterranean coast. However, building projects, as is often the case, tend to go over the budget. Solomon was under financial pressure and to make some form of payment he decided to give Hiram twenty cities from the tribe of Asher. This was despite the commandment of God that the Promised Land was not to be permanently sold (Leviticus 25:23).

The sites were not appreciated by Hiram due to their poor physical condition and Cabul or Kabul means inferior (I Kings 9:13). These cities of Cabul were in the highlands south of Tyre and down as far as the Beit Kerem Valley (refer Illus. C.06). This is how Sidon became an enclave "alongside" on the north-west border of Zebulun. This was predicted by Jacob's prophecy, showing a good example that God is all-knowing of future events.[8]

### Moses and Zebulun

Moses was one hundred and twenty years old when he made his final exhortations to the tribes before their crossing of the River Jordan and into the Promised Land. This involved blessings, warnings and some promises of inheritance. His words regarding Zebulun and Issachar found in Deut. 33:18–19 were: "Rejoice, Zebulun, in your going out, and Issachar in your

---

8 The traditional nomination at Tel Rosh Zayit does not make sense as an inferior site for Cabul. It is located near a rich fertile part of the Akko plain and it was also a strategic location. Solomon would not be so quick to give away a strategic site guarding the Galilee and in a fertile area.

tents ... for they shall partake of *the abundance of the seas* and of *treasures hidden in the sand*". What does this mean for these two tribes? (italics added)

## The abundance of the seas

Consulting this passage in different translations shows a rich variety of adjectives used for the fishing described. Moses' prophecy is well fulfilled as the Sea of Galilee has a history of profitable net fishing. There are currently eighteen freshwater indigenous species found and ten are commercially important. In the 1980s the annual catch was nearly 2,000 tonnes (2,200 US tons) and supported about one hundred and fifty fishermen.[9] It would have been even more abundant in ancient times before the effects of pollution.

## Glass manufacture – treasures hidden in the sand

The text in the prophecy uses the plural of "seas" which clearly includes the Sea of Galilee on the east. However on the western border of Zebulun there originally was a freshwater lake called *Cendevia* that was part of a short river called *Belus* in the plain of Akko.[10] These water references were described by the first century historians Pliny and Josephus.

> Belus ... described by Pliny as taking its rise from a lake called Cendevia, at the roots of Mount Carmel, which after running five miles, enters the sea near Ptolemais (36:26) or two stadia from the city according to Josephus (*War*, 10,2). It is chiefly celebrated among the ancients for its vitreous sand; and the accidental discovery of the manufacture of glass (q.v) is ascribed by Pliny to the banks of this river ... It is now called Nahr Naaman, but Lake Cendevia has disappeared.[11]

This historical report shows that Zebulun, with the help of its neighbours Issachar and Asher, provided assistance to the art of glass-making on its western border. Glass was considered a real treasure in the ancient world as it enriched culture and had many uses, as it does today. A recent discovery of an important glass-making centre dating to Roman times indicates that "the Land of Israel was one of the foremost centers for glass production in the ancient world" and this was because "the Valley of Akko was renowned for the excellent quality sand located there, which was highly suitable for the manufacture of glass".[12]

*In conclusion, all aspects of the prophecies by Jacob and Moses were fulfilled when the correct definition of Zebulun's territory is established.*

---

9  Nun, M 1989, *The Sea of Galilee and its fishermen* Kibbutz Ein Gev. Tourist Department and Kinnereth Sailing Co., p. 12.

10  Today the remains of this large drained lake basin can be seen south-east of Akko.

11  *McClintock and Strong Biblical Cyclopedia* 2016, 'Belus (2)', <www.biblicalcyclopedia.com/B/belus-(2).html>.

12  Antiquities.org.il., 2016, *An Important Archaeological Discovery at the Foot of Mount Carmel*, <www.antiquities.org.il/Article_eng.aspx?sec_id=25&subj_id=240&id=4192>.

C.09 Aerial view of the Colosseum, Rome which is a magnificent structure. A large component of the workforce to build it were Jewish slaves from the war with Rome. Credit Photo Google Earth. © 2016.

C.10 Evidence of a plaque was found on the walls of the Colosseum that indicates the building was made possible by the spoils of war, the Jewish–Roman War in 67–71 AD. Credit Photo by GraphicStock.

# CHAPTER 11
## THE ROMAN–JEWISH WAR EVIDENCE

> For days will come upon you when your enemies will build an embankment around you, surround you and close you in on every side, and level you, and your children within you, to the ground; and they will not leave in you one stone upon another, because you did not know the time of your visitation.
>
> Luke 19:43–44.

When Jesus made the above prediction in 30 AD many would not have understood it. Jerusalem at that time was a large and well-built city. King Herod had built large fortresses and palaces. The Temple stood on a huge podium of massive stones. Forty years later this was to change drastically. The Jewish–Roman War began in the Galilee and the eye-witness account of this campaign by Josephus gives vital clues on some of the sites.

## 11.1 Jewish fortifications and the Roman strategy

### The Colosseum in Rome – Jewish blood and sweat

There are an estimated five million tourists who flock annually to a very famous landmark in downtown Rome. It is the Colosseum, the massive architectural amphitheatre that still impresses today. A place of gladiatorial contests, ostentatious displays and bizarre deaths. Many are not aware of the infamy in some of its funding and much of the slave labour source for the building. Vespasian was a Roman commander who had brutally crushed a Jewish Revolt in 67–71 AD. From the circumstances of that war he quickly rose from a conquering general to become Emperor of Rome. He took over from the infamous and notorious ruler Nero who died in 69 AD. The new emperor wanted to make his mark on history and wanted to build a grand stadium for the masses. British historian Professor Keith Hopkins has noted on this project by Vespasian that he:

> decided to shore up his shaky regime by building an amphitheatre, or pleasure palace for the people, out of the booty from the Jewish War, on the site of the lake in the gardens of Nero's palace.[1]

Thus much of the finance for his massive project came from pillaging the Jewish nation. In fact evidence of an inscription placed on the Colosseum walls was recently deciphered and it stated[2]: "Caesar Vespasianus Augustus ordered this new amphitheatre erected from the spoils of war".[3]

Considering the time frame, this was most likely the Jewish War. It has been proposed that of the 97,000 Jewish war captives, an estimated 20,000 became slave labourers exploited in the construction of the Colosseum.[4] How did this come about? It requires an understanding of the religious aspect of the Romans, who worshipped many gods, including the gods of war. Their politics required Caesar to be seen as deified and supreme ruler and many of the Caesars had the title *"Pater Patriae"* – Father of the Nation. All of this was obviously odious to the Jews, compounded by high taxation and Nero's erratic and despotic rule from 50 to 69 AD.[5] These tensions along with other local clashes lead to Nero declaring war on the Jewish nation.

---

1 Hopkins, K 2011, *The Colosseum: Emblem of Rome*, <www.bbc.co.uk/history/ancient/romans/colosseum_01.shtml>.

2 BAS Library 2001, *Connecting the Dots: Deciphering the Colosseum Inscription*, The BAS Library. <members.bib-arch.org/publication.asp?PubID=BSBA&Volume=27&Issue=4&ArticleID=13>.

3 Open.conted.ox.ac.uk. 2012, *Colosseum Building Inscription*, <open.conted.ox.ac.uk/resources/link/colosseum-building-inscription>.

4 Roffe, S *Jews Built Roman Coliseum After Destruction of Second Temple*, <www.jewishgen.org/sefardsig/coliseum.htm>.

5 Goodman, M 2007, *Rome and Jerusalem*, Penguin Books, London, WC2R, UK.

## Josephus and the war in Galilee

We have the eyewitness accounts of the Jewish leader Josephus, who was the commander of the Galilean resistance to the might of Rome. He not only saw everything, but also wrote a detailed account of the sites and battles, as a historian and military leader. Josephus' command was established by Judean Jerusalem, which was not always supported by the strong-minded Galileans.

C.11 Josephus gave personal accounts of Roman attacks on Jotapata and Japhia 67 AD. Wikimedia Commons.

> Josephus' first hand writings have interesting information. He gives the reasons why the Romans were such a formidable army.
>
> There was extraordinary discipline by the soldiers and their well-organised ranks. They all practised group exercises that built morale. The army used large war machines to batter the enemy defences.
>
> The more sobering reading is his account of the disunity of the Jewish city factions. Even though they had valiant fighters they were no match for the systematic professional army of Rome. The result was inevitable.

The story of the Roman War in the Galilee supports a major thesis of this book, that is the correct identification of the site called Japhia and its nearby neighbour of Jotapata. When both of these sites are identified correctly, it has significant implications for two other sites which are explained in Section D.

## Jotapata and Japhia – military logic

Josephus had oversight of rebuilding fortification sites in the Galilee region. He was not a professional soldier by background, but he did use military logic in the selection of sites for strengthening the existing strongholds.

C.12 Vespasian, who led the Roman army. Total destruction of Jotapata was his key objective. Wikimedia Commons.

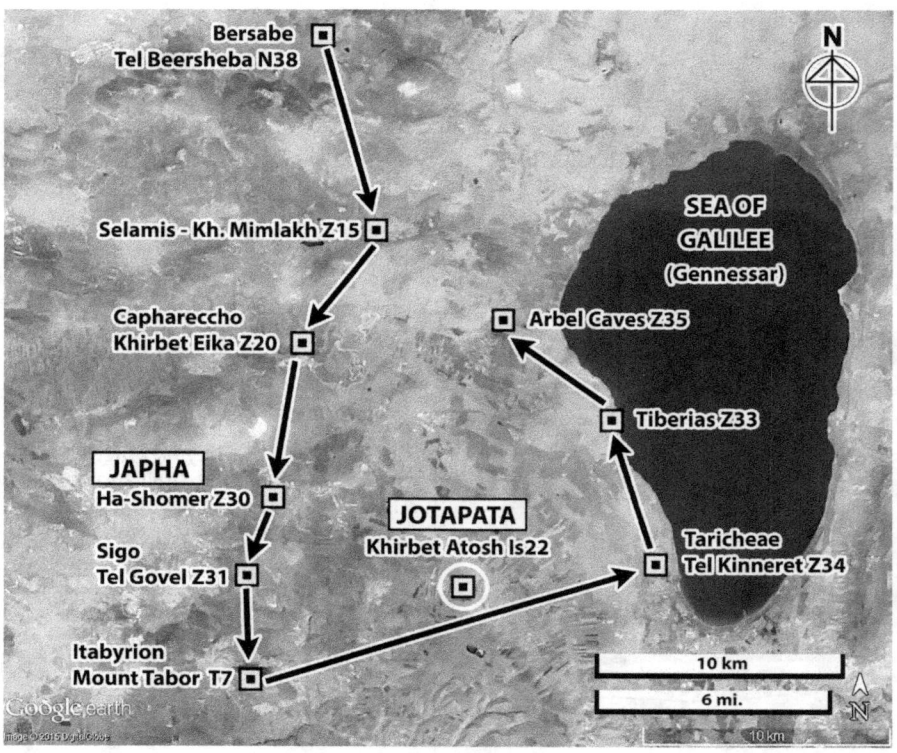

C.13 Lower Galilee showing the anticlockwise logic of Josephus' listing of his fortifications with Jotapata (HQ) in the centre. Base map Google Earth © 2015 Digital Globe.

The following list of his fortifications is explained in detail in Appendix 8 and shown in the illustration above:

> And as he knew the Romans would fall upon Galilee, he built walls in the proper places about Jotapata and Bersabe, and Salamis: and besides these about Caphareccho and Japha, and Sigo, and what they call Mount Tabor, and Taricheae, and Tiberias. Moreover he built walls about the caves near the lake of Gennesar, which places lay in the lower Galilee (*War* 2.20.573).

This listing order can be seen as having anticlockwise logic, starting with the well-known site of Bersabe, Tel Beer Sheba (N38) of Galilee. Jotapata (IS22) occupies a central position which shows the military logic and its importance. Jotapata and Japhia are not correctly located with their traditional nominations.

### Tel Yodfat is not Josephus' Jotapata

General Vespasian began his Jewish War in the Galilee and his war machine was known for its ruthlessness. Vespasian was a very experienced, shrewd soldier who knew how to create fear in the local populace with his tactics.

Josephus indicated in *Wars* 3.7.3 that Vespasian's first objective was that he was, *"desirous of demolishing Jotapata,* for he had gotten intelligence that the greatest part of the enemy had retired thither". [italics added]

Tel Yodfat was incorrectly nominated as Jotapata by Ernst Schultz in 1847. His criteria was the topographical features which did have some similarities to Josephus' description. Another reason was the discovery of evidence of a Roman attack on the site. However, not all the factors were considered and there is other evidence that refutes the claim. There is good support for an alternative site for Josephus' fortification at Jotapata.

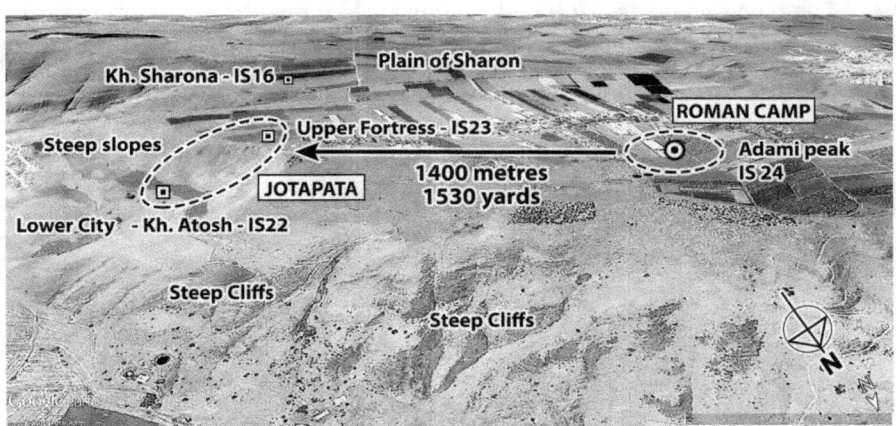

C.14 Proposed location of Josephus' fortifications at Jotapata (IS 22–23). The topography meets all the descriptions in his account of the siege.
Base map Google Earth. Image © 2016 Digital Globe.

## 11.2 Jotapata: the 'Masada' of Galilee

Proposed location: Khirbet Atosh at 32-43-29 N. and 35-28-57 E.

Located 500 metres (550 yards) east of modern Moshav Sharona and 8.5 kilometres (5.2 miles) south-west of Tiberias. There are three features to understand about this site.

1. Castle fortress on the ridge (IS23): A strategic location on a steep cliff on the eastern edge of Moshav Sharona. A natural fortification site.
2. Lower city at Khirbet Atosh(IS22): The walled city of Jotapata that was adjacent and below the castle.
3. Vespasian's camp-site on peak Har Adami: 32-43-54 N. and 35-28-0 E. The highest hill in the region (IS24) and used as the Roman base to attack the fortress. Josephus states the sites were separated by seven furlongs in *Wars* 3.7.4 (1,400 m or 1,530 yds) which is correct for the nomination.

## The evidence for the location

A range of criteria needs to be met according to information in Josephus' accounts. More detailed explanation of these factors is given in Appendix 7.

1. *The military logic:* The central location with the ring of fortifications as listed previously. Jotapata was the Jewish headquarters and intended to be the last stronghold.
2. *The Roman attack route:* Vespasian realised Jotapata was strategic and made it a priority to attack. His route from Akko on the coast to a camp-site on Har Adami can be readily plotted.
3. T*he topographic description:* Josephus gives a detailed description of the topography that suits the nominated site over that of Tel Yodfat.
4. Located near Japhia: The correct location of Japhia can be shown as nearby, as required, and is explained in the next chapter.

C.15 View from Gabara (Z23) towards the hill of Jotapata. The arrow indicates the proposed location of Vespasian's camp on the high point adjacent to the city (IS24).

## The archaeological mystery

A visit to the Jotapata sites today shows very few surface remains. The Khirbet Atosh PEF report indicates scant remains on the surface.[6] A full archaeological survey of this site has not been done but local historians at the nearby modern town of Sharona, have indicated to the author that Early Roman remains are still found from time to time in the fields of Khirbet Atosh. The proposed site of the castle fortress shows no trace on the surface, except for a few random building stones. The Roman camp-site on the hill of Har Adami is now covered and put to agricultural use.

The site meets all of Josephus' topographical requirements, so why are there scant remains? Despite a heroic resistance lasting forty-seven days, Jotapata fell and resulted in the massacre of forty thousand defenders and the taking of twelve hundred captives (*Wars* 3.7.36). The Roman aim was to erase its memory as a site of prolonged Jewish resistance, just like Masada in Judea.

---

6 'Khirbet Attusha'. *PEF Survey*. Photocopy of original hand written report provided by the Israel Antiquities Authority to the author.

To appreciate this policy requires an understanding of the ruthless Roman mindset. Josephus in *Wars* 3.7.36 stated *"Vespasian gave order that the city be entirely demolished and all the fortifications burnt down"*. [italics added] The long Jotapata siege had injured Roman pride and revenge was required. The Roman Army had a reputation of demolishing specific sites of resistance, particularly those that had political significance.

C.16 Jotapata fortress (IS23) was located on this ridge with the walled city below. Vespasian ordered the total destruction of the site after it was captured.

## Remember Jerusalem

After the campaign in the Galilee the Roman army moved south to Jerusalem. This too was the scene of an epic campaign and the outcome was the same. The victory was followed by a total flattening to ground level of all of the city. This had been prophesied by Jesus in 30 AD. He indicated Jerusalem's enemy would "level you, and your children within you, to the ground; and they will *not leave in you one stone upon another,* because you did not know the time of your visitation" (Luke 19:43–44). [italics added]

This we know the Romans did with systematic fury. Josephus has recorded Jerusalem's demise in *Wars* 7.1.1 showing how this prophecy was fulfilled: "Caesar gave orders that they should now demolish the entire city and temple". The only exception was part of Herod's towers on the western walls left to show its former glory. The building structures of the Temple and the residential city were removed stone by stone. Only the foundation stone bases were left that were below ground level after the toppling. This was Roman military policy for certain sites that defied and mocked its might.

C.17 Engraving showing a Roman attack on a Jewish fortified site in the war of 67–71 AD.
Such a scene is vividly described by Josephus in the massacre at Japhia.
Courtesy of heritage-history.com.

C.18 Roman denarius coin in Titus Augustus' reign 79–81 AD.
Titus was Vespasian's son and was involved in the attacks on
Jotapata, Japhia and Jerusalem.
It depicts the Roman victory over Jewish captives.
Credit Wikimedia Commons.

# CHAPTER 12
## IDENTIFYING BIBLICAL JAPHIA

*Then from Sarid it went eastward toward the sunrise along the border of Chizloth Tabor, and went out toward Daberath, bypassing Japhia. And from there it passed along on the east of Gath Hepher.*

Joshua 19:12–13.

---

Identifying biblical Japhia is essential to this book. The error in nominating Japhia at Tel Yafia needs to be proven. The answer lies in the detailed accounts of Josephus and a tragic attack made on the city. This, along with other historical evidence, gives a case for an alternate location. When this is established, an interesting explanation of the meaning of Japhia is revealed in the final chapter.

## 12.1 Tel Yafia is not biblical Japhia

### The tragic attack on Japhia

Josephus details the side campaign of the Romans from the main battle at Jotapata in *Wars* 3.7.31:

> About this time it was that Vespasian sent out Trajan against *a city called Japha, that lay near to Jotapata,* and that desired innovations, and was puffed up with the unexpected length of the opposition of Jotapata. This Trajan was the commander of the tenth legion, and to him Vespasian committed one thousand horsemen, and two thousand footmen. When Trajan came to the city, he found it hard to be taken, for besides the natural strength of the situation, it was secured by a double wall; but when he saw the people of this city coming out of it, and ready to fight him, he joined battle with them, and after a short resistance which they made, he pursued after them; and as they fled to their first wall, the Romans followed them closely, that they fell in; but when the Jews were endeavouring to get again within their second wall, their fellow citizens shut them out, as being afraid that the Romans would force themselves in with them. [italics added]

With these words Josephus begins the description of the brutal, tragic attack on Japha (Japhia). He implies some arrogance in the populace even though he was commander of the Jewish resistance. He explains the debacle at the gates resulted in a division of the citizens, those in the outer wall and those in the inner wall. The trapped Jews were devastated by being:

> betrayed by their own friends, which quite broke their spirits and at last they died, cursing not the Romans, but their own citizens, till they were all destroyed, being in number twelve thousand (*Wars* 3.7.31).

The remaining Jews, men and women fought a heroic defence of the inner compound but were overcome by Vespasian's son Titus' troops:

> Then did Titus's men leap into the city, and seized upon it ... there was a fierce battle between them for the men of power fell upon the Romans in the narrow streets, and the women threw whatsoever came next to hand at them, and sustained a fight with them for six hours' time ... that the number of the slain, both now in the city and at the former fight, was fifteen thousand, and the captives were two thousand one hundred and thirty (*Wars* 3.7.31).

Archaeologists and historians have located this tragedy at Tel Yafia on the doorstep of the Christian hamlet of Nazareth, where Jesus' relatives had their community in 67 AD. A careful reading of Josephus' account shows this is not correct and an alternative site must be sought to meet his requirements.

## Scholars who reject Tel Yafia's nomination

Modern-day Tel Yafia has been incorrectly labelled as Japhia and caused a serious error in understanding the geography of the gospels. Scholars from a range of disciplines have not accepted the nomination. One of them is Israeli archaeologist Professor Yigal Levin who stated regarding Japhia:

> Many scholars have identified this town with the village of Yafa southwest of Nazareth. And in fact this identification would have been perfect had Japhia appeared between Sarid and Chisloth-Tabor. However there is no evidence that the text has been emended in this way ... For these reasons many scholars remain undecided on the identification of Japhia.[1]

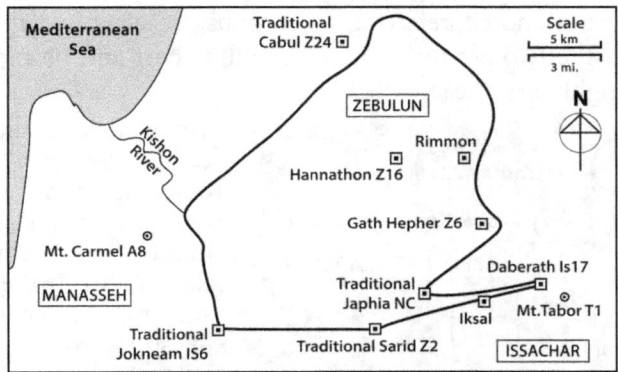

C.19 Map showing traditional Zebulun boundaries. The illogical location of Japhia is clear with the zig-zag action of the order that has been pointed out by scholars.

## The illogical zig-zag border

Some scholars have suggested that the author of Joshua's book got the order wrong. With the nomination of Yafa and the order given, an illogical zig-zag action is clearly shown in Illus. C.19. This was observed some time ago by a Bible commentator Friedrich Keil who wrote:

> it is just as certain that it cannot be the present Jafa, a place half an hour to the south west of Nazareth, as Robinson and Knobel suppose, since the boundary is running eastwards, and cannot possibly have turned back again towards the west, and run from Deburieh beyond Sarid. If the positions assigned to Chisloth-tabor and Dabrath are correct, Japhia must be sought on the east of Deburieh.[2]

---

[1] Email sent by Yigal Levin (Israeli Archaeologist and Bible Geographer) to the author on 19 February 2016. There are also other Israeli scholars who do not accept the nomination based on the topography such as Zacharia Kallai (historian/geographer), Nadav Na'aman (historian/archaeologist), Zvi Gal (archaeologist) and Ze'ev Safrai (historian/geographer). Christian scholars who have not accepted the nomination are Martin Noth (historian), Carl Keil (Bible scholar), Robert Boling (Bible scholar) and Robert Hubbard (Professor Biblical Literature).

[2] Keil, F and Delitzsch, F 2016 *Biblical Commentary on the Old Testament*, 'Joshua Chapter 19'. Sacred-texts.com. Daberath has different spellings; Dabrath, Deburieh and Daburiya.

More recently, archaeologist Zvi Gal noted "Yaffa near Nazareth, follows, but its location does not create a continuous line".[3] Bible scholar, Robert Hubbard has also stated: "The common identification of Japhia with Jafa (near modern Nazareth) is improbable because that would make the border senselessly backtrack westward".[4] This has led to efforts to nominate other sites for the location.[5]

**Traditional Japhia and Jotapata are not close**

Tel Yafia does not lie near to Tel Yodfat (Arabic Jefat). This fact had been recognised by Bible scholars soon after the traditional nominations of Yafa (Jafa) by Robinson (1841) and Jotapata (Tel Yodfat) by Shultz (1848). In 1869 Dr. William Smith noted, referring to Josephus, "if Jefat be Jotapata this can hardly be, as the two are more than ten miles apart and he expressly says they were neighbours to each other".[6]

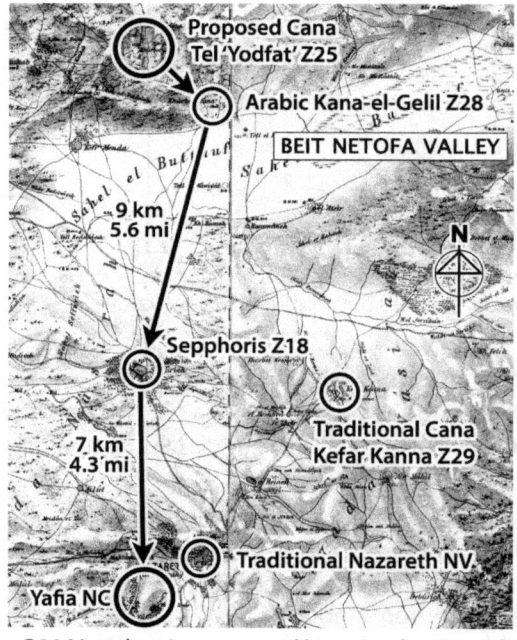

C.20 Map showing proposed locations for Cana of Galilee. Also the illogical route of Vespasian's attack on Japhia based on the incorrect traditional sites. PEF base map.

These two traditional sites cannot be seen from each other, being 19 km (12 miles) apart with two large ranges of hills between them (*refer* Map Illus. C.20). If the traditional sites were accepted a logical question would then follow. Why did the Romans conduct a military diversion over such a long distance when Jotapata was the main target?

**Searching for Japhia**

In Chapter 16 the significance and the meaning of Japhia is explained. It is an interesting Hebrew word that has to do with shining light. In order to show the logic and evidence for the correct identification of Japhia a correlation of two sources is required: first, the

---

3   Gal, Z *Lower Galilee During the Iron Age*, op. cit., p. 99.
4   Hubbard, RL 2009, *The NIV Application Commentary – Joshua*, Zondervan, Grand Rapids, Michigan, USA, p. 418.
5   Nominated sites include Mount Tabor (N. Na'aman, Y. Levin) and somewhere north-east of Nazareth near Meshed (R.G. Boling, R. Hubbard).
6   Smith, W 1869, *A Dictionary of the Bible*, p. 1212.

*Identifying biblical Japhia*

topographic sequence of Joshua as shown previously; second, the account of Josephus above who described the Roman attack. When all the factors are pieced together it becomes clear that Japhia is centred on a locality known today in Galilee as Ilaniya.

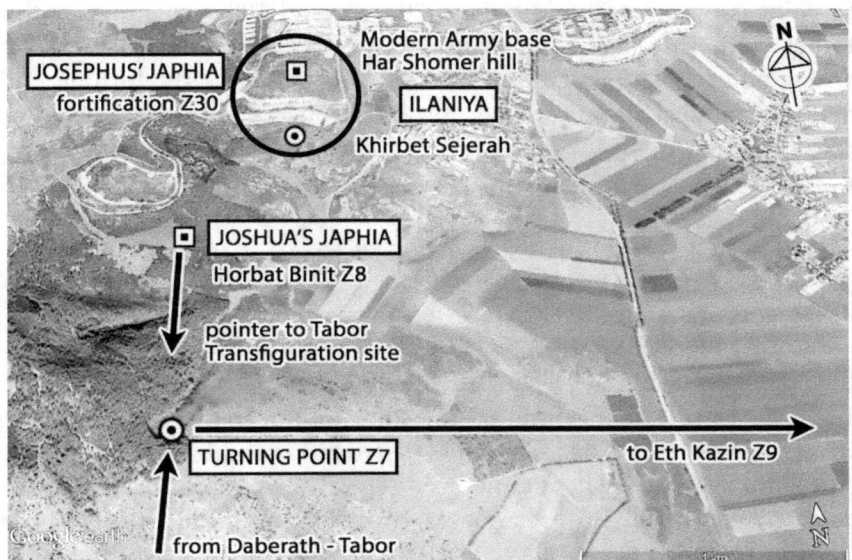

C.21 Map indicating the location of Joshua's Japhia and the turning point of the Zebulun border south of it. The proposed location of Josephus' fortification at Japhia (Z30). Base map Google Earth. Image © 2016 Digital Globe

### 12.2 Joshua's Japhia (Z8)
Proposed location: Horbat Binit: 32-44-48.5 N. and 35-23-24 E.
It is located one kilometre (1,100 yards) south-west of modern Ilaniya, on a ridge that faces south and the following locators give supporting evidence.

#### The topographic logic from Daberath
Joshua's listing states the Zebulun border "went out toward Daberath, by-passing Japhia" (Joshua19:12). This is a crucial factor in nominating this area for Japhia and follows topographic logic shown in Chapter 10. Daberath is on the northern side near Mt. Tabor. Other versions use "going up" in the passage. The elevated site of Horbat Binit is due north of the centre of Mt. Tabor. One of the options for Japhia given by scholar Robert Hubbard was "north of Mount Tabor".[7]

#### The turning point near Japhia (Z7)
Proposed location on a spur near Horbat Binit: 32-44-17 N. and 35-23-24 E.
The border turns east just before (south) of Japhia at a point "and from there

---
7   Hubbard, RL, op. cit., p. 418.

it passed along on the east of Gath Hepher" (Joshua19:13). Tel Gath Hefer is accepted by most archaeologists as correct and is located near the town today called Meshed. If the border is taken as bisecting Mount Tabor (east longitude) and meets the north latitude of Tel Gath Hepher then the turning point is on a prominent spur 1,000 metres (1,100 yards) due south of Horbat Binit. This gives confirmation as it is the closest ancient site to the turning point. A tall, whitewashed timber post to mark the turning point would be an ideal ancient marker for the shepherds in the days of Joshua.

**The archaeology of Joshua's Japhia**
Horbat Binit is a small site of one hectare (2.5 acres, 10 dunams) located on a high hill. In 1881
> The survey of Western Palestine recorded heaps of stones and several cisterns on the site ... A later archaeological survey documented wall segments and agricultural terraces on the eastern slope, a possible wall enclosing the site, as well as Persian, Hellenistic and Byzantine potsherds in association with these elements. [8]

The evidence of a former wall on the site is of interest. Unfortunately the hill site has suffered from successive destructions and extensive pillaging. A preliminary survey has found Iron Age, Late Hellenistic and Roman remains. Late Middle Bronze remains, required for a Joshua site, have been found in tombs in the locality. A full archaeological survey of the tel has not been done, and the preliminary report recommends an excavation to bedrock. [9]

C.22 The co-author of the Ilanya IAA Archaeological Survey, Eric Gould showing examples of archaeological remains in Ilanya.

---

8   Alexandre, Y and Gould, E 2011, 'Horbat Binit,' Final Report, vol. 123., *Hadashot Arkeologiyot*. Israel Antiquities Authority Report.
9   ibid.

*Identifying biblical Japhia*

## 12.3 Josephus' Japhia (Z30)

Proposed location: Ilaniya in Lower Galilee 13 kilometres (8 miles) west of Tiberias (*refer* Illus. C.21). There are two features to note:

1. Josephus' fortress: at *Havat Ha-Shomer*: 32-45-25 N. and 35-23-46 E. This is part of an existing Israeli army base that owns the site in Ilaniya.
2. Japhia settlement: *Khirbet Sejerah*: 32-45-5 N. and 35-23-50 E. Adjacent to the army base, with historic remains and a water source. It is 1,000 m (1,100 yards) north of Joshua's Japhia at Horbat Binit.

### A strategic military site

Josephus selected this site due to its strategic location at the intersection of two major ancient trade routes. Even today it is near the intersection of two major highways known as Golani Junction. The strategic location is also illustrated by its location on the historic military route known as *Darb-el-Hawarna*. This logistical advantage continues today with the large Havat Ha-Shomer army base located on the northern slopes.

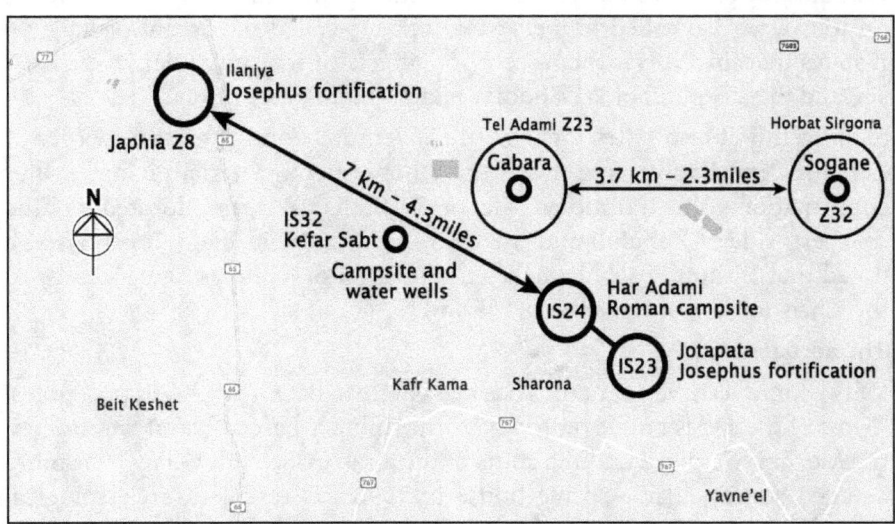

C.23. Author Map showing the proximity of Japhia to Har Adami. These two sites are within view of each other. A key water source was between them.
Base roads from Google Maps.

### The proximity of Japhia and Jotapata

Japhia is 7 km (4.3 miles) to the north-west of Har Adami, which was the camp of Vespasian. Due to the prolonged resistance of Jotapata, the nearby Jewish fortification at Japhia began to become "puffed up" and taunted the Romans (*Wars* 3.7.31). Maybe they had Jewish flags shown above upturned Roman flags on poles? The direct line of vision can be clearly seen today.

The main water supply for the Roman army was at Kefar Sabt which is between Japhia and the Roman Camp. All good reasons for the Roman side campaign to Jafa (Japhia) (*refer* Appendix 8.7).

**Japha near Gabara and Sogane ( Illust. C23).**
Josephus makes reference to his stay at Japha (*Life* 52.270). The account names the city of Gabara nearby. This is the site of Tel Adami (Z23) and is not to be confused with Har Adami (IS24). It also names Sogane as a village "twenty furlongs" (3.7 km, 2.3 miles) from Gabara (*Life* 51.265). Sogane can be identified with Horbat Sirgona whose out-skirt is the required distance east of the edge of Tel Adami (Gabara) in the Yabneel Valley. Josephus' movements are well understood with these locations of Japha, Gabara and Sogane.

**Eusebius' Jafo an elevated site in eastern Zebulun**
Eusebius (260–340 AD) was a resident of Palestine and produced a list of Bible sites. Japhia was still known in 325 AD as Jafo or Joppe. This was the start of the Byzantine era and remains of that era have been found at Ilaniya. Eusebius' *Onomasticon* described, "Japheth (Jafthie) in the tribe of Zebulun on the east. Also called Joppe. (Now Joppe is called the ascent of Iafo)". [10] It states that then it was the "ascent" of Jafo (Iafo) which implies an elevated site and the steep hill of Ha-Shomer matches that description.

Significantly it also notes that the site is definitely on the eastern border of Zebulun. The Ilaniya area meets the Onomasticon criteria, giving further confirmation. The traditional site of Tel Yafia is clearly located on the southern side of Zebulun and therefore is not Eusebius' Jafo. It can also be noted that Bishop Eusebius makes no mention of Japho as being nearby to the Christian site of Nazareth of his day.

**The archaeology**
Only a limited survey of Ilaniya has been done to date. The IAA Report notes, "Most of the site is built over today by the military base at Havat ha-Shomer, the Moshava Ilaniyya and the ruins of the Arab es-Sejerah village".[11] A more detailed survey near a spring-house in 1996 has revealed "archaeological layers from the Neolithic and Chalcolithic periods, the Early and Middle Bronze Ages, as well as the Roman period".[12]

---

10 Wolf, UC, 'Iapheth'. Onomasticon, op. cit. Some claim Eusebius was confused between Japhia and the port of Jaffa. It has various spellings including Japhet, Japhic, Japheth, Japhie, Jafo (Iafo). Further comment by Wolf is found in No. 558. The misunderstanding is due to the same root for Japhia and Joppa which is Yapho (Strong's H3305).

11 Alexandre, Y and Gould, E 2011, 'Ilaniyya', *Hadashot Arkeologiyot*, Jerusalem. Israel Antiquities Authority Report.

12 ibid.

## Conclusion to Section C

The evidence shows that some of the traditional archaeological nominations for the Lower Galilee are not correct. These sites have been based on false assumptions regarding the location of Jafia. This has led some to suggest the biblical account is in error. This section challenges that response.

We are indebted to Josephus' historical accounts as he gives much-valued information on his era of first century Palestine. His detailed description of the Galilee gives confirming evidence of two important site proposals of this book. From his accounts the traditional locations of Jotapata and Japhia require re-evaluation. His sites can be harmonised with the biblical criteria.

- The link between Jotapata and Japhia fortifications can be shown.
- The evidence supports the nomination of the Ilaniya locality for Japhia. Joshua's Japhia was on the hill of Horbat Binit based on the topography. Josephus' military site of the same name was nearby to the north on a more elevated plateau, now part of an army base.
- The topography, historical sources, biblical references and the military logic all confirm and correlate. The traditional nomination at Tel Yafia as Japhia does not meet certain crucial requirements.
- The location of Japhia is key evidence for consideration and enables Tel Yafia to be nominated as the correct location of Nazareth City.

C.24 Arch of Titus in Rome depicting the
Roman sacking of the Temple in Jerusalem.
Josephus gave graphic details of the event.
Credit Wikimedia Commons.

*Proving Biblical Nazareth*

D.01 Jesus made a profound statement to Cleopas and Luke on the road to Emmaus listed below. Part detail engraving of the event by Gustave Dore, circa 1866. Courtesy of the Pitts Theology Library, Emory University, USA.

> And beginning at Moses and all the Prophets, He expounded to them in all the Scriptures the things concerning Himself.
>
> Luke 24:27.

# SECTION D

## FOUR SITES OF THE MESSIAH

Even to a casual traveller in the Holy Land the Bible becomes, in its form, and therefore to some extent in its substance, a new book. Many an allusion which hitherto had no meaning, or had lain unnoticed, starts into prominence and throws a light over a whole passage ...
... by identifiable ancient towns of Holy Writ with the modern villages which are their successors; by bringing to light the remains of so many races and generations ...

Prospectus given at the first meeting of the Palestine Exploration Fund in London 1865.

---

With the correct location of key Zebulun sites, some very interesting connections between Old Testament and New Testament sites can be shown. The examples given relate to the two key sites associated with Nazareth, that of the incarnation and the other the declaration of the Gospel in the Nazareth synagogue.

*Proving Biblical Nazareth*

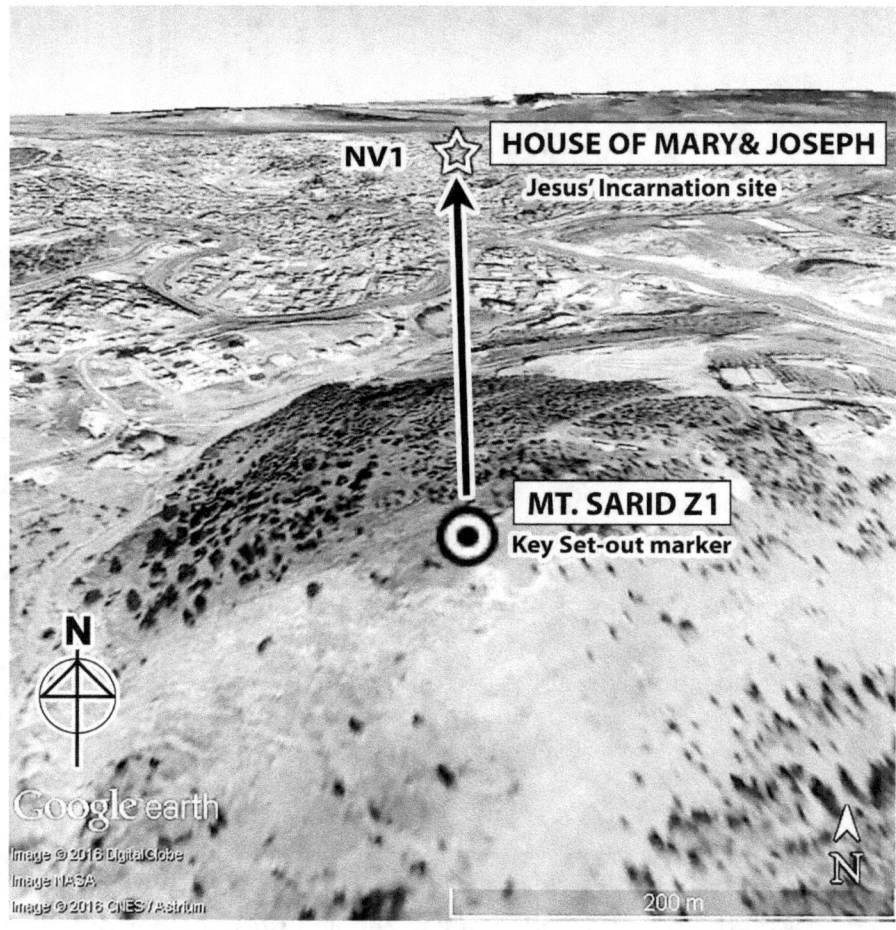

D.02 The set-out point of Sarid was on the extreme southern end of Mt. Kedumim The location prophetically points to the proposed site of the Annunciation of Mary at the traditional place in the hamlet of Nazareth.
Base Map Google Earth. Image © 2016 DigitalGlobe.

# CHAPTER 13

## PROPHETIC MOUNTAIN NEAR NAZARETH

Then Mary said to the angel, "How can this be, since I do not know a man?" And the angel answered and said to her, "The Holy Spirit will come upon you, and the power of the Highest will overshadow you; therefore, also, that Holy One who is to be born will be called the Son of God".

Luke 1: 34–35.

---

If Jesus was the promised Messiah it would be logical to expect some clues to be found in prophecies about him. Scholars have pointed out that Nazareth is not recorded in the Old Testament. However other clues associated with sites nearby show the planned location of Nazareth. One of these is a majestic peak that juts into the Jezreel Plain. The name of this peak is Sarid and the subtle Hebrew root meanings associated with the name gives prophetic clues.

## 13.1 Bible site mapping

Bible site mapping is the examination of spatial relationships involving Old and New Testament sites and the geography of the land. God made a promise to the Israelites after he gave them the Ten Commandments. At designated locations if they built a sacrificial altar made of natural earth or stones, it would become a place of blessing. "In every place where I record my name I will come to you and bless you" (Exodus 20:24). The Hebrew for "every place" is *tephillah maqown*, which means a dedicated place of prayer. The "record" in Hebrew is *zakar* which means to keep in remembrance and make a memorial. This indicates that many specially named Bible sites are spiritually significant and have some connection with the plan and blessing of God.

Bible names, including those of people and sites, can have deeper spiritual meaning. This is reinforced by the subset or Hebrew *root meanings* that can be derived from them which gives a richer understanding of the context. It can give valuable clues for the identification of sites.

When Christians consider this topic they can seek an added dimension for investigation. Jesus made a profound claim after his resurrection to two witnesses on the road to Emmaus. "And beginning at Moses and all the Prophets, He expounded to them in all the Scriptures the things concerning Himself" (Luke 24:27). Geographical correlations can be shown between some Old Testament and New Testament sites sharing the same latitude or longitude (*refer* Summary pp. 197-202). Some Old Testament sites can be seen as *signposts* pointing to the story of Jesus, as a form of *prophetic mapping*. Clues to the mystery of some sites can be solved using this mapping to:

1) Confirm existing sites that are known, giving supporting evidence.

2) Help establish a preferred site when there are a number of other options.

3) Enable new proposals for further investigation and research.

Examples of these three forms of biblical site mapping involving Nazareth are found in this section and include sites named as Sarid, Daberath, Cana and Mount Tabor. They are used to illustrate the theme mentioned in the Introduction with the quotation of St. Augustine that strongly links the Old and New Testaments.

## 13.2 Sarid: key set-out point

Sarid is an elusive site that has intrigued Bible geographers for a long time. Traditional archaeology has accepted Claude Conder's location of Sarid at Tel Shadud on the Jezreel Plain (Z2) because of the Arabic name.

*Prophetic mountain near Nazareth*

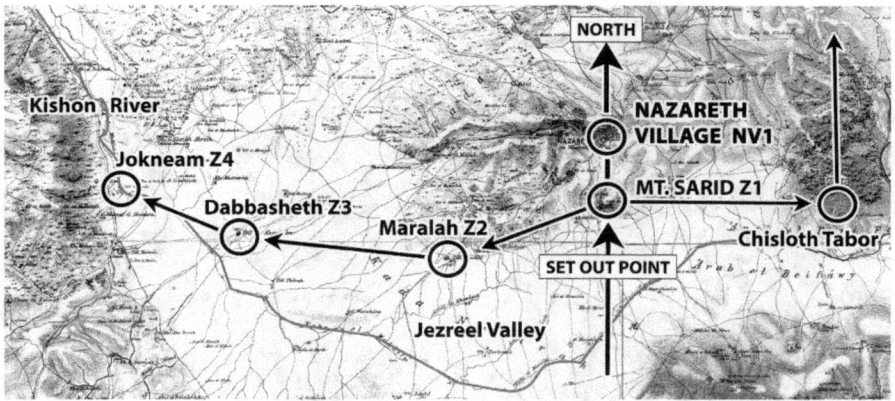

D.03 The set-out point of Sarid showing the boundary definition to the west and east. This position points due north to the house of Mary and Joseph. Base map PEF.

Others disagree with the nomination and have taken the correct logic that the possible location of Sarid is somewhere south of Nazareth. Bible scholar Carl Keil "definitely suggests that it may be found in one of the two heaps of ruins on the south side of the modern 'Mount of Precipitation'".[1] His Mount of Precipitation (Precipice) is currently known as Mount Kedumim, but a more accurate and logical nomination needs to be made and proven.

**Sarid is Mount Kedumim / Precipice (Z1)**
Location: the southern promontory at 32-40-50.4 N. and 35-17-52.6 E.

This is a key prophetic site as shown in Illus. D.03. Sarid is a very prominent mountain marker site, not one of the "twelve cities with villages" in the Joshua list. This is explained in Appendix 4. This dominant peak is located 2.3 km (1.4 miles) due south from the centre of traditional Nazareth (NV1). Sarid has an unusual method of delineation with the border described as running to the west, then returning to the marker before heading east. This is a curious part of the order which must give some important clue. It would seem logical to name Sarid the set-out point, due to its prominence and high visibility. Surveyors and planners utilise these kind of sites, as they help everyone to get orientated. The site is the ideal *flagstaff* or visual *trig point*. A visit to the Jezreel Valley today quickly shows the reason for the nominated position with the huge projection spur of Mt. Kedumim jutting its head from the Nazareth ridge.

As one travels across most of the Jezreel Valley, this peak is visible and it is clear why Joshua chose it. A question can be asked if there is a deeper meaning in the name of Sarid, and whether this name has prophetic significance.

---

[1] 'Sarid', *McClintock and Strong Biblical Cyclopedia*. *Refer* Bibliography.

D.04 Mt. Kedumim from the west showing the peak profile. The set-out point (Z1) arrowed is the olive tree on the south promontory. *Refer* Credits Wikimedia Commons.

**The Hebrew meaning**

The term *Sarid* refers to *survivor* and Strong's (H8300) indicates it means "survivor, remnant, that which is left" (H8300). Another dictionary links Sarid to "something left over, especially the righteous people of God after divine judgement".[2] The Vaticanus Septuagint version intriguingly uses another name for Sarid which is *"Esedek Gola"*. Esedek has to do with *righteousness* (H6664) and *Gola* (H1473) can refer to *exiles*. There are other opinions on the name of *Sarid* which will be commented on further.

D.05 Rocky south promontory of Mt. Kedumim with spectacular views over the Jezreel Valley.

---

2  StudyLight.org. 2016. 'Remnant', *Holman Bible Dictionary*. *Refer* Bibliography.

## Sarid's amazing cave – Neanderthals or ancient pious pioneers?

Mount Kedumim was named by archaeologists who found ancient remains in cave settlements on the hill. The name means *ancient people* in Hebrew. One of the caves on the south-west slope of Mount Kedumim is called *Qafzeh*, which is the French word for precipice. This word comes from the legend that Jesus jumped from the peak to escape his executioners and hid in this cave to escape. The cave is unique and is one of the oldest sites of human occupation in Israel. The rediscovery of this cave raised many historical questions when French archaeologist René Neuville conducted research there in 1934.[3] He found eighteen layers of habitation, attesting to the long period of occupation before the end of the Middle Bronze Age, the time of Joshua. The history plaque on the summit claims that remains date back to the Mousterian–Neanderthal era.[4] There is much debate at present about the relationship of Neanderthals with modern human ancestors as there is genetic evidence of sexual interaction. This interaction raises new questions about some of the dates: "For the first time at Qafzeh it was clearly proven that the Mousterian was the work of both Neanderthal and Modern man, at least in the Levant".[5]

Mount Sarid has been interpreted as the mount of a *remnant* and it can also mean *survivors* of a judgement of God. According to the biblical account, there is another possible explanation. Genesis explains that the ancients were survivors of a great flood. Biblical Job's name is associated with several sites in Israel according to tradition, and it is possible that a similar ancient clan may have spent some time on this mountain at a time after Noah and before Abraham. This gives another explanation of the name given by Joshua to the mount. It is a matter of speculation who the *righteous remnant* might mean for a site like this. Devout people may have occupied the locality for a period of time in the Early Bronze period. So the question remains to determine who these mysterious pioneers occupying a spiritual hill very early in Israel's history could have been. (*Refer* Appendix 8.10.1 for a radical explanation.)

## A memorial park and a prophetic tree (Z1)

A visit to the peak of Mount Kedumim today shows that it has a history of veneration. Near the peak "traces can still be seen of a Byzantine structure … an altar also dug in the rock. Opposite the cave there was believed to be a church, built it is said by St. Helen".[6]

---

3  Vandermeersch, B 2002, 'The excavation of Qafzeh', <bcrfj.revues.org/1192 p.65–70 No.10>.

4  ibid. No.20. The plaque nominates a 80,000–10,000 BC time frame. Studies have revealed Neanderthal DNA has been found in modern human genomes and they are not a different species. The Qafzeh report showed there was more complex interaction between them.

5  ibid., No.12.

6  ibid., No.2. St. Helen is Emperor Constantine's mother who was a devout Christian.

The Jewish National Fund and the Nazareth Municipality have erected a memorial plaza on the summit (Illus. D.06). This location is not the highest part of the mountain, but is the most southerly peak and by far the most visually identifiable location. Sculptures and plaques have been placed along well-made paths leading to the summit plaza. At the centre, an olive tree has been planted inside a circular ring of concrete blocks. This tree is the visual marker for the southern promontory and has an intriguing location. It aligns on the same longitude as the Catholic Church of the Annunciation with the dome above (Illus. D.07). This is the proposed location of the original house of Mary and Joseph. This mountain can now be reconsidered and its true spiritual significance revealed.

D.06 Peak plaza of Mt. Kedumim (Z1) proposed as a site of preaching by the prophets.

## 13.3 Reclaiming Mount Kedumim for Jesus

### Sarid and the Catholic celebration

In March 2000 AD Pope John Paul II celebrated the year of the Catholic Jubilee in the Nazareth Church of the Annunciation, commemorating two thousand years of Christianity. The ceremony emphasised that this church site is deemed to be the cradle of Christianity, being the place of Mary's Annunciation. This celebration was followed by Pope Benedict XVI in May 2009, who called a large assembly of the faithful in Nazareth. This time the site for the gathering was on the northern slopes of Mount Kedumim with terraces and seats providing seating for forty thousand people. The banner for this convocation stated boldly, *"Nazareth – it all began here"*. Catholics honour the event of the incarnation and it was appropriate that they chose a mount that was a prophetic pointer to that event. The location was between the peak of Mount Kedumim (Sarid) and the Church of the Annunciation.

## The mount of prophetic themes

The following section looks at aspects of Sarid in Zebulun and the significance of its location. Prophetic *themes* can be shown pointing to the relationship between the southern peak of Mt. Sarid and the proposed house of Mary and Joseph in Zebulun. Both are key sites that share the same longitude.

### 1. Zebulun – the habitation of God

There are two common aspects offered by scholars for the Hebrew meaning of Zebulun, one is *habitation* (H2194) and the other involves *honour* (H2082). This was the designated tribal location of Jesus for most of his life. However a deeper meaning can be seen in the location with Sarid. Zebulun is named as a son by Jacob's wife, Leah, when she exclaimed after his birth, "God has endowed me with a good endowment, now my husband will dwell with me" (Gen. 30:20). Zabal, the verb of Zebulun, is also used of God's dwelling in the Temple by his Spirit (2 Chronicles 6:2). The *"will dwell"* part of Leah's exclamation can be seen as describing Zebulun as a desired habitation.

**Prophetic pointer No.1:** *Leah made a very prophetic exclamation at the birth of Zebulun. In his tribal region there would be a future honoured place of habitation for the Messiah. Sarid is the set-out border marker.*

### 2. The righteous remnant

Sarid shares a similarity with the Hebrew word *shear*. Sarid is a remnant that escapes destruction. Shear is a remnant that returns to establish a pledge. This word has a rich theological connotation as stated in a Bible dictionary:

> The remnant doctrine was so important to Isaiah that he named one of his sons Shear-Jashub, meaning 'A Remnant Shall Return' (Isaiah 7:3) … Many remnant passages are closely tied with the future king, the Messiah, who would be the majestic ruler of those who seek his mercies … in that future there would be a new people, a new community, a new nation, and a strong faith in one God. This remnant would be personified in the Suffering Servant (Isaiah 53:1–12).[7]

There is a link between the two powerful theological concepts, the theology of the remnant and the theology of the coming of the Messiah. When the lens of the history of Israel is aimed at this remarkable mountain, an interesting perspective can be seen. When Joshua named the mount he was linking the past history of the site with the future significance. This is the mount of the ancient remnant, survivors of a past judgement. The archaeology supports this as an ancient site. It overlooks the Plain of Jezreel which was the scene of a crucial battle in Israel's history. The prophetess Deborah and commander

---

7  'Remnant', *Holman Bible Dictionary*, op. cit. *Refer* Bibliography.

*Proving Biblical Nazareth*

Barak made their attack on Canaanite King Jabin from Mount Tabor on this plain (Judges 4). They were a faithful remnant who were victorious against the odds. In later periods prophets like Elijah, Elisha and Malachi, part of a remnant in the region in times of apostasy, exhorted the people back to faith.

**Prophetic pointer No.2:** *The peak of Mount Sarid would be an ideal location for a devout remnant people or survivors to go and pray for God's plan of salvation and deliverance in times of struggle.*

D.07 The prophetic olive tree on the southern promontory of Mt. Kedumim (Z1) is on the same longitude as the house of Mary and Joseph (NV1) indicated with the arrow.

### 3. Isaiah's prophesy of Immanuel and a virgin

When the prophet Isaiah met King Ahaz in Jerusalem, he was told to take his son *Shear-Jashub* as a testimony. During their meeting Isaiah made his famous *Immanuel* declaration of a prophetic sign with "the virgin shall conceive and bear a Son" (Isaiah 7:14) (Hebrew *almah*, young woman). St. Matthew takes this event as prophetic and relates it to the Virgin Mary (Matthew 1:23):

> Behold the virgin [Gk. *parthenos*] shall be with child, and bear a Son, and they shall call His name Immanuel, which is translated, "God with us".

There has been fierce debate on the meaning of this Isaiah verse between Jewish and Christian theologians over the centuries, for obvious reasons. It is generally accepted that it does refer to a young girl and probably a teenager. It can be reasonably extrapolated she had not had sexual relations, which is why Christians accept the use of the word virgin, clearly denoted by the Greek word used in Matthew.

Even though the Galilee had a long period of Israelite abandonment God still had a plan for it. The exiles returned from their sojourn in Babylon and settled in Judah. Later, during the time of the Maccabees, there was a return of Jews to Galilee. Once again, devout Jews settled in the city of Nazareth. Mary and Joseph are good examples of descendants of the returned remnant They were examples of survivors.

How did Mary's parents decide on the location of a dwelling for their young teenage daughter? Did they ponder and pray on the mount of the righteous survivors and receive a divine vision of the location on the hill to the north? This is speculation, but there can be no argument that the physical alignment on the north-south longitude is there (*refer* Appendix 8.2.2 and 8.10.2).

**Prophetic pointer No.3:** *The Mount of the remnant or survivors points to the location where the conception of the Messiah occurs with the Virgin Mary.*

### 4. The hand of the Prince?

One scholar has defined Sarid as "the hand of the Prince".[8] Eusebius denoted Sarid as '*Sarith*', which St. Jerome further suggested: "For sarith, which is derived from the word Israel, means prince …"[9] He seems to use the 'sr' in 'Israel' to get the word '*sar*'. The Hebrew word *sar* (H8269) means a prince, ruler or chief. This link of Sarid to *sar* is based on an assumption and can be considered as speculative.

**Prophetic pointer No.4:** *Some scholars, such as St. Jerome, do see a link between Sarid and a ruler or prince. They would see it illustrates an aspect of the Messiah – the Prince.*

There have been other theories put forward to define Sarid and its location. Bible scholar August Knobel considered that the root letters may mean an "incision" and looked for a clue in the topography for a cutting.[10] Others have suggested it may be a misspelling of Shadud but their is no proof of that. The mystery is solved with the correct Hebrew meaning and understanding the topographic logic.

---

8 'Sarid', *Hitchcock's Bible Names Dictionary*. *Refer* Bibliography.

9 Hayward, CTR 2010, *Saint Jeromes Hebrew Questions on Genesis*, Oxford University Press, Oxford, UK, p. 70.

10 "Sarid", *McClintock and Strong Biblical Cyclopedia*, op. cit. *Refer* Bibliography. This requires an alteration of the final letter from a "d" to a "t".

## Summary: Sarid and the Messiah

Sarid is definitely not the site of the attempt to kill Jesus. However, it is important that this spiritual peak is reclaimed as prophetically significant. Joshua was naming a site pointing north to a future event that would honour the coming of the Messiah. It is an Old Testament messianic site.

- The main Hebrew root meaning seems to imply an aspect to do with the remnant or survivors. The Septuagint site name can mean *'righteous exiles'* and also a type of remnant in the Jewish understanding. Joseph and Mary can be seen as descendants of the *remnant* that are used in the plan of God.
- The location shows why Joshua defined Sarid in a very particular way. In Appendix 4 a case is made for Sarid being understood as a geographic feature, not a city.
- The peak points to the proposed house of Mary at the time of the incarnation. It is also the family home where Jesus dwelt during most of his life on earth. This is an example of biblical and prophetic mapping confirming a traditional site.
- The family may have had picnics there on occasions with friends and relatives. Jesus would have been well acquainted with the hill of Sarid in his youth as it was a short thirty minute walk south from his family home. It would have been a good devotional location with its spectacular views. He may have prayed there, reflecting on his future mission.
- A point for speculation is whether the site is a candidate for a place of public preaching by some of the Old Testament prophets like Elijah. It can also be speculated Jesus may have had theological discussions there with locals just as he had done at the age of twelve in the Temple in Jerusalem. It was in his neighbourhood (*refer* Appendix 8.10.2).
- Today, Christian groups use the mountain as a place to gather and pray. Mount Sarid should be promoted and understood as a site pointing to the first coming of the Messiah.

# CHAPTER 14

## A LEVITE CITY THAT POINTS TO JESUS

*An altar of earth you shall make for Me, and you shall sacrifice on it your burnt offerings and your peace offerings, your sheep and your oxen. In every place where I record My name I will come to you, and I will bless you.*

Exodus 20:24.

---

The Levites had a special role in Israel. They had no tribal region but instead had designated cities with pasturage. They had specific names and their borders had markers that could not be moved. A case can be made that one of these cities was prophetic in that it pointed as a signpost to an aspect of Jesus. This gives further confirmation for the location of the incarnation.

D.08 The Levites consecrated all their spiritually significant sites with prayer and sacrifice. Engraving by J. Carolsfeld c.1860 AD of dedication ceremony in Jerusalem. Courtesy of the Pitts Theology Library, Emory University, USA.

> "Thus you shall separate the Levites from among the children of Israel, and the Levites shall be Mine."
> Numbers 8:14. God's commandment to Moses.
> The Levites had a special role in the affairs of Israel.
> Their priestly function involved a broad range of activities.

*A Levite city that points to Jesus*

## 14.1 Unique city layout of the Levite priests

### The coming of the Messiah and a prophetic site

There is a Levite city that has an interesting location in reference to Nazareth. Before we can consider this, it is important to look at the special tribe of Levi, who were told to live in designated holy cities. Why was this done and for what purpose?

God had instructed Joshua to make special provisions of cities for the Levites with a unique layout. It can be assumed the city plan was symmetrical. The Exodus campsites of the Israelites after Sinai were symmetrical. The Levites did not receive a tribal region but instead were given designated locations throughout the other tribal territories. Their city plan was physically defined in a detailed way (lllus. D.09):

> They shall have the cities to dwell in; and their common-land shall be for their cattle, for their herds, and for all their animals. The common-land of the cities which you will give the Levites shall extend from the wall of the city outward a thousand cubits all round. And you shall measure outside the city on the east side two thousand cubits, on the south side two thousand cubits, on the west side two thousand cubits, and on the north side two thousand cubits. The city shall be in the middle. This shall belong to them as common-land for the cities (Numbers 35:3–5).

There is debate on interpreting the outer dimensions of the city, but all agree the inner zone is one thousand cubits from the central city walls. The debate is about whether the outer zone of two thousand cubits extend from the central city wall again or from the edge of the inner zone making it three thousand cubits. The answer lies in the Septuagint version which translates this passage thus: "And the suburbs of the cities which ye shall give to the Levites, shall be from the wall of the city and outwards two thousand cubits round about."[1] The Septuagint makes no reference to the thousand cubits, only to a ring of two thousand cubits from the central city wall. Thus the correct interpretation of the measurement for the city is to look at three zones with clear functions and areas:

- **The central walled city.** This is known in Hebrew as the '*Ir*'. This area would vary in size and shape depending on the location and topography. All the measurements were taken from the north, south, east and west extremities of the city walls. The general shape would probably have been a type of rectangular plan of approximately one to three hectares (up to 2.5 acres). This zone would consist of dense housing, probably with the synagogue.

---

1   Brenton, L 2001, *The Septuagint with the Apocrypha: Greek and English,* Hendrickson Publishing, Peabody, Massachusetts, USA, p. 226.

- **The suburban plots precinct.** This is described in Hebrew as '*Migrash*' and accurately measured for a distance of a thousand cubits or 445 metres (486 yards) from the city walls in the cardinal directions. This zone contained farmers and shepherds, the animals and their shelters and pens. This precinct also had other agricultural activity depending on the location including gardens, fruit trees and vines. Also there would be storage silos, cisterns, olive presses, and bakeries. (A zone of 110 hectares, 270 acres.)
- **The outer pastures.** These are also known as '*Migrash,*' and can also be connected to a root word *garash* meaning '*to drive out*'. This outer square was a further thousand cubits from the inner square, comprising open fields set aside for pastures for the animals. Thus the animals were contained within the city limits of zone two, but during the day shepherds would "drive them out" to feed in the open pasture land of zone three. This area may also have included some land for crops such as wheat and barley, and access to water would also be important. [2]

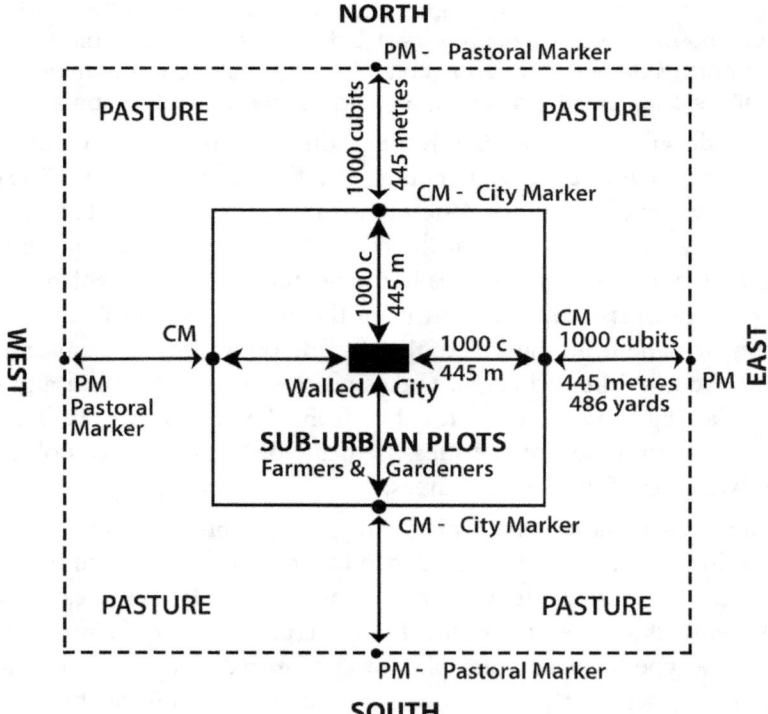

D.09 Typical city layout of the Levites showing the defined boundary points. These markers were not be moved and could be spiritually significant.

---

2  Pastures zone 270 hectares (667 acres) gives a total Levite allocation of 383 hectares (946 acres).

*A Levite city that points to Jesus*

**The unmoveable dedicated boundary landmarks**
Natural stone boundary markers would be at all four cardinal points from the city centre and would be solemnly dedicated. Ancient boundary markers were to be preserved according to the Law (Deut. 19:14). Proverbs 22:28 also commands: "Do not remove the ancient landmark which your fathers have set." So whether the Levite city population grew or declined, the boundary markers were to remain fixed. With the large distances of the pasture lands it is probable that these corner points were marked with large whitewashed timber poles to enable shepherds to have a clear view of the limits. The pasture land also could not be sold (Lev. 25:34), so these markers are indicative of a very defined and unchangeable zone of land in the plan of God.

**The consecration services at the boundary landmarks**
When the cities were marked out accurately as required by the Law, there would be a consecration service at the place of the boundary markers. This would involve priests offering up prayers and probably having an altar for sacrifice. An example cited previously on page 158 was for "an altar of earth" that was natural materials and not artificially made. It then linked this altar with "every place where I record My name *I will come to you*, and I will bless you". (italics added) This is a promise of future significance and the blessing by God. Using such sacred sites for prayer and worship would have been a part of the city's life. These special boundary markers probably had their Hebrew names inscribed on a dedicated prayer plaque. The priests may have prayed facing the four cardinal points just as Abraham had been told to do when he received the promise of inheriting the Land (Genesis 13:14).

**Spiritual signposts in the story of Jesus**
For Christians *the coming* of the Messiah was the fulfilment of the blessing of God. Some of these consecrated boundary markers may have had a further purpose in that they relate to the Messiah. The priests would have prayed for the coming of the Messiah and God's will to be done in the Land. The markers on occasions could be the location of a prophetic act and this concept has profound theological implications. The example relevant to this book is one of the Levite cities of the tribe of Issachar named Daberath, which was located on the border of Zebulun. In fact it was just inside the border with the outer pastoral markers being near the description of Zebulun's boundary in Chapter 10. This site is used to illustrate the principle of a messianic signpost and to show the intriguing connection with Nazareth.

## 14.2 Daberath and 'The Word'

There is agreement on Daberath's locality on the eastern side of Mt. Tabor at Khirbet Daburiyeh (IS18) and recorded over the centuries by historians, such as Josephus. This town's structures date to the Iron Age (c. 1130 BC), which means it does not meet the requirement to be the city in Joshua's time frame. A more precise location of Joshua's Bronze Age site can be selected, and the answer lies in another site 900 metres (980 yards) to the north-east.

Central location: *Horbat Devora* at 32-41-50.2 N. and 35-22-39 E.

If the northern city walls were 75 metres (82 yards) from the centre then adding the 1000 cubits (445 metres, 486 yards) the proposed north city marker (NCM) is at 32-42-7.4 N. and 35-22-39 E., the same latitude as the Church of the Annunciation (NV1) (*refer* Illus. D.10. and E.03).

Some scholars support this older site as that of Joshua's time. For example, Jewish historian Dr. Rivka Lissak wrote, "North-East of the Arabic village (Daburiyeh) one can see Hirbet Daboura, the site of the Biblical Davrat or Davira".[3] The site has good support from the archaeology with remains from the required Middle Bronze IIB era.[4]

### The Septuagint clue for the two adjoining sites

The mystery of the relocation of the name is found in comparing the list of Issachar's Levite sites in the Masoretic version of 1 Chronicles 6:72 with the list in the Septuagint version.[5] The original site of Daberath at Horbat *Devora* was known as *Deberi* or *Debba* in the LXX in 425 BC. Deberi spawned another city adjacent known as *Dabor*, preserved today as Khirbet *Daburiyeh*. Dabor eventually becomes the more significant site due to its strategic location.

### The meanings of Daberath – The Word, The Pasture

Daberath can have several root words. One is '*Dabar*' (H1697) which has meanings, including "speech, saying, utterance, words, acts". The Hebrew scholar Gesenius' list includes "a promise"; "a precept, an edict"; "a commandment"; "the word of the Lord, an oracle"; "proposed plan".[6] The other root word is '*Pasture*'. It must be noted that the definite article is used in the Joshua 19:12 text so it could be understood as *"The Word"* or *"The Pasture"*.

---

3 Lissak, RS 2014, *Dabburiya, an Arabic Village was formerly the Israeli/Jewish Davarita*. Refer Bibliography. Daberath has various spellings including Dabereh, Davrat, and Davora.

4 Gal, Z *Lower Galilee in the Iron Age*, op.cit., p. 14. "Middle Bronze Age IIB–9%, Iron Age I –16%. More information on the archaeology is given in Appendix 6.

5 The Masoretic has four sites, with Daberath listed second but the Septuagint has five sites with the second and third listed as Deberi and Dabor. The latter are said to be cities with suburbs indicating two separate sites but with names of similar meaning. This reference dates back to circa 425 BC when the Septuagint was compiled and there were two Levite sites close together.

6 Daberath root meaning *dabar* listed in Strong's Dictionary. Another root word is *dober* (H1699) which means pasture.

## The prophetic significance

This Hebrew meaning gives a clue to the prophetic significance, as it is one of the messianic titles given to Jesus in the New Testament. The Apostle John wrote of Jesus: "In the beginning was *the Word, and the Word was with God, and the Word was God*. (John 1:1)". [italics added]

This clearly shows that the naming of the Levite city had something to do with Jesus – the *'Word of God'* in human form. This is a powerful concept and shows the richness of the previous descriptions by Gesenius. His list includes the promise, an oracle, a proposed plan, pointing to a future event, even the coming of the Messiah. This also relates to the record of the visit of the angel Gabriel and his profound declaration or edict to Mary in Nazareth:

> "The Holy Spirit will come upon you, and the power of the highest will overshadow you: therefore, also, that Holy One who is to be born will be called the Son of God" (Luke 1:35).

This indicates that the prophetic meaning of Daberath, with its northern city marker (NCM), points as a signpost to the future incarnation site of Jesus.

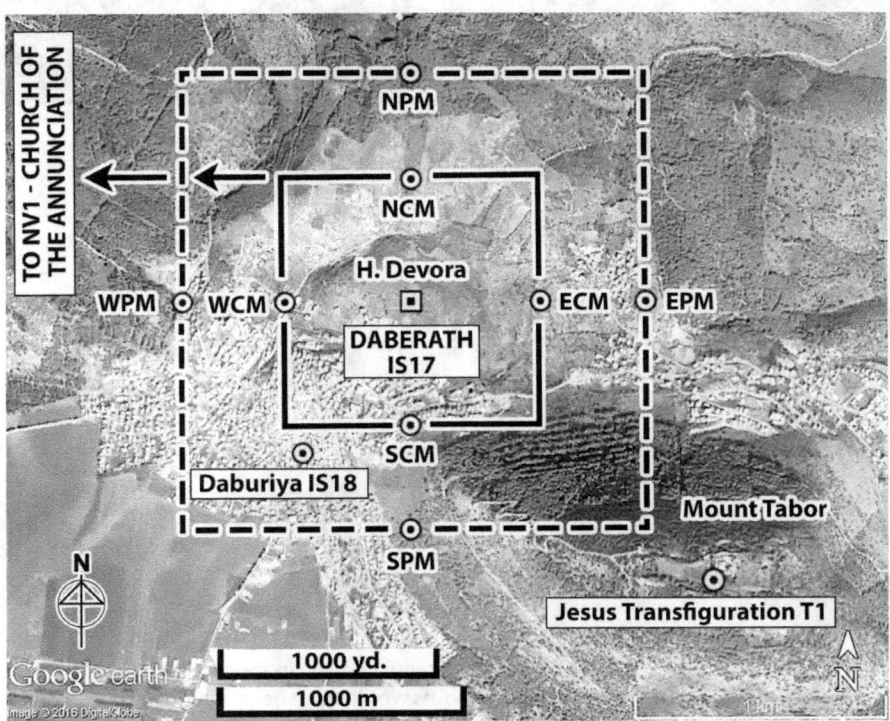

D.10 Proposed Daberath Levite city layout. The northern city marker is a messianic key site that points prophetically west to the Incarnation site. PM–Pastoral Marker CM–City Marker. Base Map Google Earth. Image © 2015 DigitalGlobe.

D.11 Jesus turning water into wine. 'Miracle at Cana' painting by Russian artist Vladimir Makovsky, 1897 AD. Credit WikiArt.org.

D.12 Stone water pots were used in the Cana miracle. Spigots would have been provided at the base to allow the easy drawing of water.

# CHAPTER 15
## CANA OF GALILEE

This beginning of signs Jesus did in Cana of Galilee, and manifested His glory: and His disciples believed in Him.

John 2:11.

> The story of the miracle at the wedding at Cana is often quoted in Christian wedding services all round the world. This event was where Jesus turned water into wine and is recorded as the first of his public miracles. There are debates about the location of Cana of Galilee, but with the help of Josephus' accounts, the correct city can be identified. With the logistics explained a locality for the wedding can be proposed.

## 15.1 The miracle at a Jewish wedding

### The eyewitness account of the Apostle John

On the third day there was a wedding in Cana of Galilee, and the mother of Jesus was there. Now both Jesus and His disciples were invited to the wedding. And when they ran out of wine, the mother of Jesus said to Him, "They have no wine". Jesus said to her, "Woman, what does your concern have to do with Me? My hour has not yet come". His mother said to the servants, "Whatever He says to you, do it." Now there were set there six waterpots of stone, according to the manner of purification of the Jews, containing twenty or thirty gallons apiece.[1] Jesus said to them, "Fill the waterpots with water". And they filled them up to the brim. And He said to them, "Draw some out now and take it to the master of the feast". And they took it.

When the master of the feast had tasted the water that was made wine, and did not know where it came from (but the servants who had drawn the water knew), the master of the feast called the bridegroom. And he said to him, "Every man at the beginning sets out the good wine, and when the guests have well drunk, then the inferior. You have kept the good wine until now!"

This beginning of signs Jesus did in Cana of Galilee, and manifested His glory; and His disciples believed in Him (John 2:1–11).

Several theological comments can be made about this account. The first being that this was the "first sign" of Jesus showing his anointing in the power of God. The second is the addressing of his mother Mary as "Woman", is not a term of rebuke or rudeness, as we would think at first. It was to mark that at this point, at the start of his ministry, he would be taking his instructions from his *Heavenly Father* not his *earthly mother*.

In the natural realm, Mary's request suggests that she probably had some responsibility in the food and wine distribution, indicating that she may have been related to the bride or groom. If the celebrations were occurring outside the city walls, then it would be normal for someone to go and order replenishment from within the city. That would be a natural explanation for Mary's suggestion that her son could organise it.

Jesus makes it clear that it was not the right way or time, that it had to be done God's way. Mary senses that and orders the servants to follow Jesus' instruction. He asks for ritually pure stone pots, not the normal clay pots called *amphora* used to store wine. He also would have instructed what source of water was to be used, as he was to bless the water in a public way, to demonstrate to all that he indeed was the reason for the transformation. There was no doubt to his disciples and to those who tasted the good wine.

---

[1] An incorrect assumption on a unit measure by translator. The quantity is explained later in the chapter. Thirty US gallons is 114 litres which is 114 kg (259 pounds) plus the weight of the pot.

*Cana of Galilee*

D.13 Cana wedding mosaic above doorway to Orthodox Church at traditional Cana. (Kefar Kanna)

**Understanding the type of "wine"**

The reason why the wine is considered is that it affects the calculation of the number of guests involved, which in turn affects the logistics of the location proposal. This segment is not supporting a case for or against the consumption of alcohol, but rather examining what type of wine may have been created by the miracle.

- Alcohol is a very emotive topic for many people. A wide range of opinion today has medical experts divided between those saying all alchohol is toxic and those saying it has health benefits. However it is agreed if taken it should be in moderation. The question is then asked whether Jesus created wine with an alcoholic content or not.

- There are three common Hebrew words for wine. First is *tirosh* which is fresh grape juice (or lightly fermented). Second is *yayin*, which has aged alcohol content.[2] This is the wine of Proverbs 104:14. "And wine that makes glad the heart of man." The third is *shekar* which is strong alcohol.

- In the gospel account the Greek word for the wine is *oinos* which is a generic term. It can be differentiated between 'new wine' and 'old wine.' When Jesus told a parable of wineskins, he explained that *new wine* was not to be put into old wineskins. The residue in the old wineskin causes the new wine to ferment further, causing the container to burst (Matt. 9:17).

---

2 There is debate over the composition and definition of *tirosh*. Scholars suggest it included grapes or a type of fresh grape juice and was non-alcoholic. Other scholars propose it could include slight fermentation from the first year harvest. There are Bible verses (e.g. Hosea 4:11) that imply some mild fermentation could be involved. Tirosh was part of the first fruit offerings of thanksgiving. Yayin is "effervescence; wine (as fermented); by implication, intoxication". (H3196). This is clearly aged alcoholic wine but with variable percentages. Shekar is "an intoxicant, i.e. intensely alcoholic liquor – strong drink + drunkard, strong wine" (Strong's).

Alcoholic or non-alcoholic wine would be appropriate to celebrate a Jewish wedding in 27 AD and in that era there was a way of storing both options.[3] In summary the Greek word *oinos* used permits an alcohol content but the percentage is unspecified. The second consideration is the moral aspect.

**Some comments that gives clues on the wine**

- The wedding is one involving devout Jews. Mary and Jesus are present along with his disciples and they were Torah (Law) observant. The Law permitted alcohol but did not endorse a drunken party.
- A large Jewish wedding would involve a large percentage of women and youth so it would be appropriate to assume that they were all partaking of the drinking. They need to be considered in the calculation.
- Jesus requested six ritually pure stone water pots for the transformation which tells us that he required containers with no contaminants. No yeast, leaven, dregs or impure residue in any form.[4] This was to show that the miracle had no residual chemicals to aid the wine creation.
- The crucial point is the wine is *"kalos oinos"*– 'virtuous wine' in Greek. 'Kalos' has a purity aspect to its meaning as "properly, beautiful, but chiefly figuratively good (literally or morally), i.e. valuable or virtuous" (G2570).
- *Agathos* the Greek word for good, is not used but rather *kalos* which is moral, excellent and beneficial. Another relevant point to emphasise is that everyone was partaking and enjoying it. The master of the feast, who would be a drink connoiseur, noted the excellent quality of the wine.
- *In conclusion the Cana wine whatever the chemical mixture is a pure, non-toxic, healthy drink and it was very refreshing and enjoyable.*

**The time frame of the Jewish wedding**

What would be the cultural expectation of a Jewish wedding in 27–28 AD Galilee? At the Cana wedding John specifically said that it was on the "third day" that the miracle occurs, and this can be interpreted in two ways. Most likely it was the third day of the week which was Tuesday. (However it could be the third day of the wedding festivities.) The travel day required for the guests would be the Sunday (after the Sabbath) and the preparations would be on the Monday. The third day is the actual wedding ceremony and the feast and celebrations would be on that day. This explains why the wine had run out as there had been consumption on the previous one or two days. A large group of relatives and friends of all ages would be there.

---

3   Bacchiocchi, S 2001. *Wine in the Bible: A Biblical Study on the Use of Alcoholic Beverages,* Biblical Perspectives, Berrien Springs, Michigan, 49103 USA, pp. 87–108.

4   Zangenberg, JK 2012, *Pure Stone: Archaeological Evidence for Jewish Purity Practices in Late Second Temple Judaism,* Brill, Leiden, The Netherlands.

*Cana of Galilee*

D.14 A typical Jewish wedding would have youths dancing as part of the celebration. Photo credit courtesy of 123 RF. Graphics Company.

**How many guests?**

The wine volume can help estimate the number of guests and the required logistics. The key is to identify what unit of liquid measure is used as detailed in John's account. Many translations mistakenly use the Greek or Roman measures called *amphora*, which results in very large-sized containers. The correct measure is the sacred Hebrew volume known as a *'bath'* which can be defined as about 22 litres (23.2 quarts). [5]

They were purification jars so the sacred measure was a requirement and the total can be calculated to 330 litres. [6] If an estimated 120 adults were in attendance, with 60 youths under the age of twenty, then nearly 1.8 litres (1.9 quarts) per person was available. This would be available on the day and also the next as they departed. So the total wedding party can be seen as about 180 people. The *'healthy wine'* factor means that all the attendees can partake and get the benefit of a totally refreshing, nutritious and invigorating drink. An appropriate drink for a devout Jewish wedding and a pointer to Jesus' messianic claims. This information can now be used to examine the nominated city of Cana and to seek out an appropriate locality for the activities.

---

5   Oxfordbiblicalstudies.com. 2016, 'Tools & Resources', *Oxford Biblical Studies*, <www.oxfordbiblicalstudies.com/resource/WeightsAndMeasures.xhtml>.

6   The original Greek text has the six water pots as containing either two or three measures. The assumption with the six pots is that three had 3 measures (66 litres) and three had 2 measures (44 litres). 66x3=198 and 44x3=132 giving a total of 330 litres (87 US gallons). Note these quantities with the weight of the jar would require two men to lift them.

## 15.2 Tel Yodfat is Cana of Galilee

There are five sites contending for the location of Cana in John's Gospel, but they are not correct. This has generated much debate over the centuries.[7] Refer Illus. C.20 for two of the traditional locations.

- *Kefar Kanna* (Z29) is the traditional site 4.7 kilometres (3 miles) to the north-east of Nazareth. With Kefar Kanna's proximity to Nazareth, it suits the pilgrim and tourist trade, but evidence of its name origin dates only to the fourth century. It has been a site important in preserving the memory of the story and should be honoured and respected for that. There are two further sites nearby to this location also offered.

- *Kanah in Lebanon* (A18) has also been proposed due to its historic name. Although it has the same name, this site is linked to Joshua's site of Kanah in the tribal area of Asher (Josh. 19:28). The gospels clearly describe the wedding at Cana in Galilee, which differentiates it from the Lebanon Kanah site. This site does not meet Josephus' requirement to be on a trade route of Galilee (*Life* 71.398).

- *Kana-el-Gelil* (Z28) are the ancient ruins that preserve the name Cana of Galilee in Arabic. This site is located on the northern edge of the Netofa Valley and has a growing list of supporters, but it does not have the military significance implied by Josephus (*Life* 16.86).

**The case for Tel Yodfat being Cana (Z25)**

Cana of Galilee: *Tel Yodfat* at 32-49-57.5 N. and 35-16-40 E.

Located 21 kilometres (13 miles) south-east of Akko. Tel Yodfat received its nomination as Josephus' Jotapata in 1847 AD from German scholar and diplomat Ernst Gustav Schultz.[8] His nomination of the site was because of Josephus' topographical descriptions, and examination of ruins on the large hill. Schultz was also influenced by Edward Robinson's nomination of Japhia at Tel Yafia six years earlier. Robinson in turn agreed with his nomination so both proposals became mutually supporting. Robinson was considered the authority on Palestinian sites of his day, so both proposals have remained in place, even though some scholars have not accepted the Japhia location (*refer* Appendix 8.4.1). The following evidence supports Tel Yodfat as Cana:[9]

---

7 Laney, J. Carl, 1977, 'The Identification of Cana of Galilee' from *Selective Geographical Problems in the Life of Christ*, Doctoral dissertation, Dallas Theological Seminary. *Refer* Bibliography.

8 EG Schultz 1811–1851. An Orientalist who was an expert in Hebrew and Arab linguistics. He had studied archaeology but did not have extensive field experience. Biblical archaeology was still in its infancy.

9 This site was examined by Claude Conder and Kitchener for the PEF in the 1870s. Extensive archaeological surveys (Rochester University 1992) showed remains of the Hellenistic period. The lack of Iron Age remains shows it does not meet the requirements of Jotapata (Jotabah).

*Cana of Galilee*

D.15 View looking towards Tel Yodfat with the proposed city of Cana city on the peak.

### 1. A strategic location
Tel Yodfat is located near a trade route that ran from Ptolemais (Akko) to Tiberias which was a strategic position in the Galilee. Josephus states Cana was on an important trade route of the Galilee (*Life* 71.398).

### 2. The Arabic name of Kana
It is of particular interest that 2.5 km (1.55 miles) to the east of the proposed site is a place with the Arabic name of Kana-el-Gelil, which means Cana of Galilee (Z28). The hill between the two sites is named as Jebel Kana on the PEF map. This is due to a historic Arabic tradition that preserves the name of Cana in the locality. This gives supporting evidence for the proposal.

### 3. A fortified site
The perimeter walls started in the Hellenistic period were followed by two phases of Early Roman walls. In 27 AD it was more a compact city before the expanded walls done before 67 AD. To the north-west are the remains of a siege ramp dating to the time of the Roman war.[10] Josephus does not explicitly state that he fortified Cana like other sites in the Galilee, but some scholars say that he did. A survey by the University of Rochester showed the walls of the three eras and the extensive evidence of the Roman era attack.[11] Josephus states that he resided in Cana of Galilee for some time (*Life* 16.86), but does not say if it was inside or outside the walls.

D.16 View of Tel Yodfat walls contains evidence of a Roman attack 67AD. It is not Jotapata.

---

10  Negev A. and Gibson, S, *'Jotapata; Jotbah; Yodfat; Shifat (Khirbet)'*, op. cit., p. 273.

11  ibid., p. 273.

### 4. The archaeology of a Jewish site

Remains found at this site show its origin in the Hellenistic era, which is why it is not mentioned in the Old Testament. It is decidedly Jewish in the Early Roman era as remains of several ritual baths (miqvah) were uncovered.[12] An important criteria for the nomination is to show the Jewish character of the site. The gospels indicate that the wedding of Cana was a Jewish event.

### 5. Jotapata is located near Japhia

In Chap. 12.3 Jotpata was located at Kh. Atosh. Tel Yodfat needs to be renamed.

### 6. The Desposyni village of Cochaba

An interesting point is what became of this devout city if it was attacked by the Romans in 67 AD. The answer may lie in the historic village of Kaukab which lies 2.5 kilometres (1.55 miles) due west of the site. This is the same name as the Judeo-Christian village Cochaba (meaning *Star* in Hebrew) mentioned by Sextus Africanus and linked to 'Nazarene' Nazareth, a site settled by Jesus' relatives as described in Chapter 3. Archaeologist Bagatti examined the site and came to the conclusion that this was correct. "The ruins that we saw prove the antiquity of the village and its Christian character in the centuries before the Arab occupation."[13]

## 15.3 The Cana wedding site: a proposal (Z26)

Proposed locality marker (Z26): grove at 32-49-57 N. and 35-16-30.3 E.

The latitude is a variable and the longitude is an assumption. A messianic site, about 180 metres (200 yards) to the west of Tel Yodfat's city walls. The locality has been determined by Josephus' account, site examination, logistical factors and prophetic mapping (*refer* also Appendix 8.4.2-4).

### The logistics

The Gospel of John only states that the wedding was "in Cana of Galilee", so the question is where exactly did this event occur? The walled city would be a compact site, not so suitable for a large group of one hundred and eighty celebrants and the associated activities. A Jewish wedding known as a *mishteh* festival would have included group dancing and games. Some of the guests came from outside the city so they would require lodging facilities. A facility is required with kitchens for large scale cooking and food preparation and a nearby dining place with many reclining tables to enjoy food and drink. The master of the feast is described as *architriklinos* (G755) (John 2:8), which means a superintendent of a banquet room with three couches. This was a typical three-sided seating plan for the main bridal group. Public conveniences and washing facilities would also be required.

---

12 ibid., p. 273. This site probably was part of the Jewish migration to Galilee mentioned in Ch.1.
13 Bagatti, B, *Ancient Christian Villages of Galilee*, op. cit., p. 104.

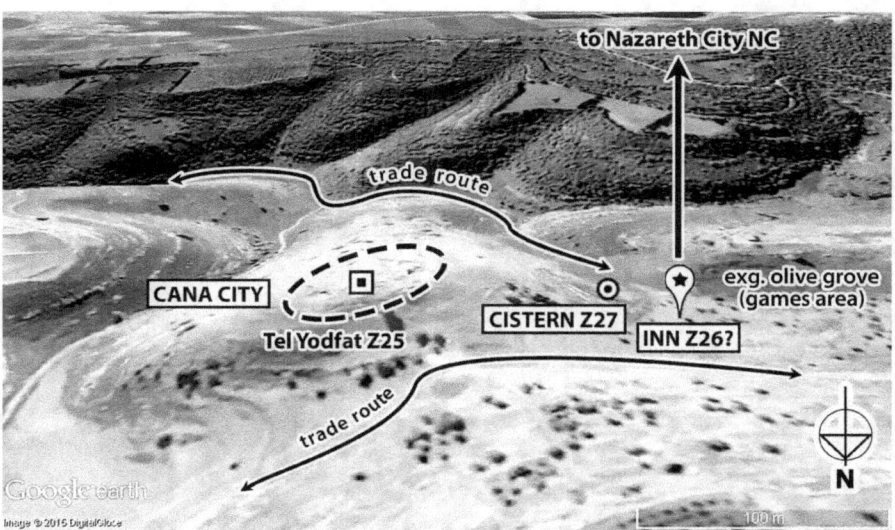

D.17 Map of Cana of Galilee showing the walled city location in reference to the proposed inn where the wedding was celebrated. A water cistern has been found nearby. Base Map Google Earth. Image © 2015 DigitalGlobe.

**The inn near the city**

An inn would be ideal, as this was a place that catered for large groups of travellers. An innkeeper had to provide for large trading caravans with their animals, and this factor suggests a location outside the city walls.

The proposed Cana city sits on a hill that is near the intersection of two trade routes. One road comes from Akko and travels towards the site from the north and then heads east towards Tiberias. Remains have been found of this road, which tends to follow the ridges. The other road passes Cana on the west side and follows the Wadi Jifat into the Netofa Valley and on to Sepphoris. If a public inn was used, its location would lie somewhere near the intersection of these two routes, which is the case for the site (Illus. D.17).

**A pleasant location**

Tel Yodfat has steep slopes on three sides and the only easy access is on the north-west side which would be the direction to the city gate. On this side is a gentle slope that leads to a saucer-shaped meadow, and currently this area is a pleasant olive grove. This location would be ideal for a public inn with areas for campers and a space for dancing and games (*refer* Appendix 9.4). The place where Jesus turned the water into wine was the ritual washing area which may have been in a compound with a tent structure. There is evidence of stone footings in the terraces adjacent (Illus. D.19).

D.18 View to Cana and olive grove where Jewish dancing would have been celebrated.

D.19 North view of the olive grove and place of the festivities. Note the stone terraces

### The large water cistern (Z27)

Underground cistern: 32-49-57 N. and 35-16-32.9 E. Located 120 metres (130 yards) from the city walls. An inn catering for large numbers of people requires a good water supply. The gospel account suggests there was a water supply on site to fill the pots. There is a very large underground cistern at the proposed locality with rendered wall sections and a small stone aperture at the top that could have been the well head with a hand pump. My investigation has resulted in an estimation of the volume as about 180 cubic metres (235 cubic yards).[14] This is a significant feature in support of the proposal of the locality of the inn and a key marker to consider (*refer* Appendix 8.4.5).

---

14 The variable height and the soil debris on the floor make it difficult to determine the volume. This gives an estimated water capacity of about 200,000 litres (52,830 gallons) which is a good storage capacity for an inn catering for travellers. The historic estimate of Galilee's rainfall is about 630 mm (25 inches) per annum. The Cana area currently receives about 580mm of rain per year so if 500mm is conservatively assumed, the roof area required to fill the cistern is 400 sq. m (43 squares). Two buildings of 20 x 10 metres meet the requirement to fill the cistern.

D.20 Stone rim with shrub in the foreground (arrowed) indicates a historic cistern (Z27) where water could have been drawn for use in the wedding ceremony. Rear arrow with figure indicates proposed wedding locality (Z26?).

D.21 The author with team investigating the large underground cistern (Z27). Evidence of render on the walls can still be seen.

## Summary and prophetic mapping

Logistics for Cana city can be correlated to information in Josephus' accounts and the archaeological requirements. The walled section in 27 AD is shown as Z25 which was extended south by 67 AD. Other dwellings would be on the slopes. The proposed location of the wedding site is based on assumptions of prophetic mapping and logistical factors. The cistern location (Z27) shown below is an important feature. The wedding area locality shown dashed in the map below requires more archaeological investigation. Its position is bisected by the longitude of Joshua's altar on Mount Ebal. This gives the hint of the spiritual significance. The messianic connections are shown in the Summary. Some will question this, but the spatial connection is there to be examined along with the site logistics.

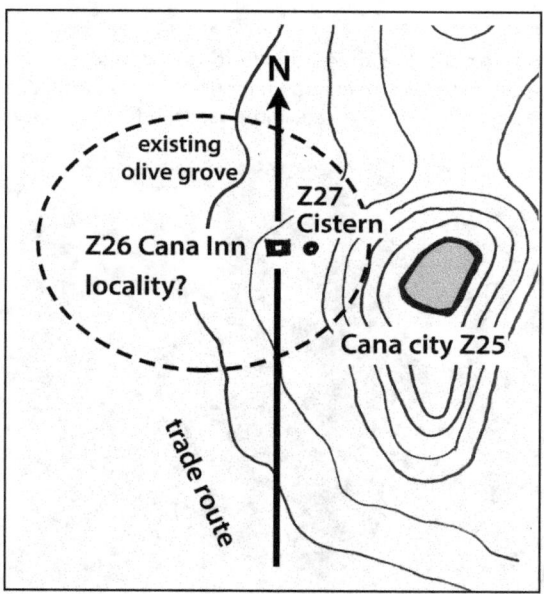

D.22 A proposed inn locality west of Cana city bisected by the longitude both of Joshua's altar on Mount Ebal and the centre of the city of Nazareth in 27 AD.

# CHAPTER 16
## LOCATING THE TRANSFIGURATION

*Now after six days Jesus took Peter, James and John his brother, led them up the high mountain by themselves, and He was transfigured before them. His face shone like the sun, and His clothes became as white as the light. And behold, Moses and Elijah appeared to them, talking with Him.*

Matthew 17:1–3.

---

This very extraordinary event has profound theological implications. The claim is that Jesus became radiated with a supernatural light that was observed by three human witnesses. He was also visited by the spirit bodies of Moses representing the Law and Elijah representing the Prophets. This would make the location of the event very holy and indeed the Apostle Peter used that adjective to describe the mountain on which it occurred. There are a number of sacred sites on Mount Tabor, and prophetic mapping gives support for a particular locality for the event.

D.23 The Transfiguration of Jesus on Mt. Tabor. Moses and Elijah appear with him in their spirit bodies representing the Law and the Prophets. The Apostles Peter, James and John were witnesses to this event.
Engraving by J. Carolsfeld. Courtesy of the Pitts Theology Library, Emory University, USA.

## 16.1 Which holy mountain?

The Transfiguration of Jesus is recorded in the Gospels of Matthew, Mark and Luke. The Apostles John and Peter wrote of the event and were eyewitnesses.

**The story of the Glory** (Matthew 17:1–9.)

> Now after six days Jesus took Peter, James and John his brother, led them up on a high mountain by themselves; and He was transfigured before them. His face shone like the sun, and His clothes became as white as the light. And behold, Moses and Elijah appeared to them, talking with Him. Then Peter answered and said to Jesus, "Lord it is good for us to be here; if You wish let us make here three tabernacles: one for You, one for Moses, and one for Elijah". While he was still speaking, behold a bright cloud overshadowed them; and suddenly a voice came out of the cloud, saying "This is My beloved Son, in whom I am well pleased. Hear Him!" And when the disciples heard it, they fell on their faces and were greatly afraid. But Jesus came and touched them and said "Arise, and do not be afraid." When they had lifted their eyes, they saw no one but Jesus only. Now as they came down from the mountain, Jesus commanded them, saying "Tell the vision to no one until the Son of Man is risen from the dead".

The Apostle Peter recalling the event:

> For we received from God the Father honour and glory when such a voice came to Him from the Excellent Glory: "This is My Beloved Son in whom I am well pleased". And we heard this voice which came from heaven when we were with Him on the holy mountain (2 Peter 1:17–18).

The Apostle John makes similar reference:

> And the Word became flesh and dwelt among us, and we beheld His glory, the glory as the only begotten of the Father, full of grace and truth (John 1:14).

These accounts make an amazing claim that Jesus was transfigured before three human witnesses. His messianic status was confirmed with his encounter with Moses and Elijah in their spiritual bodies. God the Father made some profound direct statements from heaven. Note also that Peter describes the said mountain as 'holy'– a God anointed site of the prophets.

**The tradition of Mount Tabor**

The spiritual significance of Mount Tabor is very well known. As shown previously, a quarter of the north-western hillside was allocated to the Levites of Daberath. It was also the spiritual headquarters of Deborah and Barak's campaign against the oppressive Canaanites. The belief that Mount Tabor is the correct site for the transfiguration is very old. There are other nominations, such as a hill near Caesarea Philippi, but these are all later theories with no evidence. The strong case for Mount Tabor is given in the Catholic Encyclopaedia which affirms a very long tradition.

The early Church scholar Origen (185–254 AD) said: "Thabor is the mountain of Galilee on which Christ was transfigured." (Comm. In Ps. lxxxviii, 13). This was followed by "St. Cyril of Jerusalem (Catechetical Lectures II.16) and St. Jerome (Epistles 46, 53 and 13) likewise declare it categorically."[1]

D.24 View to Mt. Tabor from Mt. Kedumim. IS18 marks modern Daburiyah and Z5 marks Chisloth-Tabor on the southern slopes.

## The sacred sites of Mount Tabor

There are four sacred precincts on Mt. Tabor, two of which are of particular interest and very historic (Illus. D.27–28). Jerome made a visit in 386 AD and noted devotional structures he describes in the plural as tabernacles. The anonymous pilgrim of Piacenza saw three basilicas in 570 AD.[2] These basilicas can be identified as the Catholic and Orthodox compounds. The other two precincts are later developments that also preserve traditions.[3]

## The Catholic Church of the Transfiguration (T4)

D.25 Mt. Tabor Byzantine church remains adjacent to the modern Catholic Church.

This massive church structure, by the famed Italian architect Antonio Barluzzi, has been built over historic remains from the Roman and Byzantine eras. It has been recorded as an early place of pilgrimage. The critical question is whether its grottos are the correct location of the transfiguration. My proposal is that this prominent site is sacred because it contains grottos probably used by Old Testament prophets. It is likely

---

1 Newadvent.org. 2016, *Catholic Encyclopedia*, 'Transfiguration'. *Refer* Bibliography.

2 Murphy-O'Connor, J, op. cit., p. 366.

3 The Cave of Melchizedek (T5) which dates to the Crusader period. It is based on a tradition at that time that this enigmatic figure may have had occasion to visit the mount in his travels. *Refer* Appendix 8.10. The other site is the Medieval Decentibus chapel (T6) which preserves the tradition of the descent of the disciples after the transfiguration.

that the grottos were used by the resident northern Israel prophets such as Elijah, Elisha, Nahum and Malachi (*refer* Appendix 8.9.1-2). The Old Testament lists Tabor as a place of devotion (Hosea 5:1). Elijah's life in the region is well known, with his connection to Mt. Carmel, and he would have spent some time on Tabor. It is no surprise that he is present with Jesus on the mount as it was near his prayer site. It must be acknowledged the Catholic site is very significant in preserving the memory of the event. [4]

**The tradition of Tabor Light**

D.26 Photo of Tabor light at St. Elias. An unusual phenomenon that occurs at the time of the Orthodox celebration of the Transfiguration. *Refer* Credits.

One of the interesting criteria that is used by the Orthodox Church to prove that their church compound has the right credentials for the transfiguration is a very unusual nightly phenomenon. During the celebration of the liturgy of the Feast of the Transfiguration on August 17–18, Christian pilgrims from many nations, mainly Orthodox, and some non-believers, gather in the courtyard. On this date, according to eyewitness accounts, a glowing soft cloud sometimes manifests above the church in the middle of the night. Aikaterini, an Orthodox nun recalls:

> This cloud however is different from other more familiar clouds which descend in the morning on our mountains. As the vigil begins, one sees on the top of the mountain, towards Nazareth, something orange in the darkness of the night. This moves perpendicularly towards the church and stands like an orange tongue ... the cloud comes toward the mountain and takes various shapes ... Words are poor to describe what you feel when these pieces, which are soft like cotton, come and you touch them with your hands, and you feel them on your face. [5]

Some will doubt this phenomenon, but there has been research on it. An Orthodox scholar has written articles on the subject and there is a website showing videos of this event. [6] The more analytical minds may be interested to know that a scientific examination has been done. The Russian newspaper

---

4 The location is very spiritual and many pilgrims over the centuries from around the world come to honour the event of the transfiguration. The Orthodox site is not so open in this regard.

5 Aikaterini, Orthodox nun 2011, *A Witness of the Holy Cloud of Mt. Tabor,* Mystagogy Resource Center, <www.johnsanidopoulos.com/2011/08/nun-aikaterini-witnesses-holy-cloud-of.html>. Johnsanidopoulos.com. The author has tried to make contact with this witness to no avail.

6 ibid.

*Pravda* and *Interfax* on 11/1/2011 featured a report by Russian and Israeli meteorologists on an investigation by the *Orthodox Synodal Theological Commission*. The findings quoted one of the participants Serey Mirov.

> According to him, summing up the results, the experts concluded that the fog cannot be generated in such dry air and temperature. Mirov stressed that the "descending of the blessed cloud" takes place only in the territory of the Orthodox monastery. He said that during the festival service ... a glaring sphere rushes over believers ... it glows in dimensions and descends on believers covering them and pouring life giving moisture to them. [7]

D.27 View indicating the sacred sites of Mount Tabor and the Zebulun boundary. T1 – Proposed Transfiguration grotto; T2 – Byzantine Church; T3 – St. Elias Church; T4 – Catholic Transfiguration Church; T5 – Cave of Melchizedek T6 – Descentilus Chapel; T7 – Tower of the Winds. Base map Google Earth. Image © 2015 DigtalGlobe.

## 16.2 St. Elias Orthodox Church

The Orthodox Church compound with the 'holy light' retains the historic name of Elijah. There are two sites in the compound that need explanation.
1. Current St. Elias Orthodox Church (T3): 32-41-16.2 N. and 35-23-25 E. The existing church and monastery date to the Medieval era and were rebuilt in 1845. This is a sacred Orthodox headquarters and many pilgrims from countries around the world come to visit.
2. Byzantine Church of St. Elias (T2): 32-41-15.6 N. and 35-23-25 E.
The remains of this church are very scant but evidence of its existence have been recorded in history. The structure was observed by the anonymous pilgrim of Piacenza in 570 AD. Archaeologist M. de Vogue wrote in 1854:

---

7   *Pravda : Interfax 11/1/2011*, "Meteorologists fail to explain descending of the cloud on supposed place of the Lord's Transfiguration", <www.interfax-religion.com/?act=news&div=8081>.

## Locating the Transfiguration

that the inside wall-face of the aisle lying south of the Greek church was covered with white plaster, on which could be distinguished traces of rinceaux painted in red. The pavement was in mosaic and made with large white and black cubes depicting a large circle and lozenges ... V. Guerin also noted that the nineteenth century church had incorporated remains of an earlier mosaic pavement into the new marble slabbed floor.[8]

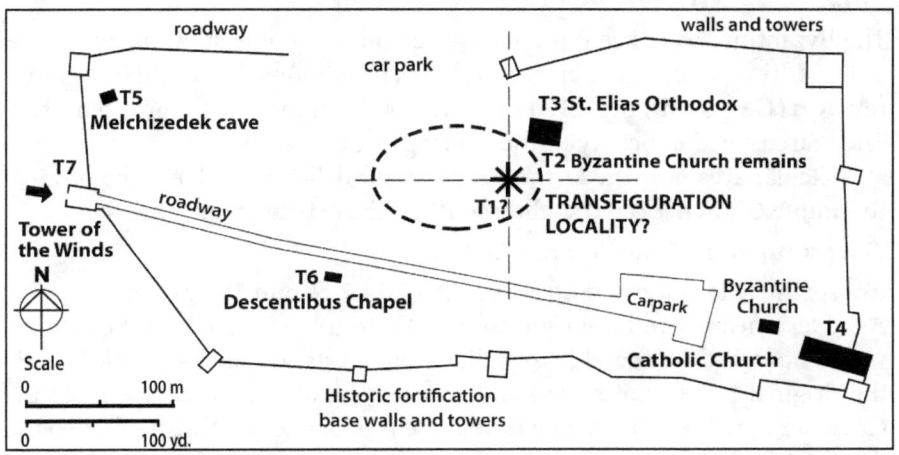

D.28 Mt. Tabor sacred sites and proposed transfiguration locality for investigation. Base Map Credit after Battista & Bagatti in Denys Pringle footnote No.8. below.

Count M. de Vogue considered these remains as Byzantine. Rinceaux is a floral frieze often used in Byzantine and Classical era artwork. The diamond shaped "lozenges" and circles are also very typical in Byzantine mosaics. In 1054 AD a historic divide or schism led to the formation of the Roman Catholic and Orthodox Churches. It would appear on Mt. Tabor there was a division of the sites with the Catholics gaining the eastern buildings. The Orthodox inherited the north-western site in what became known as the Church of St. Elias and established a monastery. In 1102 AD the pilgrim Saewulf located the site a small distance away from the other two main churches at the other (eastern) end of the plateau. His account noted:

> On the summit still remain three ancient monasteries; one in honour of our Lord Jesus Christ; another in honour of Moses; and a third at some distance from the others, in honour of Elias.[9]

---

8   Pringle, D 1993, *The Churches of the Crusader Kingdom of Jerusalem: A Corpus*: Volume 2, L-Z. Cambridge University Press, Cambridge, UK, p. 82.

9   Bohn, HG 1848. *Early travels in Palestine*, George Woodfall and Son. London, p. 46. This account would suggest that the site of Saint Elias is a historict one and could date back to the Byzantine era. This would then link it to one of the three basilicas noted in 570 AD.

*Proving Biblical Nazareth*

Abbot Daniel in 1106 AD indicated that this church was to the north.[10] Researcher Denys Pringle concluded these pilgrim accounts "appear to be referring to the medieval Church of St. Elias, whose remains are now incorporated into the Greek Orthodox Church of the same name".[11] The church and monastery were conquered by the Muslims in the Crusader wars.

## 16.3 Jesus' Transfiguration: a site proposal

The Byzantines were keen to establish the memory of past events in the life of Jesus. They would have access to the oral traditions that came from Jesus' relatives (Desposyni) that lived in the region from the first to third centuries. The search for the locality of the transfiguration can be narrowed down to a particular area near the Orthodox compound. The first clue is the original Byzantine Church located slightly south of the existing main church.

### The grotto of the Transfiguration (T1)

Approximate locality: A grotto near 32-41-14.2 N. and 35-23-24 E.
A subterranean chamber or grotto near the southern wall of St. Elias. Jesus would not want the occasion to be like a lighthouse on the mount. It is likely the original site is still sealed and this may have been the case since the Crusader era. The monks may have done this due to the threat of extensive decimation that was to occur in the Muslim attack on the site in 1183 AD.

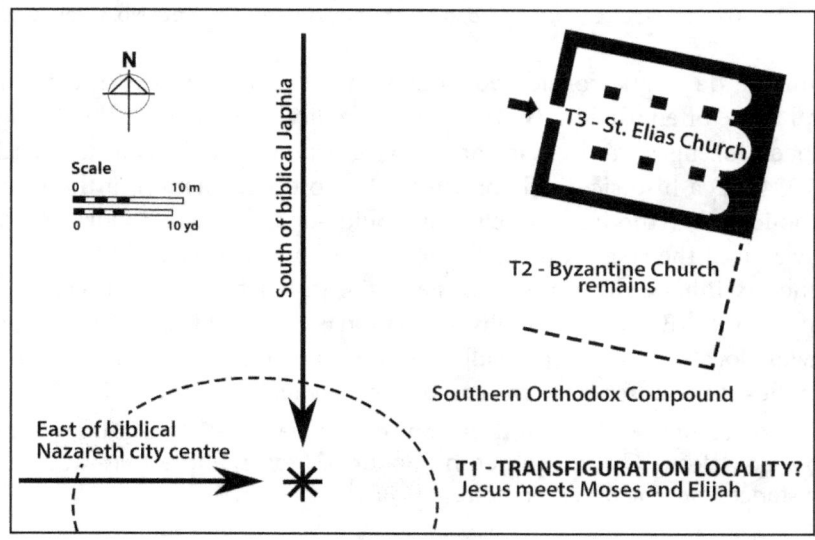

D.29 Author's plan of St. Elias Church with Byzantine remains to the south. Locality due south of Joshua's Japhia. Church plan credit Denys Pringle footnote 8.

---

10 Also in 1185 AD a pilgrim John Phocas observed the church remains as "left" of the Latin one.
11 Pringle, D, op. cit., p. 82.

*Locating the Transfiguration*

The Byzantine Church is a good marker, and the cave or grotto would be nearby. A recent report noted some preliminary investigations in this area:
> A web of catacombs recently discovered under the courtyard and church of the Orthodox contains a chapel with a 3rd century Holy Table and other important artefacts. Archaeologists surmise that these caves also served as hiding places during persecutions. [12]

This is encouraging information and a more extensive survey is required. There are a number of caves just west of this location toward T5 (*refer* Appendix 8.9.3). A second important clue is now given to seek a locality.

### The meaning of Japhia – God shines

There is the need to look again at Joshua's Japhia, shown in Chapter 12, with its Hebrew root of *yapa*. Strong's (H3309) defines it as *shining* and other dictionaries translate it as *splendid*. [13] The root meaning of *yapha* (H3313) means "to shine out, shine forth, send out beams". Gesenius significantly expands it "to cause to shine, used of God" and "to give splendour", and this is the same brillance of the *shekinah* glory (Deut. 33:2). Japhia means 'God shines' and the proposal is that this site points directly south to majestic Mt. Tabor, the mountain that is the traditional location of the transfiguration of Jesus recorded in the Gospels. Joshua's Japhia is 6.5 kilometres (4 miles) due north of Mount Tabor. The proposal is that the environs of Japhia, the city of *"God shines"*, prophetically points towards the mountain claimed by Christians as where Jesus shone (*refer* Appendix 8.9.3).

D.30 View towards the Orthodox Church compound southern wall. The bell-tower on the left is near the locality of the proposed grotto of the Transfiguration.

---

12 Koutroubas, K 2012 *Mount Tabor & The Transfiguration of Christ*. <theorthodoxchurch.info/blog/news/mount-tabor-the-transfiguration-of-christ/>.

13 *Easton's Bible Dictionary* 'Japhia' and *Smith's Bible Dictionary* 'Japhia'. *Refer* Bibliography.

## Conclusion to Section D

In Section C it was noted when archaeologists nominate sites that appear contrary to the Bible, some suggest the biblical writers got the facts wrong. There are even archaeologists who claim not only that, but that archaeology can be used to re-interpret biblical history. One of these controversial sources claimed: "Through the evidence of recent discoveries we will construct a new history of ancient Israel in which the most famous events and personalities mentioned in the Bible play unexpectedly different roles". [14] They claim that many of the traditional interpretations of Bible events and sites need revision. Sections C and D suggest that in regards to Lower Galilee, some of the archaeological assumptions are in need of revision.

Section D raises a new perspective in nominating Bible sites and that is the spiritual logic. Prophetic mapping is there to be examined and this section gives examples of the benefit:

- Mount Sarid is a confirming prophetic pointer to the traditional site of the Annunciation of Mary and the Incarnation.
- The Levite city marker of Daberath gives significance to the traditional Catholic site of the Incarnation.
- The location of biblical Cana at Tel Yodfat has been made based on Josephus and its strategic location. The western side of this site is an area of particular interest for investigation.
- Joshua's city of Japhia gives a helpful clue to investigating the site of the transfiguration on Mount Tabor. When this longitude is plotted with the latitude of the southern peak of biblical Nazareth a locality near the Orthodox compound is supported for investigation.

---

[14] Finkelstein, I and Silberman, N 2002, *The Bible Unearthed, Archaeology's new vision of ancient Israel and the origin of its sacred texts*, Simon and Schuster, New York, USA, p. 3.

# E: GEOGRAPHIC SPATIAL SUMMARY

All points on the earth can be located by latitude (parallels) and longitude (meridians). They create the cardinal points (N, S, E, W) which help us to orientate. The word *orientate* comes from the Latin word 'oriens' which means east. The *east* has significance in the Bible and for the Hebrew world view it was the main direction for orientation in the same way our modern world uses north to orientate.

**Biblical east orientation – Paradise lost?**
- East was the direction of lost Paradise (Gen. 2:8). The entrance to the garden of Eden was east (Gen. 3:24).
- The Tabernacle at all the Exodus camp-sites was required to face east with an eastern gate access (Numbers 3:38).
- Jerusalem's Temple faced eastward to the Mount of Olives (Ezekiel 43:1).

**Biblical north orientation – Heaven?**
The other primary direction is north which is significant in many cultures. There are a number of particular *north* references in the Old Testament.
- *A direction in space:* "He stretches out the north over empty space; he hangs the earth on nothing" (Job 26:7).
- *Exaltation (great joy) only from the north:* "For exaltation comes neither from the east, nor from the west nor from the south" (Psalm 75:6).
- *Holy City elevation:* "Great is the LORD, and greatly to be praised. In the city of our God. In His holy mountain. Beautiful in elevation, The joy of the whole earth, Is Mount Zion on the sides of the north, The city of the great King" (Psalm 48:1-2).
- *Satan's claim:* "I will ascend into heaven ... I will also sit on the mount of the congregation on the farthest sides of the north" (Isaiah 14:13).
- *The polar axis:* "The north and the south you have created them" (Psalm 89:12).

**Planning logic**
Urban and Regional planning involves design that incorporates elements of location and place with the human functions required. This must be related to the physical features of the land and requires certain assumed logic in the design. These functions and the logic can also be seen when analysing the planning used in historical regions.

It has been commented previously that there are particular ancient sites that God seems to have planned and are intended to be places of blessing (Chapter 13.1 and Exodus 20:24). The following section summarises some of the interesting relationships between sites identified in this book.

*Proving Biblical Nazareth*

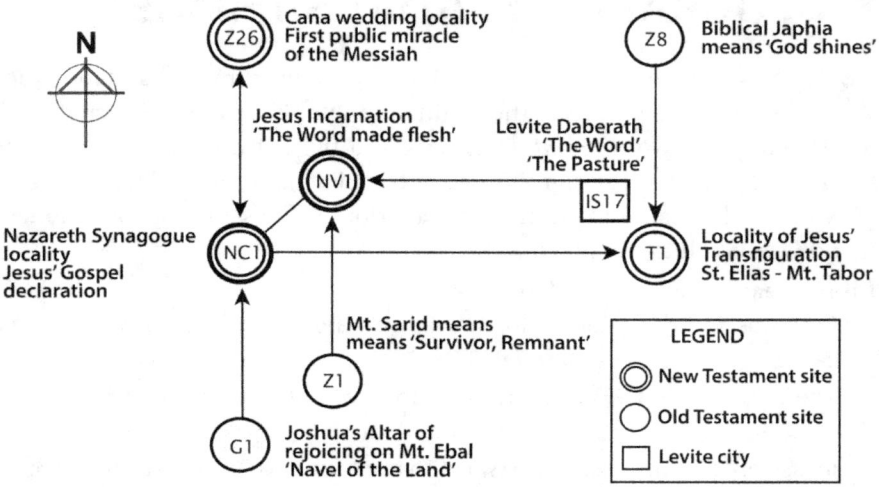

E.01 Diagram showing the spatial relationship between the eight spiritual sites introduced in the Preface.

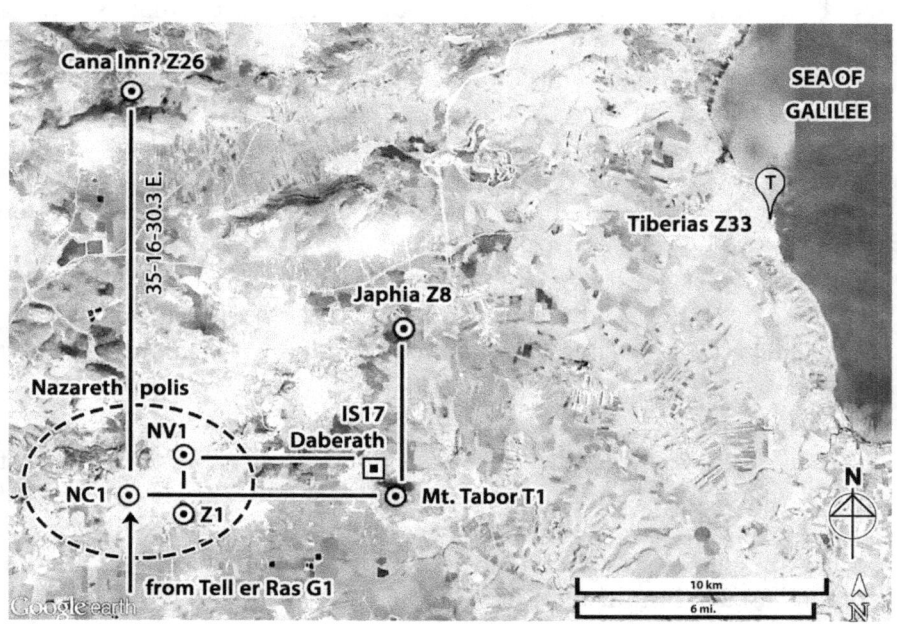

E.02 Geographical relationships of the eight sites.
NC– Nazareth city  NV – Nazareth hamlet.
Dashed outline is the locality of Nazareth polis.

*Geographic spatial summary*

**Prophetic Bible site mapping**

When the sites nominated in this text are analysed there is a discernible logic as they relate to the latitude and longitude. There appears to be spatial connections between Old Testament and New Testament sites. There also appears to be spiritual logic with some of the name selections. This mapping can be used in particular ways to help confirm and identify sites. Some sites are very specific in their coordinates and others are more indicators of a locality requiring more investigation. The following is a summary of the sites and their relationship with the city-polis of Nazareth.

**The place of the Incarnation**

- Mount Kedumim (Sarid) is the set-out point of Zebulun and means a surviving remnant in the plan of God. It is in alignment with the Church of the Annunciation, the proposed location of the Incarnation.
- The latitude of the northern marker of the Levite city of Daberath coincides with the same church. One of the root meanings of Joshua's Daberath is "The Word" in Hebrew.

This represents the intersection of two prophetic themes. The first is the faithful "remnant" illustrated by Joseph and Mary. The other is the promise of the Messiah who is described in the Gospel of John as "The Word" in human form.

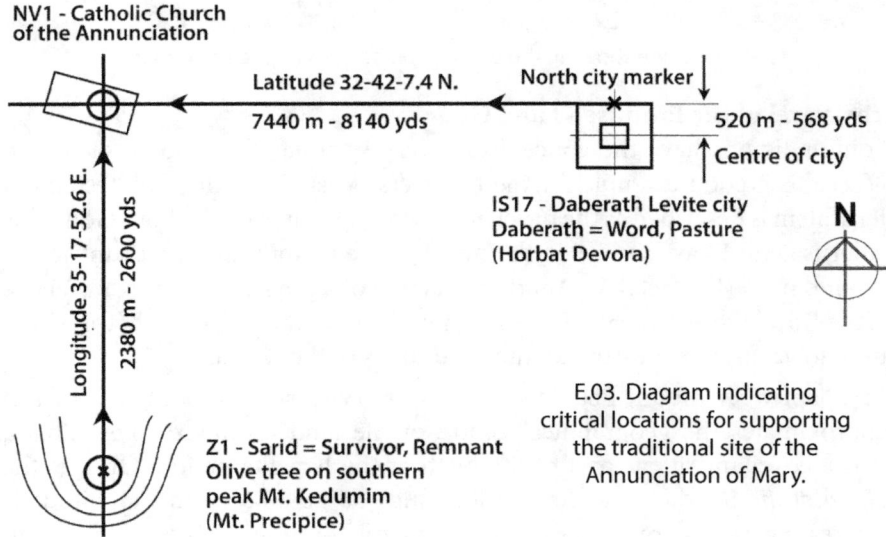

E.03. Diagram indicating critical locations for supporting the traditional site of the Annunciation of Mary.

*Proving Biblical Nazareth*

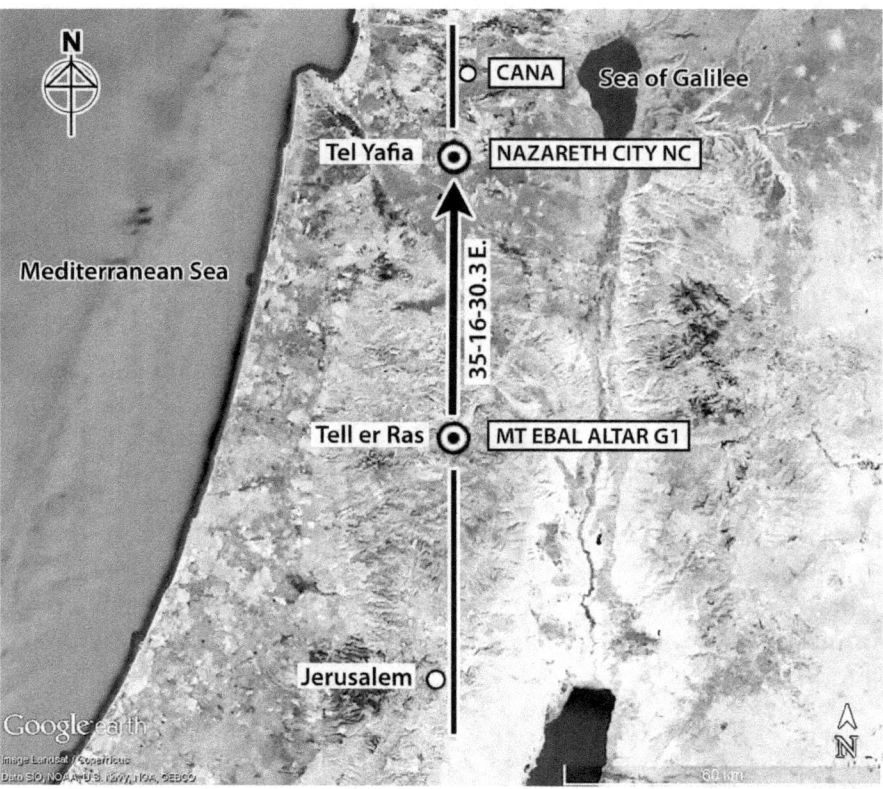

E.04 Longitude showing the connection between three key localities.

**The Navel of the Promised Land G1**

Some religions have the concept of a very spiritual 'focal point' or 'navel'. Mecca, is a good example for the followers of Islam. In the Old Testament Jerusalem is described as the navel of the world: "Thus says the Lord God 'This is Jerusalem; I have set her in the midst of the nations and the countries all around her'" (Ezekiel 5:5). Another example of a physical defining navel site is the Royal Observatory at Greenwich in the UK. The longitude of this site is used to accurately measure all the time zones of the world.

In Chapter 7.1 Mount Ebal is shown as a very spiritual mountain. The site approximates the geographical centre of the land promised to Abraham. It is a covenant site as part of the birth of the Israelite nation. On it is the *Navel of the Land* (Tell er-Ras) at longitude 35-16-30.3 E. This longitude is interesting as it corresponds to two messianic localities. It bisects the urban city of Nazareth and passes close to the western side of the city of Cana.

*Geographic spatial summary*

### Nazareth City
The urban centre is located 68 kilometres (42 miles) due north of Tell er-Ras. The longitude bisects the Franciscan Church compound and for this reason this locality is proposed as a good starting point for seeking the Nazareth synagogue which should be in the southern zone of Tel Yafia.

The longitude also comes nearby to the remains of the Byzantine church of Count Joseph. This has been speculated as a possible locality for the workshop of Saint Joseph. It is a point of interest why he chose that location. The nearby IAA excavations (NC7) did reveal remains of human occupation in the required Early Roman period.

### Cana wedding location Z26
The controversy of the location of Cana has been long-standing. It is the site of Jesus' first public messianic miracle. However, with the information provided by Josephus a more reliable nomination has been made. The wedding logistics explained in the text give support for a location just west of the city of Cana. The location is bisected by the longitude of Tell er-Ras. This gives another locality for investigation.

### The locality of the Transfiguration T1
The case for traditional Mount Tabor as the site of the Transfiguration is strong. A location due east of urban Nazareth city is supported and the preference is somewhere near the southern part of the Orthodox compound of Saint Elias. This location is also supported as it is due south of the city of Joshua named as Japhia which means "God shines" in Hebrew. A case can be made that it is a prophetic signpost to the account of Jesus' meeting with Moses and Elijah. Further investigation is required for this locality as there are a number of underground caves in this section of the mountain.

This locale also links by latitude the original city of Nazareth where Jesus pronounced the Gospel of Liberty with the meeting of Moses representing the Law and Elijah that of the Prophets.

### Prophetic site mapping as a research tool
The examples shown in this book indicate the three ways that prophetic site mapping can be used as a research tool:
1. Confirming an existing traditional site, e.g. the Catholic Church of the Annunciation in Nazareth and the location of Levite Daberath.
2. Supporting a particular locality when there are a number of alternative nominations, e.g. the location of Cana of Galilee; a locality for the transfiguration; an explanation for Zebulun's borders of Sarid and Japhia.
3. Helping establish nominations for new sites for further investigation.
    e.g. a locality for the Nazareth Synagogue; a locality for Saint Joseph's workshop and the precinct of a wedding site at Cana.

## Four spiritual sites sharing the same longitude

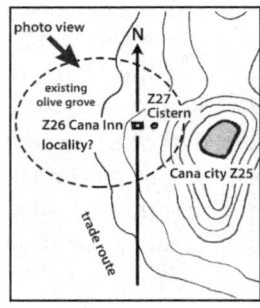 

E.05 Tel Yodfat olive grove looking towards proposed Cana wedding site locality? (Z26)

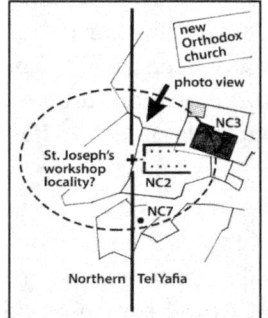 

E.06 Yafia Byzantine Church buried under building (NC2). St. Joseph's workshop locality?

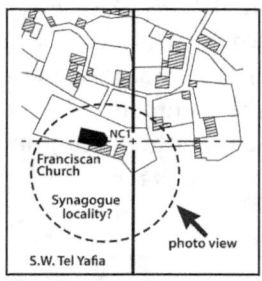 

E.07 Yafia Franciscan Church site. (NC1). Proposed Nazareth Synagogue locality?

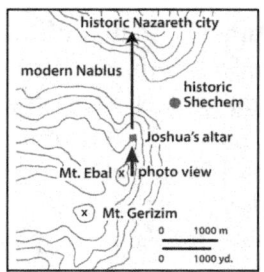 

E.08 Mt. Ebal. Traditional Mt. Gerizim. Joshua's altar proposed on Tell er-Ras knoll (G1).

# E: SUMMARY

1. THE STORY OF NAZARETH
2. SOME REFLECTIONS
3. AFTERWORD
4. CONCLUSIONS

## 1. THE STORY OF NAZARETH

Nazareth can now be summarised with all the sites. The history begins with a very ancient people who settle on a prominent mountain jutting into the Jezreel Valley in Galilee. They are replaced by Canaanites who are descended from Ham, a son of Noah. When Abraham was directed to travel to Canaan, he was given a great promise that his descendants would inherit the Land. Four hundred and seventy years later these descendants cross the Jordan river and claim the Land.

The tribe of Zebulun is given the region known as the Lower Galilee and some begin to settle the hills and valleys of the future Nazareth region. The Levites were given a mandate to stake out their unmoveable markers for their cities, such as Daberath, which were part of the plan of God. There were other sites named as Sarid and Japhia that were to point to aspects of the story of the Messiah and Nazareth later in time.

During the time of the biblical Judges there were many upheavals in the region and eventually King David was victorious in conquering this land. His son Solomon inherited a kingdom that grew in power and influence, but Nazareth was not the location of any great city. By 732 BC the moral decline in northern Israel resulted in a cataclysmic invasion by the Assyrians who leave it desolate, and the vacuum is filled by Gentiles. It is not until the Maccabees' conquest in 101 BC that Israelites return to the Galilee. A group of them known as Nazarenes founded the city of Nazareth on a hill. A pious couple known as Joseph and Mary become residents of a hamlet on the outskirts of the city. This is where the angel Gabriel made his dramatic visit in 4 BC. This was the site of the incarnation of the Messiah.

Jesus grows up in this locality and gains first-hand experience of life as a human. However he is not accepted in Nazareth as the Messiah. This does not stop him fulfilling his mission in the plan of God. His relatives founded a Judeo-Christian church in the hamlet. Despite persecution in the first three centuries AD this location eventually becomes a place of pilgrimage. The Jewish urban centre nearby was eventually destroyed in the seventh century. This resulted in the original Nazareth becoming a lost city and the hamlet site went on preserving the name for countless pilgrims over the centuries.

The original Jewish city site was called Yafa or Japha based on a Medieval tradition. The revival of Palestinian archaeology in the nineteenth century continued this misunderstanding of the site. The story of Nazareth, with the help of its archaeology, and a correct understanding of the Bible, enables the truth to be known. *Nazareth city has been found!*
- Nearly a million people each year visit modern Nazareth from all the nations of the world.

## TABLE 4: Two Nazareths: a summary through time

| Date/ Historical Era* | Nazareth Walled City NC | Nazareth Village NV |
|---|---|---|
| Pre-Canaanite | Prehistoric cave sites at Mt. Kedumim / Precipice nearby both sites | |
| Early Bronze | No occupation | No occupation |
| End Middle Bronze (MBIIC) 1450–1400 BC | Small Israelite hamlet. MBII remains found. | Small Israelite hamlet. MBII remains found. |
| Late Bronze 1400–1120 BC | Small hamlet occupation | Small hamlet occupation |
| Iron Age 1120–732 BC | Small hamlet occupation | Small hamlet occupation |
| Eastern Empires 732–332 | Abandoned | Abandoned |
| Hellenistic 332–63 BC Maccabees about 100 BC | Devout Nazarene Jewish village named Nazareth in 100–80 BC | Small devout Jewish farm area linked to main Nazarene village 2.5km (1.5 mi.) to S.W. |
| Early Roman 63 BC–135 AD Includes Jesus' Era 4 BC–30 AD | Large Jewish walled city named Nazareth starts about 80 BC. City of Joseph and Mary. | Small devout Jewish hamlet of Mary & Joseph 4 BC–27 AD. Becomes Christian after 30 AD. |
| Late Roman 135–325 AD | Decline after 70 AD. Minimal Jewish site affected by two wars. Revived Jewish city after 313 AD. | Small Judeo-Christian hamlet. Jewish & Roman opposition. |
| Byzantine 325–638 AD | 345 AD Count Joseph's church. 377 AD Devout Jewish town. Record of Nazareth priests. 630 AD Dispersal of Jews written by Jewish poet Eleazar ben Killir. | Small Christian 'Village of the Saviour' mentioned by Jerome c. 400 AD. Growth of the city and basilica of Mary's house 570 AD. Growth of pilgrims. |
| Islamic Arab Period (Umayyad, Abbasid) 640–1099 AD | Largely abandoned site with few remains. Memory of the city begins to fade, then lost. | Small Christian village visited by pilgrims. Mentioned in travellers' diaries. |
| Crusader 1099–1291 AD | Small village. Unknown name. Nearby to village 3.2 km (2 mi.) to the north called Japheth in Greek and Ophna in Hebrew. | Large Christian city. Catholic basilica at centre with pilgrims giving descriptions. Destroyed 1263 AD, remains found. |
| Islamic–Medieval (Ayyubid, Mamluk) 1291–1517 AD | Village named Safra and Saron. Proposed tradition of birthplace Apostles James & John. 1350 AD. | Small Christian village noted by pilgrims. |
| Islamic–Ottoman 1517–1917 AD | Village known as Saffa/Safra/Safa Orthodox & Catholic Churches. Robinson endorses as Yafa 1841. | Christian village with some pilgrims. Preliminary surveys by Quaresmius 1626 AD. |
| British Mandate 1917–1948 AD | Christian–Muslim village known as Yafia. 1948 receives many Arab refugees from nearby Mual area. | Christian town of Nazareth. Many pilgrims. Catholic, Orthodox, Protestant churches. |
| Modern Israel 1948 AD – Present | Muslim–Christian suburb of greater Nazareth city. IAA archaeological survey confirms a large Jewish city in 27AD. | Large Israeli city. Major rebuild of Church of the Annunciation in 1968 AD. Large numbers of worldwide pilgrims. |

\* Lower Bronze Age dates by author explained in Appendix 1. Remaining dates from 732 BC are based on Murphy-O'Connor, J Oxford Archaeological Series, op. cit., pp. 2-5.

## 2. SOME REFLECTIONS

When the gospel sites are identified this helps to gain a more accurate reconstruction of the events described and enables enriched reflections.

**Answered prayer**

Consider the teenage Mary in her newly made dwelling in an isolated hamlet, a forty minute walk from the main city centre. Her parents had prayed for the location of the dwelling. She had prayed for the coming of the Messiah. Now an angel had appeared within the dwelling!

**The close cousins**

Jesus spent a lot of time with his cousins. They were well known in the large city of Nazareth. When Jesus began his ministry they did not understand him at first (John 7:5) and he was causing some embarrassment (Mark 3:21). Yet they went on after his ascension to be strong leaders in the Church.

**Beware the Jewish stoning place**

The Apostles would know of the attempt to kill Jesus in his home city. Some would even know the location of the execution site. They would be aware of the cost of discipleship as other cities had similar sites for executing heretics.

**A tale to tell travellers**

There was excitement at the Cana inn for a wedding. When the public miracle of turning water into wine occurred it caused quite a reaction. This would result in a strong oral tradition. The many inn visitors on this trade route site would be told of the event. The story would be spread to other countries.

**No doubt in their mind**

The Apostles Peter, James and John had seen the amazing transfiguration of Jesus. As devout Jews they also had seen Moses and Elijah in their spirit bodies. As they began their ministries many people would have asked them questions about Jesus' claim to be the Messiah. They would recall the event and explain it was on a sacred hill called Tabor with no doubt in their mind.

**Facts on the ground**

Luke the historian was an early convert to the Christian faith. Before he began to write his gospel he was determined to check with many witnesses. He also travelled to the Galilee and understood the geography. He visited key sites associated with Nazareth and some associated with Jesus' ministry.

**A profound sermon setting**

Count Joseph had a powerful testimony of becoming what we would call a Messianic Jew. He earnestly desired to build a church at a Jewish Nazareth city site and eventually achieved his aim. Think of some of the sermons that could be preached in that church. How vivid would be some of the New Testament Bible readings?

## 3. AFTERWORD: By a Bible teacher and pastor

At the heart of Biblical prophecy is the voice of God addressing the hearts of people in the 'now' (forth-telling) and the 'then' (fore-telling), which ultimately points to the coming of Jesus as the fulfilment of Messianic promises. This message, when interpreted in connection with other biblical themes, helps us understand what God is saying to his people in the way of encouragement or admonition in their journey with Christ. This book brings more light on the important subject of the first coming of Christ.

As teachers and preachers, we want insights into the text that help our pathway from sound exegesis at our study desk to a powerful exposition to the audience. We are glad of any material that can help in the process. We dig deep to find clues through detailed examination of key words in the text, utilising the Hebrew or Greek texts if we have the facility; by considering the literary elements of genre, poetry and prose; and by examining the historical, geographical, political and cultural background to the passage to enrich our approach. But what if there was another element that we could add – the importance of place and the significance of place that was pronounced by God. The proposals in this book open up a new understanding on this topic.

The Bible has many examples of spiritual sites both specific and implied. Jacob "when he reached a certain place" (Gen. 28:11) dreamt of a ladder connecting heaven and earth with angels ascending and descending on it. Moses was given specific instruction about "the place the Lord your God will choose … to put his name there for his dwelling" (Deut. 12:5). Jesus gave the disciples the Lord's prayer after he had been "praying in a certain place" (Luke 11:1). It seems that God has particular places in mind when he speaks to his people. The examples given in the preceding pages give further proposals to consider.

It is not hard to imagine that places and their alignment with each other could be key pointers to the way God has spoken, and continues to speak to his people, in the same way that God used a star to direct the Magi to find the Christ child (Matthew 2:1-10). In this sense the geographical positioning of certain key sites seems to serve as signposts from God that pointed to the first coming of Christ. This book offers insight into the geography and history of other Biblical sites that relate to the life of Jesus. This is God speaking through time and place. The evidence in this book is affirming as it demonstrates that these sites do exist. It will help teachers and preachers who wish to give added illustrations to their messages.

Rev. H. Frank Eames, ThM, BSc (Hons), GradDipPS, GradDipEd.
Bible College lecturer. Senior pastor, Baptist Churches of South Australia.

## 4. CONCLUSIONS

There were four questions raised in the Preface and concluding responses can be made from them.

### 1. Nazareth city

The biblical city of Nazareth (NC) is located at Tel Yafia, a large Jewish city in Early Roman times. This city named as a polis in the gospel accounts included an urban centre with outlying hamlets and villages. The house of Mary and Joseph is located in a very rural part of the polis that was part of a small dispersed hamlet with few residences. All the archaeology of this locality fully supports this explanation. This information refutes the claims by sceptics that Nazareth was a myth in the time of Jesus.

### 2. Nazareth synagogue

Identifying Nazareth enables a locality for its synagogue to be proposed. Jesus and his family worshipped in this large city synagogue. This has to be a site of great spiritual significance as he announced his claim to be the *Anointed One* of God. The result was an attempt on his life by the rulers of the synagogue. The topography, the archaeology and the prophetic mapping enables a proposal of a locality for investigation.

### 3. Lower Galilee

Solving Nazareth and Yafia (Japhia) enables Zebulun's border sites to be accurately defined. Biblical Japhia can be identified at modern day Ilaniya. This results in establishing the correct location of other sites in the Lower Galilee. One of these is Cana of Galilee, the site of Jesus' first miracle. All these sites can be demonstrated by the archaeology, topographic logic, geography and historical accounts.

### 4. Messianic sites

When the sites are plotted and their Hebrew names understood, some of them can be linked to the Messiah. There are examples of spatial relationships between Old and New Testament sites. This can illustrate how sites can be like signposts to aspects of the life of Jesus Christ as the Messiah. This has profound theological implications in understanding the plan of God over the millennia.

# Summary

This book has information and proposals from the main disciplines of history, archaeology and theology.

### The Bible as a historical source

The biblical sites quoted are shown as logical and reliable geographically. They can also be correlated to other historical sources such as the important record made by Jewish historian Josephus. New Testament descriptions of events and references can be related to the culture and topography of Nazareth and the Galilee. Aspects of Jesus' life are more clearly understood with the examples given.

- Evidence has been shown that the ancient and historic Bible sites quoted are verifiable.

### Archaeology and the Bible

There is much controversy about the relationship of modern archaeology and the Bible. Evidence has been presented to indicate there is not a huge gap in some of the time frames from the Exodus period onwards. Information has been given that some of the traditional archaeological assumptions on sites need to be revised, particularly in the Lower Galilee. More investigation is also recommended at a number of the sites of great spiritual significance.

- Correlations between biblical events and defined archaeological eras can be made.

### Bible site mapping

Bible site identification can be a challenging discipline. Information on the spiritual aspect of this topic has been given to promote more understanding of the subject. It can be shown that some sites are part of a geographical order that is not the product of chance. They are not random or haphazard. Some of the sites can be described as having prophetic relationships. This topic, because of the implications, will generate controversy and debate.

- The spiritual aspect of biblical site mapping can be used to help identify and clarify sites.

## The Divine Plan

The title of this book claims to be proving the history of Nazareth. This is not meant to be presumptuous, but rather a defence of the reliablity of the gospel accounts. This is supported by archaeology and specific historical references. Nazareth is significant in the *salvation plan* of God being the location of the *incarnation* of Jesus Christ. The city synagogue is also the chosen place where he announced the *Gospel of Liberty* in fulfilment of Isaiah's prophecy. These two locations, in conjunction with other sites, illustrate that they are all part of a divine plan over a long period of time. If Jesus is the Messiah it could be expected to find sites that point to future events in his life.

E.09 Interior of the Catholic Church of the Annunciation facing the altar table. The proposed location of the encounter of the angel Gabriel and the Virgin Mary.

# F: APPENDICES

**1. BIBLICAL ARCHAEOLOGY: AN EXPLANATION** — 212
    1.1 The end of the Middle Bronze Age
    1.2 Dating Jericho's tumbling walls

**2. NAZARETH 27 AD: DEMOGRAPHICS AND THE CRITICS** — 217
    2.1 Calculating the city-polis sectors
    2.2 Responding to the critics and sceptics

**3. JOSHUA'S ALTAR: SACRED MT. EBAL** — 222
    3.1 Renewing the covenant: birth of the Israelite nation
    3.2 Ebal as a sacred mountain

**4. SITES OF ZEBULUN: LOWER GALILEE** — 231
    4.1 The border sites: unlocking the Galilee
    4.2 The internal cities: more sites unravelled

**5. BORDER SITES NEAR ZEBULUN** — 235
    5.1 Western border with Asher
    5.2 Southern border with Issachar
    5.3 Northern border with Naphtali

**6. LEVITE CITIES ARCHAEOLOGY** — 238
    6.1 Daberath: on the side of Tabor
    6.2 Jokne'am: the error and the archaeology
    6.3 Kartah: the mystery site

**7. JEWISH FORTIFICATIONS IN LOWER GALILEE** — 241
    7.1 The military logic of the locations
    7.2 Jotapata fortress: the logistics

**8. A CATHOLIC SOURCE FOR BIBLE SITES** — 245

## APPENDIX 1:
## BIBLICAL ARCHAEOLOGY: AN EXPLANATION
### 1.1 The end of the Middle Bronze Age

This appendix shows the required evidence for the sites associated with Joshua. Relevant to this book is the controversy about dating the end of the Middle Bronze Age.[1] Not all scholars agree on historical time frames and the interpretation of remains. One archaeology textbook preface noted commonly accepted dates but also stated that "no effort has been made to impose a rigid dating scheme on contributors".[2] There are *higher* and *lower chronologies* with most eras before the Assyrian invasion of the Northern Kingdom of Israel in 732 BC. The other area of debate is the use of Egyptian chronology which also has variable time frames.[3]

**Exodus Bible dates**

Calculations for biblical events that produce higher and lower proposals fall into two distinct categories for the Israelite Exodus date.

1. Higher chronology, with a date range of 1491–1446 BC. This time frame is accepted by most conservative Bible scholars. The dates are based on an interpretation of 1 Kings 6:1.
2. Lower chronology, with a range from 1290–1230 BC is based on different archaeological assumptions, a key one being the date for a Rameses site.

The low chronology has been challenged by archaeologist Dr Bryant Wood.[4] Bible chronologist Dr F. L. Jones is very emphatic: "Regarding the question as to whether the Exodus was a 15th (early date) or 13th century (late date) BC episode, the biblical evidence unmistakeably places the event in the 15th".[5]

His date for the Exodus is 1491 BC which has also been supported by other scholars and is accepted as correct in this book. This date is much higher than those used by secular scholars, hence the reason for the controversial differences in interpreting evidence. This matter is at the core of the debate.

---

1  Maeir, AM 2000, *Is the Middle Chronology Dead? (or are they all?)*, <www.tau.ac.il/~archpubs/projects/mbsg/maeirlecture.html>.

2  Negev, A and Gibson, S, op. cit., Preface by Shimon Gibson.

3  Rohl, D 1995, *A Test of Time: The Bible From Myth to History*, Random House, London, UK. Archaeologist D. Rohl has put a case to revise down Egyptian chronology by several centuries.

4  Wood, BG 2009, *Recent Research on the Date and Setting of the Exodus*, <www biblearchaeology.org/post/2009/10/19/Recent-Research-on-the-Date-and-Setting-of-the-Exodus.aspx.>.Also Wood, BG 2009, *The Biblical Date for the Exodus is 1446 BC: A Response to James Hoffmeier*, <www.biblearchaeology.org/post/2009/03/30/The-Biblical-Date-for-the-Exodus-is-1446-BC-A-Response-to-James-Hoffmeier.aspx.>. Wood presents the case for the Exodus in 1446 but the biblical date can be computed to slightly higher at 1491 BC.

5  Jones, FN, op. cit., p. 49. My proposal uses the higher Bible chronology of Professor Jones and the lower chronology of conventional archaeology to show Joshua's destruction of Jericho occurs at the end of the Middle Bronze II period.

## Reconstruction of the anchor dates

Comparing the higher biblical dates with the lower archaeology dates show a narrowing of the gap in the following eras. A case for the revision has been given by archaeologists Dr David Livingston and Dr John Bimson. [6]

### 1. The Middle Bronze IIB fortifications

Canaanites, Amorites and Amalekites are responsible for some of the large fortifications in Israel that are dated to the Middle Bronze IIB period. When Moses sent the spies into the Land in 1490 BC they reported back to him that some of the sites were "walled up to heaven" (Deut. 1:28).

### 2. Middle Bronze IIC or Middle Bronze III

The last phase of the Middle Bronze is labelled either as Middle Bronze IIC or Middle Bronze III. This end phase has proved very controversial in archaeological circles. Archaeologist Aren Maeir has concluded: "I believe that the dating of the final portion of the MBII appears at the present time the most problematic". [7]

There is good reason for this as this era involves the conquest of the Land by Joshua and a mixed settlement of Israelites and local Canaanites. There are variations in the dates nominated for the Middle Bronze IIC period. [8] However a growing number of archaeologists now place the end date at 1500 BC. [9] Even more controversial are the proposals by some scholars to go lower by another century (Bimson 1420 BC) and Gasche (circa 1400 BC). [10]

### 3. Conquering the Land of Canaan

From 1451–1445 BC Joshua conquered many sites, but only three were burnt with fire: Jericho (Josh. 6:24), Ai (Josh. 8:28) and Hazor (Josh. 11:11). It took seven years to subdue most of the Land and conduct a land survey.

### 4. Settling the Land

1445–1410 BC was a time of consolidation of settlements and the death of Joshua. The Bible does not record wholesale destruction of all the cities.

---

6  Bimson, J and Livingston, D 1987, 'Redating the Exodus'. *Biblical Archaeology Review*, 13:05.

7  Maeir, AM, op. cit.

8  Dever, WG 1991 'Tell el-Daba and Levantine Middle Bronze Age Chronology: A rejoinder to Manfred Bietak' *Bulletin of the American Schools of Oriental Research*, No. 281, pp. 73–79. MBIIC period M Bietak (1570–1530 BC) WG Dever (1625–1525) listed in Table. Richard, S 2003 *Near Eastern Archaeology: A Reader* Eisenbrauns, p. 83. Dates MBIII from 1650–1550 BC and a transitional phase to Late Bronze 1550–1500 BC.

9  Bunimovitz, Shlomo, 1995, 'On the edge of Empires – Late Bronze Age (1500–1200 BCE)', in Levy, Thomas (ed), *The Archaeology of Society in the Holy Land*, p. 320.

10 Bimson, J and Livingston, D, op. cit. p. 13. Archaeologist Hermann Gasche's lower date for the end of the Middle Bronze era is explained by archaeologist Y. Meitlis http://www.academia.edu/17355528/End_of_Middle_Bronze_Culture_in_Israel.

Unconquered sites were put under tribute, others were taken over by the new arrivals as the original residents fled. This 35-year window is when the Israelites reoccupied some sites but also built new ones. After Joshua died the government went to the tribal elders who were part of the covenant at Sinai. By 1410 BC most of these elders were dead or aged about 100 years. After this a new generation emerged that did not honour the laws of God.

## 5. The cruel invasion of King Cushan

The 1410–1400 BC time frame is a critical anchor period and helps prove the reconciliation of Bible dates with archaeology. One of the foreign people groups were the Hurrians, noted by archaeologist Nadav Na'aman: "in the second half of the fifteenth century BCE, we find that the number of people of northern origin in the population of Palestine has increased significantly". [11]

The judgement of God was in the form of a cruel campaign by invading King Cushan-Rishathaim who oppressed the Land for eight years from 1400–1392 BC. His origin is clear, being Aram Naharayin called *"Syria of the Rivers"* in the Septuagint, which is Upper Mesopotamia. Some nominate he is a Hurrian king who preceded the rise of the Mitanni Empire. This is a good nomination as his name means "Cushan the doubly wicked" (H763) and gives a clue that he was a ruthless ruler who would inflict much grief on the Israelites (Judges 3:8). The anchor period of the Hurrian invasion is found when:

> In Palestine, the transition from the Middle Bronze II to the Late Bronze Age was marked by a severe settlement crisis. All urban centers were destroyed, some were abandoned and resettled much later, and others suffered serious regression. [12]

The Hurrian expansion explains the conclusive *'dark age'* end of the Middle Bronze Age II in the Levant and the beginning of the Late Bronze Age. [13] In Israel it is not the destruction by Joshua as assumed by some scholars.

## 6. The Late Bronze Age

The 1400–1100 BC era is the time of the Judges from Othniel to Samson and is characterised by oscillations from independence to oppression, marked well in the archaeological record. This evidence has led some archaeologists to propose that the Exodus did not occur. Rather, it is suggested, the rise of the kingdom of Israel was the growth of local Israelites against Canaanite tribes and eventually, King David became victorious. The time of the Judges

---

11 Na'aman, N 2005, *Canaan in the Second Millennium BCE*, Eisenbrauns, Winona Lake, Indiana, USA, p. 4.

12 ibid. p.1. The sites defined as destroyed are the full extent of the Promised Land from north to south.

13 Some have mistakenly linked the extensive destruction to the campaign of Joshua or to an invading Egyptian dynasty. The Hurrian invasion of 1400 BC ushers in the Late Bronze age.

details recurrent invasions by Canaanites, Moabites, Midianites, Amalekites, and Philistines. In this period are the *Amarna letters* that record an Egyptian influence in the region. These Egyptians were ethnically and culturally related to the Philistines (Gen. 10:14) so the time of the Philistine oppression can be related to the Egyptian influence found in the archaeological profile.[14]

### 7. The Iron Age revision

The start of the Iron Age is debated. Conventional dating of the Iron Age starts at 1200 BC, but some archaeologists have advocated a lowering of the date by at least 70–80 years which gives a date of 1130/1120 BC.[15]

## 1.2 Dating Jericho's tumbling walls

The story of the walls of Jericho coming down fascinates, with the claim that the activity of the worshipping Israelites caused a seismic vibration that results in part of the massive walls collapsing (Joshua 6:20). The debate is over the time frame and the archaeological period (*refer* Table 5).

**Archaeological dating**

Archaeologist Kathleen Kenyon concluded that the City IV at Tel Sultan was definitely destroyed at the end of the Middle Bronze IIB/C period and this is supported by many archaeologists.[16] Kenyon's date was 1550 BC but more recently other scholars have lowered the time frame of this period by 50 years. My conclusion accepts this is the correct archaeological period but the time frame needs to be reduced by another 50 years. The destruction in 1451 BC is in the Middle Bronze IIC or MBIII period (1500–1400 BC).

F.01 Tel Sultan
31-52-16 N. 35-26-38.6 E.
is ancient Jericho.
Evidence of the broken walls have been found on the western side near the line of palm trees.

---

14 Rohl, D, op. cit., pp. 225–257. Rohl explains the correlations of the Levant to the start of the United Kingdom of Saul. Another thesis would link King David's early era to that of Akhenaten.
15 Sapir-Hen L, Bar-Oz, G, Gadot, Y and Finkelstein, I 2013. *Pig Husbandry in Iron Age Israel and Judah* Zeitschrift des Deutschen Palastina-Vereins 129(1), p. 4. Israel Finkelstein also confirmed his dates by personal correspondence to the author via email dated 15 Oct. 2014.
16 Bienkowski, Piotr 1990. 'Jericho was destroyed in the Middle Bronze Age, Not the Late Bronze Age', *Biblical Archaeology Society*, 16:05.

**TABLE 5: Proposed Jericho time frame**

| Bible date BC | Archaeo. period | Jericho Events: Tel Sultan |
|---|---|---|
| 1550 | MB IIB | Prosperous Canaanite and Amorite city with large walls. |
| 1491 | MB IIB–C | Rahab the resident of Jericho states that due to the Exodus it caused great fear in Jericho (Joshua 2:10). Probably resulted in hasty efforts to raise the walls and evidence of this has been found. |
| 1451 | MB IIC or MB III | A collapse of the walls on western side. A massive destruction of the city and it is burnt. Clear evidence of this has been found. Joshua puts a curse on the site and it is abandoned (Joshua 6:26). |
| 1400–1300 | LB I | King Cushan and his army invade and oppress the Israelites 1400–1392 BC. The start of the Late Bronze era. The Moabite king Eglon invades Israel. He establishes his HQ at Jericho 1360–1342 BC. A large eroded building dating to this era has been found. |
| 1300–1200 | LB II | Minimal remains. |
| 1200–1100 | LB III | Egyptian influence in Israel as part of the Philistine oppressions. Scarabs of Tutmosis IV and Amenhotep III are found in burial sites at Jericho which was used as a cemetery. |
| 1100–1000 | Iron IA–B | King David asks his servants to camp at Jericho 1038 BC. It is not a city but a campsite. Limited remains in this era. |
| 1000–586 | Iron IIA–B–C | The reign of King Ahab is 918 to 897 BC. During his reign Hiel of Bethel attempts a rebuild in defiance of Joshua's curse (1 Kings 16:34). This Iron Age II site suffers judgement. Later references to Jericho are not the Tel Sultan site. |

## Radiocarbon dating

This is not the place for debating the tolerances and accuracy of radiocarbon dating, but it must be noted there are variables in calibration curves.[17] It also has been pointed out "that there are periods with a considerable difference between radiocarbon and historical chronology which cannot be denied nor be reconciled at the moment".[18] For example, the radiocarbon range for burnt wheat at Jericho in the MBIIB destruction layer is upper (1601–1556 BC) and lower (1561–1524 BC).[19] This gives a range of 77 years from the same burnt sample and the lower reading is only 73 years from the biblical date of 1451 BC.

---

17 Singer-Avitz, L 2011, 'Does Radiocarbon Dating Accuracy Help Us Determine Bible Chronology?' *Biblical Archaeology Society*. <www.biblicalarchaeology.org/daily/ancient-cultures/ancient-israel/does-radiocarbon-dating-accuracy-help-us-determine-bible-chronology/>.

18 Bietak, M and Höflmayer, F 2007 *Introduction: High and Low Chronology*, Verlag der Österreichischen Akademie der Wissenschaften, p. 13.

19 Bruins, HJ and van der Plicht, J 1995, 'Tell Es-Sultan (Jericho): Radiocarbon Results of Short-Lived Cereal and Multiyear Charcoal Samples From the End of the Middle Bronze Age', *Proceedings of the 15th International 14C Conference*, p. 219.

# APPENDIX 2
# NAZARETH 27 AD: DEMOGRAPHICS AND THE CRITICS
## 2.1 Calculating the city-polis sectors

It is possible to determine an estimate of the total 27 AD population of the city (polis) of Nazareth based on a range of criteria. Key information is found in a book on the demographics of Galilean settlements in the Early Roman period.[1] The total population can be divided into two categories.

1. The urban city centre was estimated by Z. Gal as 5 hectares or 12.5 acres (50 dunams).[2] It can be further subdivided into the walled section at the peak and the inner suburbs on the slopes adjacent.
2. The surrounding villages and hamlets that were linked to the city centre.

**Nazareth walled sector**

Based on the topographical contour of the top plateau this is just under half of the urban area calculated as 20 dunams, 2 hectares, or 6.25 acres. With a circular shape this creates a perimeter of about 500 metres (546 yards). Proposed density is 400 persons per hectare, 160 persons per acre, or 40 persons per dunam giving a total population = 800 people.[3] The number of households is 160 if average household size is 5 persons per unit.[4] This translates as 320 adults and 480 under the age of 20 years.

**Nazareth suburbs**

The extent of the suburbs can be estimated. The density of this zone would also vary depending on the residences and their associated activity.

1. Inner suburbs based on Gal's survey is 30 dunams at density of 25 = 750.
2. Outer suburbs 25 dunams at density of 18 = 450 (est. as no survey done).

Total suburban population of 1,200 residents giving about 240 households which computes to 480 adults and 720 under the age of 20 years.

**Nazareth villages and hamlets**

Estimating the rural population is more difficult with various criteria used by demographers. The approach used is to assume the total Galilean population is 300,000 people.[5] The area of the Galilee has been digitally measured as

---

1 Fiensey, D and Strange, J 2014 *Galilee in the Late Second Temple and Meshanaic Periods*, op. cit.
2 Gal, Z, op. cit.
3 Fiensey, D, op. cit. p. 182, Footnote 25.
4 ibid., p. 182, Footnote 25. This figure is conservative but is used for this calculation.
5 There is a wide range quoted by scholars for the first century population of Galilee. Beloch gave a high figure of 400,000. Prof. C. McCown calculated a figure of 100,000, based on 150 people per square mile. Meyer had a range of 150–175,000. Harold Hoehner had a figure of 200,000. Josephus gave a figure of 41,200 at Jotapata and 17,150 at Japhia in the final battles.

2,073 sq. km (800 sq. miles).[6] This gives an average of 145 people per square kilometre for the Galilee. An estimate of the Nazareth polis region based on Illus. F.02 shows it is approximately 35 sq. km (8,650 acres) giving a total of 5,075 residents. If 2,000 are in the urban area then a figure of about 3,000 could be in villages and hamlets. Five villages of 600 residents would justify this, and possible sites are shown on map F.02.[7] This reflects the balance of the city-rural dynamic which was one of the features of a Jewish polis.

**Conclusion:** The total population of the city-polis of Nazareth is about 5,000 people. This can be estimated as 2,000 adults and 3,000 under the age of 20. This can now be compared with the sizes calculated for other Galilean cities and villages.

**TABLE 6: Galilean site demographics**

| No. of sites (1) | Acres (1) | Hectares | Population (1) | Hebrew | Greek | English |
|---|---|---|---|---|---|---|
| 5 | 0.5 | 0.2 | 80 | Kaphar | Chorio (2) | Hamlet |
| 14 | 1.7 | 0.7 | 300 | Kaphar | Kome | Village |
| 8 | 3.7 | 1.5 | 592 | Kaphar | Kome | Village |
| 7 | 7.5 | 3.0 | 1,200 | Ir | Polis | City |
| 4 | 12.5 | 5.0 | 1,900 (3) | Ir | Polis | City |
| 2 | 18.7 | 7.6 | 3,000 | Kerak | Polis | Large City |

(1) Figures from Fiensey, D, op.cit., p. 184. Liebner, U, op.cit., p. 8.
(2) Mikro chorio is Greek for a hamlet.
(3) This is the same size as Nazareth urban sector estimated at 2,000 people.

This shows that Nazareth was a good sized city by Galilean standards and therefore a quite identifiable known location in Early Roman times.

### Nazareth Synagogue attendees

An estimate of the attendees of the Nazareth City synagogue can be made. Being a Jewish polis would assume most were in attendance at some time on the Sabbath. It includes the teenagers, over the age of twelve years. Children

---

(5 cont.) This would mainly be adults and would include some from surrounding areas. The two large cities of Sepporis and Tiberias estimated each at 10–15,000 or higher. This gives a total of 88,350 for just four of the sites. The figure of 300,000 people has been based on the range given by scholars and Josephus' figures.

6  Fiensey, D, op. cit., p. 265.

7  The potential five village sites shown in Illus. F.02 adjacent. They are (1) Iksal east of Sarid, (2) Khashash at SW foot of Sarid, (3) Junjar (Ginegar) SW of Yafia and (4) Mujeidil west of Yafia. (5) Makbiyeh near Ein es Sufsafeh. Note that the hamlet of Joseph and Mary is not included as it is a very minor hamlet. The rural population of 3,000 is equivalent of 600 families. The average size of first century family rural allotment can be estimated as 30–40 dunams. (Pastor, J 1997 *Land and Economy in Ancient Palestine*, Routledge London, UK. p. 9) This would require 18–24,000 dunams. Nazareth city limits is 35,000 dunams (35 sq. km.) This gives a 50–70% arable requirement which is reasonable for the locality.

under that age would be minded by friends and relatives on a rotating roster. Large villages could have their own synagogue. Using the figures given above a calculation can be made. The urban population of 2,000 people is estimated as 400 households (800 adults and 1,200 under 20 years). The under 20 age averages 60 per year so the teenage population becomes 8 years x 60 = 480.

This gives a combined synagogue population of about 1,280 attendees for the Sabbath period. If seating was provided for about 400 then three or four services would be required. Full capacity of 426 people with three sessions, evening, morning, and afternoon services. A generous capacity of 320 people requires four sessions between the two sunsets.

**The Rabbis of Nazareth**

A congregational population of about 1,280 with a ratio of one rabbi for every hundred attendees could require at least thirteen to be based in Nazareth. This can be compared to a modern day congregation ratio (ideal average) of one clergy or rabbi for a hundred members. The central headquarters would probably give support to the five associated villages' synagogues. Added to this would be several officers and a few administrators. The total eldership and administration could be in the order of at least 20–25 men.

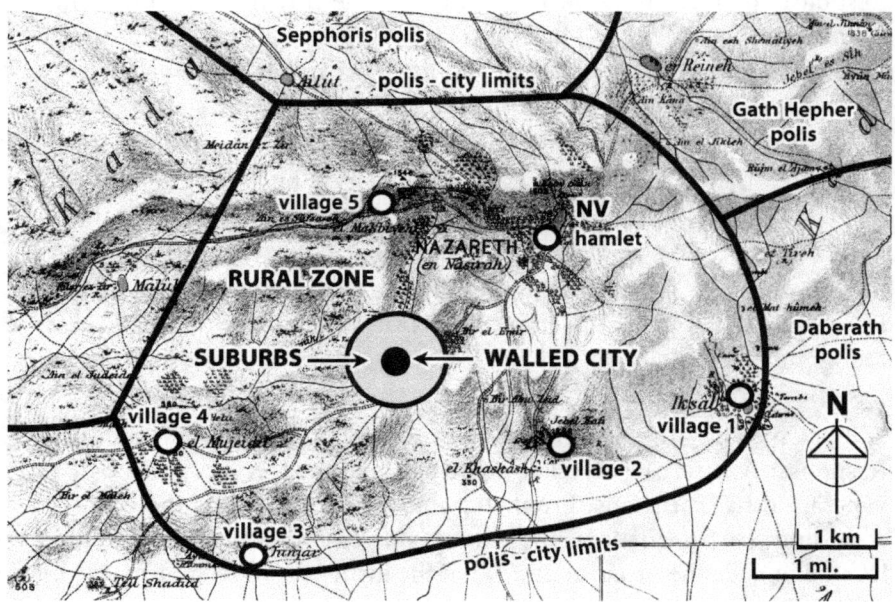

F.02 Proposed boundary map of Nazareth polis showing the relationship between the urban centre and five adjacent rural villages. PEF base map.

## 2.2 Responding to the critics and sceptics

Claims have been made about the traditional hamlet of Mary and Joseph. The following is a summary of responses to questions raised by critics.

**1. There is no mention of Nazareth in the Old Testament.**
Response: This is not a critical issue for it to be the site of the Incarnation. It is not mentioned, as the two Nazareth sites were small hamlets in Joshua's time. Nazareth city was a revived village after a long period of abandonment and it was built after 100 BC, so it could not be listed in the Old Testament.

**2. There is no archaeological evidence of a city of Nazareth.**
Response: There is ample Early Roman archaeological evidence for the required era at Tel Yafia. It was incorrectly nominated by scholars in the nineteenth century as Japhia was based on a mistaken Medieval assumption.

**3. There is no evidence of a Jewish city at traditional Nazareth.**
Response: It is agreed there is no city at the place of Jesus' residence but there was a large Jewish city centre within short walking distance. The hamlet of Nazareth has archaeological remains of the Early Roman era and is within the outer city boundaries of Nazareth polis as required by the gospels.

**4. Nazareth was a Jewish town with few Christians for many centuries.**
Response: By identifying two separate sites the true history can be shown. Both have the same name but they are separate groups. The city site stays Jewish until 630 AD. The Christian hamlet–village site starts small, but grows slowly over time. Historical records can explain why there are two sites.

**5. The threat to kill Jesus was caused by a small group of fellow villagers.**
Response: The threat to kill was real and caused by a big group of people from a large city. There was a large school of rabbis (probably Pharisees) in that city who were known to have questionable ethics by other Galileans.

**6. Nazareth village was near Japhia the site of a massacre in 67 AD.**
Response: Locating Japhia near the Nazareth area does not make sense topographically based on Joshua's list. It also does not have logic based on Josephus' account. An alternative site for Japhia can be shown.

**7. The Church of the Annunciation is not Mary's residence location.**
Response: A case can be made that this site is correct as a place of early veneration by Christians. Prophetic pointers indicate it as the correct site regarding the Incarnation. There are good reasons why the residence was located outside the urban centre when the history is understood.

## Was Nazareth an elaborate conspiracy?
Some sceptics have said biblical Nazareth was concocted or "invented" to relate to a later era site.[8] This can be shown as a false claim and there is no evidence in support of it. They appeal to the small number of documents outside the gospels mentioning the name to suggest it did not exist in the time of Jesus. This is the *evidence from silence* fallacy being demonstrated.

### 1. The archaeology.
The archaeological evidence clearly shows there was a Jewish city nearby the residence of Mary and Joseph. This site of Tel Yafia is not Japhia.

### 2. Roman Law.
Pilate placed on the Cross "Jesus of Nazareth King of the Jews". This was a legal act under Roman Law. Pilate would not do that if Nazareth did not exist. What would the Roman authorities say post 30 AD if the plaque text was indeed made up by the gospel writers?

### 3. First Century critics.
Aspects of Jesus' life were circulated in Palestine well before the close of the first century. Any glaring fabrications would come under the attention of hostile Jews or Romans. No evidence denying Nazareth has been found.

### 4. Second and third century persecution.
These two centuries were a time of great persecution. In such times the truth is important for a person who may be martyred. A conspiracy would be very risky. To claim Nazareth was a conspiracy would also involve a cover-up by many people from different cultures and countries.

### 5. Testimony of historians.
In 220 AD, Nazareth, where Jesus' relatives lived, was recorded by a visitor Africanus and confirmed by Eusebius. It was visited by Jerome in 380 AD.

### 6. Sceptics accept a Jewish City named Nazareth.
If Nazareth was "invented" when was this done? We even have the sceptics mentioning a town of Nazareth that was occupied by Jews with priestly functions in the fourth century. When was that site created? If it was the second or third century what was the name of Early Roman "Nazareth"?

### 7. What would be a motive for a conspiracy?
A claim of a conspiracy requires a motive by the originators. Some sceptics say it was the link to the *Nazarene* concept. The question is, what would be the motive for all four gospel writers? What would be the intent?

---

8 Salm, R *The Myth of Nazareth*. op. cit., p. xvi.

# APPENDIX 3
# JOSHUA'S ALTAR: SACRED MT. EBAL
## 3.1 Renewing the Covenant: birth of the Israelite Nation

This appendix gives more evidence on a covenant site of importance to Israelites and Samaritans. When Abraham made his journey into the Land of Canaan he camped close to Shechem (the valley of modern Nablus with two peaks named Ebal and Gerizim nearby). God gave him the covenant promise of the Land (Gen. 12:6–7). When Moses gave his final exhortation to Joshua before they crossed over the Jordan River they were instructed to do several important things involving an extension of that covenant.

**1. First day:** After crossing the Jordan on arrival at Gilgal near Jericho they were to make memorial stone slabs with the whole of God's Law inscribed on them (Deut. 27:2–3). This was 80,000 words which could be on twelve stones. This makes the stones a good size to have about 6,600 words each.

**2. Mount Ebal consecration:** After establishing themselves they were to travel to Mt. Ebal and make an altar and place the memorial stones of the Law there. This act of consecration makes Mt. Ebal a very important sacred mount. It is significant that they were told to rejoice at this sacred location.

> Therefore it shall be, when you have crossed over the Jordan, that on Mount Ebal, you set up these stones which I command you this day, and you shall whitewash them with lime. And you shall build an altar to the Lord your God, an altar of stones, you shall not use an iron tool on them ... You shall offer peace offerings, and shall eat there, and *rejoice before the Lord* your God (Deut. 27:4–8). [italics added]

**3. Covenant ceremony:** Following the consecration they were to relocate, with six tribes standing on the slopes of Mount Ebal and six tribes standing on the slopes of Mount Gerizim. The Ark of God and the Levites were at the saddle junction between the two assemblies. Each group made covenant declarations involving either blessings or curses (*refer* Illus. F.04):

> And Moses commanded the people on the same day, saying "These shall stand on Mount Gerizim to bless the people ... and these shall stand on Mount Ebal to curse" (Deut. 27:11–13).

Moses' instructions were carried out on the two peaks of Mount Ebal and Gerizim by Joshua:

> Now Joshua built an altar to the Lord of Israel in Mount Ebal as Moses the servant of the Lord had commanded the children of Israel, ... an altar of whole stones over which no man has wielded an iron tool. And they offered on it burnt offerings to the Lord; and sacrificed peace offerings. And there in the presence of the children of Israel he wrote on the stones a copy of the law of Moses ... Then Israel, with all their elders and offices and judges,

stood on either side of the ark ... Half of them in front of Mount Gerizim and half of them in front of Mount Ebal (Joshua 8:30–33).

This denotes sites of renewing the covenant and the birth of the Israelite nation. The key question is where was the altar on Mount Ebal? Josephus informs us that the site, according to him, was not used again for sacrifice after the first event (*Ant.* 4.8.44).

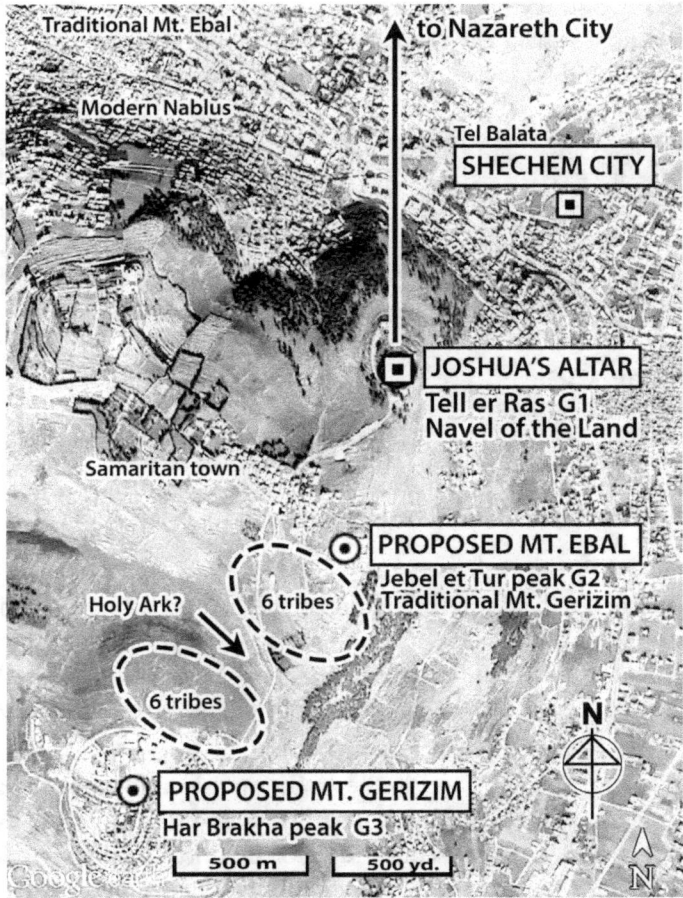

F.03 Map showing proposed Mt. Ebal and Mt. Gerizim. Tell er-Ras is part of sacred Mt. Ebal and aligns exactly with the centre of biblical Nazareth. Base map Google Earth. Image © 2016 DigitalGlobe.

## Identifying Mount Ebal and Mount Gerizim

A long tradition has proposed Mount Gerizim to be on the south side of Tel Balata (Levite Shechem) in modern Nablus. The Samaritans, historically and even today, honour traditional Mount Gerizim as sacred. This results in Ebal being allocated to the large mountain to the north of Tel Balata.

- There is no evidence of a significant altar on traditional Mt. Ebal in the required end of the Middle Bronze period (MBIIC). There is a debatable site said to be an altar on the north-east side of the hill, but it dates to the later Iron Age.[1] This site has not been accepted by all scholars.[2]
- The logic given with the traditional nominations is the 500 m (546 yds) proximity of the two mountains at a narrow pass at the eastern end of Nablus suggesting the two large congregations of Israelites facing each other are able to hear each other's responses in the ceremony. The desired acoustics would be helpful but indistinct for the whole distance involved.

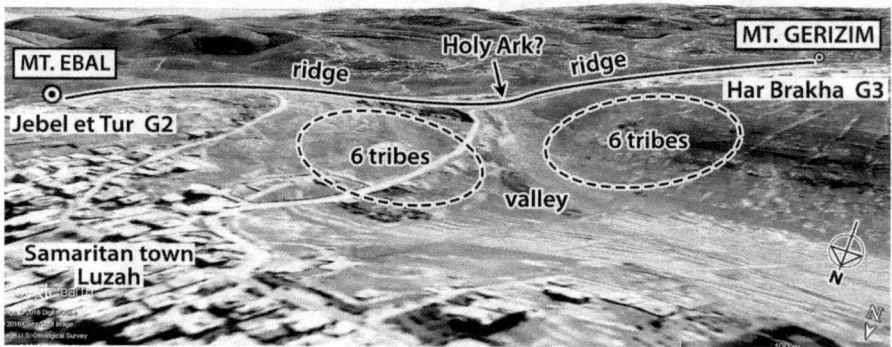

F.04 Proposed Mt. Ebal and Gerizim where six tribes of Israel gathered facing each other and made a covenant with God. Base map Google Earth. Image © 2016 DigitalGlobe.

### Alternative proposal

There is another radical interpretation of the location for the required two peaks. An analysis of the large massif to the south of ancient Shechem reveals two prominent peaks of about the same altitude (880 metres, 2880 ft.). It can be shown that they meet the biblical requirements (*refer* Illus. F.03–F.04).

**1. Jebel et Tur (G2)** peak at 32-12-4.3 N. and 35-16-24.9 E. It is commonly known as Mount Gerizim and is the traditional location of the Samaritan Mount of Blessing. However this is not correct and it is proposed as Joshua's Mount Ebal. Located on the same ridge to the north of the peak is a knoll called Tell er-Ras (830 metres) with evidence of an ancient sacred site.

**2. Har Brakha (G3)** peak at 32-11-38 N. and 35-15-53.4 E. This means in Hebrew *Mount of Blessing*. It is proposed that this peak is the original Mt. Gerizim of Joshua and the modern naming of the mount is correct. Har Gerizim means in Hebrew *Mount of the Cutoff* (H1630). It currently has a Jewish settlement on the peak.

---

1 Zertal, A 2016, *Mount Ebal – A stone mound on the notheastern ridge*, <ebal.haifa.ac.il/ebal01.html>.

2 Various articles have appeared in *Biblical Archeological Society Review* debating this site.

This explanation enables the assembly of the six tribes on either side of the Ark of God and the Levites. Between Har Brakha and Jebel et Tur is a wide valley with gentle slopes. The location easily contains the required space for a large group of people to assemble and to hear each others benedictions. The saddle ridge connection shown in F. 04 would be ideal for the Ark.

### Joshua's Altar on Gerizim or Ebal?

The Hebrew Masoretic text clearly supports the altar on Mount Ebal but the Samaritan text has the opposite. It reads:

> Therefore it shall be when ye be gone over Jordan, (that) ye shall set up these stones, which I command you this day, in Mount Gerizim, and thou shalt plaster them with plaster. And there shalt thou build an altar unto the LORD thy God, an altar of stones (Deut. 27:4–5). [3]

The whole passage reads the same as the Hebrew Masoretic except Gerizim is substituted for Ebal. The immediate question is which text is correct? This has engaged scholars for many centuries. It is proposed that the text of the Samaritans was changed about the time of the institution of their monotheistic priesthood in circa 445 BC. Their settlement involved Jews expelled from Judea who became Samaritans (Nehemiah 13:28). However, while preserving the sacredness of the mount the original name was lost, either by design, or by misunderstanding, due to the occupation gap of the Exile.

## 3.2 Ebal as a sacred mountain

Ebal can be given a number of meanings including bald, stony and heap (H5858). It can mean the *'Mount of the stone pile'*. However it must be emphasised that Mount Ebal was not an evil or cursed mountain. It is a hill that showed the outcome of rejecting God's Law, with the inscribed stones as a reminder warning of a consequent curse. The fact that it had an altar was to point to the grace and mercy of God who provides an answer to the effects of sin. Mt. Ebal must be understood as a *Mount of Grace and Mercy* requiring an acceptable sacrifice and to *"rejoice before the Lord"* (Deut. 27:8).

### Proof of Mount Ebal and the Navel of the Land

An important part of the evidence for the proposal is an account in Judges 9:35–37. Two observers named Gaal and Zebul in the city of Shechem (Tel Balata) were witnessing a two pronged attack on the city by King Abimelech from the south (*refer* Illus. F.05–F.06).

- Gaal exclaimed, "Look, people are coming down from the tops of the mountains", to which Zebul said, "You see the shadows of the mountains as if they are men." This can only be understood with the mountain to

---

3   Interlinear Pentateuch 2016 'Deuteronomy 27:1–15', *Interlinear Pentateuch*, y2 <sites.google.com/site/interlinearpentateuch/deuteronomy-devarim/chapter-27-1-15>.

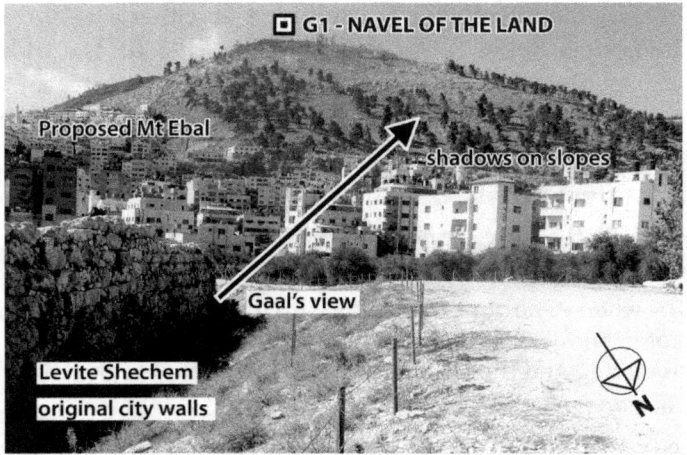

F.05 The tree shadow movement on proposed Mount Ebal. Viewed from Shechem city it is on the southern side of the Nablus valley as required in the account in Judges Chap. 9.

the south casting a shadow on the northern slopes of traditional Mount Gerizim with the observers at Tel Balata. A crucial description.[4]

- Gaal again replies and says, "See people are coming down from the center of the land". The Hebrew words for centre of the land are *Tabbur Erets* which means *Navel of the Land*. Scholars have debated this text and in the Greek LXX it is *"omphalos"* which means *navel* and implies a central marker. It makes sense that this was a reference to the sacred altar site of Joshua which would be truly the *Navel of the Land* recalling the ceremony.

This early morning description makes sense from the solar movement and the city location. The altar and compound of Joshua were a defining location in the centre of the Promised Land both physically and spiritually. *It shows convincing evidence why Mount Ebal must be south of Shechem.*

Ironically even to this day it is stated; "According the Samaritan chronicles, Mount Gerizim is the place where Joshua erected the stones on which he wrote the law and built an altar".[5]

F.06 View from the 'Navel of the Land' on Mt. Ebal towards Shechem (Tel Balata centre circled).

---

4  1,000 m (1,093 yd.) to the south-west of the observer and 280 m (918 ft.) above on Mt. Gerizim.

5  The-samaritans.com. 2016, 'The Twelve Stones' *Mount Gerizim and the Samaritans*, <www.the-samaritans.com/mount_gerizim/>.

*Joshua's altar – sacred Mt. Ebal*

F.07 Tell er-Ras. It is proposed this is the site of Joshua's altar and two subsequent sacred temple buildings.

### Joshua's sacred Altar and Memorial compound (G1)

Proposed location: Tell er-Ras 32-12-25 N. and 35-16-30.3 E.

Located on the northern ridge of Jebel et-Tur overlooking modern Nablus. A visit to this knoll shows why Joshua would choose it as a sacred site. The position has commanding views over a vast area and is strategically located. It was also located within the boundaries of the Levite city of Shechem; the Levites would be the guardians of the precinct. A survey done by American archaeologist Robert Bull in 1964–66 identified two building platforms labelled as A and B.[6] It can be explained in four stages (*refer* Illus. F.08).

**1. Joshua's sacred compound:** Proposed as a structure of ramp and elevated altar platform made with natural unhewn stones. A compound of standing stone blocks rendered with lime and Moses' Law inscribed on them. No remains have been confirmed as any stones of this complex would be buried under the subsequent Building B. This building was exposed in the survey but unfortunately not penetrated to establish what may be within or under it on the inside.[7]

**2. Building B:** This structure was of semi-hewn stones and therefore not Joshua's structure. It is proposed that this was the platform of a Samaritan Temple as it was built on bedrock.

- It was recorded as built in 328 BC "which Alexander (the Great) permitted" and stood for "two hundred years" (*Ant.* 13.9.1).

---

6   Bull, R 1968, 'The Excavation of Tel er-Ras on Mt. Gerizim', *The Biblical Archaeologist*, vol XXXI, no. 2, < https://www.jstor.org/stable/i361169>.

7   ibid., p. 63.

*Proving Biblical Nazareth*

- It originally was called by the Samaritans the *Temple of the Unknown God*. In circa 166 BC they sought the consent of Antiochus IV Epiphanes to rededicate their temple "which at present hath no name at all be named the Temple of Jupiter Hellenius" (*Ant.* 12.5.5).
- The archaeologist of the excavation raised "the possibility that it is the remains of the Samaritan temple".[8] The Temple structure was demolished in 128 BC by John Hyrcanus (*Ant.* 13.9.1).

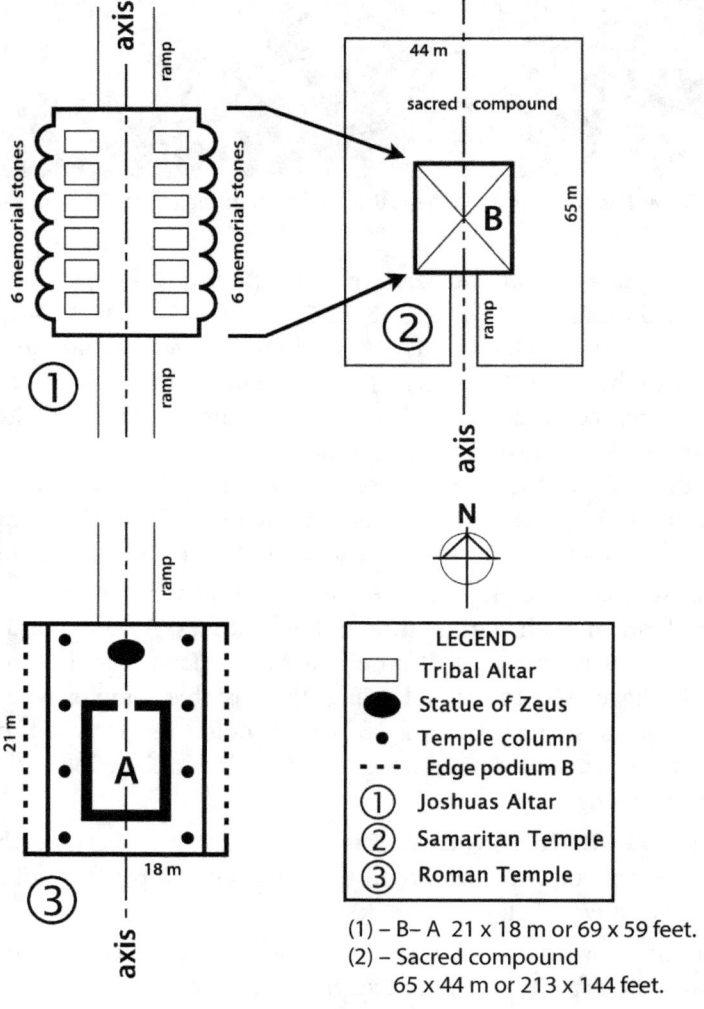

(1) – B– A  21 x 18 m or 69 x 59 feet.
(2) – Sacred compound
      65 x 44 m or 213 x 144 feet.

F.08 No.1 Joshua's Mt. Ebal site of 12 stones cluster ( Law inscribed), 12 tribal altars on top.
   No. 2 Samaritan temple built over 12 stone site (Building B) in a walled compound.
   No.3 Temple of Zeus (Building A) above podium of Building B in same compound.

---

8   ibid. p. 71.

**3. Building A:** The top of the tel is a large stone platform of dressed masonry. It was built over the remains of Building B which was covered in Roman concrete to provide a base. It supported the well known and documented *Temple of Jupiter* built in 135 AD with the consent of Emperor Hadrian after the Bar Kokhba Revolt. The monumental temple is depicted on Neapolis coins dated from 138–253 AD and mentioned by a Samaritan scholar Marinus in 440 AD (*refer* coin below). It was clearly a pagan temple site with a grand stairway access up the northern slopes of the mount from the Roman city of Neapolis below.[9]

Zeus temple and altar at the rear

Samaritan temple on adjacent peak

Large staircase

Neapolis colonnade

F.09 Roman coin showing the Temple of Zeus at Mt. Ebal. Note the statue depicted at the entrance. Also the large staircase from the city below to the front of the temple.
Image from Archaeology report. Bull, Robert op. cit. p. 60.
Courtesy American Society of Oriental Research. Article available on JSTOR.

## The sacred peak of Gerizim (G2)

There are two sacred temple sites on traditional Mt. Gerizim. The second one was the Samaritan Temple at the centre of their community on the peak. The archaeology report shows this temple and precinct dated to about 445 BC in the time of Nehemiah the archaeological Persian Period.[10] The survey showed remains that had features in "imitation of the temple in Jerusalem" (*Wars* 1.2.6). The peak has revealed remains of an extensive city in Hellenistic times before its destruction by John Hyrcanus in 128 BC. This peak was the scene of many subsequent battles. In 36 AD Roman Governor Pilate ordered a massacre there and in 67 AD Roman General Vespasian killed 11,600 Samaritans fleeing from battle. In the Byzantine era there were revolts by the Samaritans who still saw the peak as sacred and a rally point for battles against the rule of Constantinople.

---

9   Negev, A and Gibson, S, *Archaeological Encyclopedia of the Holy Land*, op. cit., p. 19.

10  Magen, Y 2015, *The Sacred Precinct on Mount Gerizim*, <www.biblearchaeology.org/post/2015/01/31/>.

### A Samaritan woman and Jesus at the Well of Jacob

The woman said to Him, "Sir, I perceive that you are a prophet. Our fathers worshipped on this mountain and you Jews say that in Jerusalem is the place where one ought to worship." Jesus said to her, "Woman, believe Me, the hour is coming when you will neither on this mountain, nor in Jerusalem, worship the Father" (John 4:19–21).

This famous encounter near the well of Jacob makes reference to a mountain sacred to the Samaritans in 27 AD with historic places of worship. It is clearly traditional Mt. Gerizim with two dedicated sacred sites on the ridge. Jesus was making reference to a new era when the Christian Church would see worship as a matter of the Holy Spirit, not limited to a geographical sacred site.

### Summary

- Tell er-Ras is on the same longitude as the biblical city of Nazareth centre.
- Tell er-Ras is Joshua's altar and stone memorial which makes Mount Jebel et-Tur (traditional Gerizim) sacred. The Samaritans have preserved this even if the naming of Ebal was changed.
- Jebel et-Tur is sacred in the Hebrew Bible as Mount Ebal. It is the *Navel of the Promised Land*. An altar and memorial covenant site showing the grace of God that can cover the curses of sin.
- The proposal illustrated in F.08 is that 12 stones were aligned together to form a platform. There are about 80,000 words in Moses Law so a total of twelve large stones would be required representing each tribe. The large platform would allow 12 sub-altars, one for each tribe, to facilitate the sacrifice ceremony involving a large number of people over several days.
- The internal examination of the base of Building B was not done by the archaeologist. Any natural stones from Joshua's altar would be hard to prove as Josephus claims it was only used once. The memorial stone's lime whitewash would be about one thousand years old (1450 to circa 445 BC) so probably eroded but any engraving may be still be traceable. The clue to the nomination is the two temples erected directly overhead.
- Acknowledgement must be made that the Samaritans, who still have a small community living today at Luzah, on the western side of the mount. They have ensured the sacred tradition has been preserved over a long period of time. UNESCO has recognised Mount Gerizim: "This sanctity and longevity, through to the present day, make this sacred mountain a place of outstanding universal value going far beyond the beliefs of a few hundred people".[11]

---

11 UNESCO, 2012 'Mount Gerizim and the Samaritans', *UNESCO World Heritage Centre*, <whc.unesco.org/en/tentativelists/5706/>. *Refer:* 'Justification of Outstanding Universal Value'.

# APPENDIX 4
# THE SITES OF ZEBULUN: LOWER GALILEE
## 4.1 The border sites: unlocking the Galilee

The border can be described in exact detail with the geography, the correct archaeology and the right orientation. The Masoretic name is listed first followed by the Septuagint name (LXX) (Joshua 19:10–16) (Illus. F.10).

### TABLE 7: Border sites of Zebulun

| Bible Name<br>Site status | Proposal<br>Coordinates | Notes<br>Site status is explained in **Note 1** p. 232. |
|---|---|---|
| Z1 Sarid<br>Sedduc, Esedekgola<br>*Geographic feature* | Mount Kedumim | *Refer* Chapter 13. Refer Note 1. Set-out point crucial to understand the logic of Zebulun's borders. |
| Z2 Maralah<br>Magelda<br>*Zebulun city 1* | Tel Shadud<br>32-39-37 N.<br>35-14-2 E. | Hebrew meaning: trembling (H4831) and earthquake (H7477). The archaeology supports this with evidence of seismic upheaval in the earlier remains. |
| Z3 Dabbasheth<br>Baitharava<br>*Zebulun city 2* | Tel Shammam<br>32-39-54 N.<br>35-8-51 E. | Hebrew meaning: a hill place. It is located at a key crossing place over the River Kishon. LXX name for the site means house of the crossing. |
| Z4 Jokne'am, Maan<br>*Zebulun Levite city 3* | Tel Qashish | Also known as Tel Qassis, Kassis. *Refer* Appendix 6. |
| Z5 Chisloth Tabor<br>Chaselothaith<br>*Issachar site* | Tel Umm al Ghanan<br>32-40-45 N.<br>35-23-30 E. | Hebrew meaning: flanks of Tabor (H3696). Site indicated on the PEF Map. Known in Roman times as Xaloth (Josephus). |
| IS17 Daberath,<br>Debba. *Issachar site* | Horbat Devora | *Refer* Chapter 14. |
| Z8 Japhia, Phangai<br>*Zebulun city 4* | Horbat Binit | *Refer* Chapter 12. |
| Z6 Gath Hepher<br>Not listed in LXX<br>*Zebulun city 5* | Tel Gath Hepher<br>32-44-17 N.<br>35-19-10 E. | Scholars are in agreement on Gath Hepher. The turning point is due east of Tel Gath Hepher. |
| Z23 Gebere (Gabara)<br>Only in the LXX<br>Not listed in MT. | Tel Adami<br>32-44-57 N.<br>35-27-34 E | Not mentioned in the Masoretic text. Hebrew meaning: a place of strength. Gabara did not exist in the time of Joshua but listed in the LXX as a site east of Japhia. Tel Adami meets that requirement (Iron Age origin). Described by Josephus. |
| Z9 Ith Kazin<br>Catasem<br>*Zebulun city 6* | Khirbet Qadis<br>32-44-8 N.<br>35-33-18 E. | Hebrew meaning: time of the Judge (H6278). It is a mystery site that has been hard to identify. The original site of Joshua may lie beneath Poriya Ilut. In the Iron Age a large settlement formed to the east of the ridge called Khirbet Qadis or Qedesh. Nearby the Hellenistic city of Taricheae developed. |
| Z11 Neah<br>Not in LXX<br>*Geographic feature* | Har Arbel<br>32-49-25 N.<br>35-29-58 E. | The border extends northward along the shores of the Sea of Galilee to the River (Nachal) Zalmon. Adjacent is Neah which describes the two seismic mountains of Har Arbel and Har Nitai. Neah means shaking, probably of the ground (H5269). |

*Proving Biblical Nazareth*

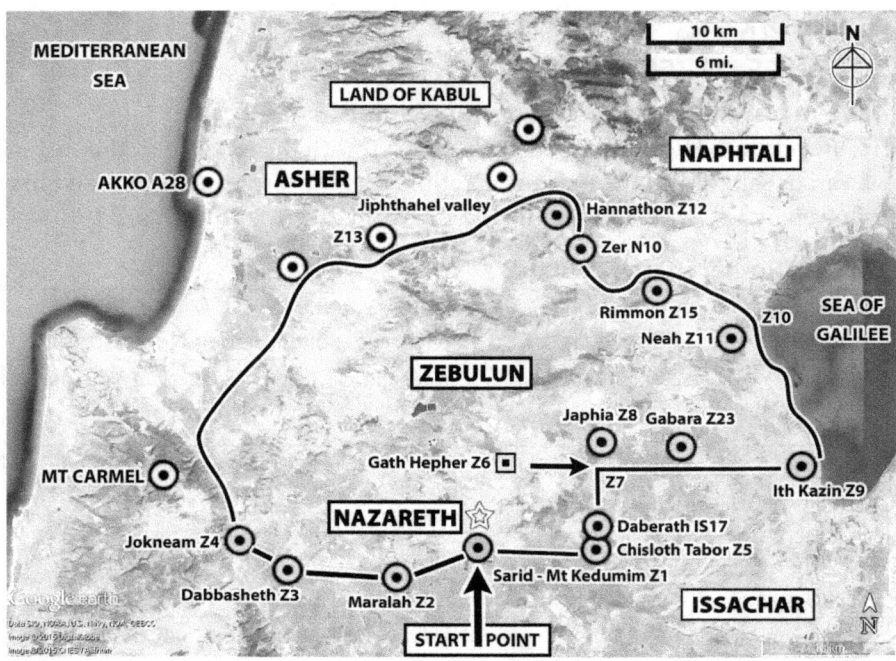

F.10 Zebulun boundary archaeological sites: Z1–Mt. Kedumim; Z2– Tel Shadud; Z3–Tel Shammam; Z4–Tel Qassis; Z5–Tel Umm al Ghanan; IS17–H. Devora; Z6–Gath Hepher; Z7–Turn point ; Z8–Horbat Binit; Z9–Kh. Qadis; Z10–Nachal Zalmon; Z11–Har Arbel; Z15–Kh. Mimlakh; N10–Tel Zalmon; Z12–Har Camon; Z13–Entrance to Beit Karem Valley. Base map Google Earth. Image © 2015 DigitalGlobe.

**TABLE 7 continued**

| Bible Name<br>Site status | Proposal<br>Coordinates | Notes<br>Site status is explained in **Note 1** p. 232. |
|---|---|---|
| Z15 Dimnah<br>Rimmono – Sella<br>*Zebulun Levite city 7* | Khirbet Mimlakh<br>32-51-25 N.<br>35-26-26 E. | The key is the LXX Rimmono linking with Rimmon Methoar used in the Masoretic text. A root word of Ramam (H7426) meaning to be exalted or be lifted up. A Levite city. **Note 2**. |
| Z12 Hannathon<br>Amoth<br>*Geographic feature* | Har Kamon<br>32-54-31 N.<br>35-21-38 E. | Hebrew meaning: Hill of grace (H2603). This site is not a city, but the highest summit in the Lower Galilee. **Note 3**. |
| Z13 Jiphthahel Valley<br>Gaiphael<br>*Geographic feature* | Valley of Beit Kerem at the entrance<br>32-54-35 N.<br>35-12-50 E. | Hebrew meaning: The Opening of God (Smith's Bible Dictionary). The Valley of Beit Kerem (House of the Vines). **Note 4** |

**Table 7 Note 1: Sarid is clearly a geographical feature, not a city.**
The site status is critical to meet the requirements of Joshua 19:10–16. This list has seven Zebulun cities which added by the five internal cities gives the required total of twelve cities (*refer* Appendix 4.2.1). The other names are Issachar sites or geographic features like Sarid.

# The sites of Zebulun – Lower Galilee

**Note 2:** This describes the whole elevated plateau bordered by the circuitous River Zalmon, a very obvious tribal boundary. Sella of Josh. 21:34 is the Remmon of 1 Chron. 6:77 and becomes Sellame mentioned by Josephus.

**Note 3:** The LXX name of Amoth is derived from Ramoth which means a high place. It is currently preserved in the nearby name of Tel Ramah which is located in the valley directly north below the peak.

**Note 4:** This is a very significant valley, wide and long, and is the traditional demarcation of the divide between Upper Galilee in the north and Lower Galilee in the south. Such a valley is aptly named the *Opening of God* with its majestic ridges and peaks.

## 4.2 The internal cities: more clues unravelled

When the correct Zebulun boundary is defined the internal cities can be identified in two categories.

1. "Included" sites: "Kattath, Nahalal, Shimron, Idalah, and Bethlehem" (Joshua 19:15). There is clockwise logic with this listing. The key site in this list is Shimron, mentioned previously in the story of how Nazareth became known as Yafia (*refer* Illus. F.11).

2. Levite Cities: Jokne'am, Kartah, Dimnah and Nahalal (Joshua 21:34–35). These cities are anticlockwise in order (*refer* Illus. F.14).

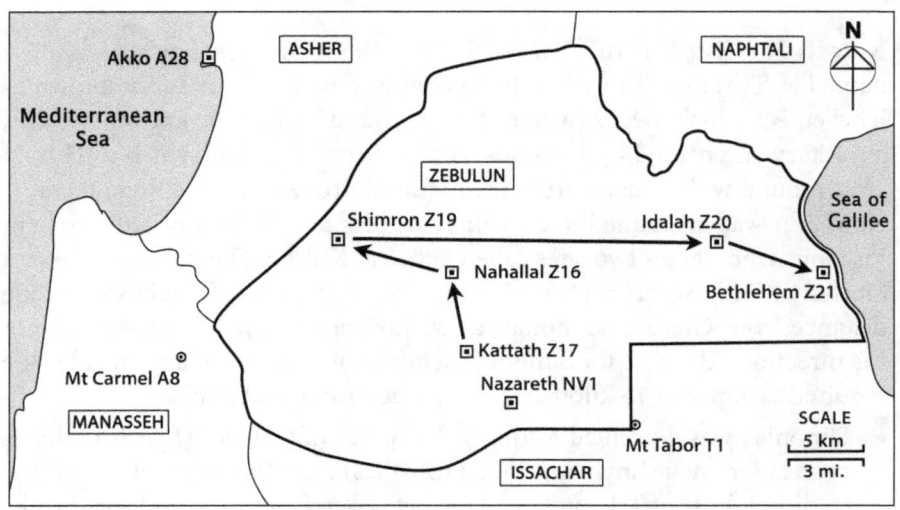

F.11 "Included" Zebulun cities showing clockwise logic.

233

**TABLE 8: Internal sites of Zebulun.**

| Bible Name | Proposal Coordinates | Notes |
|---|---|---|
| Z17 Kattath Catanath | Ein Zippori 32-43-57 N. 35-16-23 E. | On the banks of the River (Nachal) Zippori. A mystery site with the Talmud commenting that it was near Sepphoris which is just north of the site. |
| Z16 Nahalal Nabaal, Tabor | Tel Hannathon 32-47-10 N. 35-15-26 E. | Hebrew meaning: Pasture (H5096) or Watering place (H5095). This is apt for this Levite site lying in the western pasture lands of the Netofa Valley with two streams passing by. **Note 1.** |
| Z19 Shimron Symoon | Shefar'am | *Refer* Z22. Shimron means guard which suits this Galilee location watching over the coastal Plain. |
| Z20 Idalah Jericho | Khirbet Hattin 32-48-13 N. 35-27-11 E. | Hebrew meaning: God's snares or trap, that becomes Beth Arbel meaning the place of God's ambush (H1009). In Hellenistic times it is named Jer (icho) which becomes Josephus' site of Cafar(eccho). Today it is named Khirbet Eika (=icho) |
| Z21 Bethlehem Baethman | Khirbet Nasir Din 32-46-31 N. 35-31-24 E. In the time of Joshua. | Hebrew meaning: House of Bread (H1035). It becomes Beth Maon (Z42) in the LXX at 32-46-56N and 35-30-52 E. in Hellenistic–Roman times. Mentioned by Josephus as 4 furlongs (630 m, 700 yd.) from Tiberias' city limits. Not to be confused with its famous namesake in Judea. |
| Z 22 Kitron Kedron | Tel Shimron 32-42-14 N. 35-12-51 E. | Hebrew meaning: incense (H7003). This site is located 8 km (5 mi.) west of traditional Nazareth centre. **Note 2.** |

**Note 1:** Not listed in the LXX of Joshua 21:34. In 1 Chronicles 6:77 it is named as T(h)abor. This is not to be confused with Mount Tabor known as Jebel et-Tur which means "Mount of the Mound." It became known as Garis, a military site named by Josephus as near Sepphoris. Today it is a tel on a large mound with remains from the required Bronze Age and Roman era.

**Note 2:** It was misnamed due to an error of interpretation of a distance in Josephus who names two sites called Gibea at Khirbet Harishiya and Besara located at Beth Shearim (*Life* 24). The next clue is that Josephus gives the distance from Gibea to Simonias as 60 furlongs (16km, 10 miles) but not the direction. The case for Simonias being located at Shefar'am includes the required distance of 16 kilometres via a trade route and also:

- Simonias was described as on the "confines of Galilee" (*Life* 24). This is correct for Shefar'am being 2 km (1.2 miles) from the edge but not for the traditional site of Tel Shimron which is 12 km (7.4 miles) and well inside.
- Josephus stated he was a resident of Simonias and came under attack from a Roman troop which makes more sense at Shefar'am as the Romans at that stage were camped at Akko on the coast (*Life* 24).

# APPENDIX 5
# BORDER SITES NEAR ZEBULUN
## 5.1 Western border with Asher
The border sites of Joshua 19:26–27 are shown on Illus. F12. The eastern border of Asher runs anticlockwise starting from the coastal Akko Plain and makes topographic sense in the understanding of Zebulun as Lower Galilee.

**TABLE 9: Western border**

| Bible Name | Proposal Coordinates | Notes |
|---|---|---|
| A8 Mount Carmel | Main peak 32-43-47 N. 35-2-59 E. | Set-out point. The Kishon River would be a logical border. |
| A9 Sihor Libnath Sion and Labanath | Tel Kishon 32-52-23 N. 35-9-4 E. | There is a good case that it is a city located on the Sihor River which would be the ancient Belus stream known for its turbidity. |
| A10 Beth Dagon Baethegeneth | Tel Ya'anim 32-53-36 N. 35-13-18 E. | Located near the outgoing of the proposed Jiphthahel Valley. |
| A11 Beth Emek Ekgai | Tel Nahf 32-56-4 N. 35-19-2 E. | Means House of the Valley and suits this location in the Beit Kerem Valley. |
| A13 Neiel Phthaee | Tel Harashim 32-57-59 N. 35-20-19 E. | The turning point of the border and heading north in the Nachal Peki'in valley. |
| A14 Kabul/Cabul | Tel Mi'ilya 33-1-25 N. 35-15-40 E. | Also known as Tarshisha. Kabul is located in the land of Asher (not Zebulun). The border was heading for Ebron which is proposed at Iqrit (Akrith). |

## 5.2 Southern border with Issachar
Joshua 19:22. This border is quite logical as it nominates Tabor on the western side and ends at the river Jordan in the east. The direction is clockwise.

**TABLE 10: Southern border**

| Bible Name | Proposal Coordinates | Notes |
|---|---|---|
| IS14 Tabor Gaethbor | Horbat Zelef 32-41-18 N. 35-24-24 E. | Located on the NE slopes of Mount Tabor. The mount gives its name to this city. |
| IS16 Shahazimah Salim | Khirbet Sharona 32-42-47N. 35-28-28 E. | Hebrew meaning: towards the heights or double peaks (H7831). Located between two peaks in the region, Har Yabneel and Har Adami. This site is located near the fortress of Jotapata. |
| IS17 Beth Shemesh Baethsamys | Khirbet Beit Yerah 32-42-59 N. 35-34-16 E. | Many scholars nominate this site as correct. |

## 5.3 Northern border with Naphtali

Five forts of Joshua 19:35 are at the start of the circle protecting Naphtali's southern border. The border fortifications order runs anticlockwise.

**TABLE 11: Northern border**

| Bible Name | Proposal Coordinates | Notes |
| --- | --- | --- |
| N9 Ziddim<br>LXX Walled city of the Tyrians | Kh. Zeitun er Rama<br>32-55-37 N.<br>35-24-4 E. | Could also be Khirbet Jul. Later relocated nearby to Tel Beer Sheba. (Josephus' fortifications in 67 AD). |
| N10 Zer<br>LXX Walled city of the Tyrians | Khirbet Sellame<br>32-53-5 N.<br>35-22-46 E. | Tel Zalmon. City of the Gentile Tyrians noted in the LXX and named by Josephus as Cydessa. Near Roman Zar (Mughar). Misnamed as Sellame/Selamis. |
| N11 Hammath of Naphtali | Kh. Sheikh Nashi<br>32-53-3 N.<br>35-29-11 E. | The traditional location is a warm spring site just south of Tiberias. This was incorrectly nominated as the correct site was abandoned. **Note 1.** |
| N11 Omathadaketh in LXX | Khirbet Huqoq<br>32-53-6N.<br>35-28-47 E. | Khirbet Huqoq has remains from the required Hellenistic era. **Note 2.** It is nearby to Kh. Sheikh Nashi. |
| N13 Rakkath<br>Not listed in LXX | Khirbet Ghuweir<br>32-51-18 N.<br>35-30-31 E. | Hebrew meaning: elevated bank or shore town (H7557). No confirmed Middle Bronze remains at this site but it is supported for topographical reasons. Site shifted in name to near Tiberias (Z39). |
| N14 Chinnereth<br>Kenereth | Tel Oreimeh also Tel Kinerot<br>32-52-10 N.<br>35-32-23 E. | Hebrew meaning: Harp shape (H3672). The reason for the name is the Sea of Galilee which is shaped like a Jewish harp. A strategic location on the historic 'Way of the Sea'. |

**Note 1:** The traditional site near Tiberias caused an error with the east border of Zebulun. Hammath means hot or warm springs (H2575). The proposed site suits the topographic logic and has the required Bronze age remains to be Joshua's Hammath. It has evidence of fortifications and has been nominated as a fort of Josephus known as Caphar-ecco.[1] The question is where were the warm springs? Spring sites can vary in temperature over time so a site hot in the past may not be warm today. *Refer* Note 2 below and Appendix 8.6.

**Note 2:** There is a mystery with this name and it has been suggested it combines the Hammath of Naphtali with the next site of Rakkath.[2] Huqoq had two large bathing facilities (miqveh), one being an underground pool within an excavated hall.[3] There is evidence of extensive water facilities at the site. These could be part of the original warm bath locality.

---

1  Caparecco is located at Khirbet Eika. *Refer* Z20 Table 8.

2  *McClintock and Strong Biblical Cyclopedia*, 2016, 'Hammath'. *Refer* Bibliography.

3  Grey, M and Spigel, C 2015, 'Huqoq in the late Hellenistic and early Roman periods', *Galilee in the Late Second Temple and Mishnaic Periods*, Volume 2 in Fiensy D and Strange J (eds), Fortress Press. Minneapolis, USA, p. 37.

*Border sites near Zebulun*

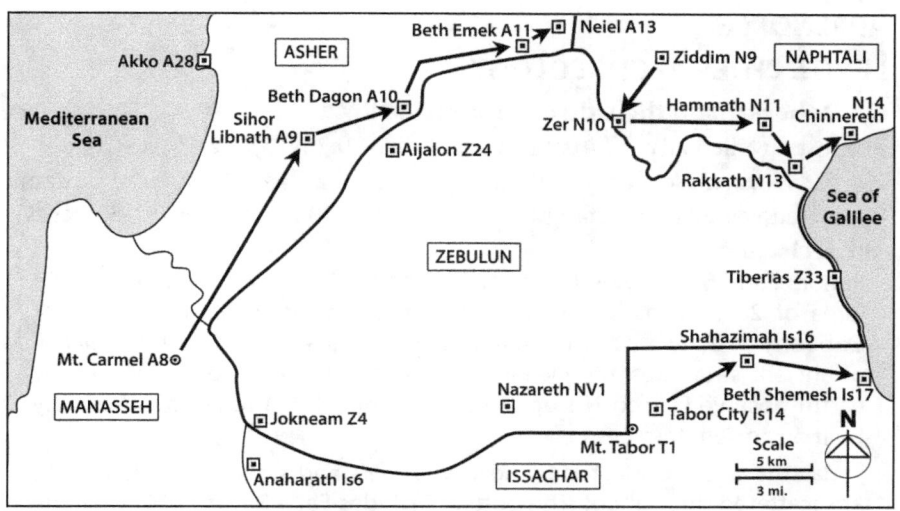

F.12 Three tribes boundary sites adjacent to Zebulun.

> The incorrect nomination of Hammath of Naphtali near Tiberias has caused the main error in defining Zebulun. There is no evidence of a Middle Bronze fortification. In the above map an alternative logical location is given at N11.

F.13 Har Nitai: Seismic mountain which was part of Neah (Z11) on the Zebulun northern border. The River Zalmon (Tsalmon) to the north was the border with Naphtali.

## APPENDIX 6
## LEVITE CITIES ARCHAEOLOGY

### 6.1 Daberath: on the side of Tabor (IS17)

Proposed walled city: *Khirbet Devora*. 32-41-50.2 N. 35-22-39 E. (Chap. 14). Horbat Devora archaeological survey area: 2 ha., 5.8 acres or 20 dunams. Estimated walled city rectangular shape 150 x 140 metres (164 x 153 yards).

**The archaeology**

> Period: Early Bronze Age I, Hellenistic, Roman, Byzantine, Mamluk ... Ruin (area of 20 dunams on knoll on spur overlooking Nahal Devora NE of Dabburiya (today a cultivated area). Stone piles – created by the collapse of ancient structures and clearance work, and cisterns (today blocked by earth) observed ... on N slope of spur – agricultural terraces, apparently built on ancient terraces.[1]

> Today the site is cultivated by nearby farmers and stones of ancient walls are scattered throughout. The pottery includes Early Bronze I 30%, Middle Bronze IIB 9%, Iron Age I 16%, Persian 24%, Byzantine 21%.[2]

This is key information as it shows a revived occupation at the end of the MB IIB period. Nearby Khirbet Daburiya has an Iron Age origin which was a later satellite site that grew to be the dominant town. (They became twin sites 900 m or 970 yards apart.) The topography of Khirbet Devora favours the Levite city dimensions far better than Daburiya which is on steep slopes.

### 6.2 Jokne'am: the error and the archaeology

Traditional archaeology nominates Tell Keimun, also known as Kammon, as Jokne'am. Eusebius lists Jokne'am and Kammon as separate sites so they are not the same in his mind. He wrote: "There is now a village Kammona in the great plain six miles north of Legeon on the road to Ptolemais".[3] Legeon is Legio, a Roman military camp of the Sixth Legion that has recently been revealed just south of Megiddo. Khirbet Tabaneh is Kammona located to the north at a distance of six Roman miles which is 8.8 km (5.5 miles) whereas Tell Qeimun is 12.6 km (7.8 miles). Clearly again the nomination is incorrect and there is another explanation for his roadway to Akko (Ptolemais). Eusebius used this definition because Kammona was an intersection of two major trade routes in the Jezreel valley (his "great plain"). From Kammona a trade route headed north-west to Akko, so Eusebius was using a well-known route from Legio-Megiddo to Ptolemais to define his site.

---

1 The Archaeological Survey of Israel, 2016, <www.antiquities.org.il/survey/new/default_en.aspx>. Site name: H. Devora, Map No: 41, Site No. 64.

2 Gal, Z *Lower Galilee During the Iron Age*, op. cit., p. 14.

3 Eusebius of Caesarea, *Onomasticon*, Translation (1971). pp. 1–75 <www.tertullian.org/fathers/eusebius_onomasticon_02_trans.htm. No.607>.

### Tell Qeimun is Anaharath – Jokne'am's neighbour (IS6)
Location: Tell Keimun at 32-39-52 N. and 35-6-32 E. (*refer* Illus. F.14).

A Crusader site known as Caymont (Mons Cain) and then the Arabic site of Khirbet Keimun (Qeimun). It was incorrectly nominated by Robinson as Jokne'am. When this error is corrected the mystery of the biblical name of Tell Keimun can be solved. With the borders of Zebulun shown previously Tell Keimun is not in Zebulun but in Issachar. It is proposed Keimun is the boundary site of *Anaharath* (IS6) (Josh. 19:19). One of the Hebrew meanings of Anaharath (H588) is a gorge or narrow pass. This describes the location of Tell Keimun which sits directly on a hill guarding the strategic road through Wadi Milek, connecting the plains of Megiddo with the Mediterranean coast.

### Jokne'am facing the Kishon River

Jokne'am is a western border site and the accurate rendering is found in some translations (KJV) [4] as the border "reached to the river that is before Jokne'am" (Josh. 19:11). It is not helped by some translations which loosely use two words in Joshua 19:11. One is the translation of *nachal* (H5158) as a ravine (NIV) when a wadi, watercourse or river is a more correct selection. The second is the word *paniyim* used with Jokne'am (H6440) which means before or facing. It is not east as some translations (ESV) offer; that would require the word *qedem*. Using east or ravine appears to be done to support the traditional nomination. The Complete Jewish Bible has "on to the wadi fronting Yokne'am" which is a correct translation that refers to the Kishon which meanders closely south of Tel Qashish.

### The name and archaeology of Jokne'am (Z4)
Proposed location: Tel Qashish at 32-41-6.6 N. and 35-6-34.3 E.

Also known as Qassis or Kassis. The name means "Hill of the Priest" which comes from a proposal it was the locality where Elijah executed the prophets of Baal described in 1 Kings 18:38-40. The Hebrew meaning is "The lament of the people" (H3362). This site is 2.2 kilometres (1.4 miles) N.E. of the traditional site. It is a large mound with a total area of about 4.45 hectares (11 acres, 44.5 dunams) making it a good size city in its early periods. The tel has been surveyed a number of times finding "a sequence of 15 strata, ranging from various phases of late Early Bronze Age I through to the Persian period." [5] This is key evidence, as the biblical requirement is of a large royal Canaanite city site at the end of the Middle Bronze which was conquered by Joshua. There is evidence of the occupation in the Middle Bronze IIC to Late Bronze period. Geographically the site is due west of biblical Nazareth city.

---

4   KJV–King James Version. NIV–New International Version. ESV– English Standard Version.
5   van den Brink, E and Ad, U 2011, '*Tel Qashish*', op. cit.

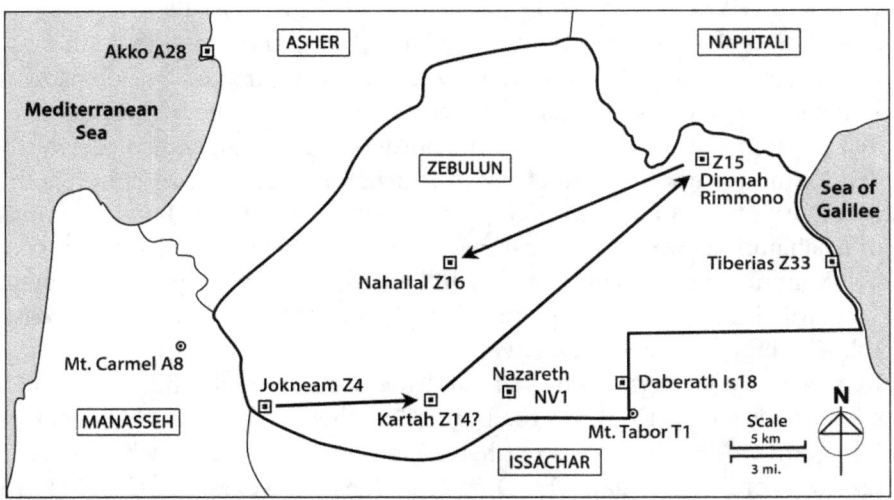

F.14 Zebulun's four Levite sites showing anticlockwise logic. Z4 Tel Qashish, Z14(?) Ein Hilu at Migdal ha-Emek, Z15 Kh. Mimlakh and Z16 Tel Khanaton.

### 6.3 Kartah mystery site?

Levite Kartah is an unknown site and there is no obvious confirmation of the location. Some scholars believe Kartah is lost. When nominations of the site are offered, they are somewhere near the western zone of Zebulun. One of the candidates that could be considered is Migdal Ha-Emek (Z14).

Centred on Ein el-Hilu at 32-40-58.6 N. and 35-14-44 E.

It meets the anticlockwise logic of the listing of the sites as shown in F.14 above. It has the required Middle Bronze Age IIB remains but the site has been affected by modern development. The Hebrew meaning of Kartah is "City of the meeting" (H7177). If it is a Levite site the northern city marker would approximate the latitude of Tel Yafia. This raises speculation that it may be a Levite signpost to a future site of a "special city"–the city of the Messiah. This cannot be proven as there is no current evidence linking the name of Kartah to Migdal Ha-Emek. The reason it is noted is the geographical position in relation to Nazareth.

# APPENDIX 7
# JEWISH FORTIFICATIONS IN LOWER GALILEE
## 7.1 The military logic of the locations

With the nomination of Yafia as Nazareth it becomes imperative to demonstrate with evidence another location for Japhia. The name can be found in the historical accounts of Josephus where information is given on Jotapata and the nearby site of Japhia. The logic can be seen with the nominations in contrast to the traditional sites which are listed below. All the sites have natural fortification features and are located on trade routes.

**TABLE 12: Summary of Josephus' fortifications.** *Refer* Illus. C13.

| Josephus' name | Traditional nominations | Proposed Locations |
|---|---|---|
| Jotapata H.Q. | Tel Yodefat | Khirbet Atosh. *Refer* Chapter 11.2. |
| Bersabe | Khirbet Beer Sheba | Khirbet Beer Sheba (N38) 32-55-48 N. and 35-26-26 E. An agreed site. Close to biblical Ziddim of Naphtali. |
| Salamis | Kh. Sellame | Khirbet Mimlakh (Z15) 32-51-25 N. and 35-22-46 E. Levite site Sella in Josh. 21:34 LXX (Appendix 5.3). |
| Caphareccho | Mystery site Khirbet Sheikh Nashi? | Khirbet Eika (Z20) at 32-48-13 N. and 35-27-11 E. Located on the Horns of Hattin. Biblical Idalah. Table 8. |
| Japha | Tel Yafia near Nazareth | Ilaniya at Har Shomer (Z30) and Kh. Sejerah (Ch. 12). |
| Sigo | Mystery site Tel Shikhin? | Tel Govel (Z31) at 32-43-39 N. and 35-23-6 E. This site has Early Roman remains. |
| Itabyrion | Mount Tabor west side | West Mount Tabor (Z32) at 32-41-15 N. and 35-23-12 E. Scholars accept this site with the Greek name for Tabor. |
| Taricheae | 1. Magdala near Arbel 2. Near Tel Kinneret | Near Tel Kinneret (Z34) at 32-43-56 N. and 35-33-43E. South of Tiberias. **Note 1.** |
| Tiberias | Tiberias | Tiberias (Z33) at 32-47-10 N. and 35-32-33 E. This site with its remains is agreed by scholars. |
| Gennessar Caves | Har Arbel Caves | Har Arbel Caves (Z35) at 32-49-24 N. and 35-29-44 E. These caves are agreed. Infamous in Jewish history. |

**Note 1.** Traditional nominations locate the site either north of Tiberias at Magdala or somewhere to the south near Tel Kinneret. There has been much controversy about this site which suffered a calamitous defeat by the Romans, and little evidence of the walls have been found. A good case has been given by a researcher Nikos Kokkinos for the southern location. He states: "In conclusion any remains of Graeco-Roman Tarichaea should be sought up to 1.5 km [0.93 mile] north and north-west of Bet Yerach".[1]

---

1 Kokkinos, N 2010, 'The location of Tarichaea: north or south of Tiberias?' *Palestine Exploration Quarterly*, 142.1, pp. 7–23.

## 7.2 Jotapata fortress: the logistics

The evidence supporting the location of Jotapata can be considered from a range of criteria including historical and topographic.

### 1. The proof in the Roman campaign route

The record of Vespasian's route to Jotapata gives good confirmation of the nominated site (*Wars* 3.6.1–4). His logic shows he moved his military juggernaut along Roman highways from Akko via Garis (Camp 1) to Gabara (Camp 2). [Josephus mentions a village nearby also known as Gabaroth]. After destroying Gabara he moved to Camp 3 at Kefr Sabt which had a good water supply. From there he had to make his own road to a hill known today as Har Adami and create his final Camp 4. Har Adami at 32-43-54 N. and 35-28-0 E. (IS 24) is the highest peak in the locality at the required distance.

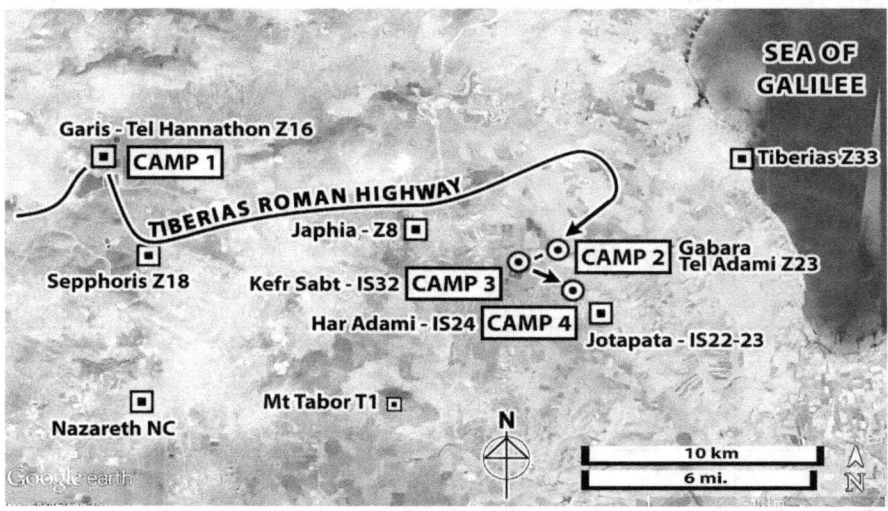

F.15 Map of proposed route of Vespasian with campsites to the fortress of Jotapata. Base map Google Earth. Image © 2015 DigitalGlobe.

### 2. The Plain of Blood

Josephus noted that Jotapata ended "obliquely at a plain" (*Wars* 3.7.7). This is not the case with the traditional site at Tel Yodfat. The Talmud makes mention of a Plain called Niddah which is the Jewish word for *impure blood*.[2] G. T. Neubauer proposes the plain called Niddah is the *plain of Jotapata*. In Byzantine times Eusebius mentions this geographical feature known as the *Plain of Saron* "between Mt. Tabor and the Lake of Tiberias".[3] However to the Jews, because of the massacre, it could be described as the Plain of Blood.

---

2  Neubauer, GT 'Jotapata' ,*Jewish Encyclopedia*, p. 203. *Refer* Bibliography.

3  *International Standard Bible Encyclopedia*. 'LaSharon'. *Refer* Bibliography.

## 3. Searching for a lost site

- The first and only direct biblical reference to Jotapata is a resident called "Haruz of Jotbah" who is the father of Meshullemeth, the mother of a King of Judah called Amon (2 Kings 21:19). This would make it an Iron Age II and possibly 'royal' site.
- There is a proposal that Jotbah existed before the Assyrian invasion and is known as *'Ia-at-bi-te'* or *'Yathbite'* in the list of conquered sites of Israel by Tiglath Pileser III in 721 BC.[4] This suggests a site on a trade-military route of some importance and such remains have been found nearby.[5]
- In the Mishnah (ar. 9.32a) Jotapata is called *"the Ancient"* and is supposed to have been fortified by Joshua.[6] The Mishnah is probably referring to Shahazimah (H. Sharona IS16) which is a site nearby on the trade route.
- Horbat Sharona's location is difficult to defend with its higher encircling slopes. When the Hasmoneans and Herod developed their site, the fortification was located 1,000 m (1,100 yards) to the north on a very steep cliff at the eastern end of the modern moshav village of Sharona.
- Josephus was re-fortifying an existing military site. As such it would have large storage facilities as well as very strong walls. An ideal military HQ.

## The City of Jotapata at Khirbet Atosh

This city had two sections, an upper and lower, with walls all round.

- Lower City at 32-43-29 N. and 35-28-57 E. (IS22). Josephus stated that: "The city is covered all round with other mountains, and can no way be seen till a man comes upon it. And this was the strong situation of Jotapata" (*War* 3.7.7). Located near Moshav Sharona.
- Upper fortress at 32-43-25 N. and 35-28-42 E. (IS23). It is logical that Jotapata had an upper level castle and a lower city support site. Josephus makes reference to the view from the top (*refer* Appendix 8.8). The almost sheer drop is spectacular and it is no surprise that this pinnacle today is popular as a hang-gliding site. The position at the end of the plain is also very applicable to this site as quoted in the next page.

The two contrasting comments by Josephus can be reconciled with the nominated site. The quote above describes the almost hidden lower city nestled in the cliff face in contrast to the elevated fortress at the ridge to which it was connected. The fortress is confirmed by Josephus' distance from Har Adami hill being seven furlongs (1,400 metres, 1,530 yards) (*Wars* 3.7.7).

---

4 These points have been listed in Avi-Yonah, M and Gibson, S 2013, 'Jotapata or Yodefat', *Jewish Virtual Library*. Refer Bibliography.

5 Lapin, H 2001, *Economy, Geography, and Provincial History in Latter Roman Palestine*, Mohr Siebeck, Tubingen, Germany, p. 90.

6 *Jewish Encyclopedia*, 'Jotapata'. Refer Bibliography.

*Proving Biblical Nazareth*

F.16 View from ridge of Moshav Sharona down the slopes to Khirbet Atosh, the proposed location of Lower Jotapata city 68 AD.

Now Jotapata is almost all of it built upon a precipice, having on all the other side of it every way valleys immensely deep and steep, in so much that those that look down would have their sight fail them before they reach the bottom. It is only to be come at on the north side, where the utmost part of the city is built on the mountain, as it ends obliquely at a plain. This mountain Josephus had encompassed with a wall when he fortified the city, that its top might not be capable of being seized by the enemies (*Wars* 3.7.7).

The logistics also support this site. The number of those killed at Jotapata was 40,000 men and the capture of 1,200 women and children. An estimate of the city and fortress area is 35 hectares (86 acres) based on a topographical evaluation, which gives a density of 118 per dunam (1,000 sq.m, 107 squares). The average density of a dense Galilean city is 40 persons per dunam. This shows that Jotapata had about three times the normal density while it was under seige.[7]

---

[7] In contrast the traditional site at Tel Yodfat with its walled site would be barely standing room for the listed occupants.

# APPENDIX 8: A CATHOLIC SOURCE FOR BIBLE SITES
## A controversial historical account

This book is a resource edition to help students, scholars and those interested in the quest for more information on Bible sites. The test with all historical material is the reliability of the author and the source of the facts. During my investigations I came across a very controversial source which does not meet the requirements of modern academic scholarship. It was the account of a German Augustinian nun named *Anne Emmerich* (1774–1824). [1] Initially I was not particularly interested in sharing it in this book aimed at scholars and students. The reason was that she claimed her information came by spiritual revelation from God and not by her intellect. Her descriptions are well known by Catholics in Europe and some Catholic scholars quote her as a source. There was controversy when Mel Gibson used her accounts in some movie scenes of *"The Passion of the Christ"* in 2004.

## Her life

Emmerich was illiterate and not able to write down her visions, so a well-known German scholar at the time, Clemens Brentano, wrote her verbatim descriptions which he later edited. Emmerich's life has been investigated by the Roman Catholic Church and her status is venerable (just below saint) in their system. She was beatified in 2004 by Pope John Paul II who said in his homily she was one of those who "let the Word of God guide them as a bright and safe beacon that never ceased to enlighten them on their way". [2]

She was very loyal to her Church, upholding traditional Catholic teachings and theology but was subject to investigations and endured much suffering with her gift. Brentano's writings have been edited by a German Catholic priest and his edition translated into English. This requires a word of caution as the quotes below are actually fourth hand. We do not know how much influence the three subsequent editors had on the final account. Some of her descriptions are a bit unclear with spiritual overtones, but much of the material is very specific and illustrative allowing for investigation.

## The challenge of her information

The time frame of her information is from 1818–1823 AD at a time when Palestinian archaeology had not developed and information on many sites was still unknown. Her descriptions and detail are very challenging and in a few accounts it requires careful interpretation geographically. There are

---

1 Vatican.va. 2016. Anna Katharina Emmerick (1774–1824), biography, <www.vatican.va/news_services/liturgy/saints/ns_lit_doc_20041003_emmerick_en.html>.
2 Libreria Editrice Vaticana, 3 October 2004: The Beatification of five Servants of God. John Paul II. <w2.vatican.va/content/john-paul-ii/en/homilies/2004/documents/hf_jp-ii_hom_20041003_beatifications.html>.

occasional errors, but overall her information on Bible sites can be shown as very reasonable. If the Bible is full of examples of prophets seeing future events, is it not possible for a person with a prophetic gift to also see past events in some way? The Bible's teaching is that all visions and revelations outside of the direct 'inspired' aspects of the authorised Bible are to be tested. This is a key consideration as no human is perfect and can bring aspects of their culture to interpretations of spiritual revelations.

**Testing with evidence**

Emmerich never travelled outside of Germany, yet her detail of topography and settlements has astonishing accuracy, even for sites still not discovered in 1818 AD! In the course of research I found many of her descriptions of sites very plausible and they corroborated with the conclusions of my research. In several cases it influenced my conclusions. The following selections are some of her visions on sites described in this book for those who may be interested. Not all will accept her source or approach, but those who have an interest in spiritual revelation may find it informative. Quoting a source does not mean endorsing their personal beliefs or theology. However, with all historical sources, discernment and confirmation of the reliability is an important aim in ongoing research.

F.19 Reconstructed Byzantine Church at Ephesus in Turkey is built over the early 'House of Mary'. The discovery was due to a vision received by Anne Emmerich.

## Site descriptions

The following information is given for the reader to discern and to decide. Below are the direct quotes that correlate with important sites in this book.[3] My responses are given to compare with this information.

### 8.1 Nazareth walled city with gates (NC)

1. Jesus with some disciples approaching the city: "They approached by the side whose gate opens to the east on the road leading to the Sea of Galilee, but they went not into the city. Nazareth had five gates" (vol. 1, p. 364–365).

2. The Synagogue was located within the city walls (NC1): "The synagogue was in the western part of Nazareth" (vol. 2, p. 236).

3. Joseph's Workshop (NC3): "Outside the city walls, where Joseph had his carpenter shop, lived several people, poor but good, who had been known to Joseph, and among whose sons were some of the playmates of Jesus' childhood" (vol. 1, p. 372).

4. The water spring/well of the city (NC6): "They offered their guests a morsel of bread and a little fresh water. The water was especially good in Nazareth" (vol. 1, p. 373).

A response: These details support the location of Tel Yafia as the walled city with the synagogue location. Joseph's workshop nearby in the suburbs is also very intriguing (*refer* NC2 Illus. A.15).

### 8.2 House of Mary and Joseph (NV1)

1. Preparation work by pious pioneers long before Mary: "Nazareth where those three men worked on the spot upon which afterward stood the house in which the angel delivered the message to Mary" (vol. 1, p. 68).

2. Provided by mother Anne: "The little house at Nazareth which Anne fitted up for Mary and Joseph, belonged to Anne. From her own dwelling, she could, unnoticed, reach it in about half an hour by a cross path" (vol. 1, p. 190).

3. Mary's house in a hamlet: "Mary's house stood on a hill outside the city, part of it extending into the hill like a cave. The top of the house however, arose above the hill, on the opposite side of which lay other dwellings". (vol. 1, p. 372).

4. Place of the Annunciation: Description of Mary's room as a prayer oratory for devotion and a sleeping area at the rear. The oratory section was where "the angelic Annunciation took place" (vol. 1, p. 191).

5. Mother Anne and a servant present at the incarnation event: "Some time elapsed, and then Anne and the other woman entered Mary's room, but when they beheld her in ecstasy they withdrew" (vol. 1, p. 195).

---

3 Emmerich, AC. 2004, *The Life of Jesus Christ and Biblical Revelations*, Tan Books, Rockford, Illinois, USA. Used with permission (www.tanbooks.com).

6. The Essene connection: "The Essenians lived very retired around here, attended the synagogue at Nazareth, and were very devoted to the Holy Family. The care of Mary's house during her absence had been entrusted to them" (vol. 1, p. 365).

7. Joseph's shed near his house (NV2): "I saw St. Joseph, out of long strips of bark – yellow, brown and green – platting [sic] screens, large surfaces, and covers for ceilings. He had a stock of his woven board-like work piled under a shed near the house" (vol. 1, p. 289).

8. The burial of Joseph (NV3): "he was wrapped from head to foot in a white winding sheet, laid in a narrow casket, and placed in a very beautiful tomb, the gift of a good man … Joseph's remains were afterward removed by Christians to Bethlehem, and interred" (vol. 1, p. 330).

A response: These interesting accounts support the traditional location for the Incarnation of the gospels. It shows there were appropriate witnesses to the event. Indicates a workshop shed of Joseph near his house. The candidate for the burial site of Joseph is the rolling stone tomb located in the Sisters of Nazareth site. It also explains why his bones have not been found there.

### 8.3 The Execution Site (NC8)

1. The distance: "A little less than a quarter of an hour's distance from the city, rose the mountain from whose steep summit they hurled people, and whence, at a later period, they wanted to cast Jesus" (vol. 1, p. 365).

2. The attempted execution: "It was already dark and two of the crowd bore torches. They led Jesus around the eastern side of the synagogue, then turned into a broad street that ran westward out of the city. Ascending the mountain, they reached a lofty spur which on the northern side overlooked a marshy pool, and on the south formed a rocky projection over a steep precipice. It was from this point they were in the habit of precipitating malefactors. Here they intended once more to call Jesus to account, and then hurl him down. The abyss ended in a narrow ravine. They were not far from the scene of action when Jesus, who had been led as a prisoner among them, stood still, until they continued their way mocking and jeering" (vol. 2, p. 236).

A response: The descriptions support the direction and location of the nominated locality and gives intriguing information on Jesus' escape. It gives a distance just over one kilometre (1,100 yd.) from the city (less than quarter of an hour).

### 8.4 Cana of Galilee (Z25)

1. The city: "Mary went to Cana in Galilee, and stopped with the parents of the bride of Cana … Their beautiful mansion stood in the heart of the clean and well built city. A street ran through the middle of it, I think a continuation of the highroad from Ptolomais; one could see it descending toward Cana

from a higher level. This city was not so irregularly and evenly built as many others of Palestine" (vol. 2, p. 19).

2. The Inn (Z26): "Cana, situated on the west side of a hill, was a clean, pleasant place ... It had a synagogue ... Near it was the public house at which the wedding was to be held ... From this house to the synagogue, the street was adorned with leafy festoons, and arches from which hung garlands and fruits" (vol. 2, p. 44).

3. The guests: "All the relatives of St. Anne and Joachim had come from around Galilee to Cana, in all over one hundred guests ... Jesus Himself brought about twenty-five of His disciples with Him" (vol. 2, p. 45).

4. The celebration: "There was also performed a kind of dance. Children played on musical instruments and sang choruses at intervals. The dancers both men and the maidens, held scarfs with which they touched one another when dancing in rows or in rings" (vol. 2, p. 47).

5. Filling the water-pots for the miracle (Z27): "Then Jesus ordered each to be filled with water. The servants took them off to the well which was in a vault in the cellar, and which consisted of a stone cistern provided with a pump. The jugs were earthen, large and so heavy it took two men to carry them, one at each handle" (vol. 2, p. 56).

A response: The description supports the nominated city on a highway from Akko to Tiberias. It supports the city on a hill and an inn located to the west of it. A key factor is a rendered underground water cistern located nearby the proposed wedding site at a distance of about 60 m (65 yds) (*refer* Illus. D22).

## 8.5 Japha – Ophna (Z47)

1. Village of Japha: Mary's elder sister: "She dwelt at Japha, a little place an hour at most from Nazareth, where Zebedee once lived and where his sons were born" (vol. 3, p. 4).

2. Village of Ophna: "About an hour's journey from Nazareth toward Sepphoris, is a little place called Ophna. There during the boyhood of Jesus, dwelt the parents of James the Greater and John. In those early years, they associated with Jesus, until their parents removed to Bethsaida, and they themselves went to the fishery" (vol. 1, p. 324).

A response: The information supports the location of Tel Ilut with its Hellenistic–Roman era remains identified in 1980. Ophna would be the Hebrew name and the Greek name was Japha. (Gophna was a name of a site identified near Sepphoris in the Talmud period.) Japheph is a site located near to Nazareth in the Crusader era which could be linked to Japha. It suggests it could be another Nazarene village if it is the location of the birthplace of the sons of Zebedee. This gives a fascinating explanation for the Japha connection with Tel Yafia–Japhia nearby.

### 8.6 Hammath of Naphtali (N11)

1. Near the River Zalmon (Nachal Tsalmon): The warm baths and pleasure gardens are described as a region known as Bethuel: "to the north side of the valley where was the fountain of Bethuel. A great many wealthy and distinguished people from Galilee and Judea owned villas and gardens here, which they occupied in the beautiful season of the year. On the south side of the lake, formed by the northern declivity of the heights of Bethuel, were rows of houses and warm baths, those towards the east being the warmer. The baths had one large reservoir in common, around which were private apartments formed by tents: in them were tanks sunk to a greater or lesser depth in the water" (vol. 2, p. 265).

2. The Roman Era hot baths at Emmaus south of Tiberias are recorded: "… and by the hot-baths of Emmaus. These baths were on the declivity of a mountain, about an hour's distance further on from Magdalum in the direction of Tiberias" (vol. 1, p. 333).

A response: This describes two hot-bath locations. One on the border of Naphtali and the other a well known Roman Era site south of Tiberias. Emmerich's account of Emmaus is accurate before its rediscovery in 1920.

### 8.7 Japhia (Z30)

1. From Daberath heading northward: "Just at the outset of His journey lay a place to the east, I think Japhia, and another directly opposite towards the west and northward from Thabor" (vol. 2, p. 461).

2. Located near Jabneel Valley: "The one on the left was called Ulama: that on the right was, I think named Japhia" (vol. 2, p. 291).

3. Bethulia is proposed at Yabneel: "Bethulia appeared to rise above and behind Japhia" (vol. 2, p. 291).

A response: These three references support Khirbet Ilaniya and a location west of the Sea of Galilee near the Yabneel Valley. The site on the north-west of Tabor would be Sigo mentioned by Josephus and located at Tel Govel.

### 8.8 Jotapata (IS22-23)

1. City location: "Jetebatha … built in the bosom of the mountains as in an immense cave. Before rose a mountain from which the descent into the city was over deep, wild ditches. It appeared to be built in a deep quarry, the mountain hanging high over it. To the north of this mountain, not quite two hours distant was Magdalum" (vol. 2, p. 269).

2. The lofty fortress (IS23): "He traversed the valley and the plain to the somewhat important city of Gabara. It lay at the western foot of the mountain on whose south-western slope was perched the Herodian eyrie Jetebatha" (vol. 2, p. 467).

3. A Herodian City: "There were numerous Herodians in Jetebatha. In a wall of the fortifications they had a secret meeting place" (vol. 2, p. 270).

A response: The Herodians were a political party. The distance to Magdalum is correct. This description supports the nomination of Khirbet Atosh with the cliff face that is formed as a vast amphitheatre with a cave located in the centre. An eyrie is a fortress perched high on a mountain similar to the lofty nest of a bird of prey like an eagle. It describes the Herodian fortress at the peak which supports Josephus' account.

### 8.9 Transfiguration on Mount Tabor (T1)

1. The southern side ascent by Jesus and the three disciples from Kisloth: "He proceeded up the mountain by a footpath. They spent nearly two hours in ascent, for Jesus paused frequently at the different caves and places made memorable by the sojourn of the Prophets ... The view from the summit of the mountain extended far and wide. On it was a large open place surrounded by a wall and shade trees ... Hidden in a rock was a reservoir which upon the turning of a spiggot poured forth sparkling water and very cold" (vol. 3, p. 296).

2. The sacred caves of the prophets on Mount Tabor (T3): "On the southeastern side of Thabor lay a cave with a garden in front. There the Prophet Malachias had often sojourned. Farther up the mountain were another cave and garden where Elias and his disciples sometimes lived retired, as upon Carmel. These caves were now held as shrines by pious Jews, and thither they used to go to pray" (vol. 2, p. 453).

3. The grotto of the Transfiguration (T1): "Then Jesus withdrew with them into a deep grotto behind a rock which formed, as it were, a door to the cave. It was like the grotto on the Mount of Olives, to which Jesus so often retires to pray, and from it a descent led down into a vault" (vol. 3, p. 296).

A response: The prayer cave on the Mount of Olives is known and is a deep hollow. Mount Tabor has a long tradition of sacredness to the Israelites. It was a place of sojourn and prayer for some of the prophets. The journey up from the south-east suggests the plateau for the water spot is near the Catholic Church site. The cave and garden here could be the precinct of Elijah. The withdrawing to another grotto is not obvious. It is not clear where the actual location of the transfiguration occurs other than it is in a deep grotto-cave. However, it would suggest some area in the central plateau of Tabor.

## 8.10 Sarid (Z1)

1. Ancient residents settled on Mount Kedumim: "Of the Samanenses [sic] whom Melchisedech [sic] settled in Palestine, I saw long before the coming of Abraham three men on the so-called Bread Mountain, in the neighbourhood of Thabor". They lived in caves "... I saw them every month assembling on this mountain where Melchisedech broke a large four-cornered loaf" (vol. 1, p. 67–68).

2. The Prophet's Seat positioned on Mount Kedumim: "An instruction had been announced for the following day, which was to be delivered on a height southwest of Thabor ... The spot upon which Jesus now taught was a beautiful plateau where, from the stone chair, the Prophets of bygone days had taught. From it one could see across the valley of Esdrelon and into the country around Mageddo [sic]" (vol. 3, p. 137–139).

A response: The description of the very ancient habitation by Emmerich preceded the discovery of the pre-historic remains in 1934. The use of the term *Samanenses* is interesting as it is a generic term that ancient historians applied to a caste of religious ascetics. They were given different titles in various cultures, but piety and self-discipline were among their traits. Some were pagan and some were godly. They cover a range of time frames and are explained by an early Church scholar Clement of Alexandria (150–215 AD).[4] He comments on their rural rustic lifestyle and sexual asceticism in some cultures. Clement wrote about a wider group of devout people with very ancient origins including "the Samanaeans among the Bactrians, and the philosophers of the Celts, and the Magi of the Persians, who foretold the Saviour's birth, and came into the land of Judea guided by a star".

Esdrelon is the Jezreel Valley. This locates and illustrates the special spiritual status of Mount Kedumim and her description of it as "Bread Mountain". She gives intriguing insight on ancient occupants of the caves. Emmerich sees this group in Israel as honouring the true God in the same tradition as biblical Job. They predate Abraham's sojourn. Her comment is that a prophet's preaching place existed at the peak with a view exactly as it is today. Candidates for the preaching would be Elijah, Elisha, Malachi and Nahum. They are part of the faithful remnant preaching of the God of Israel. This agrees with all the material in Chapter 13.

*Mary's parents may have prayed there for guidance on the location for a dwelling for their daughter!*

---

4 A quotation from Clement of Alexandria, *The Stromata, or Miscellanies*, Book I, Chap XV, <www.earlychristianwritings.com/text/clement-stromata-book1.html.>. The 'Samanaeans' are also an oriental caste listed in *McClintock and Strong Biblical Cyclopedia*. *Refer* Bibliography.

# REFERENCE SECTION
## ABBREVIATIONS, TERMINOLOGY AND GLOSSARY
### Abbreviations

| | |
|---|---|
| **PEF** | Palestine Exploration Fund |
| **IAA** | Israel Antiquities Authority |
| **KJV** | King James Version |
| **NIV** | New International Version |
| **OT and NT** | Old Testament and New Testament |
| **AD** | After the birth of Jesus Christ. Also CE in some quotes. |
| **BC** | Before the birth of Jesus Christ. Also BCE in some quotes. |
| **LXX** | Septuagint Bible. The Greek version of the OT. |
| **MT** | Masoretic Text. Authoritative Hebrew text of Old Testament. |
| **AEHL** | Archaeological Encyclopedia of the Holy Land. |
| **Bible books** | Gen.–Genesis, Lev.–Leviticus, Num.–Numbers, Deut.–Deuteronomy, Josh.–Joshua, Chron.– Chronicles, Jer.–Jeremiah, Matt.–Matthew, Rev.–Revelation. |

### Base map terminology

**Google Earth Maps:** These maps have been produced under the terms and conditions of "Google Earth". The coordinates given relate to the visual reference points and can vary slightly over time. This system has been used for ease of access for readers to view the sites. They will be at some variance to the Global Positioning System (GPS) based on the WGS84 Grid.

**Google Maps:** Produced under the conditions of "Google Maps". Information data from Mapa GISrael ORION – ME.

**PEF Maps:** The PEF maps used have been provided by courtesy the Israel Antiquities Authority.

### Measurement terminology

**Length:** c-cubit (short) = 457 mm, 18 inches. m–metre = 39.37 inches. km–kilometre =1,000 metres, 1,093 yards.

**Area:** ha–hectare = 10,000 square metres, 2.47 acres. Dunam (Arabic land measure used in Israel) = 1,000 square metres. US square = 100 sq. feet = 9.3 sq. m.

**Volume:** L-litre = 0.264 US gallon.

**Abbreviations:** ft. = foot, m = metres, mi. = mile, yds = yards, sq. = square area, c. = circa (an approximation of time or dates).

## Glossary

**Anointed**
In this book the sanctifying influence of the Holy Spirit.
**Apostolic**
Related to the Christian apostles.
**Bir**
Arabic for a water well
**Byzantine era**
313–640 AD Palestine. The rule of Constantinople capital of a mainly Christian empire of the East.
**Catholic**
The Roman Catholic Church ruled from Rome.
**Cistern**
A storage receptacle used to store water. Can be natural formed or man-made. Often used to collect rainwater.
**Crusader era**
1100–1291 AD. The rule by European powers in Palestine.
**Desposyni**
Judeo-Christians who were blood relative descendants of the mother and father of the Virgin Mary. They would be cousins to Jesus (adelphoi in the Greek).
**Essene**
Jewish sect in the Early Roman era of Palestine. Communal lifestyle and known for their piety.
**Evangelist**
In this text primarily the four writers of the Gospels of the NT.
**Fortification**
A defensive wall, rampart, fortress. Can be a walled city.

**Galilee (The)**
Traditionally divided into Upper (northern Israel and southern Lebanon) and Lower (northern Israel) above the Plain of Jezreel to Beth Kerem Valley.
**Gospel**
In this text primarily the four books of the New Testament by Matthew, Mark, Luke and John. Also used to denote the Christian message.
**Hebrew Christians**
There were different labels for Christians that came from a Jewish culture. They include those known as Judeo-Christians.
**Hamlet**
A small rural community nominally less than 500 people in Early Roman times.
**Hellenistic**
The Greek period of history. In the Near East also known as Seleucid.
**Historic vs. ancient.**
In this book the arbitrary time frame for ancient is the BC period and historic is the AD period.
**Horbat, H.**
Hebrew for historic ruined site.
**Incarnation**
Theological term for the embodiment of a divine being. In this book it has particular reference to the claim of Jesus Christ to be God the Son in human form.
**Jews**
Those who believe in the Jewish religion and the teachings of the Old Testament. Can also be cultural.

*Reference Section*

**Joshua**
The leader appointed by Moses to lead Israel into the Promised Land. Used as a generic word for the time of the entry into the Promise Land till Joshua's death (1451–1400 BC).

**Kefar, Kefr, Kfr.**
Hebrew for Village.

**Khirbet, Kh.**
Arabic word for historic ruin.

**Orthodox**
The Orthodox Church ruled from Constantinople.

**Mikvah**
Jewish purity bath allowing immersion. Other spellings used.

**Mishnah**
Jewish period of writing dated about 200 AD.

**Moses**
(1571–1451 BC) Leader of the Israelites in the Exodus. Traditional author of the Pentateuch.

**Nazareth**
A large city-polis in the Early Roman Era. Had a central urban area with surrounding rural villages and hamlets.

**Navel**
A spiritual or physical site of significance. In this book a site of the birth of the Israelite nation.

**Palestine**
Greek name for Israel (Herodotus). In 135 AD the Romans proclaimed "Syria Palaestina" joining their provinces of Judea and Syria.

**Pharisees**
Jewish sect of the Early Roman era in Palestine. Known for their many rules for living.

**Prophetic**
Information pointing to a future event. For Christians a pointing to an aspect of Jesus the Messiah. (Rev. 19:10).

**Spiritual**
The non-material realm. The Bible explains three realms: the true God, the angelic creatures (godly or evil) and the human spirit. An aspect of the sacred related to a site or event.

**Silo**
A dry storage receptacle, natural or man-made, used to store bulk items such as cereals.

**Sabbath**
The last day of the Jewish week. Observed as a day of rest.

**Talmuds**
Jewish writings (Babylonian and Jerusalem) up to 400 AD.

**Tel, Tell**
Hebrew (tel) and Arabic (tell) hill of ancient layers of human settlement.

**Torah**
The Jewish Law as recorded in the first five books of the Hebrew Bible.

**Traditional**
A historic idea, a record of a particular event, nomination of a location. Accepted over time by a large number of sources.

**Transfiguration**
The transforming of a person into a higher state of existence or splendour. Used in this book in reference to Jesus Christ.

**Vulgate**
St. Jerome's Latin translation of Bible that dates to the fourth century AD.

## ALPHA-NUMERIC CODE FOR SITES

Nazareth City sites (NC): Nazareth Hamlet/Village sites (NV)

Asher tribe sites (A), Naphtali tribe sites (N), Zebulun tribe sites (Z), Issachar (IS), and Gerizim (G).

**Nazareth city sites (Tel Yafia)**

NC1 – Nazareth city synagogue (proposed) Franciscan site.
NC2 – Yafia Byzantine site–Count Joseph's Church (proposed).
NC3 – Yafia Orthodox Church (historic).
NC4 – Yafia Catholic Church.
NC5 – Yafia Melkite Church.
NC6 – Nazareth spring/well.
NC7 – IAA excavation site in Tel Yafia (30 m or 33 yd. south of NC2)
NC8 – Nazareth execution site on east bank of Yafia valley.

**Nazareth hamlet/village sites**

NV1 – House of Joseph and Mary – Catholic Church of the Annunciation.
NV2 – St. Joseph's Workshop Church.
NV3 – St. Joseph's burial site – Sisters of Nazareth Convent.
NV4 – Synagogue Church (traditional)
NV5 – International Mary Center – Mary's neighbour's house?
NV6 – Orthodox Church of the Annunciation.
NV7 – Mary's Well – historic site.

Zebulun sites – Table 7 and 8.
Asher sites – Table 9.
Issachar sites – Table 10.
Naphtali sites – Table 11.
Other Lower Galilee sites – Table 12.

## LIST OF TABLES

1. Historical periods of the Galilee.
2. Bible verses explaining the two Nazareth sites.
3. Sacred sites at traditional Nazareth.
4. Two Nazareths: a summary through time.
5. Jericho time frame.
6. Galilean site demographics.
7. Border sites near Zebulun.
8. Internal sites of Zebulun.
9. Western border with Asher.
10. Southern border with Issachar.
11. Northern border with Naphtali.
12. Summary of Josephus' fortifications

## SUMMARY: ALTERNATIVE SITE NOMINATIONS

### Galilee proposals with Bible names in italics

- Tel Yafia (incorrectly nominated as biblical Japhia) is a suburb of modern Nazareth. It is the original urban centre of *Nazareth* in the time of Jesus.
- Biblical *Japhia* was located at Horbat Binit in the vicinity of Ilaniya near the Golani Junction. Josephus Japhia located at Har Shomer hill.
- Josephus' *Jotapata* was located at Khirbet Atosh near the modern town of Sharona south west of Tiberias.
- *Sarid* of Zebulun is Mt. Kedumim south of traditional Nazareth.
- Levite *Daberath* was located at Horbat Devora near the northern side of Mt. Tabor.
- Levite *Jokne'am* was located at Tel Qashish on the Kishon River.
- Tel Qeimun was the city of *Anahareth* of Issachar.
- Tel Yodfat is not Jotapata. It is the location of *Cana of Galilee*.
- *Shimron* was located at modern Shefar'am on the edge of the Akko Plain.
- *Kitron* was located at Tel Shimron due west of Nazareth.
- *Hammath of Naphtali* was located near Huqoq west of the Sea of Galilee.
- Josephus' *Cydessa* fortification was at Khirbet Sellame on the Nachal Tsalmon (River Zalmon).
- Joshua's *Kabul* was located as Khirbet Mi'ilya (NE of Akko) and not Tel Rosh Zayit. Tel Rosh Zayit is a candidate for *Aijalon* of Zebulun.
- Levite *Kartah* was located at Migdal Ha-Emek west of Tel Yafia.
- Levite *Nahalal* was located at Tel Hannathon.
- Levite *Dimnah* or *Rimmono* was located at Khirbet Mimlakh.
- *Kattath* was located at Tel Ein Zippori.
- *Idalah* was located at Khirbet Hittin – The Horns of Hattin .
- *Bethlehem of Zebulun* was located at Khirbet Nasir Din and Beth Maon.
- *Gabara* (LXX) of Josephus is located at Tel Adami in the Yabneel Valley.
- Issachar site of *Tabor* was located at Ein Zelef on NE side of Mt. Tabor.
- *Shahazimah* of Issachar was located at Khirbet Sharona.
- *Beth Shemesh* of Issachar was located at Tel Beit Yerah.
- Fortified *Zer of Naphtali* is Khirbet Sellame.
- Fortified *Ziddim of Naphtali* is Khirbet Zeitun er Rama.
- Fortified *Chinnereth of Naphtali* is Tel Kinarot on the Sea of Galilee.
- *Ith Kazin* at Poriya and Khirbet Qadis near the Sea of Galilee (south).

## CREDITS FOR ILLUSTRATIONS

Unless indicated below all maps, plans and photos used in the book are by the author who holds the copyright. No part for reproduction without permission.

Some illustration credits have been given in the captions which is why some numbers are missing below. The following information is further acknowledgement of some of the credits with any conditions.

**SECTION A**

A.01 Plaque of Jesus' cross. No source for this image has been found.

A.02 Nazareth 1920's. Fadil Saba photograph. Wikipedia Commons. Public domain.

A.04 Painting of Babylon city. Wikipedia Commons. Source unknown.

A.05 Photo of author's copy of the book by René Salm.

A.06 St. Luke. Artist G. Reni. Bob Jones University Library. WikiArt.org. Public domain.

A.07 Icon St. Matthew. Courtesy Convent of St. Elizabeth. Canada. www.conventofsaintelizabeth.org.

A.15 Town plan based on information in Sukenik E.L. 1951, *The Ancient Synagogue at Yafa near Nazareth,* Preliminary Report. The Hebrew University of Jerusalem. p.12.

A.16, 17, 18, 19, 20 Illustrations used courtesy of Israel Antiquities Authority Report Vol 124 – 2012. Photo credits Assaf Peretz.

A.25 Map by author. Base Map 'Nazareth Survey 1946', Courtesy National Library of Australia, ref. yn1117986-sd-cd. Used with permission.

A.30 International Mary Center aerial photo. Courtesy of the International Mary Center, Nazareth. www.cimdn.org.

A.31 James the Less icon. Credit Wikimedia Commons. Public domain.

A.34 St. Paul's conversion. Artist Gustave Dore. WikiArt.org. Public domain.

A.35 Engraving of 'Eusebius of Caesarea, church historian'. Wikipedia Commons. Public domain.

A.36. Detail 'St. Jerome in his study', Wikipedia Commons. Public domain.

A.37 Detail 'The Caesarea inscription as reconstructed by Avi-Yonah', Source: *Caesarea, Queen of the Coast,* Israel Nature and Parks Authority, 2009. Reproduction by author of text supplied by Israel Exploration Society.

A.39 'El'azar Hakalir' street sign Tel Aviv. Wikipedia Commons. Public domain.

A.41 Edward Robinson. Wikipedia Commons. Public domain.

## SECTION B

B.01 'Jesus unrolls the book in the Synagogue'. Artist James Tissot c.1886. Credit Brooklyn Museum. Public domain.

B.04 Part detail Mary and Joseph. Engraving by Julius Carolsfeld. Courtesy Pitts Theological Library, Candler School of Theology, Emory University, USA.

B.06 King Janneus. Wikipedia Commons. Public domain.

B.07 King Herod. Wikipedia Commons. Public domain.

B.08 Herod Antipas. Artist J.Tissot. Wikipedia Commons. Public domain.

B.14 Authors' plan of Gamla Synagoue based on Horbury, W (ed.) 1999, *The Cambridge History of Judaism*, vol. 3, 'The Early Roman Period'. Cambridge University Press, Cambridge, UK, p. 272.

B16 Author's town plan based on plan in Archaeology report. Refer A15.

B.20 Jewish shofar. Wikipedia Commons. Public domain.

B.21 Isaiah Scroll. Wikipedia Commons. Public domain.

B.22 'Jesus rejected in his home town'. Engraving by Jerome Nadal 1595 AD, <http://catholic-resources.org/Nadal/040.jpg>.

B.27 Author's sketch showing the proposed scenario of the attempt to kill Jesus south west of the city.

B.28 Photo of excavation of Yafia synagogue 1953. Credit 'Japhia NEAEHL Vol 2'. Courtesy Israel Exploration Society.

B.29 Yafia synagogue plan by author based on information in Archaeology report. Refer A.15.

B.34 Author's plan of Byzantine site based on town plan in Archaeology report. Refer A 15.

B.35 Detail 'Emperor Constantine I, presenting a model of the city to the blessed Virgin Mary', Wikipedia Commons. Public domain.

B.39 Yafia synagogue mosaic. Permission for reproduction given by Hebrew University. Overlay notes and interpretation by author.

B.40,45 St. John the Evangelist in the Lindisfarne Gospels' (London, British Library, MS Cotton Nero D IV, f. 209v). Manuscript Book cover to Lindisfarne Gospels. Courtesy the British Library.

B. 41 Author's photo of original Yafa mosaic in IAA Museum Jerusalem.

B.44 Zidan, Omar, 2015, Yafi'a, Hadashot Arkheologiyot, Volume 127, p.3. Courtesy of the IAA.

## SECTION C

C.01 'Dividing the land of Canaan', Henry Davenport Northrop 1894 AD, Engraving from Treasures of the Bible. Permission to reproduce from La Vista Church of Christ, Omaha, Nebraska, USA.

C.02 Map <http://www.mideastweb.org/northernisraelmap1949.htm>.

C.04 Detail 'Map of Canaan as divided among the tribes'. Bible map p. 266 in King James Version Bible owned by author. Publisher details missing.

C.07 Rembrant painting. Credit Wikipedia Commons. Public domain.

C.11 'The woodcut engraving of Flavius Josephus appearing in William Whiston's translation of his works'. Electronic version. Public domain.

C.12 Vespasian the Roman general. Wikipedia Creative Commons. Public domain. Russian source. Pushkin Museum. Author Shakko.

C.17 Engraving of Roman attack on Jewish fortification 67 AD. 'Roman Jewish Wars 66–135'. Courtsey of heritage-history. com.

C.18 Titus, Denarius' reverse side. <http://www.wildwinds.com/coins/sear5/s2505.html>. Public domain.

C.24 Detail the Arch of Titus. Rome. Wikipedia Commons. Public domain.

## SECTION D

D.01 Road to Emmaus. Engraving by Gustave Dore. Courtesy Pitts Theology Library, Candler School of Theology, Emory University, USA.

D.04 Mount Kedumim. Free photo from Almog. Wikimedia Commons.

D.08 Levite ceremony engraving. Artist J. Carolsfeld. Courtesy Pitts Theology Library, Candler School of Theology, Emory Univesity, USA.

D.11 'Miracle at Cana', by Vladimir Makovsky 1887 AD. WikiArt. Public domain.

D.23 Transfiguration engraving by J. Carolsfeld. Courtesy Pitts Theological Library, Candler School of Theology, Emory University, USA.

D.26 St. Elias church Mt. Tabor. Photo source unknown.

D.28 Author's plan based on information in Pringle, D *The Churches of the Crusader Kingdom of Jerusalem,* Cambridge University Press, UK, p. 67.

D.29 Church plan St. Elias by author based on information in Pringle, D *The Churches of the Crusader Kingdom of Jerusalem,* p. 82.

## SECTION F APPENDICES

F.08 Author's plans based on dimension in Bull, R 1968, 'Excavations of Tel er-Ras on Mt. Gerizim', *The Biblical Archaeologist,* vol. XXXI, No.2.

F.09 Roman coin. Reproduced from Archaeology report noted in F.10. Courtesy of American Society of Oriental Research.

# BIBLIOGRAPHY

All electronic references have been accessed and checked from June to October 2016 in this Bibliography. The online addresses are given for encyclopedias, dictionaries and some references quoted in the footnotes.

## Bibles

*The NKJV Study Bible*, 1997, 2007, Copyright © by Thomas Nelson Inc., Nashville, TN, USA.

Brenton, Sir Lancelot 1851, *The Septuagint with Apocrypha: Greek and English*, Samuel Bagster & Sons. Ltd, London, UK.

Green, Jay (ed.) 2005, *The Interlinear Hebrew–Aramaic Old Testament*, Volumes 1–3, 2nd Edition, Hendrickson, Peabody, Massachusetts, USA.

Green, Jay P(ed.) 2005, *The Interlinear Greek–English New Testament*, Volume 1, 2nd Edition, Hendrickson, Peabody, Massachusetts, USA.

## Bible Dictionaries, Encyclopedias & Commentaries

*Smith's Bible Dictionary*, Available at: http://www.biblestudytools.com/dictionaries/smiths-bible-dictionary.

*McClintock and Strong Biblical Cyclopedia*, Available at: http://www.biblicalcyclopedia.com/

*Holman Bible Dictionary*, Available at: http://www.studylight.org/dictionaries/hbd/

*Easton's Bible Dictionary*, Available at: http://www.biblestudytools.com/dictionaries/eastons-bible-dictionary/

*Hitchcock's Bible Names Dictionary*, Available at: http://www.biblestudytools.com/dictionaries/hitchcocks-bible-names/

*International Standard Bible Encyclopedia*, Available at: http://www.internationalstandardbible.com/

*Jewish Encyclopedia*, Available at: http://www.jewishencyclopedia.com/

*Jewish Virtual Library*, Available at: https://www.jewishvirtuallibrary.org/

*New Advent Catholic Encyclopedia*, Available at: http://www.newadvent.org/cathen/

Sacred-texts.com. (2016). *Biblical Commentary on the Old Testament by Carl Friedrich Keil and Franz Delitzsch:* Joshua: Joshua Chapter 19. [online] Available at: http://www.sacred-texts.com/bib/cmt/kad/jos019.htm.

## Books

Aharoni, Y 1979, *The Land of the Bible: A Historical Geography* (ed.) Rainey AF, The Westminister Press, Philadelphia, USA.

Bagatti, B 2001, *Ancient Christian Villages of Galilee*, Franciscan Printing Press, Jerusalem, Israel.

Bagatti, B 1969, *Excavations in Nazareth Volume One*, Franciscan Printing Press, Jerusalem, Israel.

Bagatti, B 2002, *Excavations in Nazareth Volume Two*, Franciscan Printing Press, Jerusalem, Israel.

Briand, J 1994, *The Judeo-Christian Church of Nazareth*, 4th Edition, Franciscan Printing Press, Jerusalem, Israel.

Bauckham, R 1990, *Jude and the relatives of Jesus in the Early Church*, T&T Clark International, London, UK.

Charlesworth, JH 2006, *Jesus and Archaeology*, Eerdmans.

Fine, S, (ed.) 1996, *Sacred Realm- The Emergence of the Synagogue in the Ancient World*, Yeshiva University Museum, Oxford University Press, Oxford, UK.

Fiensey, D and Strange J 2014, *Galilee in the Late Second Temple and Mishnaic Periods*, in 'Life, Culture, and Society,' Fortress Press, Minneapolis, MN 55440, USA.

Finkelstein, I and Silberman, N 2002, *The Bible Unearthed, Archaeology's new vision of ancient Israel and the origin of its sacred texts*, Simon and Schuster, New York, USA.

Flavius, Josephus 1987, *The Works of Josephus*, New Updated Edition, Whiston, W. (trans.), Hendrickson Publishers Inc., Peabody, MA, USA.

Frend, W and Stevenson, J 1987, *A New Eusebius– Documents illustrating the history of the Church to AD 337*, Society for Promoting Christian Knowledge, London, UK.

Gal, Z 1992 *Lower Galilee during the Iron Age*, Eisenbrauns, Winona Lake, Indiana, USA.

Horbury, W (ed.) 1999, *The Cambridge History of Judaism*, vol. 3, 'The Early Roman Period', Cambridge University Press, Cambridge, UK, <http://books.google.com.au/books?id=MA-4VX5gWS4C>.

Jones, FN 2005, *The Chronology of the Old Testament*, Master Books, Green Forest, AR, USA.

Lapin, H 2001, *Economy, Geography, and Provincial History in Latter Roman Palestine*, Mohr Siebeck, Tubingen, Germany.

Levine, LI 2005, *The Ancient Synagogue – the first thousand years*, Yale University Press, London, UK.

Leibner, U 2009, *Settlement and History in Hellenistic, Roman, and Byzantine Galilee*, Mohr Siebeck, Tubingen, Germany.

Maier, PL 1999, *Eusebius – The Church History*, Kregel Publications, Grand Rapids, MI, USA.

Mazar, A 1992, *Archaeology of the Land of the Bible 10,000-586 BCE*. Yale University Press, New Haven, USA.

Murphy-O'Connor, J 1998, *The Holy Land*, Oxford Archaeological Guides, Oxford University Press, Oxford, UK.

Negev, A and Gibson, S (eds) 2001, *Archaeological Encyclopedia of the Holy Land*, Continuum, New York, USA.

Pixner, B 2001, *Paths of the Messiah and Sites of the early Church from Galilee to Jerusalem*, Ignatius Press, San Francisco, USA.

Pringle, D 1998, *The Churches of the Crusader Kingdom of Jerusalem*. vol. II, Cambridge University Press, Cambridge, UK.

Reed, JL 2002, *Archaeology and the Galilean Jesus*, Trinity Press International, Harrisburg, Pennsylvania, USA.

Robinson, E and Smith, E 1841, *Biblical Researches in Palestine, Mount Sinai and Arabia Petraea*, Vol III, Crocker and Brewster, Boston, USA.

Rohl, D 1995, *A Test of Time – the Bible from Myth to History*, Century Ltd, London, UK.

Safrai, Z 2005, *The Economy of Roman Palestine*, Taylor and Francis, Florence, Kentucky, USA.

Salm, R 2008, *The Myth of Nazareth*, American Atheist Press, Cranford, New Jersey, USA.

Schmoger, C (ed.) 2004, *The Life of Jesus Christ*, vol. 1-4, Tan Books and Publishers Inc., Rockford, Illinois, USA.

Spigel, C 2002 *Ancient Synagogue Seating Capacities*. Mohr Siebeck, Tubingen, Germany.

Stemberger, G 2000, *Jews and Christians in the Holy Land*, T&T Clark Ltd, Edinburgh, UK.

Taylor, J 1993, *Christians and the Holy Places – The myth of Jewish–Christian origins*, Clarendon Press, Oxford, UK.

Urman, D and Flesher, P 1995, *Ancient Synagogues – Historical Analysis and Archaeological Discovery*, Brill Academic Publishers, Leiden, Netherlands.

Wolf, CU 2006, *The Onomasticon of Eusebius Pamphili*, <http://www.ccel.org/ccel/pearse/morefathers/files/eusebius_onomasticon_01_intro.htm>.

## Archaeology Reports

Alexandre, Y 2012, *Yafi'a*, Final Report, vol. 124, Israel Antiquities Authority, Jerusalem, <http://www.hadashot-esi.org.il/report_detail_eng.aspx?id=2084>.

Alexandre, Y and Gould, E 2011, *Horbat Binit – Final Report*, Israel Antiquities Authority, Jerusalem, <http://www.hadashot-esi.org.il/report_detail_eng.aspx?id=1887&mag_id=118>.

Alexandre, Y and Gould, E 2011, *Ilaniyya*, Israel Antiquities Authority, Jerusalem,<http://www.hadashot-esi.org.il/report_detail_eng.aspx?id=1885&print=all>.

Atrash, W Nazareth (West) (2009), Israel Antiquities Authority. [online] Available at: http://www.hadashot-esi.org.il/report_detail_eng.aspx?id=1073&mag_id=115.

Aviam, M *Yodfat*, Israel Antiquities Authority, Jerusalem, <http://www.antiquities.org.il/site_Item_eng.asp?id=126>.

Bienkowski, P 1990, 'Jericho was destroyed in the Middle Bronze Age, Not the Late Bronze Age', *Biblical Archaeology Society*, 16:05.

Bietak, M and Höflmayer, F 2007, *Introduction: High and Low Chronology*, Verlag der Österreichischen Akademie der Wissenschaften.

Bull, R 1968, 'The Excavation of Tell er-Ras on Mt. Gerizim', *The Biblical Archaeologist*, Vol XXXI, no. 2. < https://www.jstor.org/stable/i361169>.

Dalali-Amos, E 2009, *Ilut*, Israel Antiquities Authority, Jerusalem, <http://www.hadashot-esi.org.il/report_detail_eng.aspx?id=1038&mag_id=115>.

Dark, K 2012, 'Early Roman-Period Nazareth and the Sisters of Nazareth Convent', *The Antiquaries Journal*, 92, 2912, The Society of Antiquaries of London, UK.

Dark, K 2012, 'The Byzantine Church of the Nutrition in Nazareth rediscovered' *Palestine Exploration Quarterly* 144 (3):164-184.

Dark, K and Ribak, E 2009 *A report on the unpublished excavation by Roland de Vaux at the 'Synagogue Church' in Nazareth, Israel*, Reading Medieval Studies, p. 35.

Covello-Paran, K 2015, *Ein el-Hilu (Migdal Ha-'Emeq)* [online]. Available at: http://www.baslibrary.org/new-encyclopedia-archaeological-excavations-holy-land/0/0/46/ein-el-hilu-migdal-ha-emeq.

Grey, M and Spigel, Chad 2015, 'Huqoq in the late Hellenistic and early Roman periods', in *Galilee in the Late Second Temple and Mishnaic Periods*, vol. 2, Fiensy, D and Strange J (eds), Fortress Press, Minneapolis, USA.

Sukenik, EL 1951, *The Ancient Synagogue at Yafa near Nazareth*. Preliminary Report, The Hebrew University of Jerusalem, Jerusalem, Israel.

van den Brink, E and Ad, U 2011, *Tel Qashish,* Israel Antiquities Authority [online] Available at: http://www.hadashot-esi.org.il/report_detail_eng.aspx?id=1894.

Zidan, O 2015, *Yaf'ia*, Israel Antiquities Authority, Jerusalem <http://www.hadashot-esi.org.il/Report_Detail_Eng.aspx?id=24841>.

## Articles and Theses

Avi-Yonah, M 2011, *The Caesarea Inscription of the Twenty-Four Priestly Courses,* <http://www.textexcavation.com/priestlycoursesinscription.html>.

Avni, G 2010, *The Persian Conquest of Jerusalem (614 c.e.)—An Archaeological Assessment,* p. 35. (accessed via: https://www.jstor.org/stable/27805159).

Bacchiocchi, S 2001, *Wine in the Bible: A Biblical Study on the Use of Alcoholic Beverages.* Biblical Perspectives. Berrien Springs, Michigan, USA.

Bimson, J and Livingston, D 1987, 'Redating the Exodus'. *Biblical Archaeology Review,* 13:05.

Dever, WG 1991, 'Tell el-Daba and Levantine Middle Bronze Age Chronology: A rejoinder to Manfred Bietak' *Bulletin of the American Schools of Oriental Research,* No. 281.

Goranson, SC, 1990, *The Joseph of Tiberias Episode in Epiphanus',* Department of Religion, Ph.D thesis, Duke University, <http://people.duke.edu/~goranson/Joseph_of_Tiberias.pdf>.

Jenks, G 2013, *The Quest for the Historical Nazareth,* School of Theology, Charles Sturt University, St. Francis Theological College, Brisbane, Australia. <http://www.academia.edu/3988852/>.

Laney, JC 1977, *The Identification of Cana of Galilee from Selective Geographical Problems in the Life of Christ,* Doctoral dissertation, Dallas Theological Seminary,<http://www.bibleplaces.com/Identification_of_Cana_of_Galilee,_by_J_Carl_Laney.pdf>.

Lissak, RS 2014, *Dabburiya, An Arabic Village was formerly the Israeli/Jewish Davarita* [online] Available at: http://archive.is/I23Z.

Maeir, AM 2000, *Is the Middle Chronology Dead?* [online] Available at: http://www.tau.ac.il/~archpubs/projects/mbsg/maeirlecture.html.

Miller, JM 1983, *Site Identification: A Problem Area in Contemporary Biblical Scholarship,* Zeitschrift des Deutschen Palästina-Vereins (1953-) Bd. 99.

Pritz, R, 1985, *Joseph of Tiberias – The Legend of a 4th Century Jewish Christian,* Mishkan – A Theological Forum on Jewish Evangelism, <http://caspari.com/new/images/stories/archives/Mishkan/mishkan02.pdf>.

Stein, J 2013, *Josephus' Fortifications in the Galilee,* <http://www.academia.edu/6390419/Josephus_Fortifications_In_the_Galilee>.

Tuccinardi, E 2010, *Nazareth the Caesarea Inscription, and the hand of God,* Salm, R (trans.), <https://archive.org/details/NazarethTheCaesareaInscriptionAndTheHandOfGod>.

Vandermeersch, B 2002, *The excavation of Qafzeh,* Bulletin du Centre de recherche Francais a Jerusalem No.10, <http://bcrfj.revues.org/1192> pp. 65–70.

Wood, B 2009, *Recent Research on the Date and Setting of the Exodus.* [online] Biblearchaeology.org. Available at: http://www.biblearchaeology.org/post/2009/10/19/Recent-Research-on-the-Date-and-Setting-of-the-Exodus.aspx.

# INDEX

**Abbreviations**
archeo.– archaeologist; arch.– architect; Gk.–Greek word Heb.–Hebrew word; hist.– historian; Kh.–Khirbet; J.– Josephus site; rel.– family relative of Jesus. St.– saint; S.– Septuagint site; site – biblical site; mt.– mount.

## A

**Abbasid Era,** 13, 205
**Abraham,** patriarch x, xiv, 15, 126, 132, 161, 171, 204, 222, 252
**Adami,** Har hill 141, 142, 151, 152, 235, 242
**Adami,** Tel site 152 ,231, 257
**adelphoi,** Gk. 47, 49, 254
**Aeolic,** style 114
**Africanus,** hist. 47, 50, 56, 57, 182, 221
**Ahab,** King 216
**Ahaz,** King 164
**Aikaterini,** nun 191
**Ailut,** Tel site *see* Ilut
**Akko,** Ptolemais, city 62, 75, 131, 133–135, 142, 180, 181, 183, 234, 235, 238, 242, 249, 257
**Akrith,** Tel site 235
**Alexander the Great,** 13, 227
**Alexandre,** Y. archaeo. 28, 30, 33, 46, 88, 150, 152, 264
**alignment,** geographical 165, 197–202
**almah,** Heb. virgin 164
**Alphaeus,** rel. 47–49
**altar,** 90, 92, 93, 120, 130, 158, 161, 162, 167, 171, 210, 222, 225–229, 230
**Amalekites,** ethnic 213, 215
**Amarna,** Egyptian 215
**Amenhotep,** pharoah 216
**Amidah,** prayer 67, 73, 85
**Amon,** King 243
**Amorites,** ethnic 213

**Amoth,** Tel S. site 232, 233
**amphora,** vessel 176, 179
**Anaharath,** site 239
**angel,** 4, 5, 17, 21, 35, 41, 67, 70, 107, 119, 157, 173, 204, 206, 210, 247
**Angkor Wat,** Cambodia 6
**Anna,** prophetess 70
**Anne,** Virgin Mary's mother 42, 47, 49, 247, 249
**Annunciation** of Mary, 4, 6, 247
**anoint,** 81, 82, 91, 94, 95, 121, 176, 189, 208, 254
**Antiochus IV,** ruler 228
**Antonia fortress,** 77
**apostolic,** Christian 43, 45, 48
**Arab & Arabic,** 17, 34, 44, 61, 63, 108, 118, 128, 158, 180, 182, 205, 255
**Aram Naharayin,** region 214
**Arbel,** hill and J. site 131, 231, 232, 234, 241
**Archelaus,** King 70
**architriklinos,** Gk. 182
**Ark of God,** 80, 222–225
**Asher,** tribal xiv, 13, 116, 131, 133, 134, 135, 180, 235, 256
**Assyria,** Assyrian 7, 13, 30, 204, 212, 243
**Atonement,** religious 94, 95, 99, 104
**Atosh,** Kh. site 141, 142, 241, 243, 244, 251, 257
**Augustine,** St. schol. xii, 158
**Augustus,** Caesar 58
**Avigad,** N. archaeo. 109

**Avi-Yonah,** M. archaeo. 59, 243, 258, 265
**Awakening,** Great revival, 126
**Ayyubid Era,** 13, 205

## B

**Babel,** tower & city 6, 7, 127
**Babylonia,** 13
**Bactrians,** ethnic 252
**Baethegeneth,** S. site 235
**Baethman,** S. site 234
**Bagatti,** B. archaeo. 40, 41, 42, 48, 63, 89, 108, 182, 193,
**Bagdad,** Iraq 13
**Baitharava,** S. site 231
**Balata,** Tel site 222, 223, 225, 226
**baptism,** 19, 43, 70, 78, 96, 111, 112
**Barak,** Israelite 71, 163, 189
**Bar Kokhba revolt,** 229
**Barluzzi,** A. arch. 190
**Bar Mitzvah,** ceremony 72
**Barsabas,** rel. 49
**baths,** purity 24, 182, 250
**Beer Sheba,** Kh. site 140, 236, 241
**Beit Kerem,** valley 131, 134, 232, 235
**Berlin,** Germany 60
**Bersabe,** *see* Beer Sheba, J. site 140, 241
**Bethlehem** of Judea, site 11, 19, 36, 46, 54, 70
**Bethlehem** of Zebulun, site 132, 233, 234, 257
**Bethsaida of Galilee,** site 13, 249
**Bethuel,** site 250

**Bimson,** J. archaeo. 213, 265
**Binit,** Horbat site 149, 150, 151, 153, 231, 257, 264
**Bir el-Amir,** water well 29
**Bread Mountain,** Sarid 252
**Brentano,** C. schol. 245
**British Mandate,** 13, 124, 205, 260
**British Library,** 117–118,
**British Museum,** 8
**Bronze Age,** 13, 172, 212-216, 234, 236
**brow** of hill, 97, 99, 101
**Brueghel,** P. artist 6
**builder,** 14, 41, 73–75, 115, 120
**Bull,** R. archaeo. 227, 229, 264
**Burckhardt,** J. explorer 7
**burning bush,** Moses 127
**Byzantine Era,** 13, 21, 33, 37, 39, 51, 60– 62, 81, 82, 108, 110, 114, 118, 190, 193, 194, 205, 229, 238, 242, 254
**Byzantine churches,** 22, 37, 41, 44, 45, 57, 81, 82, 108, 109, 113, 161, 190, 192, 193, 194, 195, 201, 202, 246, 256

## C

**Cabul/Kabul,** Land of 134, 235
**Caesar,** Roman ruler 55, 138, 143
**Caesarea Inscription,** 58, 59
**Caesarea Maritima,** 55, 58
**Caiaphas,** High Priest 17
**Calvary,** Jesus' crucifixion 54, 127
**Camon,** Mount 131, 232
**Cana** of Galilee, site vi, 148, 158, 174–186, 201, 202, 206, 208, 257
**Canaan,** Land of 122, 204, 213, 222

**Capernaum,** site 19, 84, 86, 99, 105, 125, 130
**Caphareccho,** J. site 241
**Carmel,** Mount 71, 133, 135, 235, 251
**carpenter,** Joseph & Jesus 27, 45, 46, 55, 67, 73–76, 97, 99, 104, 107, 108, 110, 119, 120, 247
**Catanath,** S. site 234
**Catholic Church,** viii, 6, 21, 32, 35,–37, 40–42, 44, 46, 47, 71, 90, 162, 189, 190, 191, 192, 193, 205, 210, 245, 251, 254, 256
**Cedron,** site 25
**Cendevia,** Lake 135
**Center, Mary International** 46, 47, 256
**certain place,** 207
**Charlesworth,** J. schol. 70, 73, 262
**Chinnereth,** site 236, 257
**Chisloth Tabor,** site 130, 147, 190, 231
**Chosroes II,** Persian king 60, 61
**Church of St. Joseph,** 45, 256
**Church of the Annunciation** xi, 6, 21, 36, 37, 40–42, 45 – 47, 51, 52, 100, 156, 162, 196, 199, 201, 205, 210, 220, 247, 256
**Church of the Nutrition** 41
**Church, St George** Orthodox, Yafia 108, 109
**Church of the Transfiguration,** Catholic 190–193
**Cilicia,** region 111
**cistern,** storage 8, 29, 42, 46, 150, 170, 183–186, 249, 254
**Clement** of Alexandria, historian 252
**Cleopas,** disciple 17, 154
**Clopas,** rel. 49
**cloud on Mt. Tabor,** 189, 191, 192

**Cochaba,** village 47, 50, 182
**Colosseum,** Rome 136, 138
**Conder,** C. surveyor 127, 158, 180
**Conon,** martyr 51
**conspiracy of Nazareth,** viii, 6, 17, 36, 65, 221
**constancy,** Law of 88
**Constantine,** Emperor 57, 60, 112, 229, 254, 255
**Constantinople,** capital 33, 57, 60, 112, 129, 254, 255
**Cornelius,** Centurion 55
**Count Joseph,** 110–121, 205, 206, 256
**covenant with God,** 72, 126, 214, 222–224, 230
**cross of Jesus,** xii, 2, 3, 6, 17, 58, 74, 221
**Crusader Era,** 34, 37, 44, 46, 63, 81, 190, 194, 205, 239, 249, 254
**Curses,** Mount of 92
**Cushan,** Hurrian ruler 214, 216
**Cydnus** River, 112
**Cyril,** St. bishop x, 190

## D

**Dabbasheth,** site 130, 231
**Daberath,** Levite city 130, 145, 147, 149, 158, 172, 173, 189, 196, 199, 201, 231, 232, 238, 250, 257
**Dabor,** see Daberath 172
**Daboura,** see Daberath 172
**Dabrath,** see Daberath 147
**Daburiya,** site 25, 190, 238
**Dagon,** Beth site 235
**Dalley,** S. historian 8
**Darb el Hawara** route 151
**Dark,** K. archaeo. 26, 45, 81
**David,** King 5, 15, 16, 17, 30, 35, 38, 50, 67, 72, 73, 119, 204, 214, 215, 216
**Davira, Davrat,** site 172
**Debba,** see Daberath, S. site 172, 231

**Deberi,** *see* Daburiya, S. site 25, 172
**Deborah,** prophetess 71, 163, 189
**Deburieh,** *see* Daburiya 147
**Decius,** Emperor 51, 54
**dedication,** of sites and plaques 83, 108, 168, 171
**denarius,** coin 144, 260
**Descentilus chapel,** 190, 192
**Desposyni,** Jesus' relatives 50, 51, 55, 57, 182, 254
**Dever,** W. archaeo. 213, 265
**Devora,** *see* Daberath 172, 231, 238, 257
**Dimnah,** Levite city 132, 232, 233, 257
**Diocletian,** Emperor 54
**Diocesarea,** *see* Sepphoris 112
**Domitian,** Emperor 50, 54

# E

**Early Bronze Era** 161, 205, 238, 239
**Early Roman Era,** 13, 20, 21, 24, 28, 30–32, 38, 39, 42, 44–46, 119, 120, 142, 182, 205, 208, 217, 218, 220, 221, 241, 254, 255
**Eastern Empires,** 13, 205
**Ebal,** Mount vi, 91, 92, 93, 120, 130, 200, 202, 222, 223, 224– 226, 230
**Ecumenical Council,** 43, 44
**Eden,** Paradise 197
**Egeria,** pilgrim 43
**Egypt & Egyptian,** 14, 19, 42, 43, 55, 70, 71, 132, 212, 214, 215, 216
**Eika,** Kh, site 234, 236, 241
**Ein Hilu,** site 240
**Ekgai,** S. site 235
**Eleazar ben Killir, poet** 61, 205
**Elias,** St. church 191, 192, 193, 194, 260
**Elijah,** prophet 41, 71, 164, 166, 187–189, 191, 200, 206, 251, 252
**Elisha,** prophet 164, 191, 252

**Elizabeth,** rel. 5, 19
**Emek,** Beth site 235
**Emmaus,** warm bath site 154, 158, 250
**Emmerich,** A. nun 245–252
**Encyclopedia Biblica,** 1, 9
**Ephesus,** Turkey, site 12, 43, 44, 47, 246
**Ephraim,** tribal 116
**Epiphanius,** bishop & historian 34, 111–113
**Erez Tabbur,** Heb. Navel of Land 93, 200, 255
**Esdrelon,** Plain (Jezreel) 252
**Esedek Gola,** *see* Sarid, S. site 160, 231
**Essene,** sect 15, 75, 83, 248, 254
**Eth Kazin,** site 130, 231, 232
**Europe,** 6, 13, 126, 245, 254
**Eusebius,** bishop & historian 12, 50, 56–58, 152, 165, 221, 238, 242, 262, 263
**Eustochium,** pilgrim 43
**Evangelist,** Christian proclamation 10, 11, 116–118, 254, 259
**execution site,** 19, 100–105, 256
**Exodus,** book & event 70, 85, 115, 127, 169, 212, 214, 216, 265, 266
**eyrie,** nest *see* Jotapata 250, 251
**Ezekiel,** prophet 116, 197, 200

# F

**Feast,** religious 72, 176–179, 182, 191
**Fiensy,** D. schol. 38, 236, 264
**Finkelstein,** I. archaeo. 13, 196, 215, 262
**fishing,** Galilean 13, 135
**focal point,** spiritual 5, 85, 200

**fortifications,** 132, 138–143, 149, 151, 153, 254, 266, 180, 181, 213, 236, 237, 241–244, 251, 256
**Francis,** St. of Assisi 44
**Franciscans,** Catholic 22, 34, 37, 41, 43–45, 81, 82, 85, 89, 90, 103, 202, 256
**Fright,** Church of Mary's 52, 100

# G

**Gaal,** Shechem observer 225, 226
**Gabara,** J. site 142, 152, 231, 250, 257
**Gabaroth,** J. site 242
**Gabriel,** angel ii, 4, 5, 35, 41, 42, 55, 119, 173, 204, 210
**Gaiphael,** Japhia S. site 232
**Gal,** Z. archaeo. 24, 28, 30, 38, 148, 172, 217, 238, 262
**Galilean** 13, 14, 23, 24, 28, 33, 38, 39, 77, 83, 118, 139, 217, 218, 220, 244, 256
**Galilee,** region ix, x, xii, 5, 11–15, 23, 38, 47, 50, 51, 55, 56, 59, 60, 63, 64, 69, 70, 71, 73, 75, 76, 77, 79, 83–85, 86, 89, 110, 112, 113, 114, 121–124, 130, 131, 137, 139, 140–143, 149, 151, 153, 165, 178, 180, 181, 184, 206, 217, 218, 231–234, 249, 250, 254, 256, 257
**Gamla,** J. site 84, 86, 87, 259
**Garis,** J. site 234, 242
**Gasche,** archaeo 213
**gates of city** 25, 27, 28, 75, 120, 146, 247
**Gath Hepher,** Tel site 75, 130, 131, 145, 150, 231, 232
**Geisler,** N. schol. 10
**Genesareth,** Lake 133
**Genesis,** Book 6, 132, 161
**Gennessar,** Lake, J. site 140, 241

269

Gentile  13, 14, 48, 51, 55, 56, 57, 60, 82, 130, 204
Gerizim, Mount  vi, 92, 93, 202, 222–230, 256
Gesenius, W. schol.  172, 173, 195
Ghuweir, Tel site  236
Gibson, Mel  245
Gibson, S. archaeo.  8, 109, 116, 181, 212, 229, 243, 263
glass making,  135
Global Positioning System, GPS  xiv
glory, radiant  175, 176, 189
Google Earth coord.  xiv
Gophna, site  249
Gospel, Christian message and books  vi, ix, x, xii, 1, 3– 6, 10–13, 16, 20, 24, 27, 32, 41, 47, 49, 50, 55–60, 65, 67, 69, 73, 80, 82–85, 91, 94, 95, 99, 100, 101, 104, 112, 116, 118, 121, 125, 130, 147, 177, 180, 182, 184, 189, 195, 206, 208, 220, 221, 248, 254
Gould, E. schol.  150, 152, 264
Govel, Tel site  241, 250
grace, God's mercy  71, 77, 92, 189, 225, 230, 232
graffiti, Church  43
Greek words,  x, xiv, 3, 5, 7, 11, 15, 16, 24, 28, 38, 44, 47, 50, 58, 70, 72, 73, 99, 101, 102, 116, 127, 165, 177, 178, 179, 205, 218, 241, 249, 253
Greenwich, UK  200
grotto sites, sacred  37, 42, 194, 210

## H

Hadrian, Emperor  54, 229
Ha-Horesh, site  51
hamlet, small settlement, Nazarth  ix, 6, 8, 10, 18–21, 24–26, 35, 38, 39, 41, 51, 55, 58, 62, 65, 68, 74, 80–82, 97, 101, 108, 119, 146, 156, 204–206, 208, 217, 218, 220, 247, 254, 255, 256
Hammath, Naphtali site  236, 237, 250, 257
hanging gardens, ancient site  7, 8
Hannathon, site  130, 131, 232, 234, 257
Hapizzez, priests  59
Har Arbel, site  131, 231, 232, 241
Harashim, site  235
Har Brakha, mount  224, 225
Har Nitai, mount  131, 231, 237
Ha-Shomer, hill  151, 152
Hasmonean kingdom,  30, 76, 86, 243
Hattin, Horns of  234, 241, 257
Hazor, site  213
Heavenly Father,  73, 176
Hebrew Christians,  21, 37, 48, 55, 57, 82, 107, 110, 113, 116, 118, 121, 254
Hebrew root, Heb. meanings  16, 128, 157, 166
Hegesippus, hist.  48, 50
Helen, St.  161
Heli, rel.  42, 47, 49
Helios, pagan  115, 116
Hellenistic era,  13, 14, 30, 39, 63, 150, 180, 182,205, 229, 231, 234, 236, 238, 249, 254
Heraclius, Byzantine General  61
Herod Agrippa II,  14, 70, 71, 76
Herod the Great, King  14, 58, 70, 71, 76, 137, 143
Herod Antipas,  14, 25, 54, 71, 77

Hiram, King  134
Holy Apostles, Church of, Yafia  89
Holy Land,  58, 155
Holy Spirit,  5, 78, 107, 119, 157, 173, 230, 254
Homer, historian  7
Hopkins, K. historian  138
Hubbard, R. schol.  24, 147, 148, 149
Huqoq, site  83, 236, 257
Hurrians, ethnic  214
Hyrcanus, J. King  228, 229

## I

Iafo, see Japhia  152
Idalah, site  132, 233, 234, 241, 257
Ilaniya, historic  151–153, 250, 257
Ilaniya, moshav  149, 151, 152, 208, 250, 257
Ilut, site also Aiut  51, 63, 231
incarnation of Jesus,  ix, 5, 11, 16, 19, 36, 39, 41, 44, 56, 129, 155, 157, 162, 166, 173, 196, 199, 204, 210, 220, 247, 248, 254
Inn of Cana,  249
Iraq,  7, 51
Irenaeus, theologian  116
Iron Age Era,  13, 30, 38, 41, 148, 150, 172, 180, 205, 215, 216, 224, 231, 238, 243, 262
Isaiah, prophet  16, 81, 87, 91, 94, 95, 96, 99, 125, 130, 163, 164
Islamic Era,  viii, 13, 61, 108, 200, 205
Issachar, tribal  xiv, 116, 133–135, 172, 231, 235, 239, 256, 257
Istanbul, Turkey  13, 112
Itabyrion, see Mt. Tabor, J. site  241

## J

**Jabin,** King 72, 163
**Jacob,** patriarch 5, 132, 133, 134, 135, 163, 230
**Jacotin,** P., surveyor 126
**Jafthie,** *see* Japhia 152
**James,** Desposyni 49, 50
**James the Less,** rel 47–49
**James the Greater,** 13, 29, 47–49, 54, 63, 89, 90, 117, 118, 187–189, 205, 206, 249
**Jamnia Jewish Council,** of 55
**Janneus,** King 30, 76
**Japheph,** site 63, 64, 249
**Japhia,** site 20, 24, 123, 130, 131, 139, 140, 142, 144–149, 150–153, 196, 201, 208, 220, 231, 241, 249, 250, 257
**Jebel et Tur,** mt. 224, 225
**Jebus,** Jerusalem 127
**Jefat,** *see* Jotapata 148
**Jericho,** site 13, 78, 84, 86, 213, 215, 216, 222, 256
**Jerome,** St. schol. x, 43, 47, 48, 58, 60, 165, 190, 205, 255
**Jerusalem,** city viii, x, 17, 32, 48, 49, 54, 58, 61, 70, 72, 77, 78, 83, 85, 86, 94, 116, 127, 134, 137, 139, 143, 144, 153, 164, 166, 168, 187, 200, 229, 230
**Jesse,** King David's father 16
**Jesus,** *see* Messiah, Son of God, Redeemer, The Word
**Jesus Christ,** ix, xi, 13, 111, 193, 208, 210, 247, 253, 254, 258
**Jetebatha,** *see* Jotapata 250, 251
**Jewish War,** xiv, 13, 137–140
**Jezreel,** Plain of 25, 51, 52, 72, 77, 100, 157, 158, 159, 160, 163, 252, 254

**Jiphthahel,** valley 232, 235
**Joachim,** Virgin Mary's father 42, 49, 249
**John,** apostle, Gospel writer 3, 6, 9, 11–13, 17, 47, 84, 89, 90, 111, 116–118, 173, 176–180, 182, 187–189, 205, 249, 254
**John the Baptist,** 19, 78
**Jokneam,** Levite city 130–233, 238, 239, 257
**Jones,** F. schol. 13, 96, 212, 262
**Joppe,** *see* Japhia 152
**Joseph,** St., (Mary's spouse) 5, 8, 11, 14, 16–18, 20, 21, 26, 27, 30, 32, 35, 38, 39, 41, 42, 45, 46, 48, 50, 51, 70–75, 80– 82, 94, 96, 107, 108, 110, 119, 247, 248
**Josephus,** historian xiv, 9, 15, 20, 33, 83, 123, 124, 131, 133, 135, 139, 140, 141–143, 145, 153, 175, 209, 220, 223, 230, 231, 233, 234, 241–244, 250, 251, 257
**Joshua,** Israelite leader vi, 13, 20, 30, 38, 91–93, 96, 122, 126, 128, 131, 145, 147, 149 –151, 153, 159, 161, 163, 166, 169, 172, 202, 212–214, 216, 220, 222, 225, 227, 236, 238, 239, 243, 254
**Jotapata,** J. site 77, 123, 139, 140–144, 146, 151, 153, 180, 235, 241–244, 250, 257
**Jotbah,** *see* Jotapata 243
**Jubilee,** Jewish celebration 19, 67, 91, 94– 96, 99, 104
**Judah III,** rabbi 111
**Judas Iscariot,** disciple 49
**Jude,** rel. 48, 49, 50
**Judea,** region 13, 14, 19, 30, 41, 59, 61, 70, 225, 234, 250, 252

**Judeo-Christian,** 21, 35, 37, 43, 48, 50, 51, 82, 121, 182, 204, 205, 254
**Judges,** Book of 13, 72, 204, 214, 225, 226
**Julian the Apostate,** Emperor 33, 113
**Juttah,** Judean site 19

## K

**Kammona,** site 238
**Kamon,** Har mount 232
**Kana-el-Gelil,** site 180, 181
**Kanah,** site 180
**kangaroo court trial** 104
**Kanna,** Kaphar site 177, 180
**Kaphar,** Heb. 218
**Kattath,** site 132, 233, 234, 257
**Kartah,** Levite city 132, 233, 240, 257
**Kassis,** Tel site 239
**Kedumim,** Mount 22, 90, 156, 158–166, 164, 190, 205, 231, 232, 252, 257
**Kefr Sabt,** site 242
**Keil,** F. schol. 24, 132, 147, 159
**Keimun,** site 238
**Kenereth,** S. site 236
**Kenyon,** K. archaeo. vi, 215
**Kerak,** Heb. 218
**Kinerot,** Tel site 236
**Kingdom,** Messianic 5, 75, 77, 95
**Kingdom,** Northern 13, 14, 114, 212, 214
**Kingdom** Southern 13, 14, 76, 114, 204, 214
**Kinneret,** Tel site 133, 241
**Kishon,** River 130, 231, 235, 239, 257
**Kisloth,** *see* Chizloth 251
**Kitron,** site 25, 132, 234, 257
**Knobel,** K. schol. 147, 165
**kokhim,** tombs 43
**Kokkinos,** N. schol. 241
**kome,** Gk. village 24, 38, 218

## L

**Lamentations of Eleazar,** 61, 62
**landmark border,** 171
**Land-use,** sacred 88
**Late Bronze Era,** 13, 205, 213-216, 239
**Late Roman Era,** 13, 58, 109, 205
**latitude,** geographical xiv, 150, 197
**Leah,** Jacob's wife 163
**lectern,** pulpit 86, 87
**Legeon,** site 56, 238
**Levin,** Y, schol. 24, 147, 148
**Levine,** L. schol. 85, 263
**Levite priests,** 93, 132, 167-173, 196, 204, 227, 232-234, 238, 241, 257
**Libnath,** Sihor site 235
**Liebner,** U, archaeo. 24, 218
**Lindisfarne Gospels** 117, 118
**Lissak,** R. schol. 172
**Livingston,** D. archaeo. 213
**longitude,** geographical xiv, 93, 150, 162-165, 197 230
**Loreto,** Italy 44
**Lower Galilee,** region vi, 114, 123, 124, 131, 140, 151, 153, 196, 204, 208, 209, 231-235, 241, 256
**Luke,** Gospel writer 4-6, 10-12, 17, 19, 35, 41, 49, 55, 69-73, 76-80, 94, 96, 97, 99, 101, 116, 137, 143, 154, 157, 158, 173, 189, 206, 254

## M

**Maccabees,** 13, 14, 30, 76, 165, 204, 205
**Maeir,** A. archaeo. 213
**Magdala,** site 77, 241, 250, 251
**Mageddo,** *see* Megiddo 252
**Magi,** learned caste 252
**Malachi,** prophet 63, 164, 191, 251, 252
**Mamluk Era,** 13, 205
**Manasseh,** tribal 115, 116
**Mandate,** British 13, 205
**Maon,** S. site 234, 257
**Maralah,** site 130, 231
**Mark,** Gospel writer 11, 12, 17, 19, 47, 49, 73, 75, 116, 189, 206, 254
**Mary,** Saint, Virgin 4, 5, 8, 11, 14, 16, 18-21, 23, 26, 27, 35, 36, 38-52, 57, 67, 70, 72, 75, 80-82, 100, 107, 119, 156, 157, 159-166, 173, 176, 178, 196, 204-206, 208, 218, 220, 221, 246-249, 252, 256
**Mary's Well,** site 8, 52, 256
**Mar Ya'akub,** see Yafia 29, 63
**Mary Clopas,** rel. 49
**Mary Heli,** rel. 49
**Mary International Center,** Nazareth 46, 47
**Masada,** site 84, 85, 141, 142
**Masoretic,** Heb. text x, 172, 225, 231, 232, 253
**Matthew,** Gospel writer 10, 11, 12, 16, 17, 19, 23, 38, 42, 49, 70, 73, 75, 77, 81, 99, 107, 111, 116, 119, 125, 130, 164, 165, 177, 187, 189, 253, 254
**meadow at Cana,** 183
**Mecca,** Saudi Arabia 13, 200
**medallion,** Nazareth 59, 60
**Medieval Era,** 20, 34, 44, 52, 63, 64, 82, 100, 190, 192, 194, 204, 205, 220
**Mediterranean Sea,** 55, 75, 133, 134, 239
**Megiddo,** site 56, 238
**Melchizedek,** 190, 192, 252
**Melkite Church,** 82, 256
**memorial stones,** 222
**Meshullemeth,** Jewish queen 243
**Messiah,** Jesus Christ ix, x, xii, 5, 16, 36, 37, 41, 55, 66, 67, 73, 84, 91, 93, 94, 99, 107, 116, 119, 120, 125, 157, 163, 165, 166, 169, 171, 173, 204, 206, 208, 255
**Methoar,** Rimmon, Zebulun border 232
**Micah,** prophet 36
**Middle Bronze Era,** 13, 30, 128, 150, 152, 161, 172, 205, 212-216, 224, 236-239
**Middle Roman Era,** 60
**Midianites,** ethnic 215
**Migdal ha-Emek,** site 240, 257
**Mi'ilya,** Kabul site 235, 257
**mikvah,** mikveh 24, 236, 248, 255
**Milek,** Wadi route 239
**Miller,** J. schol. 128, 129
**Mimlakh,** site 232, 240, 241, 257
**miracles of Jesus,** 56, 81, 174-178, 206, 208, 249
**Mirov,** S. schol. 192
**Mishnah,** Jewish 13, 33, 71, 102, 243, 255
**Mitanni,** ethnic 214
**Moabites,** ethnic 94, 215
**mosaic tiles,** 43, 51, 106, 109, 112, 115-118, 193
**Moses,** Israelite leader 53, 83, 86, 92, 122, 127, 132, 134, 135, 154, 158, 168, 187, 188, 189, 193, 201, 206, 213, 222, 227, 230, 254
**Mosul,** Iraq 7
**Mousterian Era,** 161
**Mughar,** site 236
**Murray,** D. schol. 85
**Muzio,** G. arch. 37
**myth of Nazareth,** xii, 6, 9, 220, 221

## N

**Na'aman,** N. archaeo. 24, 75, 135, 147, 148, 214
**Naaman River,** 75, 135, 235
**Nablus,** site 222-224, 227

*Index*

**Nahalal,** Levite city 132, 233, 234, 257
**Nahf,** Tel site 235
**Nahum,** prophet 7, 191, 252
**Naphtali,** tribal xiv, 13, 116, 125, 130, 236, 237, 241, 250, 256, 257
**Napoleon,** emperor 126
**Nasara,** Arabic for Christian 17
**Nasir Din,** Kh. site 234, 257
**Nathanael,** apostle 84, 104
**Navel,** spiritual site 92, 93, 200, 225, 226, 230, 255
**Nazara,** Nazareth 16, 47, 56, 57, 58
**Nazarenes,** Jewish 13, 15, 30, 50, 51, 54, 56, 83, 204
**Nazarenos,** Jesus' title 16
**Nazareth city** 1, 10, 16, 18–27, 30–33, 36, 41, 42, 56, 61, 60, 63, 64, 66, 67, 70, 79, 81, 86, 92, 93, 100, 101, 108, 118, 121, 123, 153, 204–206, 208, 218, 220, 256
**Nazareth Inscription,** 58
**Nazareth synagogue,** vi, 32, 34, 80, 82, 83, 85, 86, 96, 99, 103, 202, 218
**Nazareth Village,** 39
**Nazoraios,** Jesus' title 16
**Nazorean,** clan 15, 16
**Neah,** site 130, 131, 231, 237
**Neanderthal,** ancient people 161
**Neapolis,** Nablus, site 229
**Nebi Sain ridge,** 100
**Neiel,** site 235
**Netofa valley** 77, 180, 183, 234
**Neubauer,** G. schol. 242
**Neuville,** R. schol. 161
**nezer,** Heb. branch 15, 16
**Nicea,** Council of 57
**Niddah,** Plain of 242
**Nineveh,** Iraq 7, 8
**Notzrim,** Heb. Christian 17
**North,** significance 197

**O**

**Olives,** Mt. of 127, 251
**Omathadaketh,** S. site 236
**Onomasticon,** Bible site book 56, 58, 152, 263
**Ophna,** site 205, 249
**oratory,** Mary's prayer room 247
**Oreimeh,** Tel site 236
**orientation,** geographical 85, 90, 114, 130, 197
**Origen,** theologian 55, 190
**Orthodox Church,** 41, 108, 109, 110, 113, 114, 120, 177, 191–195, 255, 256
**Othniel,** Israelite judge 214
**Ottoman Era,** 13, 34, 63, 108, 126, 205

**P**

**Palestine,** 14, 33, 37, 38, 44, 55–58, 60, 61, 64, 82, 112, 118, 124, 126, 128, 150, 152, 153, 180, 204, 214, 221, 245, 249, 252, 254, 255
**Palestine Exploration Fund** 126, 127, 128, 155
**Pamphylia,** region 51
**Panarion,** Book 112
**Papias,** historian 12
**Paradise of God,** 197
**Passover,** celebration 32, 72, 77, 96
**Paul,** apostle 17, 54, 55
**Paula,** pilgrim 43
**Persia,** Persian 13, 44, 60, 61, 150, 229, 238, 239, 252
**Peter,** apostle 12, 17, 187, 188, 189, 206
**Peter the Deacon,** 43, 81
**Petra,** Jordan 7
**Pfann,** S. archaeo. 39
**Phangai,** *see* Japhia, S. site 231
**Pharisees,** sect 75, 83, 84, 104, 220, 255
**Philip,** apostle 17, 53, 84
**Philistine,** ethnic 215, 216
**Phillipi,** Caesarea 189

**Phthaee,** S. site 235
**Piacenza,** pilgrim 44, 190, 192
**Pilate,** Pontius Governor xii, 3, 6, 17, 77, 221, 229
**pilgrimage,** 13, 21, 36, 44, 51, 58, 63, 190, 204
**Pixner,** B. archaeo. x, 10, 15, 263
**Pliny,** historian 135
**polis,** Gk. city 5, 12, 18, 21, 24–28, 30, 32, 58, 208, 217, 218, 220, 255
**Pompey,** Roman General 76
**Pope Benedict XVI,** 162
**Pope John Paul II,** 162, 245
**Poriya,** site 231
**Pravda,** Russian news 192
**Precipice Mt.,** Sarid 52, 100, 102, 161
**Priestly Course,** 59
**Promised Land,** vi, x, xiv, 13–15, 92, 122, 126, 132, 134, 226, 230, 254
**prophecy,** 16, 23, 95, 99, 130, 132, 133, 134, 135, 143, 207, 210
**Prophetic Bible site mapping** ix, 16, 36, 37, 67, 79, 90, 92, 93, 107, 157, 158, 162–165, 167, 171, 173, 186, 187, 195, 196, 199, 201, 208, 209, 220
**prophetic sites,** xii, 41, 70, 90, 93, 119, 125, 156, 157, 159, 161, 163, 164, 166, 169, 173
**Protestant,** denomination viii, 205
**Protoevangelium of James,** 2nd century document 42

**Q**

**Qadis,** Kh. site 231
**Qafzeh,** Mount see Sarid 161, 266
**Qashish,** Kh. site 239, 265
**Qedesh,** Kh. site 231
**Quaresmius,** schol. 81, 205
**Qumram,** site 96

273

# R

**Rabbis,** Jewish teachers 84, 219, 220
**Radiocarbon dating,** 216
**Rakkath,** Tel site 236
**Ramah,** Tel site 233
**Redeemer,** Jesus Christ 5
**Red Sea,** 127
**Rekhesh,** Tel site 84, 85
**remnant,** from the Exile 161, 163, 164, 165, 166
**revelation,** spiritual 73, 245, 246
**Revelation,** Book of 247
**Rimmon,** Rimmono, site 130, 232, 257
**Robinson,** E. explorer 14, 20, 24, 64, 129, 147, 148, 180, 205, 239, 263
**rolling stone tomb,** 45, 248
**Roman Era,** 29, 33, 38, 43, 90, 181, 234, 238, 249, 250
**Rome,** 54, 71, 136, 138, 139, 153, 254
**Russian,** 191, 192

# S

**Sabas,** rel. 49
**Sabbath,** rest day 79, 80, 81, 86, 94, 99, 178, 218, 255
**Sabt,** Kefr, site 152
**Safa,** see Yafia 64
**Safra,** see Yafia 63, 205
**Safrai,** Z. archaeo. 24, 26, 147, 263
**Salamis,** Kh. J. site 140, 241
**Salm,** R. schol. vi, xii, 9, 10, 59, 60, 65, 221, 263
**Saltis,** Domini. Lord's Leap 100
**Samanaeans,** ancient caste 252
**Samaria,** Samaritans 78, 91, 93, 112, 222-230
**Samson,** Israelite judge 214
**Sanhedrin,** Jewish Court 17, 84
**Sappha,** see Yafia 52, 64

**Sarid,** Mount 130, 145, 147, 156-158, 159, 161-166, 196, 199, 201, 252, 257
**Sarith,** see Sarid 165
**Saron,** see Yafia 63, 205
**Satan,** Devil 197
**Saul,** King 13
**Saul,** of Tarsus, apostle 54
**Saviour,** Jesus Christ 5, 50, 56, 205, 252
**sceptics,** of Nazareth vi, 8, 10, 60, 220, 221
**Schism,** Great Church 90, 120, 193
**schools in Nazareth,** 28, 70, 71, 84, 220
**Schultz,** E. schol. 141, 180
**Scythopolis,** site 111
**Sea of Galilee,** vi, 13, 129, 130, 131, 133, 135, 231, 236, 247, 250, 257
**seismic,** 102, 113, 131, 215, 231, 237
**Sejerah,** see Japhia 151, 152, 241
**Seleucid Era,** 76, 254
**Sellame,** Kh. site 233, 236, 257
**Sennacherib,** King 8
**Sepphoris,** site 14, 25, 26, 32, 75, 77, 86, 183, 234, 249
**Septuagint,** Gk. OT x, 160, 166, 169, 172, 231, 253, 261
**seven wonders of ancient world** 8
**Shadud,** Tel. site 158, 165, 231, 232
**Shahazimah,** site 235, 243, 257
**Shammam,** Tel site 231, 232
**Sharona,** site 141, 142, 235, 243, 244, 257
**Shear-Jashub,** Isaiah's son 163, 164
**Shechem,** Levite city 93, 222-227
**Shefar'am,** see Shimron 62, 63, 132, 234, 257

**Sheikh Nashi,** Kh. site 236, 241
**Shemesh,** Beth, site 235, 257
**Shikhin,** Tel site 241
**Shimron,** site 25, 62, 63, 132, 233, 234, 257
**Sidon,** site 133, 134
**siege warfare,** 141, 143, 181
**Signposts,** pointers 157, 171, 167, 201, 207, 208, 240
**Sigo,** J. site 140, 241, 250
**Simeon,** prophet 70
**Simon,** rel. 47, 48, 49
**Simonias,** J. site 63, 234
**Sinai,** Mount 127, 169, 214
**Sirgona,** Kh. site 152
**Sisters of Nazareth Convent** 41, 45, 248, 256
**Sogane,** site 152
**Solomon,** King 13, 30, 38, 87, 134, 204
**Son of God,** Jesus Christ 5, 157, 173
**Spigel,** C. schol. 86, 236, 259, 263, 264
**spiritual bodies,** 189
**Stemberger,** G. schol. 110, 112, 263
**stoning area,** execution 102, 206
**Sufsafa,** spring of 29
**Sukenik,** E. archaeo. 109, 114, 115, 116, 118, 258, 265
**Sultan,** Tel. Jericho 215, 216
**Sumerian** 6
**Symoon,** see Shimron, S. site 234
**synagogue,** general ix, 38, 39, 54, 55, 58, 59, 62, 71, 73, 86, 88
**Synagogue Church,** Nazareth 80, 81, 82, 256
**Synagogue,** Byzantine, Yafia 108-118, 200, 202, 208

# T

**Tabaneh,** Kh. site 238
**tabernacles,** shelter 189, 190

# Index

**Tabor, Mount** 22, 130, 133, 140, 145, 147, 149, 150, 163, 172, 187, 188, 189, 190–196, 206, 231, 234, 235, 238, 241, 242, 250, 251, 257

**Talmud,** Jewish 1, 9, 13, 27, 28, 33, 59, 73, 85, 101, 128, 234, 242, 255

**Tarichaea,** J. site 241

**Tarshisha,** Kh. site 235

**Taylor,** J. archaeo. 43, 48, 61

**Tell er-Ras,** site 93, 201, 223, 224, 227, 230

**Tel Yafia,** 22–34, 64, 256

**Temple of Jerusalem,** 227, 228, 229, 230

**Temple, Samaritan** 93, 222–229

**Tertullian,** theologian 57

**Theotokos,** Gk. Mother of God 43

**The Word,** Jesus 172, 173, 189

**Tiberias,** site 77, 86, 110–112, 121, 124, 140, 141, 151, 181, 183, 218, 234, 236, 237, 241, 242, 249, 250, 257

**Tiglath Pileser III,** King 243

**Titus,** General & Emperor 144, 146, 153

**topography,** ix, 27, 28, 86, 88, 97, 104, 128, 141, 142, 147, 153, 165, 169, 208, 209, 246

**Torah,** Jewish Law xiv, 9, 72, 80, 178, 255

**Tosefa,** Jewish book, 84

**Trajan,** Roman General, Emperor 48, 50, 54, 123, 146

**Transfiguration of Jesus,** 188–196, 201, 206, 251, 255

**Troy,** Troas NT site 7

**Tsalmon,** River and site. *see* Zalmon. 131, 237, 250

**Turkey,** country 7, 12, 17, 47, 51, 111, 246

**Tutmosis,** pharoah 216

**Tyre,** site 134, 236

## U

**Ulama,** site 250

**Umayyad Era,** 13, 205

**Umm al Ghanan,** site 231, 232

**UNESCO,** UN body 230

**Upper Galilee,** region 233

## V

**Vaulx,** pilgrim 90

**Vaux R.** archaeo. 81, 82

**Vespasian,** General & Emperor 123, 138–144, 146, 148, 151, 229, 242

**Vincent,** L. archaeo. 109

**Virgin Mary,** 4, 5, 11, 14, 46, 49, 57, 164, 165, 166, 210, 254

**Vogue,** M. de archaeo. 192, 193

**Voss,** R. archaeo. 39

## W

**Way of the Sea,** 130, 236

**Wedding at Cana,** 175–186, 206

**wine,** 76, 176, 177, 179, 178, 183

**Wood,** B. archaeo. 212, 266

**Workshop of Saint Joseph,** 19, 20, 27, 32, 41, 42, 45, 52, 71, 74, 75, 96, 108, 110, 119, 120, 121, 201, 202, 248

## X

**Xaloth,** J. site 231

## Y

**Ya'anim,** site 235

**Yabneel Valley,** 152, 235, 250, 257

**Yafa,** *see* Yafia 148

**Yafia,** 9, 22–24, 27–34, 52, 59, 63, 64, 65, 71, 79, 85, 88–90, 100, 101–103, 106–110, 113, 114, 117, 118, 120, 123, 145–48, 152, 153, 202, 208, 218, 220, 221, 233, 241, 247, 249, 256, 257, 259

**Yerah,** Beth site. *see* Beth Shemesh 235, 257

**Yeshua,** Heb. Jesus & Joshua 16, 17, 93, 121

**Yodfat,** Tel 50, 140, 141, 142, 148, 180–183, 242, 244, 257

**Yom Kippur,** Jewish 94

## Z

**Zalmon,** (Tsalmon) River & site 131, 133, 237, 250

**Zebedee,** father James and John 13, 54, 63, 89, 90, 118, 249

**Zebul,** Shechem observer 225

**Zebulun,** tribal vi, x, xiii, xiv, 20, 62, 123–125, 129, 130–135, 147, 149, 152, 155, 163, 191, 192, 208, 231–234, 237, 239, 240, 256, 257

**Zeitun,** Tel site 236

**Zelef,** Kh. site 235, 257

**Zer,** site 236

**Zeus,** pagan 228, 229

**Ziddim,** site 236

**Zion,** Mount 48, 197

**Zippori,** site. *see* Sepphoris 234, 257

**Zodiac,** symbols 115

**Zoker,** rel. 49, 50

275

# Books in: THE NAZARETH SERIES

**Book 1: Nazareth - Mystery City Unlocked**
By Trevor Harris
Key-line Christian Research
Non-fiction/Academic/Christian
ISBN: 978-0-9925506-0-8
Limited edition only, 2014

*Nazareth – Mystery City Unlocked* is a Review Edition for scholars. It reveals that the lost city of Nazareth did in fact exist if the correct definition of the city was made, debunking the myth that the city never existed. It provides historical and archaeological evidence for Nazareth described as a polis (city) in 27 AD. Also included is information on other sites of the Lower Galilee.

**Book 3: Nazareth Gospel Sites**
By Trevor Harris
Key-line Christian Research
Non-fiction/Christian/Guidebook
ISBN: 978-0-9925506-4-6  Print colour soft cover
ISBN: 978-0-9925506-6-0  ebook

*Nazareth Gospel Sites* reveals locations in the life of Jesus based on a correct understanding of the city he grew up in. The mystery of the lost city where he preached in the synagogue is explained. This easy to read booklet contains extensive illustrations and maps including compelling evidence that traces the footsteps of Jesus in Nazareth. An ideal guide for Nazareth visitors and those interested in a description of Jesus' hometown in 27 AD.

**Further books and booklets**
Refer Key-line Christian Research: www.biblekeylines.com